Books are to be returned on or before
the last date below.

J
A
tl

de

Ed

LIBREX–

Council of Europe Publishing

Layout: Documents and Publications Production Department (SPDP), Council of Europe
Cover design: Council of Europe Publishing

Council of Europe Publishing
F-67075 Strasbourg Cedex
http://book.coe.int

ISBN 978-92-871-6723-1
© Council of Europe, June 2010
Printed at the Council of Europe

List of authors[*]

Pablo Acosta
Associate Professor of Administrative Law
Rey Juan Carlos University, Madrid, Spain

Bruno Aguilera
Professor of Legal History
Rey Juan Carlos University, Madrid, Spain

Rainer Arnold
Professor of Public Law
University of Regensburg, Germany

Dacian Dragos
Jean Monnet Associate Professor of European and Administrative Law
Babes Bolyai University, Romania

Gunilla Edelstam
Associate Professor of Administrative Law
Sodertorn University, Sweden

Susana Galera
Associate Professor of Administrative Law
Rey Juan Carlos University, Madrid, Spain

Francisco Jiménez
Associate Professor of Public International Law
Rey Juan Carlos University, Madrid, Spain

Péter Kovács
Judge at the Hungarian Constitutional Court
Budapest, Hungary

Céline Lageot
Associate Professor of Public Law
University of Poitiers, France

Dimitra Nassimpian
Research Fellow
University of Exeter, United Kingdom

[*] Special thanks to Kevin Word, in charge of the English edition of the manuscript.

Julia Ruiloba
Associate Professor of International Law
Rey Juan Carlos University, Madrid, Spain

Sonia Skulová
Associate Professor of Administrative Law
Masaryk University, Brno, Czech Republic

Contents

Foreword

Pedro González-Trevijano
President of Rey Juan Carlos University

Since the adoption of the Bologna Declaration in 1999, by which more than thirty countries pledged to establish a European Space of Higher Education, European universities have assumed the complex challenge of reform and interconnection with each other, establishing common objectives with regard to quality, compatibility of studies and degrees, and mobility of students and staff. In this way, the European idea of the university has been infused with new elements, or, at the very least, new elements have been specifically promoted, such as a necessary connection with the greater society and the idea that the university is an instrument to increase employment and the competitiveness of Europe.

Adapting to an increasingly international and interdependent environment has enriched the centuries-old European university tradition, in a process that European institutions have shepherded. Therein, a focus that is both pragmatic and mindful of Europe's academic tradition fosters not only the interrelation of studies, teachers and studies in the EU area but also between the EU and the rest of the world, as witnessed in the numerous collaboration and exchange programmes adopted within the framework of European education policies.

The Rey Juan Carlos University readily assumes this challenge, pushing for and supporting teaching and research endeavours which connect, in a stable framework of co-operation, members of our university with similar institutions in other parts of the world. The present publication, which as Rector and full professor of Constitutional Law it is my distinct pleasure to introduce, neatly fits into this context of co-operation. This work is the result of a research project supported by this university and by the regional government; this is a project that was begun in the *European Law Research Center* of Harvard University and has the aim of analysing one of the classical themes of Public Law – judicial control over public power – from a new and timely perspective that takes into account the cohabitation of the European legal tradition – in which we include the work of the Council of Europe – with the recent organisational plan created by the European Union. The research group, led by Professor Galera, is composed of twelve participating authors representing a variety of professional fields – academic and judicial – such as Public Law jurists from across Europe: Czech Republic, France, Germany, Hungary, Romania, Spain, Sweden and the United Kingdom.

To the entire research team, and to the publications service of the Council of Europe and the research service of Rey Juan Carlos University, I extend sincere congratulations for their thorough and highly valuable work, which set its sights on interchange, collaboration and enrichment that could be achieved only by stepping across national boundaries. In any case, national boundaries are difficult to reconcile with a strict understanding of the role of the university, characterised since its beginnings by an unalienable vocation to universality. At its core, this universal vocation is underpinned by an idea close to the one known since Roman times, that is, the law of nations. According to Montesquieu in his work, *The Spirit of Laws*, "The law of nations is naturally founded on this principle: that different nations ought in time of peace to do one another all the good they can, and in time of war as little injury as possible, without prejudicing their real interests."

The guiding principle and main idea underlying this work identify "European Law" as a complex legal system, understood in its general sense as a unity made up of different interacting units. This conception is thus quite distinct from those not infrequent positions that associate the idea of "European Law" with European Union Law. What's more, this work considers the European legal system to be a reality made up of two subsystems. The first is the European legal system, in which two elements are pre-eminent: national traditions and the "regional" European tradition, based on the legal tradition elaborated in the Council of Europe. Both elements are informed first and foremost by the other, but it is above all the legal construction of the Council of Europe that has created an identity of "European Law" that harmonises to some extent the national laws with respect to essential elements characteristic of the Rule of Law tradition. The second subsystem of the European legal system is born of the previous context and in its own way is made up of two distinct components. On one hand, European Union Law (which is imposed with most obvious effect on national laws and which nowadays involves law of a mainly economic nature) and, on the other hand, the acts and activities adopted in the framework of intergovernmental pillars, whose nature is much closer to policy and political acts than to legal norms.

The primary topics researched here are some of the characteristic elements of the European tradition of the Rule of Law: separation of powers, judicial independence, appealable actions and access to the courts, among others. These elements are analysed in each of the legal systems examined: national, Council of Europe, European Community and intergovernmental pillars. This analysis concluded that the "European legal system" – that is, national regulations and the doctrine of the Council of Europe – appears more compact and homogenous than the legal framework that has recently been adopted for these elements within the context of the European Union. The final part of the work elaborates a comparative perspective that underscores what has already been established, but still not remedied, namely, the existing deficient access to the European Court of Justice in Luxembourg, as well as the lesser known deficient judicial review of political and normative acts conforming to the doctrine of "acts of government" elaborated by the European Court of Human Rights in Strasbourg.

On this evidence, the authors hold that in matters of human rights, the European Union adheres to the system of the Council of Europe, rather than develop its own system under the Charter of Fundamental Rights proclaimed at Nice. The author's principal argument is that the Strasbourg Court's interpretation of the Rome Convention of 1950 has "stretched" the convention's original spirit to the point that the ECHR has exceeded its strict function as a protector of human rights and has become the essential reference of "European public order". In this way, and from the broad concept of human rights found in the Rome Convention, the Strasbourg Court has delimited the content of the essential elements of the Rule of Law which are the object of this research (judicial independence, access to the courts, jurisdictional exemptions). This delimitation has led to a close harmonisation in European Law in this regard, much more because of the *"auctoritas"* of its pronouncements than by the *"potestas"* in the execution of its sentences.

For all of these reasons, from the articles included in this excellent body of work, the following two conclusions arise: a) that the eventual reduction of "European Law" into "European Union Law", besides being dogmatically incorrect, necessarily means the reduction of the essential guarantees of our legal tradition; and, b) that such restriction is however understandable, if one considers the strikingly powerful instruments granted to European Union Law – primacy, direct effect,... – compared to the more modest tools invested in 1949 in the Council of Europe – international character and the absence of "executive power" over the rulings of the European Court of Human Rights.

This imbalance can explain why European Union Law, instead of simply coexisting with what is here called "European legal tradition", has subordinated this tradition. Nevertheless, such a reduction is not such a bad thing in a context which now recognises that a "global Public Law" is emerging. In this regard, the European imprint can not be reduced to the elements normally used to characterise the experience of integration known as the European Union (freedom of movement, competition law, primacy...). Rather the process necessarily must comprehend the legal principles and values established by the Council of Europe on the basis of age-old European legal history. In short, it must make real the words of Victor Hugo in *Les Burgraves*: "There is today a European nationality, as there used to be, in times of Aeschylus, of Sophocles and of Euripides, a Greek nationality."

Part I
Preliminary

Chapter 1
Law as a limit to power – The origins of the rule of law in the European legal tradition

B. Aguilera

1.1. Power and law

Power and law are concepts that can be separated intellectually, but in fact, from the dawn of time, they have been intimately tied together in the human reality. By virtue of our birth we live in a society ruled by power, the force that imposes on us the law.

Aristotle (384-322), the first Western thinker who tried to explain society as a phenomenon, considered that living in society is an intrinsic part of human nature. He conceived man as a political animal (*zoon politikón*), one who lives "naturally" in society. And he thought that man, because of this natural sociability, tends to submit to power and follow the norms that essentially the law consists of. This reasoning, taken up by Thomas Aquinas (1225-1274), became one of the pillars of scholastic philosophy, at least until the crisis of the War of Religions brought in the 17th century the idea of a common "natural law" independent of personal convictions or beliefs.

Nevertheless, if it is true that power and law have been inextricably tied to the social phenomenon since the origins of humanity, it is no less true that historically law has tended to differentiate itself progressively from power. That differentiation has never been obvious or evident, because power and law are such complementary realities.

1.2. A first step: the appearance of written law

From an early stage in legal history it is possible to appreciate evidence of this process, by which law tends, if not to disengage from power – this would be impossible – at least become a distinct, differentiated reality. The first step was the appearance of written laws. In the history of all civilisations there is a moment when laws begin to be written down: in some cases by individuals – monarchs like Hammurabi (18th century BC) or the legendary King Habis in Iberian Tartessus (6th century BC), or wise law-givers like the Athenian Solon or the Spartan Lycurgus (7th and 6th centuries BC) – or in other cases as a result of political processes, as with the Law of the Twelve

Tables (450 BC), written by a legislative committee. Indeed, the political aim of the Law of the Twelve Tables was to satisfy a plebeian demand: that the law should be known by all and not only by priests, who generally sprang from the patrician landholding class.

Today it is still an essential principle that laws must be publicly known; and cannot be applied until they are made public – either orally, like municipal by-laws that an officer of the local council shouts out after warning the village with a bugle call, or written in an official gazette to which every country assigns the essential function of publishing laws.[1]

1.3. The law of God as a limit to power

The second means by which the Western legal tradition tried to impose limits on power came from the realm of religion. Soon after the Spanish-born emperor Theodosius I, by the Edict of Thessalonica (380), made Christianity the official religion, the Roman Empire faced the problem of the relationship between the civil and religious powers.[2]

According to the Christian conception, the submission of humans to a social structure dominated by power is the consequence of original sin. The Bible myth – as found in the first book of the Pentateuch, Genesis – tells us that the man and the woman were expelled from Paradise for disobeying God's law. This idea led the first interpreters of the Bible, the church fathers (Patristic Exegesis), to distinguish between a state of nature (*status naturae*) or "state of grace", coinciding with Paradise, and a later social state (*status societatis*) derived from original sin. In the former, women and men lived in peace without the need to submit to social power or laws; in the latter, they began to fight each other, and the existence of authority and law became necessary. The law needed to be set down in rules that have restricted man ever since freedom derived from the "state of nature" disappeared.

This concept of the social state as punishment from God assumed that, in the final analysis, the Roman emperors of the Dominate[3] who wielded power

---

1. Article 2.1 of the Spanish Civil Code expressly establishes that norms will not take effect until their publication ("Laws will take effect twenty days after their full publication in the Official State Gazette, if no other dispositions are contained therein") in the *Boletín Oficial del Estado*; after three hundred and forty-seven years on paper, from 1 January 2009, this is published only electronically, apart from a few printed copies for the archive; each Autonomous Community also has its own official publication, as does the European Union.
2. When followers of the Pharisees, showing Jesus a coin, asked him if tributes should be paid to Caesar, "He said to them, 'Whose image and inscription is this?' They said to him, 'Caesar's'. And he said to them, 'Render therefore to Caesar the things that are Caesar's, and to God the things that are God's'." Matthew 22: 20-21.
3. From the time of Augustus until the end of the 3rd century, Rome had a *princeps* at the head of political power, but from Diocletian (r. 284-305) he became a *dominus* ("lord, owner"), which therefore is the logical term for the governors of the early Dominate. The shift in terminology

should submit to the power of divine will. This explains why the relationship between the Roman emperors and the Church, the voice of the official religion, was troubled from the very start (*Cesaropapism*). The Roman emperors were able to preserve their independence politically in the face of ecclesiastical pressure, but they could not prevent the Church from developing its own law, canon law, with its own norms (conciliar canons and papal decretals) and its own jurisdiction, alongside Roman civil law.

At the fall of the Western Roman Empire (476), the Catholic Church finally prevailed by Christianising some of the Germanic kings, a process that began at the end of the 4th century. The kings succumbed to the pressure of bishops set up as representatives of the Roman majority. Some years after the fall of Rome, at the time of the Frankish king Clovis (*r.* 481-511), the invaders started feeling obliged to abandon the Arrian "heresy" in favour of the majority Catholic belief. From that time the Church, through its bishops, began to participate more or less openly in civil government. The best known case occurred in Visigothic Spain, where, after the conversion of Reccared (589), the Church became a crucial pillar of the state, as demonstrated by the council's meetings in the capital of Toledo, which adopted far-reaching legal measures that went beyond the religious sphere. That the Visigoth kings found their power limited by the Church is evident in the work of Isidore of Seville, who wrote that "the laws oblige the prince" and "it is just that the prince obeys his own laws". This was because royal power is of divine origin and kings are the vicars of God. In fact, Isidore believed that kings deserve their name when they act justly (*recte igitur faciendo, regis nomen tenetur*); otherwise they will lose their royal position (*Rex eris si recte facies, si non facies non eris*).[4]

Christian influence in government was consolidated in the mid-8th century when the Papal States were created, by an agreement between the Frankish King Pepin the Short and Pope Stephen II. When popes became secular rulers, the Church tended to separate itself from civil power. The evolution was especially notable after the reform begun by Gregory VII (*r.* 1073-1085), which brought the papacy into direct confrontation with the emperors. It was the famous Conflict of Investitures from which the pontiffs emerged victorious. In fact, between the pontificate of Innocent III (*r.* 1198-1216) and that of Boniface VIII (*r.* 1294-1303), the popes established themselves as the supreme rulers of Western Christianity (pontifical theocracy) and came to legitimise the power of kings and emperors through the rite of coronation and could

---

for the position of chief among the citizenry is extraordinarily relevant from the perspective of Roman constitutional history.

4. Isidore of Seville, *Etimologías*, BAC, Madrid, 2004; English edn: S. Barney et al., *The Etymologies of Isidore of Seville*, Cambridge UP, 2006. See also: Pérez de Urbel, Justo, *San Isidoro de Sevilla. Su vida, su obra y su tiempo*, León: Ed. Isidoriana, 1995; Fontaine, Jacques, *Isidore de Séville: genèse et orginalité de la culture hispanique au temps des Wisigoths*, Brepols, Turnhout, 2000 (Spanish edn: *Isidoro de Sevilla: génesis y originalidad de la cultura hispánica en tiempos de los visigodos*, Madrid: Encuentro, 2002).

delegitimise them through "excommunication", a punishment that freed their subjects from the duty of obedience.

The civil power of the pontiffs began to decline when Philip IV of France (r. 1285-1314) asserted his independence from the papacy. After the captivity of the papacy in Avignon and the Western Schism, papal power found itself under siege. The crisis reached its peak with the Protestant Reformation, instigated by Luther (1483-1546). It may be noted that, whereas in 1493, after Columbus' discovery, Pope Alexander VI could distribute the New World between the Spaniards and Portuguese, just a year later, in the Treaty of Tordesillas (1494), the limits of Castilian and Portuguese expansion were defined by an international treaty between the two crowns, without papal intervention. This was, however, no obstacle for eminent thinkers of the School of Salamanca to study the legitimacy of the Spanish dominion over the Indies and its inhabitants in light of canonical laws (Doctrine of the Just Titles).

Nevertheless, the popes could do nothing to halt the laicisation of European societies. Henry VIII of England – excommunicated in 1533 by Clement VII for divorcing Catherine of Aragon, youngest daughter of the Spanish Catholic kings, and then marrying Ann Boleyn – was the first monarch who dared to break with the Roman Church and raise himself as head of a national church. The triumph of Protestantism threw Europe into religious conflicts like the French Wars of Religion (1562-1598); the Thirty Years War (1618-1648) spread the fight to almost all Europe.

1.4. Iusnaturalism and the first secular justifications of political power and law

These continual religious conflicts tore apart the religious unity of Europe. When God ceased to be the essential foundation of society, another explanation had to be found to justify the submission of men to power and law.[5] A new current of thought grew up that explained social submission as the result of universal, natural legal principles – that is, rules whose validity was independent of religious beliefs or political authorities. This was the "natural law" or "iusnaturalism", first formulated clearly by the Dutch legal thinker Hugo Grotius (1583-1645),[6] though its antecedents can be found in Spain, in

---

5. The direct impact of the religious conflicts on the legal field has been brilliantly studied by Roelker N. L. in his work *The Parliament of Paris and the religious reformations of the sixteenth century*, Berkeley/Los Angeles/London: University of California Press, 1997.
6. This idea of natural law was expressed by Grotius in his two best-known works: *Mare liberum* (1609) and *De iure belli ac pacis* (1625). The first was a brief treatise in which he asserted the sea was the property of no one and so all nations could reap benefit from it. This dispute had an undeniable economic significance since it affected maritime mercantile traffic when Holland was a budding naval power. In fact, the thesis of Grotius was answered by John Selden, a partisan of English naval supremacy, in *Mare clausum* (1635). *De iure belli ac pacis* was the first

the neo-Thomism of the School of Salamanca, and specially in the works of Francisco de Vitoria (1486-1546), whom Grotius cites constantly.[7]

This idea of the existence of internationally valid laws, developed "naturally" and independently of the positive law applied by the nation-states, is what led Thomas Hobbes (1588-1679), a fervent believer, to reject the Aristotelian-Thomist theory of man's natural sociability as the justification of power and law, and to inspire his own theory, also of Christian origin, that distinguishes between the state of nature or grace and the social state. From this arose the idea of the social pact as justification for Leviathan,[8] a term Hobbes used to refer to the power imposed on civil society. This social pact does not however constitute a limit to power, since once it is subscribed and accepted voluntarily by all men it becomes irreversible – Hobbes thought this was the only way of guaranteeing the social order and avoiding permanent chaos and war.

Despite the fact that Hobbes is generally considered a defender of Absolutism, the idea of the social pact was in itself revolutionary, to the extent that it supposed that the social state was reached as a consequence of an agreement between members of civil society. These persons renounced forever their liberty and accepted in perpetuity subjugation to Leviathan, as the price to pay for achieving social peace. Nevertheless, it is important to point out that initially the coactivity of power was voluntarily accepted. The next step was to convert the pact into a "social contract". This idea was developed by authors like Locke, Montesquieu and Rousseau, whose thought established the basis of the liberal state model that triumphed in America, after 1776, and in Europe starting in 1789.[9] Generally speaking, for these thinkers the social pact was in reality a contract because it contained two limitations: first, there would be clauses exempt from subjugation to Leviathan, specifically the "fundamental rights" that remained outside the scope of the agreement and were thus "immune" to power; second, submission to power was not irreversible

---

systematic treatise of international law, based on the ideas of Francisco de Vitoria and the School of Salamanca.

7. Francisco de Vitoria, of the Dominican order, studied in Paris and was professor of theology at the University of Salamanca where he gained a chair in 1526. His most famous writings concern the nature of political society and authority, more specifically the question of the Crown's legal title of ownership over newly discovered Spanish domains in America. His main work on his topic was *De iure belli Hispanos in barbaros* (1532) and *Relectio de Indis* (1539); Madrid edition by CSIC, 2007. See also Puig Peña, F. *"La influencia de Francisco de Vitoria en la obra de Hugo Grocio. Los principios del derecho internacional a la luz de la España del siglo XVI*, Madrid: Tip. De Archivos, 1934 and Albert Marquez, Marta María, "El principio de la libertad de los mares en la *relectio de indis*: ¿Se enfrentó Francisco de Vitoria a los intereses españoles?" in *Derecho y opinión*, ISSN 1133-3278, No. 6, 1998, pp. 169-184.

8. Leviathan is a great sea monster created by God; it appears in the Old Testament, in Genesis 1: 21; also in Psalm 74: 13-14, Job 41 and Isaiah 27: 1. The term is an allusion to any aquatic creature of great size and in the Bible it is usually related to Satan. In modern Hebrew, *lewyatan* simply means "whale".

9. On the evolution of the Social Pact: Macpherson, C. B., *Political Theory of Possessive Individualism: Hobbes to Locke*, Oxford/London: Oxford UP, 1st edn 1962; Spanish edn: Madrid: Trotta, 2005.

19

since the members of society could enter into a new pact or contract when the earlier agreement became inoperative.

1.5. Law versus power: feudalism and the origins of the laissez-faire state model

1.5.1. The medieval origins of the rule of law

This idea of the social pact was not entirely original. With our historical perspective, we can see now that, long before the idea was articulated by Hobbes and perfected by Locke, Montesquieu and Rousseau, political power in the Middle Ages also depended on a pact: the vassalage agreement. The possibility of finding the origin of the social pact in feudalism is generally overlooked because the French Revolution, in its zeal to overthrow absolute monarchy, erased feudal society, or at least what was left of it: its tripartite estates structure of nobility, clergy and citizenry. For this reason ever since, feudalism has had a clearly negative connotation in the Western legal tradition.

However, to the extent that we can distance ourselves from the mental frame-work of the ideas of 1789, it is clear that it was the feudal agreement that really dissolved the concept of the power of absolute monarchy developed in the Roman Empire, reaching its high point in the period of the Dominate during the fourth and fifth centuries. The disappearance of the sovereign–subject relationship and its replacement by pacts of a legal nature between lord and vassal resulted primarily in former subjects occupying the same legal level as the sovereign, who became *primus inter pares*. In fact, through the feudal agreement, the king assented to a relationship of a contractual nature with his vassals that attributed to him rights but also obligations.[10]

Feudalism profoundly transformed the concept of monarchy inherited from the Roman Empire, basically because in the new feudal monarchy the king was obliged to consider the opinion of his vassals when making important decisions. This participation of the vassals in general affairs began to be insti-tutionalised through the *curia regis*, a sort of advisory council, whose origin perhaps can be found in the ancient Germanic *aula regia*. In this *curia*, the great nobles, barons and bishops talked and discussed general affairs of the realm with the king. English kings from 1066 spoke Norman French, and this is why meetings of the monarch with the barons became the parliament (based on the French judicial institution the *parlement*, from *parler*, "to

---

10. On the details and constitutional consequences of the model of the Feudal Monarchy, the classic work is Petit-Dutaillis, Charles, *La monarchie féodale en France et en Angleterre, Xe-XIIIe siècle*, Paris: La Renaissance du Livre, 1933, new ed., Paris: Albin Michel, 1998. Also, from the Anglo-Saxon perspective, see Pocock, J. G. A., *The ancient constitution and the feudal law* (1st edn 1957), Cambridge: Cambridge University Press, 1987, 2nd edn.

talk").[11] The English Parliament was almost from the beginning a political assembly, initially composed of barons and bishops, who were able to impose the Magna Carta on Lackland King John in 1215. This first constitutional text in Western history spelled out in writing a series of limitations on the Royal Prerogative that have been observed ever since by the long succession of English monarchs.[12]

Royalty would try to counteract the considerable influence of the nobility by the simple strategy of admitting representatives of the cities into the *curia regis*. This initiative was adopted for the first time in European constitutional history in the Spanish Kingdom of Leon in 1188, when Alfonso IX convoked the urban representatives, forming another court alongside the traditional court of nobles and bishops. This led to assemblies of the estates, called *cortes* (in plural because the king met with more than one curia, or *corte* in Spanish).[13] The pattern was repeated in other European kingdoms: representatives of English cities were incorporated in the parliament of Westminster at the end of the 13th century, and those of French cities into the Estates-General from 1302, when Philip IV the Fair called them to ensure his supremacy against Pope Boniface VIII.

In this way, little by little, the old *curia regis* was transformed in European kingdoms into an estates assembly, whose essential function was to approve the extraordinary subsidies the monarch needed (origin of today's budgetary laws) and to give consent, with the monarch, to the most important legislative measures. Incorporating the cities into the estates assemblies was of the utmost importance because city members were designated or elected; thus they acted as representatives and were called deputies. This was another important advance on the road to legal control over monarchical power.[14]

---

11. Henry II Plantagenet (1154-1189) still used all his life primarily the French language. However, the French *parlements* were of a different nature, as they were not political councils but judicial courts.

12. See Clarke Holt, James, *Magna Carta and medieval government*, No. 68 in the series Studies presented to the International Commission for the History of Representative and Parliamentary Opinion (published in various works, 1955-1982), Hambledon, London, 1985, 2nd edn, Cambridge UP, 1992.

13. On this extremely interesting and important process in European constitutional history, see O'Callaghan, J. F., "The beginning of the cortes of Leon-Castile" in *American Historical Review*, ISSN 0002-8762, LXXIV (June 1969), pp. 1503-1537, and Procter, E. S., *Curia and Cortes in Leon and Castile, 1072-1295*, Cambridge/New York: Cambridge UP, 1980. Spanish translation, Madrid: Cátedra D. L., 1988.

14. For the constitutional history of early examples of the medieval state, see Below, Georg von, *Der deutsche Staat des Mittelalters: ein Grundris der deutschen Verfassungsgeschichte*, Leipzig: Quelle & Meyer, 1914. See also Hintze, O., *Historia de las formas políticas*, Madrid: Revista de Occidente, 1968 (English version in *The historical essays of Otto Hintze*, ed. Felix Gilbert with Robert M. Berdahl, New York: Oxford UP, 1975) and Fedou, René, *L'État au Moyen Age*, Paris: PUF, 1971 (Spanish translation Madrid: EDAF, 1977). On limits on royal power Blythe, J. M., *Ideal government and the mixed constitution in the Middle Ages,* Princeton NJ: Princeton UP, 1992 (French translation: *Le gouvernement idéal et la constitution mixte au moyen âge*, by Ménard,

Absolute monarchy, a model of state that also appeared for the first time in European history in Spain, specifically in Castile, at the end of the 14th century, was intrinsically quite incompatible with the idea of the king sharing power with the estates assemblies. In the end, during the 16th century the kings ended up imposing themselves on the estates assemblies in almost all of Europe, except in England and in the Hispanic kingdoms of the Crown of Aragon – where "pactism" (so called because government depended on the pact traditionally established between the king and the representatives of his realm) dominated the constitutional tradition until the early 18th century, when it was abolished by the *Nueva Planta* or "new (judicial) structure" decrees.[15]

1.5.2. From vassals to parliamentarians

The English experience had nevertheless a greater impact in the history of European public law, because the English Parliament ended up limiting more efficiently the king's power. This was partly because the final defeat in the Hundred Years War had weakened the monarchy in front of a Parliament that, from the middle of the 14th century, was divided in two houses – Lords and Commons – unlike the tripartite state assemblies found in the other European kingdoms. The English arrangement gave the Commons, the representative house, half the parliamentary power. This is why, after the gap of the Tudor years, the Stuarts were impotent to maintain absolutism and the English Parliament was able to impose effective limitations on Royal Prerogative. This was consolidated after the two revolutions which, between 1642 and 1689, transformed forever the English system of public law. These political-constitutional events spread across Europe thanks to John Locke (1632-1704), who set the theoretical foundations for a new model of state based on legal limitations on political power.

Locke was not just a thinker and theorist. As doctor and secretary to Lord Shaftesbury, one of the owners of the colony of North Carolina, Locke had the opportunity of trying to put his ideas into practice in the Fundamental Constitutions for the Carolina territory.[16] Locke's thought had also a great

---

Jacques, Paris: Cerf, 2005), and Canning, Joseph, *A history of medieval political thought*, 300-1450, London/New York: Routledge, 1996.

15. For an overview of this transition, see Henshall, N., *The myth of absolutism. Change and continuity in early modern European monarchy*, London: Longman 1993. For the Spanish constitutional tradition, see *El pactismo en la Historia de España*, Madrid: Instituto de España, 1980. For relations between cities and the monarchy in Catalonia, the territory most inclined to "pactism" in the Crown of Aragon, see Sabaté I Curull, Flocel, "Municipio y monarquía en la Cataluña bajomedieval" in *Anales de la Universidad de Alicante. Historia Medieval*, No. 13 (2000-2002), ISSN 0212-2480, pp. 255-282.

16. Looking for a career, Locke moved in 1667 into Shaftesbury's home at Exeter House in London, to serve as Lord Ashley's personal physician and resumed his medical studies under the tutelage of Thomas Sydenham, who had a major effect on his thinking on natural philosophy. The *Fundamental Constitutions of Carolina* was adopted in March 1669 by the eight lords proprietor of

and decisive influence on the political education of one of the founding fathers of the United States, Thomas Jefferson (1743-1826), author of the Declaration of Independence and third president of the Federal Union from 1801 to 1809. Locke's most influential work, *Two Treatises of Government* (1690), displayed his political ideas.[17] He asserts that society is based on a contract, but this arises only to rectify lacks in the state of nature ("Civil government is the proper remedy for the inconveniences of the state of nature"). For this reason civil society (commonwealth) is born, with the essential function of guaranteeing the free exercise of basic human rights (natural rights), such as liberty, equality, life and property.

Locke's individualism was developed further by the Geneva-born Jean-Jacques Rousseau (1712-1778) in his work *The Social Contract* (1762), which clearly defines the principles of government based on a reversible contract of submission, from which are excluded some natural rights of men which are inviolable (fundamental rights). The idea of a law arising beyond the limits of the power of the state, which appears as a set of natural rights adapted to reality and to the needs of men, is also expressly detailed by Montesquieu (1689-1755) in his best known work, significantly titled "The Spirit of the Laws" (1748). Here, he offers a very broad concept of the word "law" ("Laws, in their most general signification, are the necessary relations arising from the nature of things") and distinguishes between laws made by men and pre-existing laws ("Before laws were made there were relations of possible justice"). As God gives the laws of religion, the philosophers give the moral laws, and legislators the political and civil laws.[18]

Law as conceived of by Locke, Montesquieu and Rousseau therefore clearly appears as a reality distinct from power because it precedes power – since power is based on the social contract – and because it is different from power. Political and civil laws are a manifestation of the natural order and for this reason they cannot be established in an arbitrary way by the authority.[19]

---

the Province of Carolina, which included most of the land between modern Virginia and Florida. It replaced the *Charter of Carolina* and *Concessions and Agreements of the Lords Proprietors of the Province of Carolina* (1665). Unpopular with many of the early settlers and never ratified by the assembly, the *Fundamental Constitutions* were largely abandoned by 1700. They are usually attributed to John Locke, in collaboration with his patron Anthony Ashley-Cooper, 1st Earl of Shaftesbury, a leading lord proprietor with a long-standing interest in colonial affairs. There is some question about how far Locke, as Shaftesbury's secretary, was responsible for their final form, but the pair were probably the document's principal architects, with minor contributions from other proprietors. See Milton, J. R., "John Locke and the Fundamental Constitutions of Carolina" in *Locke Newsletter* (now *Locke Studies*) No. 21 (1990), pp. 111-133.

17. Locke, John, *Two Treatises of Government*, ed. Peter Laslett, Cambridge Texts in the History of Political Thought, Cambridge: Cambridge UP, 1989. For his legal ideas, see Brooks, Thom (ed.), *Locke and law*, Aldershot: Ashgate, 2007.

18. Montesquieu, *De l'Esprit des Lois*, 1st edn, 2 vols., Barillot et fils, Geneva, 1748 (I consulted the edition in *Œuvres complètes*, Paris: Seuil, 1964, pt 1, bk 1, No. 1, pp. 530-531). English translation by Thomas Nugent (1st edn 1752), Whitefish (Mont): Kessinger Publishing's Rare Reprints, 2005.

19. As Catherine Larrere ("Montesquieu" in *Dictionnaire de philosophie politique*, 3rd edn, Paris: PUF, 2003, p. 529) points out, Montesquieu's main criticism of Hobbes is that, if law depends

The differentiation of law as something separate from power is no doubt the essential pillar on which the liberal state is supported. It is a laissez-faire model of state in which political power plays a limited role, because its function is restricted to maintaining order and guaranteeing the free development of individuals' basic rights. Politically it guarantees bourgeois access to power, weakening the power of absolute monarchy and the privileged classes traditionally represented on the clerical and noble estates. Thus, in the new regime, the bourgeoisie could control the state through a national representative assembly (Jacobinism) that was itself controlled, thanks to restricted suffrage that gave a vote only to those having adequate property and wealth, and a constitution that set the rules of political practice and the limits of state intervention.

1.5.3. Constitution v. law: the appearance of judicial review

It was still necessary to find a way of guaranteeing legal respect for the pact spelled out in the constitution, to arrest any political attempt to alter the constitutional regime. This was achieved in the United States of America, a nation born totally *ex novo* from a constitutional text; and, in the frame of the Federal Constitution of 1787, the Supreme Court adopted the principle of judicial review for the first time in the famous *Marbury v. Madison* case (1803).[20]

Judicial review is a system by which the principle of the supremacy of law – which is an expression of the people's will, because the legislative norm is dictated by a representative body such as parliament or Congress – finds itself supplanted by the supremacy of the Constitution. This supposes a limit to the tyranny of majorities and legally guarantees respect for minorities in the framework of the underlying constitutional pact. In this way, a new model

---

on the will of the power, it can be changed at any moment (see *The Spirit of the Laws*: Book V, 10-14). The idea is expressed very clearly by Montesquieu himself: "the political and civil laws of each nation ought to be only the particular cases in which human reason is applied. They should be adapted in such a manner to the people for whom they are framed that it should be a great chance if those of one nation suit another. They should be in relation to the nature and principle of each government; whether they form it, as may be said of politic laws; or whether they support it, as in the case of civil institutions. They should be in relation to the climate of each country, to the quality of its soil, to its situation and extent, to the principal occupation of the natives, whether husbandmen, huntsmen, or shepherds: they should have relation to the degree of liberty which the constitution will bear; to the religion of the inhabitants, to their inclinations, riches, numbers, commerce, manners, and customs" (*De l'Esprit des Lois*, 1748, Book 1, chapter 3; 1964 edn, op. cit., p. 532).

20. For the important consequences of this decision for the constitutional model of the US Federal State, see Nelson, W. E., *Marbury v. Madison. The origins and legacy of judicial review*, Lawrence, KS: University Press of Kansas, 2000, and O'Neill, J., "*Marbury v. Madison* at 200: revisionist scholarship and the legitimacy of American judicial review", *Modern Law Review*, Vol. 65 (2002), pp. 792-802. See also www.marshall.edu/pat/Journal/Volume2_1/Hartman_Richard_3.htm.

of state arose, for which legal doctrine has coined the term "constitutional state of law".

This model is based on two principles. First, to modify the constitution – or add to it – it is necessary to have a very sizeable majority, which obliges taking minority views into account. Second, if a law approved by the majority contradicts the constitution it may be declared unconstitutional, through the so-called constitutional control, a competence that in the United States is attributed to all judges. This check is thus "diffuse" and "incidental" because it comes into play in the course of a proceeding when a judge decides that in a particular case the applicable statute contradicts a superior statute at constitutional level. The judge may declare the law unconstitutional only in one specific case, because in another situation the same norm could be compatible with the constitution. However, if higher courts declare a law unconstitutional, their decision binds lower jurisdictional bodies. If the Supreme Court declares it unconstitutional, the ruling is *erga omnes* because of the principle of *stare decisis*. This has a retroactive effect, as *ex tunc* applies, since it is understood that the norm declared unconstitutional was inapplicable from the time it was passed.

By contrast, the liberal state model put in place by the French Revolution, consolidated by Napoleon and the most widely practised form of government in Europe after 1848, did not adopt this system of judicial review. The legal limits for controlling the executive power were not substantiated in the political sphere, thanks to the emergence of the administrative jurisdiction. This new, special jurisdiction had new, specially appointed judges, partisans of the new regime and thus predisposed to guarantee the jurisdictional application of the legal principles of the new state. The paradigmatic example is France, where the administrative jurisdiction was peeled away from the competences of the ordinary courts and inserted fully into that of the executive itself through the jurisdictional authority of the Council of State.[21]

1.6. The social question and its constitutional response: the total state

The liberal model described, based on the principle of limiting the power of the state through law, was shaken by the grave social conflict that accompanied the worker movement arising from the transforming changes in European societies brought on by the Industrial Revolution. This is what historians call the "social question", posed by a new class known as the fourth estate, or simply as the proletariat because its members had no more patrimony than

---

21. For a solid comparison between the Anglo-American tradition and the continental European concept of the rule of law: Chesterman, S., "An international rule of law?" in *New York University Public Law and Legal Theory Working Papers*, New York University School of Law, Year 2008, Paper 70, pp. 5-10.

their own descendants.[22] This human group would acquire for the first time in 1848 a consciousness of themselves as a class thanks to Marx and Engels' *Communist Manifesto* ("Workers of the world, unite").[23]

From that time there appeared a new political philosophy based on the argument that the state ought to abandon the principle of laissez-faire and take action to prevent the exploitation of one human by another, which implied giving the lie to one of the basic individual rights on which the liberal state rested: property. Rousseau, in his *Discourse on the origin of inequality between men* (1755), had already pointed out that private property was at the root of social inequality. In the same vein, the French socialist Romantics, such as Count Saint Simon (1760-1825) and Charles Fourier (1772-1837), established the basis for economic authoritarianism, fought against inheritance and defended the state's acquisition of the "instruments of production" to achieve social justice. They based their ideas on the principle "to each according to his ability, to each ability according to its work". The movement became more radical with Pierre Proudhon (1809-1865), Louis Blanc (1811-1882) and above all Karl Marx (1818-1883).

After the publication of the *Communist Manifesto*, socialism acquired a decidedly political thrust and became an international movement directed at destroying the liberal state. To this end, the International Workingmen's Association (IWA), sometimes called the First International, was founded in London in 1864. However, the failure of the Paris Commune (March to May 1871) led Marx to renounce violence in the Hague Congress of 1872, from which he expelled Bakunin's anarchists. From that point onwards the socialist movement attempted to achieve control of the state by legal means, through elections (social democracy). This was the founding time of the first workers' parties, such as the German Social Democratic Party (1875), the Spanish Socialist Workers' Party (1879), the Italian Socialist Party (1892), the English Labour Party (1900), the Russian Socialist Revolutionary Party (1901) and the French Section of the Workers International (1905), the forerunner of today's French Socialist Party.

The socialist frontal attack on the Liberal State brought in constitutional history a new model of state in which political power became again exorbitantly influential. It is not an accident that Alexis de Tocqueville (1805-1859) proclaimed in the French Constituent Assembly of the Second Republic, on 12 September 1848, his "Discourse against the Right to Work", in which he rejected completely certain social rights as being directly incompatible with the individual rights that the liberal state was obliged to guarantee. In his

---

22. From Latin *proletarius*, belonging to the lowest class of Roman citizens, the ones who contributed to the state only by having children (*proles*).
23. For a recent edition: Marx K. and Engels F., *The Communist Manifesto*, translated into English by Samuel Moore and Edward Aveling, Penguin Classics, 2003.

opinion, it amounted to a restoration of absolutist authoritarianism of the political class.

Nevertheless, state interventionism advanced implacably after the triumph of Lenin and the Bolsheviks in the first congress of the Russian Socialist Revolutionary Party in 1902, setting in motion the events that would culminate in October 1917 with the victory of the Soviet revolution and the creation of the Communist International (Komintern) in 1919. This led the Western ruling classes to support the formation of workers' parties that proposed the application of a social programme, as a way to avoid the triumph of Bolshevism. The problem was that this initiative also swept Mussolini (1922) and Hitler (1933) into power. After the First World War an ominous period in the history of constitutional government unfolded. All-powerful states were allowed to flourish as a means to once and for all resolve the "social question". In this respect, the justification of this state totalitarianism given by Carl Schmitt (1914-1985) is most interesting. Although he eventually ended up losing Hitler's favour, Schmitt's ambition was to "legalise" the model of the German National Socialist state. It is quite surprising that, despite these antecedents, Carl Schmitt's works continue today to attract interest, essentially because they lucidly describe the features of the contemporary state in the post-liberal period that begins after 1918.[24]

For Schmitt, the limits imposed by the liberal model on the state allowed intermediate bodies to appear that then completely denaturalised the function of the state. This is why he considers it necessary to rediscover the direct relationship between the individual and the state, because during the 19th century "the old adversaries [of the state as defined by Hobbes], the indirect powers of the Church and interest groups had appeared under the modern figure of political parties, trade unions, associations, in a word: the powers of the society". Through parliament, they had appropriated the power to legislate and fortify the rule of law and believed that they had been able to tame Leviathan. Their work was made easier by a constitutional system whose fundamental scheme was a catalogue of individual liberties. The supposedly free private sphere

---

24. On Schmitt's influence, see Muller, Jan-Werner, *A dangerous mind: Carl Schmitt in post-war European thought*, Yale UP, New Haven, CT, 2003. The thinking of Carl Schmitt had an especially great impact in Spain. As detailed by Manuel García Pelayo, it was no doubt in the Spain of Franco's time (1939-1975) that the work of Schmitt had its most extensive diffusion and reception. See his "Epílogo" in the Spanish version of *Teoría de la Constitución,* Madrid: Alianza Editorial, 1982, p. 373. Schmitt's relationship with Spain was doubtless nourished by the marriage of his only daughter Ánima with a Spanish professor of legal history, Alfonso Otero Varela. For a general view of the influence of Schmitt in Spain, see López García, Jose Antonio, "La presencia de Carl Schmitt en España", *Revista de Estudios Políticos* (Nueva Época) No. 91 (January to March 1996), pp. 139-168. Francisco Sosa Wagner, professor of administrative law, has published new details on the relationship of Schmitt with Spain in *Carl Schmitt y Ernst Forsthoff: coincidencias y confidencias* Madrid: Marcial Pons, 2008. This is clear evidence of the interest that this German jurist continues to inspire in contemporary legal science.

(guaranteed by these liberties) ended up liberating the state to the private, that is, "the uncontrollable and invisible powers of society".[25]

For this reason Schmitt was against the rule of law, because he understood the "law" to be at the mercy of private powers in society that had denaturalised the first function of the state as an instrument that protects civil society. Hence, Schmitt rejected the law in the liberal, Jacobin sense because in his opinion it had been converted into a way of putting "a hook into the nose of the Leviathan".[26]

The theories of the total state fortunately fell apart after the defeat of Hitler in 1945, at least with respect to fascism and Nazism, since Soviet totalitarianism persevered until 1991. The good thing was that the totalitarian period convinced Western legal scholars that it was indispensable to return to a framework in which the state submitted to law, although among its functions by necessity would appear now the one of intervening in society to correct and limit social injustices.

1.7. The contemporary reappearance of the social pact and the resurgence of the rule of law

In the Western world, the collapse of fascist (1942) and Nazi totalitarianism (1945) was an indictment of the doctrines that had criticised the principles of the liberal state and the mechanisms to limit state power. For this reason, in the second half of the 20th century, eminent Western jurists threw themselves into defining a new model of state, one which, without renouncing its social aims, was compatible with the democratic system.[27] The most representative figure was without a doubt the Austrian jurist Hans Kelsen (1881-1973), founder of the Vienna School of Legal Theory. He propounded the "pure theory of law" (*Reine Rechtslehre*), which developed the "fundamental principles for the validity of law" (*Geltungsgrund der Rechtsnormen*).

The case of Kelsen is very interesting because in his younger years he had been a firm defender of the subjugation of law to state power. In fact, in the first stage of his career, the Austrian jurist fully identified law with the state. In particular, in his first work, entitled "Fundamental problems of the science of public law" (*Hauptprobleme der Staatsrechtslehre*), published in 1911 in the

---

25. Schmitt, Carl, *The Leviathan in the state theory of Thomas Hobbes: meaning and failure of a political symbol* (1938), translated by George Schwab and Erna Hilfstein, foreword by Tracy B. Strong, University of Chicago Press, 2008. For a commentary on the text, see Baume, Sandrine, *Carl Schmitt, penseur de l'État*, Paris, Lausanne: Sciences Po., Les Presses, 2008, p. 58.
26. Schmitt, Carl, *The Leviathan* (1938). See S. Baume, op. cit., p. 55.
27. In this respect, see the very interesting pp. 155-173 on the "return to liberal understanding of Fundamental Rights" in Grimm, D., *Die Zukunft der Verfassung*, Frankfurt am Main: Suhrkamp, 1991. In Spanish: *Constitucionalismo y derechos fundamentales*, ed. Antonio López Pina, Trotta, Madrid, 2006.

Austro-Hungarian Empire, he considered the basis of a law should be found only in the mandate that made it fundamentally necessary, by virtue of what Kelsen called the principle of "imputation" (*Zurechnung*), according to which a given event (the illegal action) led necessarily to a specific reaction (the sanction). To the extent that for the young Kelsen law did not require any other justification than its simple legal recognition by the state, the legislator became the leading player in the legal world, to the clear detriment of the judges whose function was nothing more than the automatic application of the law.[28] In this period, Kelsen was profoundly influenced by the prevailing statism spread in Europe between 1870 and 1914, which was manifestly reinforced during the inter-war period (1914-1939) by the emergence of the Stalin, Hitler and Mussolini dictatorships. Under this doctrine, the legal system was whatever the state considered to be the law. European jurists in general, and those of the German-speaking area in particular, defended the need for a strong state and for this reason the law was irretrievably tied to the state.

The political events that culminated in the coming of Hitler's Third Reich (1933-1945) led Kelsen – who fled the Nazi regime and took refuge first in Switzerland and then in the United States – to modify his thinking to the point of disengaging law from political power. This was the feeling that inspired his works "General doctrine of the state" (*Allgemeine Staatslehre*, 1925), the "Theory of pure law" (*Reine Rechtslehre*, 1934), a work rewritten in 1960, and, above all, the "General theory of law and state" (published in English in North America).[29] During this second period of his thinking, Kelsen formulated his well-known theory of logical structure, which, when applied to the general legal system, led to formulation of the principle of normative hierarchy. Kelsen structures legal order as an imaginary pyramid in which legal norms are supported one upon another, constituting an ascending step structure (*Stufenbau*) in whose upper vertex is located the "basic norm" (*Grundnorm*), characterised by being self-sufficient and therefore representing the final fundamental principle that sustains the validity of the whole legal system.[30]

Placed in historical perspective, the thinking of Kelsen is indisputably a rediscovery of the idea of the social pact, since the basic norm (*Grundnorm*) is the product of it. Agreed norms constitute the basis of the legitimacy of the legal order, like the rules that society agrees to submit to. The great novelty is that in this system the state stays in the background, since it once again depends on the law and is subject to law, which becomes the protagonist of the social pact. The law forms an independent category that justifies itself. Thus, law is

---

28. On this first scientific period of the young Kelsen, see Serra Jimenez, F., "Kelsen en Kakania (Cultura y Politica en el joven Kelsen)", *Boletín de la Facultad de Derecho de la UNED*, No. 1 (autumn 1992), ISSN: 1133-1259, pp. 211-227.
29. Kelsen, H., *General theory of law and state*, translated by Anders Wedberg, Cambridge, MA: Harvard University Press 1945. Reed. The Law Book Exchange Ltd. 2007.
30. There is a more recent translation by Max Knight of Kelsen's *Pure theory of law*, from the 2nd German edition, Berkeley, CA: University of California Press, 2002.

"pure", according to the terminology coined by Kelsen, because it is separated or differentiated from the state and not at its mercy, as occurred in the times of absolute monarchies or in the 20th century during the totalitarian period.

1.8. The European reception of the constitutional rule-of-law model

As a result of the public law theories most in vogue in Europe after the French Revolution, establishing a legal procedure aiming to guarantee the constitutionality of laws created a conflict between the political and the legal. It was necessary to resolve the dilemma of how a norm approved by a body legitimised by citizens' suffrage, such as a parliament, could be judged by an unelected institution like the courts of justice.

In Europe the solution to this contradiction, as Francisco Rubio Llorente recalls,[31] was the creation of a jurisdiction within the sphere of executive power called the "administrative contentious". Affairs that involved activities of the state administration could not be examined by ordinary courts, but rather by special administrative judges. Hence, it was inconceivable that the ordinary jurisdiction could oversee the law, understood as a decision reached by the only elected power: the legislature.

Even in England the absence of a written constitution and the consolidation of the legislative hegemony of parliament (which can do all things but turn a woman into a man, and today even that) made it very difficult to apply the American principle of judicial review. Of course in continental Europe it was even more complex because of the consolidation of the monarchical principle since the times of Machiavelli and Bodin. This created such great inertia, even after 1789, that when monarchs grudgingly accepted the constitutional principle, they did so only partly, as García de Enterría states.[32] Therefore the constitution in this phase was no more than a list of limits against a pre-existing monarchical power or a simple formal code of the structure of the powers of state. So, the first liberal constitutions either did not contain rights and liberties or they were limited to recording excessively general formulations that in all cases needed later legislative development to be applied by the courts of justice.

It is true that monarchical power was eventually replaced by legislative power, in Jacobinism, but this did not reduce in the least its strength as authority. In fact, it increased political power in that it converted legislative norms into a political mandate imposed by the parliamentary majority. Law was thus

---

31. Rubio Llorente, F., "Tendances actuelles de la Juridiction Constitutionnelle en Europe" in *Annuaire International de Justice Constitutionnelle*, XII, 1996, p. 13.
32. García De Enterria, E., *La constitución como norma y el Tribunal Constitucional*, 4th ed., Madrid: Thomson-Civitas, 2006.

subject to power, while judges were powerless to question it. Furthermore, judges were the product of the old regime where the post of judge in general was bought or depended on royal appointment. This was in clear contrast to what was occurring in the United States where judges were being elected and not designated by the state. This gave American judges an undeniable democratic support which continental European judges lacked. To this it must be added that in continental Europe, at the beginning of the 19th century, judges were the natural defenders of the monarchy and the aristocracy. So it was understandable that once the bourgeoisie had by revolution established the primacy of the National Assembly, it was not disposed to letting judges question legislative decisions. This led to reticence in the new model of the rule of law against a possible government of the judges and to a ferocious defence of the principle of absolute submission of the judiciary to the law.

For all these reasons, in continental Europe the model of the rule-of-law state that initially triumphed was substantially different from the American model of the constitutional rule of law. Indeed, the bourgeois oligarchs in Europe only considered the principle of judicial review to protect their constitutional system after the "social question" came to a head, when they discovered that a new social class (the fourth estate) was trying to occupy their place at the top of the political order. This may explain why attempts to establish constitutional control over the law coincided in some cases with broadening of the right to suffrage.[33]

The first serious attempts in continental Europe to establish the principle of constitutional control over law came to fruition after the First World War, when the triumph of the Soviet Revolution caused a major crisis in the liberal model of state.[34] One example is the 1919 Weimar Constitution, which included a Constitutional Court whose primary function was to rule on conflicts between the various constitutional powers and between the federal territorial units. However, the system failed because the principle of judicial review was still repugnant to the European public law tradition, owing to the abovementioned historical inertia. Hence, constitutional control followed a different path from that of the United States. The European model of the constitutional rule-of-law state, that defined from the point of view of legal dogma for the first time by Hans Kelsen, was the "concentrated constitutional jurisdiction".

Kelsen was not its creator. In fact he only began to study the subject in 1928, and the Austrian Constitution of 1920 already included this system of constitutional jurisdiction. The mechanism was improved in the reform of 1929, inspired by the Czechoslovakian Constitutional Court. Kelsen was a member

---

33. Stjernquist, N., "Judicial review and the rule of law: comparing the United States and Sweden" in *Policy Studies Journal*, Vol. 19, 1990, pp. 106-115.

34. An aspect studied by Cruz Villalón, Pedro, in his classic work *La formación del sistema europeo de control de constitucionalidad, 1918-1939*, Madrid: Centro de Estudios Constitucionales, 1987.

of the Austrian Constitutional Court and, as he himself admitted, his doctrinal development owed much to his personal experience in that body. The idea then was not original, though Kelsen enjoys the merit of having been the first to formulate it as a legal dogma in a clear and operative way.

1.8.1. Concentrated constitutional jurisdiction versus judicial review

In the original Kelsenian system, control over the constitutionality of norms was not in the hands of judges – servants of the state, who are not democratically elected – but rather belonged to a specific body created ad hoc: the Constitutional Court. Kelsen originally conceived this court not as a jurisdictional body but as an element of legislative power, which in his view was made up of two organs: parliament, which was charged with drafting norms (the positive legislator), and the Constitutional Court, whose function was to remove from the legal order laws that conflicted with the constitution (the negative legislator). For this reason the rulings of the Constitutional Court had the same effect as the law and its members were named by parliament. This court was not a jurisdictional body because it did not judge specific situations or facts, as ordinary courts do. Instead it limited itself to resolving questions of compatibility between two norms. Being a body of a legislative nature, its decisions were to apply *ex nunc*, that is, in the future, and not *ex tunc* with retroactive effects. Consequently, the problem of unconstitutionality did not lead to absolute nullity but rather to annulment. In this first Kelsenian system of concentrated constitutional jurisdiction, conceived of as ensuring the subjugation of judges to the law, the Constitutional Court was not able to revise a norm approved by the political power through the legislature.[35]

Kelsen's original system decisively influenced some European constitutionals. Spain's was one of them, as shown by Cruz Villalón with respect to the Tribunal Constitutional Guarantees created by the 1931 Constitution of the Second Spanish Republic.[36]

The deficiencies of concentrated constitutional jurisdiction meant that in the first half of the 20th century judicial control over state actions continued to occur essentially by the administrative contentious route. In this regard the far-reaching Spanish reform of the Law of 5 April 1894 was significant because it opted for a return to judicialism, unlike the laws promulgated by the conservative General Narváez in 1845 which regulated review essentially through the administrative route. Judicialism was solidified by the Law

---

35. Kelsen himself expressly criticised the American experience with judicial review on this point in his classic article "Judicial review of legislation: a comparative study of the Austrian and the American Constitution" in *Journal of Politics*, ISSN 0022-3816, Cambridge UP, Vol. 4, No. 2 (1942), pp. 183-200.

36. For a comparison of the Austrian and Czechoslovakian systems, see P. Cruz Villalón, *La formación del sistema europeo de control de constitucionalidad*, op. cit., pp. 341-419.

of 5 April 1904, a norm that signified the integration of the administrative contentious jurisdiction into the Supreme Court.[37]

1.8.2. The European approach to judicial review

After the Second World War, once the totalitarian period had ended, at least in most of Western Europe, a review was made of the system of control over the actions of political power. It is quite understandable that at that time the constitutionalists turned their attention to the United States' system of judicial review. The Kelsenian system did not disappear formally because the principle of "concentration" was maintained, instead of the American "diffusion", and only one specialised body, the Constitutional Court, had the authority to declare unconstitutionality.

Nevertheless, the new constitutional courts in Europe were radically different from those existing before the Second World War, because they stopped being legislative organs and became more judicial institutions. The fact that the constitutional court became a true jurisdiction, constituted, as Francisco Rubio Llorente states, an authentic "revolution" in European legal tradition.[38] This was essentially because the new constitutional jurisdiction altered the division of powers, entailing the appearance of a new front in the creation of law: constitutional jurisprudence. This new field meant the introduction in countries with a continental legal tradition (civil law) of the Anglo-Saxon principle of *stare decisis* into the jurisdictional area.[39] Thus, the new constitutional jurisdiction was not limited to comparing abstract norms. It also delved profoundly into matters when there were violations of norms, specifically in the case of fundamental rights, by examining appeals for legal protection.

1.8.3. The constitutional rule of law as European public law principle

This joint evolution of legal systems towards what we could call common European public law is seen in the process of European integration initiated in the middle years of the 20th century with the Treaty of Paris (1950), which

---

37. The full judicialisation of the administrative contentious process did not occur, paradoxically, until the Franco period with the López Rodo Law of 27 December 1956.

38. "The introduction of constitutional jurisdiction in Europe has not been the product of evolution but rather of revolution." Rubio Llorente, F., "La ley como garantía de los derechos del ciudadano" in *La forma del poder: estudios sobre la Constitución*, Madrid: Centro de Estudios Constitucionales, 1993, p. 507.

39. Rubio Llorente, F., "La Jurisdicción constitucional como forma de creación del derecho", *Revista Española de Derecho Constitucional*, ISSN 0211-5743, Year 8, No. 22, 1988, pp. 9-52 and more recently in "Divide et obtempera? Una reflexión desde España sobre el modelo europeo de convergencia de jurisdicciones en la protección de los Derechos" in the *REDC*, Year 23, No. 67, January to April 2003.

created the European Coal and Steel Community (ECSC). Today there is no doubt that European integration since 1950 has deepened the tendency to establish a system of judicial control over public power.

The history of European public law we have illustrated here shows that jurisdictional control was first instituted in some states by the administrative contentious route, which did not directly infringe on political power. Today, in European legal integration, jurisdictional protection against abuse of power is beginning to be effective via the administrative route, although this is less consolidated internally in member states.[40]

Nonetheless, the establishment of the principle of control of constitutionality of laws is far from consolidated at the level of Community law.[41] Of course, the exception of the European Court of Human Rights in Strasbourg must be mentioned, in spite of the fact that its rulings are not binding. This lack of coercive power is the result of Europe not being a united state (yet) in the area of constitutional law. However, it is undeniable that a common European constitutional legal order is beginning to exist *in fieri*. As Peter Häberle points out, it is necessary to look into the deepest reserves of the legal culture of each of the constitutional states to bring to light common factors, areas of agreement and familiarity, going beyond mere legal positivity. This is possible because the national states belong to a common type of "constitutional state". Recognising that the European national states have analogous systems "permits each state to follow its own path and simultaneously find itself immersed in the common European context".[42] On the same lines, Albrecht Weber considers that the rule of law has become a common European constitutional principle, particularly in such essential aspects as the supremacy of the constitution, the submission of public authorities to the law and the right to judicial protection.[43]

---

40. See Aguilera Barchet, "Preliminary Study" in Susana Galera Rodrigo, *Sistema Europeo de Justicia Administrativa*, Madrid: Instituto de Estudios Jurídicos Internacionales and Dykinson S. L., 2005, especially pp. 49-62.

41. "If judicial control becomes widespread on the American continent, either in its original form or subject to different degrees of 'rationalisation', its adoption on the European continent has always been marginal and in all cases, hardly representative": Cruz Villalón, P., *La formación del sistema europeo de control de constitucionalidad*, op. cit., p. 32.

42. Häberle, Peter, "Derecho constitucional común europeo", translation by Emilio Mikunda Franco, in *Revista de Estudios Políticos* (Nueva Época), No. 79, January-March 1993, pp. 12, 13. Also in Perez Luño (ed.), *Derechos humanos y constitucionalismo ante el tercer milenio*. Madrid: Marcial Pons, 1996. Nevertheless it is significant that the author assumes an essentially legalistic conception. According to him, the DCCE should arise from two routes, "the legal-political path of legislation" and the "exegesis of jurisprudence". This signifies that, for him, judges still do not have the right to create law, only to interpret it. In this case the diversity of the states impedes greatly advances in this field, as in some cases, like Germany or Spain, the constitutional courts have a wide margin of action; in others, like France, the Constitutional Council can only act under the framework of previous control.

43. Weber, A., "El principio de Estado de Derecho como principio constitucional común europeo" in *Revista Española de Derecho Constitucional*, Year 28, No. 84, 2008, particularly pp. 48-53.

In the sphere of "constitutionalisation" of the model of the state based on law, however, as Marian Ahumada Ruiz points out, until now European constitutional courts have not tried to guarantee the effectiveness of constitutional precepts themselves, but instead have kept their interventions limited to the political level with the objective of consolidating the system of constitutional democracy through the route of constructing and spreading a "constitutional culture".[44] This explains the relative politicising of the constitutional courts, which affects very directly the objectivity of their function. It "seems all too clear that when the exercise of the action of unconstitutionality is left to the discretion of bodies with a political nature, these tend to exercise it according to political criteria and strategies".[45] It is interesting also to see how Manuel Aragón stresses that the European model should be considered as a transitional model, destined to progressively move towards a model of diffuse control more like judicial review, while preserving some unique characteristics from the old Kelsenian concentrated model.[46]

On this same matter, Hélène Gaudin forthrightly defends the transformation of the justice system in the European community into a super-constitutional tribunal. It is seen as the necessary consequence of the ever clearer change in the nature of the community legal order, which occurred first in the arena of international law and which is now spreading to national law.[47]

As shown in this work, it has become increasingly necessary to study the undeniable influence that Community law has had in the formation of European public law. And equally important is analysing the ways in which concepts are diverging, as a result of that influence – especially considering the perspective of the long history of relations between power and law forged in the peculiar destiny of our long European legal tradition.

---

44. "In this sense, constitutional doctrine, above all in its beginnings, is less the result of the requirements of the constitutional text than of the effort to define the consequences of the compromise acquired by the community that bases itself on a democratic constitution": Ahumada Ruiz, Marian, *La jurisdicción constitucional en Europa,* Cizar Menor (Navarre): Thomson Civitas 2005, p. 304.
45. Ibid., p. 308.
46. Aragón Reyes, M., "La aplicación judicial de la Constitución. Algunas consideraciones sobre la Justicia Constitucional" in *Estudios de Derecho Constitucional.* Madrid: Centro de Estudios Políticos y Constitucionales, 1998, pp. 130-135.
47. "La qualification de la Cour de Justice comme juridiction constitutionnelle relève de l'hypothèse d'une mutation pour ne pas dire d'une transmutation, c'est-à-dire d'un changement de nature de l'ordre juridique communautaire. C'est le passage d'un droit international à un droit de type interne": Gaudin, Hélène, "The Community judicial system – La Cour de Justice, juridiction constitutionnelle?" in *Revue des affaires européennes. Law and European Affairs*, ISSN 1152-9172, No. 3, 2000, p. 218.

Chapter 2
European constitutionalism after the Second World War

R. Arnold

Historically the first pillar erected in the construction of the rule of law – the core element of modern constitutionalism – was the primacy of legislation over executive action. The administration was no longer an instrument exempt from the law, as it had been for a long time in the hands of monarchs. This first step towards legality was a victory of parliament over monarchical power, an important event in an early phase of constitutionalism when the formal concept of the rule of law was emerging.[48]

Judicial review of administrative action is the procedural consequence of this first step and is of great significance even today when a new understanding of the rule of law – a more substantive concept – has evolved. This new approach, orientated towards constitution and values, is based on the formal dimension which has maintained its original significance. Formal and substantive rule-of-law concepts are interdependent and comprise the basic aspects of constitutionalism.[49]

The evolution of the rule of law, together with judicial control of the administration, is a fundamental element in the development of European constitutionalism and therefore of European legal culture.

2.1. Periods of constitutional development

Constitutionalism in Europe can be divided into two significant periods: from the beginnings of the idea to create normative basic orders for existing regimes, mainly from the 18th century onwards, until the turning point in constitutional thinking, the new beginning after the Second World War. The first period was characterised by the preponderance of the state over

---

48. See Reinhold Zippelius and Thomas Würtenberger, *Deutsches Staatsrecht*, 32nd edn 2008, pp. 105-106.
49. See Rainer Arnold, "Rechtsstaat und Normenkontrolle in Europa" in *Essays in Honour of Bodo Börner*, Cologne, 1992, pp. 7-28; Rainer Arnold, "Das Verfassungsprinzip gerichtlicher Kontrolle von Legislative und Exekutive – Gemeinsamkeiten und Unterschiede" in Peter-Christian Müller-Graff and Eibe Riedel (eds), *Gemeinsames Verfassungsrecht in der Europäischen Union* (Schriftenreihe des Arbeitskreises Europäische Integration e.V., Bd. 43), Baden-Baden, 1998, pp. 123-146.

the individual, the normative weakness of the constitution and the focus on a closed nation-state. In contrast, the emancipation of the individual is significant in the second period, based on the idea of the primacy of the constitution (the orientation of which is clearly anthropocentric), the growing importance of fundamental rights, a new value-orientated concept of the rule of law, and the tendency to an "open state" with a more relevant understanding of sovereignty.

This second period can itself be divided into three phases. The first was the immediate post-war phase, marked by the German constitution of 1949 with a manifestly individual-orientated structure and a strong constitutional justice system. The second phase was the 1970s, when transformation constitutions were created in Spain, Portugal and Greece after the end of authoritarian regimes. All these constitutions have modern attributes: they express provisions on the dignity of man and the rule of law as well as an anthropocentric orientation and institutional or functional constitutional justice structures. The third phase took place after the fall of communism in central and eastern Europe, where new democracies based on an advanced standard of constitutionalism were created after 1989. This phase was characterised by a significantly anthropocentric approach and recognition of the modern rule-of-law concept based on constitutional jurisdiction, with review of legislation at the centre, an important instrument in transformation. Furthermore, the new constitutionalism of the 1990s took account of the international level, referring in particular to the fundamental and human rights embodied by the European Convention on Human Rights. Thus, the concepts of the national constitutions were confirmed on the European level and this corresponded to the intention of the new democracies to Europeanise their legal concepts.[50]

2.2. European constitutionalism

Pluri- and multi-state interactions have increasingly absorbed concepts which have been developed in internal constitutional law. The elements of a modern concept of the rule of law are of particular interest in this context. Plurinational organisations, such as the European Community/European Union, can be qualified as constitutional. This qualification can also be made for the European Convention on Human Rights, which is in its form an international treaty, but in its substance is constitutional law. Therefore we can identify three levels of constitutional law in Europe: (1) the constitutions of the member states of the Council of Europe, which includes all member states of the European Union, (2) the basic provisions of the EC legal order, which forms the first pillar of the European Union, and (3) the European Convention on Human Rights.

---

50. For the historical development, see Rainer Arnold, *La unificación alemana. Estudios sobre derecho alemán y europeo*, Madrid, 1993, pp. 142-155.

The notion of constitution and constitutional law has been reserved for a long time to the state.[51] With the transfer of national functions to the European Communities, a newgroßbritannien situation came about: former intra-state fields have been "Europeanised" – supranational institutions legislate and administer these matters in a new, European dimension. The main functions of a constitution have also been attributed to the EC legal order, namely: the creation of an institutional system by establishing organs with specific competences and by determining values for the protection of the individual. These two dimensions of a modern constitution can easily be found at EC level. Whereas most provisions on institutions are embodied in the EC Treaty, values have been developed by jurisprudence and have now been listed in a written document: the European Union Fundamental Rights Charter. This charter, not yet in force, will gain normative existence by ratification of the Lisbon Reform Treaty. These arguments justify the qualification of these essential parts of the EC law as constitutional.[52]

As to the European Convention on Human Rights, the same qualification is legitimate because the charter rights complement the national constitutional rights and have a functional interconnection. The constitutional law solution of the state is functionally not final and may be subject to further review by the Court of Strasbourg. The convention can therefore be regarded as complementary to the national constitutions and – as far as the values it represents are concerned – a constitution in itself.

This pluri-level constitutional system is to a high degree interdependent and exercises mutual influence, both vertically and horizontally.

2.2.1. The interdependence of the three constitutional levels

It is significant that European Community law has an important impact on the national legal order, including national constitutional law. This is a consequence of the unwritten fundamental principle of the primacy of Community law over national law, developed, since a very early stage, by the European Court of Justice.[53] However, it is also manifest that the national constitutional law of the member states has influenced the formation of the general principles of Community law, which have the function of EC fundamental rights. The European Court of Justice has developed, through comparative and selective

---

51. See Dieter Grimm, "Does Europe need a constitution?" in Peter Gowan and Perry Anderson (eds), *The question of Europe*, London, 1997, pp. 239-257.
52. See also Rainer Arnold, "Begriff und Entwicklung des Europäischen Verfassungsrechtes" in *Staat – Kirche – Verwaltung*, Essays in honour of Hartmut Maurer, ed. M.-E. Geis and D. Lorenz, München, 2001, pp. 855-868.
53. See *Costa v. ENEL*, case 6/64, European Court Reports 1964, p. 1251.

steps, supranational fundamental rights which are drawn from member states' constitutions as well as from the European Convention on Human Rights.[54]

The third level of constitutional law, the Convention as interpreted by the Judges in Strasbourg, has a significant impact on national law. The national courts try to avoid a conflict between national and convention law. Though, in Germany for example, the Federal Constitutional Court judgments almost never refer to Strasbourg or the Convention,[55] it seems that in preparation of the national decision a comparison is made with regard to the potential Strasbourg decision. In many member states, the Convention has a specific status: it is constitutional law in Austria, has the rank of constitutional law in Switzerland and serves, according to Article 10 paragraph 2 of the Spanish constitution, as an interpretation document for internal fundamental rights.

In a significant number of countries, the Convention is ranked between legislation and the constitution. Thus traditional systems like the French are very much influenced by the Convention, and courts are applying it and choosing not to apply the national law in case of conflict between the two. Many central and eastern European countries have assumed this system, and the Convention is often referred to by their constitutional courts. This is true even in systems where international treaties are transformed into internal law, and consequently the treaties are qualified, as is the case for the federal constitution of Germany, as a help to interpret constitutional concepts such as the rule of law. Even in Great Britain, the Convention has been introduced by the Human Rights Act into national law. The courts (of higher instance) have the right to deliver a declaration of incompatibility if they regard the British law to be applied by the courts as incompatible with the Strasbourg Convention. This puts the procedure in the hands of the minister, who can modify the existing law by an order with prior consent, and in urgent cases, with subsequent consent of the Houses of Parliament.[56] The Strasbourg Convention has become a sort of constitutional document in Great Britain. These examples show the outstanding importance of the European Convention on Human Rights and make clear that it is legitimate to qualify it as constitutional.

2.3. The dynamics of European constitutional law

This three-level, mutual influence system is about to create convergent principles for constitutional law all over Europe. These principles may be considered European constitutional law.[57] Convergent processes are going on,

54. See Takis Tridimas, *The general principles of EC law*, 2001.
55. But see also German Federal Constitutional Court Rep., Vol. 35, pp. 311, 320; Vol. 74, p. 358.
56. See Aileen Kavanagh, *Constitutional review under the UK Human Rights Act*, Cambridge UP, 2009.
57. See Rainer Arnold, "European constitutional law: some reflections on a concept that emerged in the second half of the 20th century", *Tulane European & Civil Law Forum*, Vol. 14,

especially in the fields of fundamental rights and the rule of law. The influence of the Strasbourg Convention is very great, and a judicial dialogue is increasingly taking place. General characteristics are appearing, such as in particular the efficiency of the fundamental rights protection of the individual, demonstrating the ongoing emancipation of people from public power.

Efficiency means that the fundamental rights, understood as values, constitute a comprehensive objective order which encompasses all new issues arising from new technology and contemporary developments. Efficiency of fundamental rights also means that they are conceived of usually as subjective rights, which permit the individual to evoke them directly before the court. Besides that, the theory of the obligation of the state to protect the values embodied by fundamental rights has been put forward in various countries. Efficiency signifies also the constitutionalisation of all branches of law, in particular of the field of civil law. Thus fundamental rights influence the general provisions of civil law, and fundamental values are incorporated into the horizontal inter-relations between individuals. Efficiency means furthermore that the legislator cannot restrict fundamental rights, even with a high qualified majority, without any limits. The German constitution has developed, in Article 19 paragraph 2 of the Basic Law, the guarantee of the very essence of a fundamental right, a guarantee introduced later in the constitutions of Spain and Portugal and in the constitutional orders of central and eastern Europe. Although it is difficult to define what the very essence of a fundamental right is, the existence of such a limit moderates the legislator.

The principle of proportionality[58] is also applicable. It was created first by the Federal Constitutional Court of Germany, then transferred to the European Court of Justice, and thereafter exported from the supranational area to the other member states of the European Union. This principle is an expression of the basic freedom the individual possesses from birth. Let us remember the explanation of Jean-Jacques Rousseau: "men are born free and give up a part of their freedom, by a social contract, to institutions in order to be governed by them. Society transforms into a constituted state, with a constitution as a basic order, a sort of 'social contract'."[59]

The relationship between individuals and the institutions with the power to govern them must focus on the maintenance of freedom in a constituted order. The principle of proportionality is a limit of the exercise of power over the

---

New Orleans, 1999, pp. 49-64; R. Arnold, "The different levels of constitutional law in Europe and their interdependence" in J. Nergelius, P. Policastro and K. Urata (eds), *Challenges of multilevel constitutionalism*, Kraków, 2004, pp. 101-113; R. Arnold, "L'exposition des constitutions européennes aux influences externes" in *Vingtième anniversaire de la Constitution portugaise*, ed. Jorge Miranda, Coimbra, 1997, pp. 673-694.

58. See Hartmut Maurer, *Staatsrecht I*, 5th edn, München, 2007, pp. 224-227; for the European Court of Justice, see case 18/63, Rep. 1964, pp. 175, 204; case 265/87, Rep. 1989, p. 2237.

59. Jean-Jacques Rousseau, *Du contrat social* (1762), chapter 6.

individual, restricting such exercise of power to cases in which the application of public power is indispensable for the (total or partial) realisation of a legitimate public interest. This minimum of intervention corresponds to the original freedom of the individual. Proportionality also means an adequate relationship between the instrument used for the intervention and the aim to be achieved. An important aim can be realised by an instrument which has serious consequences. If less significant aims are pursued by the public power, the instruments applied must not be so powerful.

There is a second field where the dynamics of convergent processes are manifest: that of the rule of law. This concept was developed in continental Europe, by German authors in particular, in the 19th century.[60] *Rechtsstaat* was conceived at the time in a formal way: the submission of the executive branch to parliament's laws as the general will of the people. Separation of power and judicial review of administrative actions – either by special administrative courts or, more frequently, by ordinary courts – was an additional element of formal rule of law.

The rule of law was transformed into a substantive, value-orientated concept in the mid-20th century. After the Second World War, the new anthropocentric orientation of constitutional law transformed the concept of *Rechtsstaat* and gave it a new dimension: as clearly expressed by the Conseil constitutionnel in 1985, the general will of the people is no longer expressed simply by legislation, but only by the type of legislation that conforms to the constitution. The primacy of the constitution is the essential progress which has been made by the modern concept of rule of law. As the classic 1985 dictum of the Conseil constitutionnel put it: "la loi n'exprime la volonté général que dans le respect de la Constitution."[61]

It can be said that the supreme values of a society are contained in its constitution, either explicitly or implicitly. It is a characteristic of modern European constitutionalism that the dignity of man, fundamental rights and the rule of law are expressly mentioned in constitutional texts. Values expressing individuals' freedom are strictly interconnected with the primacy of constitutional law.

One element of an advanced concept of rule of law is the existence, institutional or functional, of constitutional jurisdiction. Austria and Czechoslovakia had constitutional courts from 1920, but they were rare predecessors of those of today. In the youngest phase in the development of European constitutionalism, the creation of democratic constitutions in central and eastern Europe, a significant preference was given to having specific constitutional courts. The American system attributing constitutional review of legislation to the supreme ordinary courts has, in part, been realised only in Estonia. The

---

60. See Otto Bähr, *Der Rechtsstaat*, 1864; Rudolf von Gneist, *Der Rechtsstaat*, Berlin, 1872.
61. Conseil constitutionnel, 85-197 DC of 23 August 1985, Rec., 70, 76.

core function of constitutional jurisdiction is the review of legislation. This means an intervention into the function of parliament, the most important institution of a state. In states in transformation, this review has obtained an essential importance.

Review of legislation is the very nucleus of constitutional justice, whereas an individual constitutional complaint is dedicated to the defence of fundamental rights. The types of legislation review are very similar: the distinction between an abstract and a specific review, one launched by state institutions to guarantee the compliance of the legislator with the constitution, the other initiated by judges to check the constitutionality of legislation in a determined case. The review function is usually given to a constitutional court, but some countries, like Greece or Portugal, adhere to the system of decentralised legislation review which can be exercised by any court. Of course, only a constitutional court can nullify an existing act of parliament. If other courts have the power to challenge legislation, they may only choose not to apply this act but they have no competence to nullify it.

In the new constitutional orders of the central and eastern European countries, the abstract review of legislation has obtained a new dynamic:[62] in many of these countries, the ombudsman, an independent institution elected by parliament with the task of being the guardian of the individual, can launch such a review, prompted by an alleged violation of individual rights. This is frequently done in Poland and Ukraine, where the proceedings-related review is not used as frequently; in fact, quite the opposite is true. This differentiates them from, for example, Germany where this type of constitutional action is the second most frequent after the individual constitutional complaint.

The protection of fundamental rights is a basic task of all tribunals, especially those to which the control of administrative action is entrusted. The constitutional courts also have this task, though in most cases as a subsidiary task. In the first instance the normal courts, if competent in the particular case, are obliged to remedy the violation. Thus, the individual complaint alleging a fundamental rights violation is an extraordinary remedy addressed to the constitutional court. In the case where a specific form of individual complaint exists – a complaint against a piece of legislation, the application of which would constitute such a violation – access to the constitutional court is not subsidiary but primary. The aim of the complainant is to ask the constitutional court to examine the constitutionality of the law which shall be applied to him. In truth this action is a sort of review of legislation initiated by an individual.

Other competences are also regularly attributed to constitutional courts, such as the competence to make a decision on controversies between state

---

62. Rainer Arnold, "Constitutional courts of central and eastern European countries as a dynamic source of modern legal ideas", *Tulane European & Civil Law Forum*, Vol. 18, New Orleans, 2003, pp. 99-115.

institutions, a dispute on specific competences between state authorities, regional or federal controversies, the prohibition of political parties, and many other functions. As a whole, it can be said that it is a characteristic tendency in Europe that formal constitutional jurisdiction is established with the core competence of legislation review and, generally speaking, with a broad range of other functions. Indeed, it can be said that the new concept of the rule of law has been complemented by an efficient constitutional justice – "perfectionnement de l'Etat de droit" in the words of Dominique Turpin.

The third dynamic of modern constitutionalism, parallel to fundamental rights and the rule of law, is internationalisation – specifically, in Europe, the supranationalisation of the internal legal order. This means that the globalisation of formerly purely national tasks must be recognised by constitutional law. This has consequences; in particular the reach of fundamental rights has to be extended because it is not only violation by national institutions that must be covered by fundamental rights protection. Thus, the extradition of an individual could be contrary to fundamental rights if torture would be applied in the state to which the person is conveyed. The decision to extradite a person in such a case constitutes a fundamental rights violation. This is only one example of many which show the internationalised dimension of constitutional law.

Supranationalisation means that EC/EU law has an enormous impact on national constitutional and ordinary law, due to the principle of primacy of Community law over national law. Through this process, European concepts are increasingly replacing national ones; the famous Tanja Kreil case is a significant example. In the United Kingdom, a very traditional and rigid concept of parliamentary sovereignty has reigned for two centuries; however, the Factortame case has seriously altered this doctrine. In addition, the Europeanising process can also be seen in the introduction of the European Convention on Human Rights into the British legal order by the Human Rights Act, which introduced new mechanisms (the declaration of incompatibility: an amending order of the minister to ensure that British legislation conforms to the Convention).

A fourth tendency of European constitutional law is the differentiation of power in a vertical and horizontal sense. Vertical differentiation is seen in the growing regionalisation of state territory, sometimes even tending towards federalism. This vertical differentiation of power is also recognisable in central and eastern Europe where the unitary structure of the territory is often mentioned expressly in the constitution. This must be understood as a constitutional guarantee against separatist tendencies and secession of parts of the territory.

Independent of that, a strong tendency exists to strengthen local autonomy all over Europe. Even in systems where local autonomy corresponds to what is guaranteed by legislation, the core of autonomy is being increasingly developed by the constitutional jurisdiction, which does not allow autonomy to be essentially reduced by legislation itself. As to federalism, ethnic-based federalism seems to be alive; other federal systems, such as those of Germany and Austria, underlie developments towards regionalism. The distinction between the phenomena of territorial differentiation is rather fluid; for example, Spanish regionalism is often qualified as being quasi-federal.

There is also a horizontal differentiation of power: public power is given back to society by privatisation, or political power is relativised by decisions of expert commentaries which are de facto independent and not submitted to democratic control. Besides that, transnational regional co-operation of various countries creates extra-state power centres. Transnational administrative networks, the new phenomena of globalised decision making, are increasingly replacing the traditional system of one state, one government. Multi-level governments are also an expression of power differentiation.

2.3.1. Dynamic and static elements in European constitutions

As analysed above, the tendencies in European constitutional law are very dynamic as far as fundamental rights, the rule of law and constitutional jurisdiction are concerned. Vertical power differentiation – seen in forms of federalism, regionalism and localism (the strengthening of local autonomy) – can be added to this. Their dynamic nature means that overall processes, on the abovementioned three levels of constitutional law with mutual influence, are taking place quickly and leading to the emergence of convergent general principles. The international dimension runs parallel to internal constitutionalism and is also a fast-developing dynamic process.

A static character can be found, especially in the institutional systems of states, reflecting a particular tradition. Thus, the position of a state president and the structure of parliament are consolidated structures without significant changes. Here divergences in Europe are more common than in other fields of constitutional law.

2.4. Constitutionalism and legal culture

Law is cultural. A constitution has a weighty cultural effect. A constitution, as shown above, is the basic legal order of a society and forms the behaviour of state institutions as well as of individuals, orientates the structuring of the legal order, realises certain concepts either traditional or new, establishes a framework for political activity and determines values which, themselves, have a large impact on culture.

If culture is derived from Latin *colere* – the planned arrangement of an existing reality of nature – then constitutional law corresponds in a great degree to this definition. Through its basic features, constitutional law creates national identity, at least in its legal dimension. National identity is also related to further dimensions of culture, to pieces of art and literature in the language of the country in particular.

If culture and its legal dimension are more and more influenced by foreign law, and if the mutual impact of the various constitutional law levels in Europe is increasing, national identity will be complemented or, in part, replaced by a European identity.

Politics can aim at a balanced co-existence of national and European identity, which the Reform Treaty of Lisbon intends to do. That the art-related particularity of a state shall be conserved is quite clear. Supranational competences are not full competences, only complementary ones. Unity by plurality, the motto of the ongoing integration, can only be achieved by such co-existence.

2.4.1. The principles of constitutional law as expressions of legal culture

The important elements of European legal culture include the basic legal thinking and the acceptance of certain values – especially the dignity of man, which is a supreme value of society and state as well as of supranational power – alongside distinct elements of the rule of law, democracy and openness to the international community.

It seems that the rule of law is the concept on which most contemporary legal culture focuses.

2.4.2. The rule of law as characteristic of legal culture

The concept of the rule of law unites all the basic elements of modern constitutionalism in an anthropocentric sense. Democracy is not possible without the rule of law, and a rule of law based on democracy is indispensable. A pure majority rule is not sufficient in modern constitutional thinking. If majority rule is detached from values, it can be contrary to justice and human dignity, both of which are basic tenets of contemporary legal culture. As democracy is indispensably linked with a value-orientated concept of the rule of law, majority rule must be in conformity with a constitutional order which is, in itself, anthropocentric. Primacy of the constitution is, therefore, the new dimension of the rule of law as well as of democracy.

As political self-determination of the individual is part of the individual's autonomy and dignity, the rule of law – even if it is value-orientated – cannot exist without a real democracy. Thus, the rule of law combines democratic values with human dignity, autonomy and freedom of the individual as a basis. The rule of law is the very essence of contemporary constitutionalism.

Because traditionally the rule of law contains judicial review of administrative action, it can be said that this also belongs among the core elements of a European constitutional culture.[63]

---

63. See Rainer Arnold, "Constitutional courts of central and eastern European countries as a dynamic source of modern legal ideas", *Tulane European & Civil Law Forum*, Vol. 18, New Orleans, 2003, pp. 99-115.

Part II
The European legal tradition

Chapter 3
National legal tradition – Czech Republic

S. Skulová

To understand the constitutional foundations of the judicial review system and how it is currently practised in the Czech Republic, a detailed explanation is necessary. Judicial review in the sense of submission of public power bodies to review by truly independent judicial bodies has a relatively long, but not entirely continuous, tradition dating back to the last quarter of the 19th century in the Czech Republic (formerly a part of the Austrian and Austro-Hungarian empires and, from 28 October 1918 to 31 December 1992, part of Czechoslovakia).

The existence, the means to establish and the actual execution of independent judicial review over public power was organically connected with creating and respecting, either in theory or in practice, the principles of a legal (constitutional) state, the foundations of which include public power being bound by legal acts and by the principle of democracy. In this area, from the end of the 1940s to the end of 1989, traditional standards were abandoned and, logically, progress toward the development of a modern legal state and its institutions and procedures was interrupted.

These facts and factors inevitably had an effect on both constitutional foundations and regulations and also on the specific legal regulation of judicial review. The effect was to reduce judicial review both in form and content, to the point where it survived only as a residue (for example, the fundamentally minimised review of administrative acts by ordinary courts after the dissolution of the Supreme Court in 1952, the regulation and activity of which had before been a natural continuation of the Austrian Administrative Court). These facts, originating during the establishment of (actual or non-existent) democracy and legality, and in the regulation of the public power system, necessarily had an effect in the field of constitutional documents and practice.

Although a modern system of constitutional regulations, institutions and procedures has now been created (or is being completed), elements of the previous, problematic period can still be seen in the attitudes of some public bodies and in the way the current legal provisions are applied. Knowledge of certain aspects of the problems can give a better understanding of specific facts and details of judicial review in the Czech Republic, especially the complicated phenomena, situations and procedures explained here.

3.1. The constitutional framework

The basis for separation of the different parts of public power is set out in Constitutional Act No. 1/1993 Coll., Constitution of the Czech Republic (hereinafter referred to as "the Constitution"), as amended. However, this is not a so-called mono-legal constitution, because the more comprehensive term is "constitutional order" (established by Articles 3 and 112 of the Constitution), in which other legal acts of the Parliament of the Czech Republic also have the highest legal force (according to Article 112, paragraph 1, of the Constitution), particularly the Charter of Fundamental Rights and Freedoms and several constitutional acts (for example, Constitutional Act No. 347/1997, creating higher territorial self-governing units, on which the current regions called *kraj* have been based).

According to the Constitution, as regards the form of power, the Czech Republic is a democracy, with the prevailing representative form of power execution (that is, the people execute public power through legislative, executive and judicial bodies). The Constitution allows, and Act No. 22/2004 Coll. (apart from the acts on municipalities and on the capital, Prague) regulates, a local referendum at the level of municipalities. The constitutional order does not regulate any other forms (levels) of direct democracy.

As regards relations between public bodies, it is a parliamentary form of power, in which the government as the supreme executive body is responsible to the Assembly of Deputies. The separation of powers is established in the form of mutual co-operation of legislative and executive powers. The concept of the Constitution is based on the traditional tripartite (trialistic) theory supplemented by other elements (Supreme Auditing/Control Office, Czech National Bank, territorial self-governmental units).

Legislative power is represented by the Parliament of the Czech Republic with two chambers – the Assembly of Deputies (200 deputies; elections based on a system of proportional representation) and the Senate (81 senators elected by simple majority). The Senate is established rather as a stabilising and auditing body, while the Assembly of Deputies is the actual decision-making (political) body to the decisions of which the Senate can express its opinion in the manner allowed in the Constitution. The Constitution sets out the procedure for formulating the conclusions of the Assembly of Deputies and the Senate in the legislative process (Article 47, Constitution: the ability of the Assembly of Deputies to reverse a rejecting resolution of the Senate).[64]

Owing to the direct voting legitimacy of parliament, the other organisations and activities of the state are based on it. However, parliament is naturally

---

64. In other cases, this possibility is not established. The code of procedure regulating the relation of the two chambers has not been adopted yet (unlike the legal regulation of each chamber's code of procedure).

controlled by other bodies and their competences are mutually balanced. Parliament's power is at the constitutional level, at the legislative level and at the level of the formation of governmental bodies (election of the president, confidence in the government, election of the Public Law Defender). Parliament has power in matters of foreign and interior policies, and in auditing the government and other executive bodies.

The power of parliament is limited by the ability of the Constitutional Court to examine the constitutional aspect of laws and to preventively review international agreements discussed in parliament. The Constitutional Court also hears the Senate's charges against the president in the case of high treason and it resolves possible disputes on the incapacity of the president to perform his duties.

Executive power is represented by the president as the head of state, central (usually ministries) and territorial administrative bodies (usually subordinate to a ministry or another central state body),[65] and the government as the supreme body, in which the Constitution includes the department of the state attorney as the public prosecutorial body, particularly in criminal affairs.

In practical terms, the executive power oversees territorial self-governmental bodies (of municipalities and regions) which are, however, dealt with in the Constitution separately in Chapter Seven. The "mixed model" is applied in the Czech Republic, where municipalities and regions, apart from their self-governing competencies, also execute parts of state administration transferred to them by law. The system of state administration thus does not include territorial authorities with a general competency, only specialised ones. The Constitution establishes the authority (power) for ministries, regions and municipalities to issue by-laws or specific laws and, in the area of self-government, it gives the assemblies of regions and municipalities the power to issue legal regulations in the form of statutes (generally binding notices).

The president is elected by parliament, but the president does not answer to it constitutionally and politically. The president enjoys wide immunity and may only be prosecuted for high treason.[66] The president as the head of state has representative duties. The president may dissolve parliament under certain conditions, has the right of suspensory veto and may seek redress in the Constitutional Court if deprived by parliament of the ability to perform the presidential duties.

---

65. This framework also includes so-called independent administrative bodies which are not subject to instructions from a central administrative body or the government, as in the case of, for example, the Office for Personal Data Protection. Also, this includes legal entities and individuals authorised by law to execute public administration, and also armed (Police) and other units (for example, the Fire Rescue Service).
66. "Actions directed against the sovereignty and integrity of the Republic, as well as against its democratic order." See Section 96, Act No. 182/1993 Sb., on the Constitutional Court, as amended.

Dualism is typical of the relationship between the president and the government, because the government has wide latitude in its actions and the president may do only what is entrusted specifically to the office by the Constitutional Act or an ordinary act. The president appoints the prime minister and nominates, and may dismiss, the members of the government. The countersignature authority of the prime minister is required for some acts (this does not apply to vetoing laws). Countersignature does not make the president answerable to parliament; the responsibility belongs to the government. In such cases, when countersignature is not required, the president takes the role of arbitrator and moderator (the right to participate, on request, in the sessions of both chambers with the right of advisory vote, and in sessions of the government).

In relation to judicial power, the president has the rights of amnesty (with countersignature), remission, mitigation, abolition and rehabilitation. The president and parliament work together to appoint judges to the Constitutional Court and the president of the Supreme Audit Office. The president appoints the judges (with countersignature), the chair and vice-chairs of the Constitutional Court and the Supreme Court (without countersignature). The president may file a motion with the Supreme Court to dissolve or suspend the activity of a political party unless the government has done so.

The government, as the highest body of executive power with general competency, must answer to the authority of the Assembly of Deputies; the government may request a vote of confidence from the assembly. The assembly may adopt a resolution of no confidence. The government is established by the following procedure: appointment of the prime minister by the president, appointment of the other members of the government, request of the government for a vote of confidence in the Assembly of Deputies. In the case of repeated failure, the Chairperson of the Assembly of Deputies proposes someone as prime minister to the president. The situation is then resolved by the president dissolving the Assembly of Deputies and announcing new elections.

The number of members of the government is not fixed. The list of ministries and their competencies is regulated in the Act of Competencies (Act No. 2/1969 Coll., as amended). A member of the government may also perform the function of senator or deputy of the Assembly of Deputies.

The government acts as a board, collegiately. The Constitution does not give the exact list of competencies of the government, but at the basic level it establishes that they include setting state policy objectives, taking the initiative in parliament (legislative) and with the president, management of the state by resolutions (internal acts) and orders of the government (legal regulations, issued and based on a law within its limits, published in the Collection of Laws), and management, control and co-ordination of the state machinery's activities (including ministries). One key responsibility of the government is to draft and submit bills on the state budget and final state accounting.

In the field of security and foreign policy, both chambers address the government. In this area, the so-called legislative veto can be applied in certain matters against government policy.[67]

Judicial power is represented by the structure of district, regional and high courts, and the Supreme Court as the highest within this system, and also by the Supreme Administrative Court and the Constitutional Court. The Constitutional Court is not part of the general system of courts because it has a specific mission and powers, as described below.

The judicial system is independent, executed by a special system of bodies, exclusively by courts. There are no other bodies of a judicial type in the Czech Republic (for example, specialised tribunals). Individual judges make decisions in courts, with tribunals of judges deciding only where stipulated by law.

Apart from regulating the foundations of judicial power, its organisation and its jurisdiction, the Constitution's significant feature is a guarantee of individuals' rights to judicial protection, which comprises one-fifth of the Charter of Fundamental Rights and Freedoms (hereinafter referred to as "the Charter").[68] The basic competencies of courts are to make decisions on cases dealing with rights, to make decisions on guilt and punishment (civil- and criminal-law competencies: Article 90, Constitution) and to protect against the interventions of public administration bodies (administrative-law competency: Article 36, paragraph 2 of the Charter). The courts also have a constitutional-law competency to make decisions on the lawfulness of legal regulations and other aspects of protecting the constitutional order (Articles 83 and 87 of the Constitution). The Constitutional Court decides in the form of findings, and the other courts in the form of judgments (of merits) or rulings (in other cases including questions of a procedural nature).

Judicial review of administrative bodies' decisions belongs to the field of administrative justice. In certain cases, however, review by general (civil-law) courts can occur (see below, sections 3.3.2.2 and 3.3.3).

The system of judicial review of public administration is, for specific cases, also supplemented by constitutional justice. It is only the Constitutional Court (based in Brno) that may review the constitutionality of laws; it is thus a specialised court. According to the wording of the Constitution, the

---

67. For example, the necessity of assent of an absolute majority of deputies and senators to declaring a state of war and also assent to sending the armed forces outside the territory of the state, with adoption of a resolution on participation in the defensive systems of an international organisation, etc. (Article 39 paragraph 3 and Article 43 paragraph 6 of the Constitution).
68. Declared as part of the constitutional order of the Czech Republic under No. 2/1993 Coll.

Constitutional Court is "the judicial body responsible for the protection of constitutionality" (Article 83).

The Constitutional Court uses constitutional standards as the basic criterion for the evaluation of a particular case, either a provision of a legal regulation – apart from laws, these include legal regulations issued by the government, ministries and territorial self-governing bodies (municipalities and regions), which are the only ones with the power to issue legal regulations – or a decision or another intervention of a public body on the rights and freedoms of individuals protected by the Constitution. The Constitutional Court only acts at the proposal of authorised entities, not on its own initiative. No recourse is possible to decisions of the Constitutional Court; however, international bodies can be appealed to (in cases involving protection of individuals' rights, most often appeals are made to the European Court of Human Rights).

Proposal for the repeal of a law may be lodged by the president, a group of at least 41 deputies, a group of at least 17 senators, the bench of the Constitutional Court, the plenum of the Constitutional Court (for a decision on a constitutional complaint), an ordinary court (if it decides that the law in question is in conflict with the constitutional order), and also the person who lodged a constitutional complaint (in relation to the law whose application caused a result leading to the lodging of a constitutional complaint). With other legal regulations (which are always issued by executive bodies), proposals for the repeal of by-laws and statutes may be lodged by the government, a group of at least 25 deputies or 10 senators, the bench of the Constitutional Court or the person who filed a constitutional complaint under similar conditions as mentioned above. There is no time-limit for filing such a proposal.

The legal regulation annulled by the Constitutional Court ceases to be valid on the day determined by the Constitutional Court, otherwise on the day of the announcement of the finding in the Collection of Laws. If implementing regulations have been issued to the annulled law, at the same time the Constitutional Court determines which provision(s) of these ceases to be valid.

The Constitutional Court is also competent to decide on constitutional complaints of individuals against final decisions of public authority bodies and other interventions in constitutionally guaranteed fundamental rights and freedoms (Article 87, paragraph 1, letter d) of the Constitution; also see Act No. 182/1993 Coll., on the Constitutional Court, as amended).[69]

---

69. The Constitutional Court has repeatedly pronounced its opinion on the issue of the binding effect of its findings (Article 89, paragraph 2, Constitution) issued in specific cases. These decisions are not of a precedent nature, but they dispose of cassation effects. So they are binding for public authority bodies and parties in particular proceedings, including the legal opinion expressed in a finding, with respect, among others, to the principle of legal certainty (for example, finding No. II ÚS 355/02, No. III. ÚS 495/05).

3.2. Government and public administration

The organisational structure of the public administration system, based on constitutional regulation, is supplemented by a number of legal regulations. There are several subsystems of public administration. These include central public administration bodies, specialised territorially devolved public administration bodies as a lower level of state administration, territorial administrations with a general competency (currently only self-governing) and the sphere of interest and professional self-government.

The other executive bodies – except for the president, independent administrative bodies and self-governing bodies – are subordinate to the government, which can also appoint the heads of these bodies (with the exception of the Chairman of the Czech Statistical Office and the Chairman of the Office for the Protection of Competition).

In relation to ministries, the government performs the functions of managing (by government resolutions),[70] auditing and unifying their activities.[71] The government establishes a legislative board as its advisory body, which is chaired by a minister. The highest (central) level in the execution of public administration is the ministry (ministers are always members of the government) and other central administration bodies (headed by a person who is not a member of the government). Ministries are established by law.

At the constitutional and political level, the minister is responsible for the activity of his/her ministry. In this respect, ministerial actions are regulated by the usual means of parliamentary democracy – interpellations of deputies in the assembly, the citation right of the assembly and its bodies (boards, commissions) and possible investigative commissions established by the assembly. However, the assembly cannot vote no-confidence for an individual minister, only for the government as a whole. The prime minister may propose to the president the dismissal of a member of the government.

The designation of competencies of ministries is based on the departmental principle. The names and determination of the competencies of individual ministries and their general tasks (apart from the basic constitutional determination) are regulated by the Act on Competencies, by which the central administration bodies were created at the level of the Czech Republic within the then newly established Czechoslovak federation. The details of their activities are then established by special laws and by-laws issued by these ministries, based on the express legal authorisation and within the limits of law (as required by Article 79, paragraph 3, Constitution).

---

70. See Constitutional Court's finding No. 207/1994 Coll.
71. See Section 28 paragraph 1, Act No. 2/1969 Coll., on the establishment of ministries and other central administration bodies of the Czech Republic, as amended ("Act on Competencies").

The general tasks of the central bodies are to create policy in their areas of responsibility, acting as co-ordinators, preparing bills, negotiating with EU authorities, and so on. Along with other activities, the ministerial offices oversee subordinate entities performing state administration in their areas.

Some special offices, usually subordinate to a central office, have been constituted within the competency of some central administrative bodies (for example, Czech School Inspection subordinate to the Ministry of Education, Youth and Sport; or Czech Energy Inspection, Czech Trade Inspection, Assay Office and Licence Office subordinate to the Ministry of Industry and Trade).

The lower, devolved (derived from a central office) level of state administration is performed by administrative bodies with a materially determined competency. The basis of their competency may be always found in corresponding special laws.

The territorial competency of these offices is neither unified nor does it follow the territorial division of the state (regions, districts), and not all levels are applied in all individual sectors. In some sectors, they are only at a single level of territorial competency (for example, labour offices, or area mining offices with a quite specifically established territorial competency). In others they are at two levels (for example, land registry).

Until 2002, territorial administration with general competency was represented by both state administration bodies and territorial self-governing entities. However, since the district offices were closed in 2002, general territorial administration has been formed only by self-governing regions and communities, as territorial self-governing units.

Territorial self-governing units are established in Chapter VII of the Constitution, and the regulation of their organisation and activity is contained in the law on communities (Act No. 128/2000 Coll., as amended) and the law on regions (Act. No. 129/2000 Coll., as amended). Also important is the Act on the Capital Prague No. 131/2000 Coll., as amended, according to which Prague is a statutory community, with the general competencies of a region.

After many years' interruption, the existence of communities as self-governing units – and not only state administrative bodies (as was the case from the late 1940s, with so-called "national committees" at the local, district and regional levels) – was restored in 1990 by the first law on communities, or specifically by the first municipal elections in autumn 1990. A new law on communities was adopted, within the territorial administration reform that brought into effect the second level of territorial self-government – the regions – by adopting the law on regions in 2000.

Regions and communities are primarily a sign of the decentralisation (subsidiarity) principle and enforcement of territorial self-government. Communities and regions are both administered independently by their boards of representatives (assemblies), elected by the citizens of a community or a region. The assembly is the supreme body in the field of the so-called independent competencies (territorial self-government). The board of representatives elects the municipal or regional council as the executive body for the sphere of independent competency, and also the mayor (lord mayor) of a community or the president of a region, who represents their territorial self-governing unit to the world beyond. Another body of the assembly is the committee, for initiating actions and for oversight (financial and control), along with boards for education and employment at regional level. In areas with a higher percentage of national minorities, there are boards for national minorities.

Independent competency underlies the development of territorial self-governing units and satisfaction of their citizens' needs. Self-government has a personal basis, represented by the work of a community's or region's citizens, an economic basis, since territorial self-governing units manage their property independently (they are legal entities – public corporations), and also a territorial basis, as shown by their self-governing authority over the territory of a community or region.

In their independent competency, territorial self-governing units (boards of representatives) may issue legal regulations – generally binding statutes, by which they regulate, in ways stipulated by law, matters of municipal or regional self-government. To ensure public order, municipal councils may establish a municipal police force.

The relations between communities and regions in the field of independent competency are based on the principle of co-operation. Regions are obliged to inform communities of intended actions for the region that may affect the community.

One method (traditional in central European countries) applied in communities and regions is transfer of the performance of part of state administration agendas to territorial self-governing units as a so-called delegated competency.

Apart from their self-governing activities, communities and regions thus become the executors of state administration to the extent specified by special laws. In this activity communities and regions are bound not only by laws and other legal regulations, but also by internal acts of public administration – government resolutions and directives of central administrative offices to which they are subordinate within the performance of their delegated competency. Within their delegated competency, communities and regions (or municipal councils and regional councils) issue another type of legal regulation – by-laws – which are always based on a specific legal authorisation.

Within the organisational structure of the community, the performance of delegated competencies is assigned, in particular, to the municipal office and its departments and sections, and to special municipal bodies (established according to special laws, for example misdemeanour commissions). Councils may authorise commissions for a certain activity or establish them as its initiative and advisory bodies. However, these bodies also function as executive bodies for the field of independent competency.

Communities are not assigned the same extent of delegated competencies. The basic extent of delegated competency is assigned to all communities (for example, in the field of proceedings of particular types of offences). Such communities are called type I communities. Since the beginning of the restoration of community bodies, communities with a delegated municipal office have been established to provide some of the state administration's routine services (for example, regarding the building law) for several communities in their administrative district. These are called type II communities. Since the district offices closed, most routine work (for example, the administration of identity cards and travel documents, driving offence proceedings) has been transferred to selected communities of type III – with an extended competency ("small districts"), the number of which totals 205.

The appeal authority for decision-making in administrative proceedings (whether within independent or delegated competency) for communities is the regional office. The regional office controls communities methodically in matters of performing delegated competency. It also performs a supervisory function over the legality of communities' activities as regards delegated competencies. For independent competencies, this role is fulfilled by the Ministry of the Interior. A similar task in the regions is fulfilled by the competent departmental central offices. The methodical competency of individual ministries in the regions is co-ordinated by the Ministry of the Interior (it also issues the "Governmental Bulletin for Regional and Municipal Authorities"), which has important tasks in supervising the legality of legal regulations of communities and regions (after a specified preceding procedure, it files a proposal for cancellation to the Constitutional Court).

Interest-group and professional self-government was restored after 1990 and regulated by individual laws for various public corporations of an interest character with their own self-governing bodies (primarily the professional chambers or associations, including those of physicians, dentists, veterinarians, tax advisers and lawyers). A future development in the sphere of tradesmen's associations may be expected. The authority of chambers applies solely to their members or membership applicants (if membership is obligatory, which usually is the rule), but always and strictly in conformity with a law or with professional regulations adopted on the basis of a statute. A similar character and basis applies to the self-government of universities, established by the law on universities.

These bodies do not have authority to produce legal regulations. All of their decisions (in individual matters) which affect the rights of persons and private entities can generally be examined by courts, after exhausting the administrative appeal procedure.

In the sphere of public administration, other types of entities may exercise authority in certain areas. These may be public institutions established by law that are not a direct part of public administration even though they belong to the sphere of executive power (for example, the Council for Radio and Television Broadcasting), always based on a law with strictly specified authority.

The sphere of public administration also includes the armed (security) forces; usually subordinate to the corresponding ministry (for example, Police of the Czech Republic or state police, related to the Ministry of the Interior).

Also individuals or legal entities may be assigned to perform public administration, always based on and to the extent of the relevant special law (for example, wildlife officers, school headmasters or the General Health Insurance Company).

3.3. Judicial review of government and administration

3.3.1. Judicial independence from the executive

The independence of courts is one of the bases of the state's legal system, established in Article 1 of the Constitution. Courts are independent of the legislative power, organisationally and functionally; parliament does not vote them into office (as it used to). The Constitution also guarantees the independence of judges. Judges shall be independent in the performance of their duties; no one may threaten their impartiality and they must not be bound by any instructions. No petitioner may prejudice the independence of courts. It is forbidden to hold public meetings within 100 metres of the building in which the Constitutional Court debates (Section 25 of the Constitutional Court Act).

Judges are only subject to laws and international treaties that form part of the legal order of the Czech Republic according to Article 10 of the Constitution, and also to by-laws if a judge concludes that they are not in conflict with the law; otherwise the judge is not bound by them. If a judge concludes that a law is in conflict with the Constitutional Act, he or she must submit the case to the Constitutional Court for decision in proceedings on repeal of laws (Section 64 paragraph 4 of the Constitutional Court Act).

An individual must not be kept from appearing before his/her legal judge (Article 38 paragraph 1 of the Charter). Proceedings before courts are oral and public, and judgments are always pronounced publicly. The decisions of courts may only be reviewed by a court.

Judges may not be removed against their will unless they commit such a serious disciplinary infraction that it would be the reason for their discharge (Article 82, paragraph 2, Constitution). Judges cannot be transferred to another court arbitrarily. The judges of ordinary courts are appointed for an indefinite period of time, while the term of judges of the Constitutional Court is a period of 10 years.[72]

The conduct of judges is subject to a special code of disciplinary responsibility according to Act No. 7/2002 Coll. on proceedings in the matters of judges and state attorneys, as amended. The amendment of 2008 brought (after long debate) a relatively new composition of the body (at the Supreme Administrative Court) that resolves disciplinary infractions of judges; apart from judges, the body should include lawyers, state attorneys and other legal professionals (for example, from universities), to contribute to a higher level of objectivity, while still respecting the independence of judges.

The law on courts and judges (Act No. 6/2002 Coll., as amended) has created so-called judicial councils, from judges of the competent court, which are advisory bodies to the presiding judges, particularly in matters of appointing chairpersons and vice-chairpersons of boards or benches; they also express their opinions on judges who are to be assigned or transferred to a particular court, and on fundamental issues of administration of a particular court. A more detailed regulation has been incorporated into the Code of Administrative Justice (Act No. 150/2002 Coll., as amended), relating to the judges performing administrative judiciary.

The legislative attempt (at the president's initiative) to use the above-mentioned Act No. 6/2002 Coll. to subordinate, to certain degree, the administration of courts to executive power (in matters of periodical evaluation and assessment of the professional qualification of judges by a special body with the representation of persons outside the court) was cancelled by the Constitutional Court (Finding No. 349/2002 Coll.).

---

72. The problem of relations between executive power and judicial power is illustrated by the president not appointing a probationer to be a judge, simply because of his relatively young age, although this condition was not set in the wording of the law applicable at that time. The Supreme Administrative Court first substantiated its authority to review this procedure of the president, who was ranked in the category of administrative bodies for the execution of his competency, and then it stated a breach of legitimate expectation principle on his side, as well as the right to issue a justified decision to a participant – the probationer (Judgment Reference No. 4 Aps 3/2005-51, No. 905/2006 of the Collection of Decisions of the Supreme Administrative Court). Despite the participant's suggestions, the president remained (and still remains) inactive in that case; he perceives the further decision of the administrative court, which required him to issue a justified decision in that case, as a serious intervention in his competencies, and he declares, without specifying any articles of the Czech Republic's Constitution, that appointment of judges by the president of the Czech Republic cannot be reviewed by judicial power bodies (Judgment of the Supreme Administrative Court 4 Ans 9/2007-197).

3.3.2. The scope of judicial review

3.3.2.1. Political and security questions

The rulings of the government (as a whole) are not subject to ordinary judicial review, with the exception of orders (statutory instruments) issued by the government, which are legal regulations and are subject to a general review of constitutionality by the Constitutional Court. This resolution is based on the character of the government's activities and powers as mentioned in 3.1 and 3.2 (above), which do not intervene directly in the sphere of rights and obligations of individuals.

A different case applies to specific rulings of individual ministries which are carried out in the respective procedural modes and thus subject also to judicial review. This decision-making power of ministries may reflect political and, by implication, security issues. This could be seen in the cases of reviews of some rulings of the Ministry of the Interior in the cases of (not) granting state citizenship, when the crucial question was the range of discretional power of the Ministry of the Interior (or the state) – that is, whether or not the state (ministry) has unlimited (absolute) discretion.[73]

In the security area, from the point of view of judicial protection, the regulation of classified information is also important (Act No. 148/1998 Coll., or 412/2005 Coll.). The Constitutional Court decided that:

> with regards to the specifics and importance of decision-making in the cases of classified information when the security interest of state is very evident, it is not always possible to guarantee all common procedural guarantees of a fair trial (for example, public hearing). However, also in this type of proceeding, the law-maker's task is to enable, in a legal form, to realise adequate guarantees for protection by court (or another independent and impartial tribunal acc. to Article 6, paragraph 1 of Convention) though by the nature of the case and taking into account the character of the respective function, for an even very special and differentiated protection.[74]

3.3.2.2. Administrative resolutions

Administrative resolutions are not subject to judicial review in general, because they are usually understood as provisions with (mostly) an internal nature, without direct effect in the sphere of individual rights. A rather different solution was adopted for the resolutions of bodies in self-governing communities and regions, which can be audited by the Ministry of Interior;

---

73. The Supreme Administrative Court has concluded correctly that unlimited administrative discretion does not exist in the legal state and that, in such matters, not all basic principles of administrative bodies can be followed in all cases, particularly principles of legitimate expectation, legal safeguard, prohibition of arbitrariness and discrimination, and proportionality. See, for example, the judgment of the Supreme Administrative Court No. 906/2006 (in this case an extended bench, to resolve a dispute between two benches) or No. 950/2006 of the Collection of Rulings of the Supreme Administrative Court.
74. Constitutional Court's finding No. Pl. ÚS 11/2000.

the applicable laws establish procedures for such resolutions to be revised by the relevant organ itself or annulled by the administrative court.[75]

Judicial reviews of administrative decisions should lead to fulfilment of the right of judicial protection guaranteed by the (Article 36, paragraph 2, Charter of Fundamental Rights and Basic Freedoms) against unlawful (incorrect) decisions or procedures of administrative bodies and other entities executing public administration. Generally, reviews of administrative body decisions fall within the realm of administrative justice. In certain cases, however, review by ordinary (civil) courts comes into consideration.

The Czech situation is thus a duality of judicial review. Formally, justification for judicial review was given by the necessity to fulfil the requirement of full jurisdiction according to Section 6, paragraph 1 of the European Convention for cases of "civil rights and obligations", but in actual fact it is based on the classic and already obsolete strict duality of private law and public law.

The system of judicial review of public administration is, for specific cases, also supplemented by constitutional justice. It must be stressed that the Constitutional Court was the first institution in the Czech Republic to apply argumentation by using legal principles, including the principles of proportionality and legitimate expectations.[76]

The Constitutional Court admittedly drew inspiration particularly from the European Court of Human Rights and certain constitutional or supreme courts of European states. It also applied the paradigm of a constitutional basis for the interpretation of ordinary laws and the paradigm of spreading constitutional principles throughout the entire rule of law – not excluding the public administration sphere.[77]

For the sphere of administrative judiciary, even at the turn of the millennium, it was difficult to argue for these principles, and especially for the leading principles in the sphere of administrative discretion – the principles of proportionality or legitimate expectations from an administrative authority or during a judicial review (with the abovementioned exception of the Constitutional Court) – and it became necessary to formulate major qualitative standards for the decision-making procedure of administrative authorities (if not for the general requirements of the rule of law and the constitutional principles, at least for the reason that the time of admission of the Czech Republic to

---

75. From such resolution can result the responsibility for damage or immaterial detriment according to Act No. 82/1998 Coll., as amended (which contains special provisions in addition to the general Civic Code), on compensation of damages caused within the execution of public power through an unlawful decision or incorrect official procedure. These cases (compensation, satisfaction) are resolved by the general courts, not by the administrative judiciary.
76. Although more frequently in the field of legislative acts – for the first time comprehensively in the case Pl. ÚS 4/94, then Pl. ÚS/15/96, Pl. ÚS 16/98, III. ÚS 256/01, and others, including unwritten principles (for their legal liability are important grounds of the finding Pl. ÚS 33/97).
77. Findings III. ÚS 139/98.

the EU was approaching, and many cases from the Czech Republic were being submitted at the European Court for Human Rights, some having been launched by administrative authorities). In this situation, adoption of a new Code of Administrative Procedure in 2004 was prudent (the act has been in force since 2006).

With respect to the scope of judicial review, the first, general part of the law has been important because it contains the "basic principles" of public administration procedure and has a general application to the execution of public administration. Thus, the principles are not only of a procedural, but partly also of a material, character (in some aspects they control the content of adopted decisions). Here we find a certain cataloguing of legally binding principles of modern public administration, including the principle of proportionality and the principle of legitimate expectations (not explicitly designated as such, but described quite adequately).[78]

Regulations of judicial review enable (generally speaking) the review in the case of a breach of the monitored principles. As regards the principle of proportionality, such cases may be encountered.[79] We find still some hostility and certain constraints to arguing and applying a breach of the principle of legitimate expectation, although in some cases the principle is applied in terms of arguments.[80]

Judicature has also, on a general level, defined the term "abuse of administrative discretion".[81] This can be considered as a high point in the long process of developing the judicial review of public administration.

Administrative justice

In the current regulation of 2002 (Act No. 150/2002 Coll., as amended), administrative justice is a relatively new matter. On 1 January 2003, a new conceptual system was introduced, quite different from the previous system. The previous legal regulation of administrative justice was contained in the Civil Procedure Code (amended in this respect by Act No. 519/1991 Coll.). Due to conflicts between Section 6, paragraph 1 of the Convention and some provisions of the Charter of Fundamental Rights and Freedoms of the Czech Republic, the need for this new provision arose from the Finding of the Constitutional Court No. 276/2001 Coll., effective 31 December 2002.

According to the previous regulation (adopted in 1991 as a "temporary" restoration of administrative justice after nearly 40 years of its almost com-

---

78. See Section 2-8, Act No. 500/2004 Coll., Administrative Procedural Act, as amended.
79. See, for example, judgment of the Supreme Administrative Court No. 4 As 71/2006-83.
80. See, for example, judgment of the Supreme Administrative Court No. 398/2004, 905/2006 of the Collection of Decisions of the Supreme Administrative Court.
81. See, for example, decisions No. 906/2006, 950/2006 of the Collection of Decisions of the Supreme Administrative Court.

plete replacement by a supervisory system of state prosecution), the ordinary (civil) courts reviewed decisions of public administration, in one instance at the level of regional courts (of district courts in some cases), without the possibility of unifying judicature, with a limited review of administrative discretion, and with a limited (not full) jurisdiction of the court for all kinds of matters uniformly.

The Code of Administrative Justice has already fulfilled the intent of Section 91 of the Constitution by establishing the Supreme Administrative Court and creating a second tier of administrative justice with specialised benches of regional courts.

The Supreme Administrative Court is (generally) supposed to ensure the uniformity and lawfulness of public administration decisions (by fundamental rulings and binding statements) and it decides in cases of cassation complaints (and in some other matters, such as electoral issues or local referenda). Administrative justice is thus performed as single-instance but, as extraordinary remedies and in the interest of unifying decision making, it is possible to file a cassation complaint, if a violation of lawfulness in court decision-making is alleged, or to begin new proceedings.

The Code of Administrative Justice has established the review of decisions of administrative bodies which are subject to regulation under Section 6, paragraph 1 of the European Convention for the Protection of Human Rights and Fundamental Freedoms (which the Czech Republic adopted in 1992) in full jurisdiction.

According to the applicable legal regulation, the administrative justice courts decide:

– complaints against decisions issued in the field of public administration;

– requests for protection against inaction of an administrative body;

– requests for protection against unlawful intervention of an administrative body;

– jurisdiction complaints (on division of competencies in public administration).

Also, administrative courts decide (apart from the abovementioned specific areas) on cancellation of measures of a general nature or their parts due to conflict with a law. There are also some special provisions on matters relating to elections, local referenda, political parties and political movements.

At the same time, judicial review of decision-making or decisions of administrative bodies in matters of private law which fall to the jurisdiction of ordinary courts is excluded from the jurisdiction of the Code of Administrative Justice.

Review of administrative decisions by general (civil-law) courts

In general justice, the decisions of administrative bodies are reviewed on the basis of how they were decided with respect to the rights and obligations of individuals and legal entities in the matters of private law.

According to this regulation, contained in the fifth part of the Civil Procedure Code, if an administrative body has decided according to a special law on a dispute or other legal matter resulting from civil law, labour, family or business relations and if such decision of the administrative body has become legally effective, the same matter can be heard on a petition in civil proceedings.

3.3.3. Access to the courts

3.3.3.1. Citizens' standing to sue

Reviewing the lawfulness of an administrative act is not the aim of the administrative (or civil, in cases where it is competent) judiciary itself, but the court has to find out whether the subjective law of the claimant (that is, the addressee of the original administrative decision) was broken by an administrative body's decision or whether the challenged violation of right did not occur.

The claimed unlawfulness must have led to an infringement of the claimant's subjective rights, and not an infringement in another area – for example, the rights of other persons or a certain public interest protected by law.

Unless provided by law, the protection of rights can be claimed only on the submission of a complaint and after the exhaustion of all appropriate remedial actions, if admissible under a special law (the Administrative Procedural Act establishes this possibility as a general principle for cases of administrative decisions).

The Code of Administrative Justice determines time limits for filing individual complaints (for complaints against a decision it is generally two months after the complainant was notified of the decision) and some other special conditions for different types of complaints. So, for a complaint against a decision (for example, counts of charges), it must be clear for which factual and legal reasons the complainant considers the statements of the decision illegal or null.

The law also requires payment of judicial fees (for a decision, 2 000 Czech crowns or 80 euros; in other cases, 1 000 Czech crowns or 40 euros).

Citizens are not allowed to challenge normative resolutions/regulations (see Section 3.1, last paragraph). In matters concerning individuals, these normative by-laws or statutes can be subject to the scrutiny of the Constitutional Court only within a review of the individual decision, and then only if the relevant law was the cause of the decision infringing constitutional order, international agreement or law (parliamentary act).

3.3.3.2. Public interest litigation

In a separate provision, the current regulation gives the possibility of public interest protection based on an action against entities authorised by law, in particular against public power bodies.[82]

A citizens' association may be the plaintiff in proceedings before an administrative court, but only on condition that it was a party in the corresponding proceedings before the administrative authority according to the relevant special laws (for example, Building Act No. 183/2006 Coll.). This possibility was established for the first time by the law on nature and landscape preservation (Act No. 114/1992 Coll.).

In such cases, the plaintiff's legitimacy is based on the plaintiff's procedural rights in administrative proceedings.[83]

References

Baxa, J., and Mazanec, M., "Reforma českého správního soudnictví" ("Reform of Czech administrative justice"), *Právní Rádce* ("Legal Adviser"), No. 1, 2002, p. 10.

Filip, J., "Ústavní právo České republiky. 1. Základní pojmy a instituty" in *Ústavní základy ČR*, 4. vyd. ("Constitutional law of the Czech Republic: basic concepts and institutions" in *Constitutional Rudiments of the Czech Republic*, 4th edn), Masarykova univerzita (Masaryk University), Brno, 2003.

Filip, J., Svatoň, J., and Zimek, J., *Základy státovědy* ("The basics of political science"), Masarykova univerzita (Masaryk University), Brno, 1999.

Hácha, E., [entries on] "Supreme Administrative Court" (Vol. II, pp. 827-880) and "Administrative Justice" (Vol. III, pp. 589-605) in *Slovník veřejného práva československého* ("Dictionary of Czechoslovak public law"), Brno, 1929-1948.

Hendrych, D. et al., *Správní právo, Obecná část* (Administrative law: general part), 7th edn, C. H. Beck, Prague, 2007.

Holländer, P., *Ústavněprávní argumentace, ohlédnutí po deseti letech ústavního soudu* (Constitutional law argumentation: a look back after ten years of the Constitutional Court), Linde, Prague, 2003.

---

82. The law set up the administrative body (no body was authorised by law until that time), the Supreme State Attorney and "he who is expressly authorised by a special law or an international convention that is part of the legal order" (see Section 66, paragraphs 1 to 3, Code of Administrative Justice).

83. See, for example, Judgment No. 291/2004, Collection of Decisions of the Supreme Administrative Court.

Kadečka, S. et al., *Správní řád* (Code of administrative procedure), Meritum, 1st edn, ASPI, Prague, 2006.

Klíma, K., *Ústavní právo* (Constitutional law), 3rd edn, Aleš Čeněk, Plzeň, 2006.

Klíma, K. et al., *Státověda* (Political science), Aleš Čeněk, Plzeň, 2006.

Macur, J., *Správní soudnictví a jeho uplatnění v současné době* (Administrative justice and its application in the present time), Acta Universitatis Brunensis, Masaryk University, Brno, 1992.

Mazanec, M., *Správní soudnictví* (Administrative justice), Linde, Prague, 1996.

Merkl, A., *Obecné právo správní* (Common administrative law), Vol. II, Orbis, Prague/Brno, 1932.

Pavlíček, V., and Hřebejk, J., *Ústava a ústavní řád České republiky* (The constitution and constitutional order of the Czech Republic), Parts 1 and 2, Linde, Prague, 1998.

Pítrová, L., and Pomahač, R., *Evropské správní soudnictví* (European administrative justice), C. H. Beck, Prague, 1998.

Průcha, P., *Správní právo, obecná část, Doplněk* (Administrative law, general part: amendment), Masaryk University, Brno, 2007.

Skulová, S., *Správní uvážení, základní charakteristika a souvislosti pojmu* (Administrative discretion: basic characteristics and contexts of the term), Masaryk University, Brno, 2003.

Skulová, S. et al., *Správní právo procesní* (Administrative procedural law), 2nd edn, Aleš Čeněk, Plzeň, 2008.

Sládeček, V., *Ústavní soudnictví* (Constitutional justice), 2nd edn, C. H. Beck, Prague, 2003.

Sládeček, V., Mikule, V., and Syllová, J., *Ústava České republiky, komentář* (The constitution of the Czech Republic: commentary), C. H. Beck, Prague, 2007.

Sládeček, V., *Obecné správní právo* (Common administrative law), ASPI, Prague, 2004.

Svoboda, P., *Ústavní základy správního řízení v české republice, právo na spravedlivý proces a české správní řízení* (Constitutional bases of administrative proceedings in the Czech Republic: the right to a fair trial and Czech administrative proceedings), Linde, Prague, 2007.

Šimíček, V., *Ústavní stížnost* (Constitutional complaint), 3rd edn, Linde, Prague, 2005.

Websites

The chambers of the Parliament of the Czech Republic: www.senat.cz, www.psp.cz

The Government of the Czech Republic: www.vlada.cz

The Constitutional Court of the Czech Republic: www.concourt.cz

The Supreme Administrative Court: www.nssoud.cz

The Ministry of Justice of the Czech Republic: www.justice.cz

The Ministry of the Interior: www.mvcr.cz.

Chapter 4
National legal tradition – France

C. Lageot

4.1. The constitutional framework

4.1.1. The constitutional regime

After the events in Algeria and the subsequent collapse of the Fourth Republic, France adopted a new constitution in 1958 and asked General de Gaulle to become the head of state. The Fifth Republic promoted expressly the principle of separation of powers between the three branches of the state, namely:

– Title II (the head of state) and III (the government) – the executive power;
– Title IV (Parliament) – the legislative power;
– Title VIII – the judicial authority.

This principle has prevailed in France since the adoption of the Revolutionary Act of 16 and 24 August 1790 on the Separation of Administrative and Judiciary Bodies. The French Constitution has recently been modified (Constitutional Revision of 23 July 2008) to reduce some of the very important powers allowed by the architects of the constitution to the executive power. The balance of power has always been strongly in favour of the executive, although the principles of a parliamentary regime remain, and this is not reversed by the changes of July 2008.

The executive power is exercised by both the head of state (the President of the Republic) and the prime minister. Until 1962, the president was elected by an assembly of greater electors, but Charles de Gaulle changed the type of election in order to reinforce the power of the head of state as a prominent figure of the regime. Since this major constitutional reform, the Constitutional Act of 6 November 1962, which led to the majority fact (or coincidence of the majorities for the executive and the legislature), the president has been directly elected by the people. Until 2000, the mandate was for seven years. Since the constitutional revision of 24 September 2000, the term has been reduced to five years, in order to avoid the risks of a new "cohabitation". The direct consequence is, once again, intensification of the presidential primacy.

When the President of the Republic enters office, the first thing he or she has to do is appoint the prime minister. Another singularity of the French Constitution is that the head of state is not bound by anyone for this appointment (the constitution speaks of "proper power" or *pouvoir propre*). The president appoints whoever she or he wants in a discretionary way (Article 8 al. 1).

Beyond the power to choose the prime minister, the president has also, as proper powers, the capacity to dissolve the National Assembly (Article 12), to exercise full powers in exceptional times (Article 16), to send messages to parliament (Article 18), to organise legislative referenda (Articles 11 and 88-5), to nominate three members of the Constitutional Council (one of whom is the president) (Article 56) and to refer to this council for judicial review the constitutionality of ordinary acts and international treaties (Articles 61 and 54).

Despite this, the main criteria of the parliamentary regime remain: the prime minister is the head of the government and is politically responsible before the National Assembly, which can theoretically dismiss the prime minister and his entire government. However, the conditions of censure are so strict in the French Constitution that only one government has been dismissed by the National Assembly, on 5 October 1962.

The legislative power is exercised by a parliament composed of two houses, the National Assembly and the Senate. Deputies are directly elected by the citizens for five years whereas senators are elected for six years by a college of local representatives. (A constitutional reform in 2000 has reduced their mandate to three years.) The two houses are not equal in terms of representation or powers: the National Assembly represents the people; the Senate, the local communities. The National Assembly has more power than the Senate to expand and improve parliamentary acts because the government can give the last word to the assembly in case of disagreement and, as has been said previously, the assembly can theoretically dismiss the government. The only real power which remains in the Senate's hands is the veto, which it can use during the procedure of a constitutional revision.

All this makes the French regime a very singular one, a very odd mixture of parliamentarian and presidential systems.

4.1.2. Administration of justice

Judicial power is exercised by the courts of law, courts of first instance, courts of appeal and supreme courts. The Constitutional Council stands apart because it is charged with exercising judicial review of the constitutionality of acts and treaties and also has to observe the national elections for any irregularities. Its decisions are supposed to be binding for every single court, even the Cour de Cassation and the Conseil d'Etat (Article 62). In France, a dual system has existed since the Revolutionary Act of 1790 on the separation of administrative and judicial orders. On one hand, there is the administrative organisation of justice with Administrative Tribunals (TA), as courts of first instance, Administrative Courts of Appeal (CAA) and the Supreme Court, the Conseil d'Etat (CE). On the other hand, the judicial administration of justice presents the same structure: first-instance tribunals, appeal and cassation.

However, the judicial degree is separated into the civil and criminal divisions. For the civil division, the first instance is represented by the High Tribunal of Instance (TGI) or Tribunal of Instance (TI) for minor cases. For the criminal division, it is necessary to distinguish whether the offence is a minor one (*contravention*), an indictable offence (*délit*) or a crime (*crime*). In the first case, the Police Tribunal is competent; in the second case, it is the Correctional Tribunal; and in the third case, it is the Assizes Court. At the upper levels, there are civil and criminal divisions for both Appeal Courts and Cassation Court. In 2000, an appeal for Assizes Courts was set up. For a long time, the consensus was that verdicts given by citizens could not be discussed.

Judicial review of administrative decisions has a long tradition in France, but has been confronted at times with challenges: 1830, 1870, 1940 and 1962. The Conseil d'Etat, created by the Consulate (Constitution of 22 frimaire An VIII), has benefited from its great administrative continuity, independent of political regime changes. In each French *département*, the 28 pluviose An VIII Act created a prefectorial council. This institution was transformed in 1953 (Order of 30 September) into an administrative tribunal (TA). On 15 December 1799, Napoleon Bonaparte set up a new administrative institution called the Conseil d'Etat but, at first, he gave it only consultative powers. It has to be said that, surprisingly, the revolutionaries did not think of such an institution. It is probably because they had an infinite trust in the administration and because they did not want any judge to control public bodies. The Conseil d'Etat then won its independence from the executive power and became a proper court in its own right.

The Conseil d'Etat was set up, at first, as a first-instance degree, an appeals division and a supreme court. As a first-instance degree, it was competent to consider an application for judicial review, the remedy for abuse of power (*recours pour excès de pouvoir*). Its direct competency for such a remedy derived from the Act of 7-14 October 1790. It was also a court of appeal for the purpose of challenging decisions taken by ministers or the decisions provided by the prefectorial council. Finally, it could act as a supreme court for all decisions given by such jurisdictions.

Over time, the judicial competence of the Conseil d'Etat has been affected by three major reforms:

- After the end of the Second Empire, it received directly (by the Law of 24 May 1872) the power to judge by itself and absolutely. The head of state no longer had the power of veto on its decisions. This is generally known as the change from the "retained justice" (*justice retenue*) of the head of state to the "delegated justice" (*justice déléguée*) of the Conseil d'Etat. Even if the head of state did not use its control power in reality, this reform was a major one: the Conseil d'Etat became sovereign to judge from 24 May 1872. Later, the Constitutional Council would find, on 22 July 1980 (validation Acts Decision), that the independence conferred by this Act of 1872 is one of the fundamental principles recognised by the republican acts.

– The Conseil d'Etat also became in 1889 (the Cadot case) the normal judge of first-instance degree cases. In 1953, this competency was transferred to the new administrative tribunals.

– Finally, the Conseil d'Etat was largely discharged of its appeal competency by the Act of 31 December 1987. It was at this time that the administrative courts were created.

Nowadays, both its existence and its independence are constitutionally proclaimed by the constitutional decisions of respectively 23 January 1987 (Conseil de la Concurrence) and 22 July 1980 (*Lois de validation*).

In order to decide which of the judicial or administrative judges would be competent in controversial cases, the Conflicts Tribunal (*Tribunal des Conflits*) was set up in 1848 by Article 89 of the Constitution of the Second Republic. The court was abolished by the Second Empire, but restored by the Act of 24 May 1872. This court still has an important jurisdiction competency.

It is when decrees, orders and delegated legislation are applied that the administrative judges challenge them – for example, after the Second World War. This has been the case almost everywhere in Europe, when the executive gained the power to enact law. The French constitutions of the Third Republic (1875-1940) and the Fourth Republic (1946-1958) had given secondary legislation to the executive, but it remained in large part subject to the will and control of parliament: secondary legislation needed to allow the application of acts. With the Fifth Republic, things changed radically: parliament could no longer legislate in any field, being strictly constrained by Article 34 of the constitution. In contrast, the government was able to enact law in any other field (Article 37); such laws are called autonomous decrees. All the decrees, however, remain under the authority of higher norms: first, the constitution, followed by treaties, and then acts, in that order. It is the administrative judge who challenges the conformity of all decrees to the upper sources of law.

4.1.3. Administrative organisation

Thanks to Napoleon I, France has long been a unitary state and a very centralised country with elements of de-concentration. From 1980, however, the country started to change this tradition and become decentralised. It was under the presidency of François Mitterrand that local democracy, in terms of autonomy of competencies and finances, became real. The 2 March 1982 Act remains one of the most important legislative measures of the first mandate of the president. From that date, the communes, *départements* and regions, together commonly called local bodies (*collectivités locales)* or territorial communities (*collectivités territoriales*), have received proper competencies and greater autonomy in areas such as local finance. The communes are given charge of proximity actions (*actions de proximité*), the *départements* take on the social actions, and the regions are responsible for the economic actions.

In 2003, a constitutional revision largely promoted by the former prime minister, Jean-Pierre Raffarin, consolidated the 1982 Act on decentralisation. It introduced at the local level, under certain conditions, the referendum, the right of petition, more autonomy for public bodies, without however supplementary financial means. Local finances were finally dealt with in a specific statute in the Constitutional Revision of 29 March 2003. The principle of autonomy of local bodies is now equally stated in the constitution at every local level. This has always been the case for communes and *départements* since the adoption of the constitution of 1958, but it was only in 2003 that the regions received constitutional recognition.

4.2. Government and public administration

According to the constitution, French public administration is structured between, on one hand, a central administration with de-concentrated bodies and, on the other hand, a decentralised administration.

At the central level, the government, consisting of the prime minister, ministers and secretaries of state, has the duty to ensure implementation of the domestic and foreign policy of the country and to exercise general management of public administration. According to Article 20 of the French Constitution, the government has at its disposal the administration and the armed forces. In the main areas there are organised ministries, as well as specialised agencies, subordinated to the government or to one of the ministries. These central agencies have a different nature from the Independent Administrative Authorities (AAI), such as the Superior Council for the Audiovisual (CSA) or the Defendant of Rights (the new Ombudsman since the constitutional reform of July 2008), because they are subordinated to the government. These central agencies can have a control role, such as the General Inspections (*Inspections Générales*), or a mission role, such as the General Plan Commission (*Commissariat Général au Plan*) or the Territory Planning and Regional Action Commission (DATAR), and also a consultative role, such as the Economic and Social Council (*Conseil Economique et Social*) or the Conseil d'Etat. Furthermore, every ministry has territorial units in the regions, *départements* or communities (de-concentrated territorial agencies), which perform the tasks of the ministry in that area, for the purpose of being closer to the citizens, to make the administration efficient and to affirm the work at the central level.

The state is divided territorially into regions, *départements* and communes. The existence of *départements* and communes as decentralised bodies or territorial communities has always been set up at the constitutional level since 1958. It took longer to recognise the regions. Until 1982 they were known as public establishments (*etablissements publics*). Then, the great Act on Decentralisation of 2 March 1982 recognised them as proper territorial communities. But it was only in July 2008 that this statute was inserted in the constitution as it had been for the *départements* and communes. Regions have become more and more important, especially because it is the favoured level for European Community action. *Départements* find it harder nowadays to survive as decentralised bodies, but they remain the general level for all de-concentrated agencies of the state. Communes are far more numerous in France in comparison to other European countries (36 763) and are formed by communes, towns and cities. Politicians try to find solutions by encouraging communities to co-operate because, for instance, 32 000 communes have fewer than 2 000 inhabitants and over 4 000 communes have fewer than 100 inhabitants! With similar populations, Italy has 8 097 communes and England has 10 832 parishes. This is why co-operation between communes (*co-opération inter-communale*) is widely encouraged, even if it has not yet produced all the results expected.

The commune has a long tradition of autonomy, since the French Revolution, but more specifically since the adoption of the Commune Charter of 1884. It has local autonomy and is run by a commune council, elected directly by the inhabitants, ranging from 9 to 69 members, according to the commune's population. This is to the advantage of little communes in France. The executive body of the commune is the head of the commune council and the mayor of the commune, elected by an absolute majority of the council in a two-round election, and then, if necessary, with a simple majority in the third-round election. The council is elected a bit differently, depending on whether or not the town has 3 500 or more inhabitants, but in all cases for six years.

If the town has fewer than 3 500 inhabitants, the election regime is flexible. The list can be incomplete; the elector can vote for candidates from different parties instead of for the set list of one party and can change the ranking of the candidates. Election requires a "first-past-the-post" majority: if one list obtains an absolute majority in the first round, it wins the election; if not, a relative majority is enough for the second round.

If the town has more than 3 500 inhabitants, the election regime is less flexible. The list has to be complete; the elector has to vote for the set list of one party and cannot change the ranking of the candidates. Elections use both majority and proportional systems. If a list wins the first round with an absolute majority, it gains half of the seats and the rest of the seats are distributed in a proportional way between all the lists which had at least 5 % of the votes. If it is necessary to organise a second round because none of the lists has an absolute majority, the division of the seats occurs in exactly the same way.

At the commune level, there is also a representative of central government, the prefect, who has the duty to ensure that the administrative activity of mayors, local councils and commune councils is carried out according to the law, and also to co-ordinate the administrative units of the ministries in the territory. Since the great 2 March 1982 Act on Decentralisation, the prefect no longer has the power to annul an unlawful act of the local authorities (opportunity control), but can challenge it in court (legal control). The prefect can refer the act to the administrative court (it is called the *déféré préfectoral*) within two months after the act has been published. The Decentralisation Act of 1982 marked the end of control *a priori* and definitely set up control *a posteriori*.

The prefects in France are appointed in the Council of Ministers by both the head of state and the prime minister, after being proposed by the home secretary. Four fifths come from the corps of district prefects (*sous-préfets*) or the civil administrators of the home secretary, and the remaining one fifth are appointed under the discretionary power of the executive. The prefects are subordinate to the home secretary and their rights are not as great as the normal rights of civil servants. Their political, philosophical or religious opinions can be mentioned in their records; they cannot go on strike and/or become a member of a trade union; however, they can create associations.

The local level is where the local autonomy principle brings public authorities close to the people. Communes, villages, towns and cities are all public legal entities, generally called decentralised bodies. The French are very attached to this level, even if the majority of small communes, villages or towns regularly run into problems.

The current system could be criticised because, unless members of the local council are not re-elected and/or convicted of criminal pursuits, they are safe from being held accountable. It should be noted that the mayor has both the initiative and the authority to implement decisions, whereas the local council votes to approve them. Mayors, depending on their personality, can greatly influence a local council. The mayor's party, especially in medium-sized and large towns, has a majority on the council. In such cases, the decision-making process is quite effective and not the result of compromises.

At the departmental level, France is divided into 100 *départements*, four of which are in the overseas territories. The *département* covers two different realities: on the one hand, it is an administrative division of the state, with the prefect as responsible authority, and, on the other hand, it is a decentralised body with, at its head, the president of the General Council (or Departmental Council). Confusion between the two has existed for a very long time, probably because the prefect was also the head of the executive of the *département*, until the great Act on Decentralisation of 1982. The 10 August 1871 Act gave the *département* its modern status, which in 1982 was not really questioned. It was confirmed as both an administrative division of the state and also a decentralised body. This was logical because the *département* is mentioned in the Constitution of 1958 beside the communes. This was confirmed in the 6 February 1992 Act. The debate on the future of the *départements* is nowadays less intense than in the 1990s, probably because the *départements* are allotted a large amount of resources to take care of public services and to apply adequate public policies.

As a decentralised body, it functions quite simply, with a General Council (or Departmental Council), a president of the General Council and a departmental administration. The general councillors are elected in the proportion of one per canton (or district, playing the role of electoral division), for six years, by a two-round majority system. Half of the council changes every three years.

Like the local council, the General Council meets at least once every trimester, to discuss the questions set down by the president of the council. The meetings are public. The prefect can be called upon by either the council or the prime minister. This hearing is interesting because the prefect directs all the de-concentrated bodies of the state in the *département*. Agreements of the Departmental Council become obligatory Decisions as soon as they are publicised and transmitted to the prefectoral services. Control of judicial review of the prefect operates in the same way as seen before. The president is elected in the same way as the mayor, but for a three-year term. After the decentralisation of 1982, the function of the president completely changed, because of the transfer of the executive power to him/her. (Let us remember that it was exercised before by the prefect.) Like a mayor, the president sets the business of the day and presides over the deliberations, and also prepares and executes the decisions. His function is influential.

Like the communes, the *départements* have a "general clause of competency". Their power of interpretation is very large. However, it must not conflict with the competencies of the state or other territorial bodies. Since 1982, proximate actions (such as town planning) are part of the competency of the commune; solidarity (or social) actions belong to the *départements*; and economic actions to the regions. In a case of infringement, the illegality of any local decision can be challenged before an administrative court.

At the regional level, the functioning is almost the same, but the region is the most recent territorial body and the one most adaptable to the European Union. Since 1982, France has started to regionalise its country, following its European neighbours. There are nowadays 22 regions in France and four overseas.

The Regional Council is elected for six years by the citizens, using both the majority system and the proportional one. The electoral system is comparable to the system followed by the communes. Its functioning is similar to what has been described here for the Departmental Council. The president of the region has gained in terms of powers since 1982. He is today the real head of executive power of the region. He is elected in the same way as mayors or departmental presidents, and for six years. He has the same powers as his colleagues. Besides the regional institutions there exists an important consultative council, the Regional Social and Economic Council.

4.3. Judicial review of government and administration

4.3.1 Judicial independence from the executive

Unlike many European countries, a judicial power does not exist in France; only a judicial authority is mandated (Title VIII of the French Constitution). It is, however, the basis of the principle of independence of courts (Article 64 C).

According to Article 64 of the constitution, guaranteeing the independence of the judicial authority remains with the President of the Republic. This independence derives from the principle of irremovability of bench judges (*siège*) in Article 64 subsection 3, but not state prosecutors (*parquet*). A third instrument of independence is the Superior Council of Magistracy (CSM), an autonomous constitutional authority created in 1946 (Article 65). In order to consolidate the independence of the magistracy from the executive power, the constitutional revision of 23 July 2008 modified for a third time its composition and mission. The head of state no longer presides over the CSM, nor is the minister of justice a member, and judges are nowadays in a minority in order to open the judiciary to the society.

Tribunals are composed of the First President of the Cour de Cassation, five bench judges, one state prosecutor, one *conseiller d'état*, one barrister and six qualified persons (who are members neither of parliament nor of the judiciary) chosen in an equitable way by the President of the Republic and each of the presidents of the two assemblies. The composition of tribunals dealing with state prosecutors is almost the same, apart from the Attorney General of the Cour de Cassation acting as the president and a bench judge sitting there (Article 65, subsection 3).

In the disciplinary field, there are as many professional judges as non-professional judges. After the judicial disaster of the Outreau affair, a new provision is that citizens can submit complaints to the CSM for disciplinary reasons.

The CSM monitors the careers of judges, which differ if it is a bench judge or a state prosecutor. The latter are subordinate to the Minister of Justice. They are also appointed by the President of the Republic (Article 13). For bench judges, the CSM has real power: it makes suggestions to those in the highest posts and gives advice to other judges, which must be followed (*avis conforme*). For state prosecutors, the CSM only gives consultative advice (*avis simples*).

4.3.2. The scope of judicial review

4.3.2.1. Political and security questions

In France, administrative acts are subject to review by the administrative courts: at first instance, the administrative tribunals (TA); at appeal, the administrative courts (CA); at cassation, the Conseil d'Etat (CE). In some few cases, the Conseil d'Etat can be a first-instance jurisdiction or an appellate jurisdiction. "Administrative acts" mean normative acts in the sense that they contain norms of law. Non-normative acts (recommendations, preparatory acts) are analysed by the courts only indirectly, when they serve for issuing a normative act. "Normative act" also means an obligatory act. In French administrative law, there exist two types of normative acts: regulations and decisions. Regulations are general, whereas decisions are individual.

The government issues two types of administrative acts: regulations and ordinances. Ordinances are permitted by Article 38 of the Constitution and allow the government to legislate in the field of parliament (Article 34 of the Constitution) in order to gain time. An ordinance is a regulation until parliament passes an act of authorisation. Ordinances are issued on the basis of an express delegation from parliament, in exceptional and/or urgent situations. Nevertheless, the practice of issuing ordinances has been widely used by all Western governments since the end of the Second World War.

Review of all normative acts issued by any administrative authority is granted to the administrative courts of first instance. There is a two-month period, from publication of the normative act, in which to apply to the administrative judge to ask for nullity of the act. This is called the remedy for abuse of power (*recours pour excès de pouvoir, REP*). The other type of remedy in French administrative law is the remedy of full jurisdiction (*recours de plein contentieux* or *recours de pleine juridiction*). For this form or cause of action, the judge has the power to pronounce financial sanctions and to substitute the court's own decision for the administrative decision. For the remedy to be available, the plaintiff has to have a legitimate interest to act (*intérêt à agir*), must follow the rule of the preliminary decision (*règle de la décision préalable*) and has to respect delays. Judges are liberal on the first condition, that the interest should be sufficiently certain and direct. On the second condition, the necessity to present a preliminary decision is not hard to do when the plaintiff exercises a *recours pour excès de pouvoir*. This remedy is meant to nullify the administrative act because of its illegality. It is when the plaintiff wants to exercise the other remedy (*recours de plein contentieux*) that this second condition is necessary. As for the third condition, the delay of two months from the day the administrative act is published is common (*délai de droit commun*). Some exceptions exist: delays can be shorter or longer, or the exemption of delay can be linked to the exemption of preliminary decision: that is the case for damages due to civil engineering. The remedy in this case is available at any time.

The judicial review of administrative acts in France is not absolute. The exceptions are provided either by the constitution itself, or by parliament, or by the different judges.

The first category of exceptions can be based on the doctrine called the theory of acts of government. They are acts which are non-reviewable by the courts owing to their nature (governmental as opposed to administrative acts) or because the authorities involved in their issuance cannot be subjected to the administrative court's jurisdiction (parliament, foreign states, etc.). The case law of the Conseil d'Etat used to consider that there are two types of acts of government: those in national law and those in international law. In the first category, there are acts involving the government and parliament, or the head of state and the government. In the second, there are acts which permit the execution of an international agreement and acts necessary for the conduct of foreign relations. The question whether or not an act is an act of government or an administrative act can be referred to the Conflicts Tribunal (*Tribunal des conflits*). Under the influence of the European Convention on Human Rights of 1950 and the right to an effective remedy, acts of government are becoming less and less influential, especially in the foreign affairs field. Thanks to the theory of detachable acts (*théorie des actes détachables*), administrative judges have taken to themselves the right to oversee some of these acts and to find the state responsible even if without fault.

Regarding military acts, they are excluded from review only if they are of a command nature. The decision to intervene in an armed force conflict remains, in theory, the decision of parliament. In 1991, however, the executive power decided, without the agreement of parliament, to intervene in Kuwait. Thanks to the theory of "detachable acts", for instance, the destruction of an abandoned boat on the high seas by the national Navy has been examined by an administrative judge (Conseil d'Etat, Sect., 23 October 1987, *Société Nachfolger Navigation*).

Within this large category of acts of government, there is in French law a constitutional provision on exceptional powers. Article 16 of the French Constitution allows the President of the Republic in troubled periods (armed forces conflict or civil war, for example), to exercise at the same time all the executive power, all the legislative power and all the judicial power. This article has been commonly baptised the temporary dictatorship. It is supposed to be temporary and the president should stop using it when the imminent danger ceases. But the appreciation of this element remains subjective and that is probably why General de Gaulle used this article from April 1961 until September 1961, the period that encapsulated the threat of a putsch in Algeria, which was aborted on 23 April.

The Conseil d'Etat adopted a very liberal and very courageous decision that reportedly triggered the anger of de Gaulle. In its decision *Rubin de Servens*

(Conseil d'Etat, Ass., 2 March 1962), the Conseil d'Etat decided that any decision to use Article 16 is an act of government and cannot therefore be reviewed by the courts. For acts carried out in the application of Article 16, it is necessary to distinguish those taken within the field of parliament's competence (Article 34) and those which have an administrative nature (Article 37 of the Constitution). For the earliest acts, the Constitutional Council was the only tribunal competent to examine their constitutionality, and then only before their promulgation by the head of state. This was the case until the constitutional revision of July 2008. Since the constitutional revision, the issue of constitutionality can be raised after presidential promulgation also in the matter of a prejudicial question (*question préjudicielle*) when addressed by the Cour de Cassation or the Conseil d'Etat to the Constitutional Council. These acts, because of their administrative nature, remain within the competence of the administrative judges.

Other exceptional regimes exist in French law. Some of them are established by an act; others have been established by case law.

The old regime of a state of siege (*état de siège*), under the Act of 9 August 1849, modified on 3 April 1875, was no longer suitable to modern forms of subversion. The French Parliament was obliged by the war in Algeria to reform the law. It adopted therefore, on 3 April 1955, the State Emergency (*état d'urgence*) Act. The application of the State Emergency Act is quite large because it is not linked only to cases of armed conflict; it can also be applied in case of imminent threat resulting in a serious breach of the peace, or in case of public calamities. The decision is taken by the Council of Ministers. However, its extension beyond 12 days can only be decided by parliament. It was applied in 1985 in New Caledonia. Then, on 8 November 2005, the Council of Ministers decided to apply the State Emergency Act because of the riots in the Paris suburbs; the Council itself halted its application on 4 January 2006. These exceptional acts are not necessarily incompatible with the European Convention on Human Rights. In theory, all the common law of judicial review applies, but, because of the broad competencies settled by the act and the vague conditions attached to them, the efficiency of any checks and balances is really reduced.

The French administrative judge has completed the range of exceptional regimes by one of its own creation, the theory of exceptional circumstances. Facing the necessities of war between 1914 and 1918, the administrative judge recognised that, in certain circumstances, the administrative authorities are allowed to take decisions that infringe the normal law. These decisions are not, however, illegal. In fact, the administrative judge settled a special regime that applies to these periods of exceptional circumstances. The judge checks if the measures are proportionate to the gravity of the circumstances (Conseil d'Etat, 28 February 1919, *Dames Dol & Laurent*).

4.3.2.2. Administrative resolutions (acts)

Judicial review can only apply to administrative acts which have the nature of decisions (expressions of public power that produce legal effects). This condition is meant to preclude actions against administrative operations which may be:

- interpretative acts (circulars, directives, guidelines, etc.), which most of the time are considered not to produce legal effects – though when, exceptionally, they produce legal effects, review is possible, because they become in substance administrative acts (for circulars, see in French administrative law, Conseil d'Etat, Ass., 29 January 1954, *Notre-Dame du Kreisker* for the distinction between interpretative and normative circulars; for directives, refer to Conseil d'Etat, Sect., 11 December 1970, *Crédit foncier de France*);

- procedural tools necessary for the adoption/issuance of administrative acts: consultations, proposals, recommendations and suchlike;

- purely informative and declaratory acts which have the role of acknowledging a fact without any addition to the effects associated by the law to the fact.

4.3.3. Access to the courts

4.3.3.1. Citizens' standing to sue

The plaintiff has to have the capacity to go to court. Legal personality is recognised in any physical person but also in any private or public legal person. There are many private moral persons in French law, such as associations, foundations, and civil and commercial firms. There are fewer in public law: the state; territorial bodies (communes, *départements*, regions) and public corporations (such as public hospitals and universities).

The plaintiff also has to have a "legitimate interest" – a personal interest in obtaining what he/she claims. It is easy to establish when the plaintiff asks for the recognition of a subjective right. For the rest, and especially in the field of the remedy of abuse of power (*recours pour excès de pouvoir*), it can be less obvious. However, the interpretation of this condition by the judge and the appreciation by the judge that the interest is enough, certain and direct are both liberal (see Conseil d'Etat, Sect., 14 February 1958, *Abisset*; Conseil d'Etat, Sect., 28 May 1971, *Damasio*). This liberal approach is seen in several things, for example, the moral interest or the collective interest. The fact that an association can go to justice and obtain a remedy for abuse of power is crucial for the protection of the collective interests of its members (see Conseil d'Etat, 28 December 1906, *Synd. des patrons coiffeurs de Limoges*).

Although the French Ombudsman (before the constitutional reform of July 2008, the *Médiateur de la République*; since July 2008, the *Défenseur des droits*) has recently gained increased independence and powers, she/he cannot go to court in the name of the applicant. The *Médiateur de la République* could only refer cases to the public prosecutors' department, but this has never been done. Will the *Défenseur des droits* do it? No one knows at the moment because the organic act has not been passed yet and things are rather blurred even in the Constitution (Title XI bis).

In the context of the two-month deadline for challenging decisions (from the date of notification for individual decisions or the date of publication for general administrative acts), the law states that the exception of illegality can normally be invoked at any time. The exception of illegality can be raised in any judicial procedure and empowers the judge to disregard the act at issue as being unlawful. Technically, the plaintiff can challenge a later decision, proceeding from the original one which became definite, by invoking an "exception" based on its illegality.

For general administrative acts, the exception of illegality can be invoked at any time. The nullity of the latest act can be pronounced by the judge, and in consequence, the original administrative act will be paralysed by this judicial decision.

For decisions, the exception of illegality does not remove particular situations and individual rights resulting from the previous decisions. In consequence, the exception of illegality is allowed only in two cases: damaging decisions (Conseil d'Etat, 3 December 1952, *Dubois*) and decisions which are part of a "complex operation". For example, in a procedure of expropriation, it is possible to invoke the exception of illegality of the latest decree of transferability (*arrêté de cessibilité*) and to obtain its nullity by declaring that the previous act, the declaration of public utility (*déclaration d'utilité publique*), was illegal (Conseil d'Etat, 6 July 1977, *cons. Girard*).

4.3.3.2. Public interest litigation

An *actio popularis* does not exist in French administrative law, because, as stated earlier, the plaintiff has to have at least a public legitimate interest to challenge an act before administrative courts. However, as has also been said before, the public legitimate interest has received a liberal interpretation by judges. As long as a group, association or NGO has the legal personality and a public legitimate interest, it can go to court. The rule of preliminary decision and delays will also have to be respected.

References

Auby, Jean-Bernard, *La décentralisation et le droit*, Librairie Général de Droit et de Jurisprudence (LGDJ), 2006.

Chapus, René, *Droit administratif général*, Vols. 1 and 2, Montchrestien, 2001.

Chapus, René, *Droit du contentieux administratif*, Montchrestien, 2006.

Laubadère, André de, and Gaudemet, Yves, *Traité de droit administratif*, Vol. 1 [Droit administratif général: l'administration, la juridiction administrative, les actes administratifs, les régimes administratifs], Librairie Général de Droit et de Jurisprudence (LGDJ), 2001.

Lebreton, Gilles, *Droit administratif général*, Dalloz, 2007.

Long, Marceau, *Les Grands arrêts de la jurisprudence administrative*, Dalloz, 2006.

Ricci, Jean-Claude, *Droit administratif général*, Hachette supérieur, 2007.

Chapter 5
National legal tradition – Hungary

P. Kovács

5.1. The constitutional system

Hungary has had a written constitution since 1949. Before that year, Hungary had no charter-like constitution: instead, constitutional conventions, customs and basic acts had built up a constitutional regime, more or less similar to the constitutional monarchies and semi-autocratic regimes of the nineteenth and twentieth centuries. After the comprehensive reformulation of the Hungarian Constitution in 1989, which eliminated the communist wording from the 1949 text and its modification in 1972, the current text can be considered as a typical example of a central or eastern European constitution.

It is often stated that virtually no sentence is the same in the 1949 and 1989 versions of the constitution. However, the situation is somewhat more complex because in 1989 there was a political agreement that the promotion of human rights could not be proportionally less important or less efficient than before. In fact, so-called political and civil rights were taken *quasi verbatim* from the text of the International Covenant of Civil and Political Rights or the European Convention on Human Rights and were substituted for the former "citizens' rights" (using the technical term of the former marxist phraseology), but the formulation of so-called economic, social and cultural rights, relatively rather generous as a result of their inspiration in marxist ideology, were not altered noticeably in 1989. For this reason, constitutional promises and aims (called *Staatsziel* in the German constitutional law) are still spelled out in wording that maintains the existence of subjective rights. This would not be too problematic if the economic situation of the country allowed satisfaction of the exigencies based on the rights-type formulation of these articles.[84]

Of the approach of the Hungarian Constitution vis-à-vis international law commitments, we can say that it is rather close to that of the German adoptionist school. According to Article 7(1) of the Hungarian Constitution, "The legal system of the Republic of Hungary accepts the generally recognised principles of international law and should harmonise the country's domestic law with the obligations assumed under international law."

---

84. This problematic approach to terminology can be seen in other eastern and central European countries too.

Hungary's constitutional system is a democratic, parliamentary republic with a constitutionally weak president, but with a prime minister enjoying a position similar to that of the German Chancellor: even though he must answer to a monocameral parliament, he cannot be overturned except by a "constructive motion of confidence". The country is divided into 19 departments, but some current efforts aim to introduce a new regional division of the country. Given that the total area of Hungary is rather small, about 93 000 sq. km, the seven new regions would not complement but rather replace the existing historical departments founded more than a thousand years ago by the first king of Hungary. However, the competence of the departments diminished considerably during the change of political regime in 1989. Since then, the settlements have been autonomous, that is, they are not controlled by the departments. On the other hand, the legality and constitutionality of the activity of the departments are checked, *inter alia,* by the commissioner of public administration, an office rather similar to the French *préfet*. Currently, one commissioner is appointed per region; these exist as statistical units.

The same can be said about the transformation of the judiciary, which creates a highly uniform system: there is no separate structure for administrative tribunals and civil and criminal judiciary. The structure of all three main fields follows the same architecture, and they are composed of city, departmental and regional courts, with the Supreme Court on the top. The former judicial system of three levels, that of city courts, department courts and the supreme court, was recently changed by the introduction of regional courts. These regional courts received competency over dispute settlement, and the courts' main duty in this regard is to ensure that a uniform judicial policy pervades the network of courts. Previously this competency had been the domain of the supreme court.

On the following pages, I try to give an overview of the promotion of access to justice and judicial review in the main fields of Hungarian legal practice, that is to say, civil law, penal law and administrative law.

5.2. Treaty law in justice and judicial review

In the Constitution of the Republic of Hungary, access to justice and judicial review are assured in Article 57, in the first and fifth paragraphs respectively.[85] There is a manifest similarity between the formulation of these paragraphs (a result of the comprehensive constitutional reform of 1989) and the wording of Articles 6 and 13 of the European Convention on Human Rights[86] and in some aspects also the text of Article 14 of the International Covenant on Civil and Political Rights.[87]

---

85. Article 57 of the Constitution.
86. Articles 6 and 13 of the European Convention on Human Rights.
87. Article 14 of the International Covenant on Civil and Political Rights.

This similarity is not a coincidence. One can see an obvious tendency in the post-communist constitutionalisation of central and eastern European countries: most of them preserved the relatively generous formulation of economic, social and cultural rights inherited from the marxist period, but changed the restricting formulas of civil and political rights ("citizens' rights" in the marxist phraseology) and used genuinely liberal wording. Very often, *quasi verbatim* quotations can be discovered in national constitutions stemming from the Universal Declaration of Human Rights or the International Covenant of Civil and Political Rights (hereafter "the Covenant"), or the European Convention on Human Rights ("the Convention").

Not only did the Constitutional Court not deny, but it expressly recognised the reasons and consequences of this similarity: for instance, in a resolution adopted concerning a complaint on the legal limits of making photocopies of certain documents shown to the accused and his legal counsel in a criminal procedure (where no copy could be made, *inter alia,* of "secret documents", minutes of the court or the dissenting opinion of the judge), the Constitutional Court analysed "the articles of the Covenant and the European Convention on Human Rights, which were taken as examples for the structure and the content to Article 57 of the Constitution".[88]

Even if this similarity between constitutional dispositions and treaty law commitments is obvious, it should be borne in mind that the constitutional position of international law and national law is shaped – more or less, and not without contradictions – according to the concept of dualism.[89]

All in all, three main questions arise. How has the Hungarian Constitutional Court dealt with cases related to access to justice? What are its landmark decisions? What kind of jurisprudential evolution can be discovered in the matter?

5.3. Access to justice and the Constitutional Court

Concerning the first problem, that is to say, access to justice, the position of the Constitutional Court can be illustrated by its decision adopted in a case[90] linked to membership and admittance procedures of the medical certifying boards. In fact, the Constitutional Court analysed here the relationship between access to justice and the autonomy of professional organisations. It

---

88. Case 6/1998 (III.11.) AB, *Az Alkotmánybíróság Határozatai* [Yearbook of Resolutions and Decisions of the Constitutional Court] (hereinafter ABH) 1998, p. 95.
89. Article 7(1) of the Constitution: "The legal system of the Republic of Hungary accepts the generally recognised principles of international law, and harmonises the country's domestic law with the obligations assumed under international law." For its interpretation, see, *inter alia*: Péter Kovács, "Commentary to the decision of the Supreme Court on humanitarian law cases", *Yearbook of International Humanitarian Law 1999*, The Hague, pp. 375-377; idem, "Commentary to the decision of the Supreme Court on humanitarian law cases", *Yearbook of International Humanitarian Law 2000*, The Hague, pp. 518-519.
90. Case 39/1997 (VII.1.) AB.

pointed out that Article 50 on judicial control over administrative decisions[91] should be interpreted in light of Article 57:

> in the manner that the procedure in question should lead to the real adjudgement of the rights sued for and obligations by the judiciary; all the criteria listed by the Constitution, that is, the establishment of the court by law, its independence and impartiality and the exigency that the procedure should be conducted according to the principle of justice (or as international treaties put it: fair, *équitablement, in billiger Weise*) serving this aim. A final decision is constitutional only when it has been passed after the fulfilment of all these exigencies. The judicial control of administrative decisions cannot be limited constitutionally to the observance of formal legality.[92]

From the ECHR jurisprudence, the Constitutional Court referred[93] to the Le Compte, Van Leuven and de Meyere cases, and also to the Albert and Le Compte cases.[94]

In a case concerning some aspects of the procedural law on petty offences, the court pointed out the unconstitutionality of the lack of access to justice. According to the law on penal procedure, if an offender was previously sentenced to suspended imprisonment and committed another crime during the probation time, the judge was entitled to decide whether to transform the suspended punishment into real imprisonment. However, in the case of a petty offence, the judge was not obliged even to hear the offender and could pass judgment in the offender's absence if he/she considered that the documentation in itself was sufficient. The Constitutional Court annulled this possibility and, in the reasoning of the resolution, references were made to Article 14(1) of the Covenant, Articles 5(1-a) and 6(1) of the Convention and the jurisprudence of the European Court of Human Rights.[95] The Constitutional Court cited the Deweer case[96] and the Hakansson and Sturesson judgment[97] in order to prove that the jurisprudence of Strasbourg allows the accusee to be absent from the trial only when it is the accusee's own decision not to attend the trial and not to benefit from the procedural advantages offered by penal law.[98] Hereby, the Constitutional Court confirmed its position adopted a year before in another case related to a petty offence, namely that in procedures which are of a criminal nature (whatever the proper name of the procedure), the totality of criminal procedural guarantees linked to the principle of the

---

91. Article 50 of the Constitution reads: "(1) The courts of the Republic of Hungary shall protect and uphold constitutional order, as well as the rights and lawful interests of natural persons, legal persons and unincorporated organisations, and shall determine the punishment for those who commit criminal offences. (2) The courts shall review the legality of the decisions of public administration".
92. Case 39/1997 (VII.1.) AB, ABH 1997, p. 272.
93. ABH 1997, p. 274.
94. European Court of Human Rights, judgments of 23 June 1981 and 10 February 1983.
95. Case 5/1999 (III.31.) AB, ABH 1999, pp. 79-80, 85.
96. European Court of Human Rights, judgment of 7 February 1980.
97. European Court of Human Rights, judgment of 21 February 1990.
98. Case 5/1999 (III.31.) AB, ABH 1999, p. 88.

fair trial should be observed.[99] In this case, the court cited the Belilos judgment[100] of the European Court of Human Rights as proof of the same way of legal thinking.[101]

Similarly, the appeal procedure is also unconstitutional if the condemned is *ex lege* excluded from participating in this phase of the trial. The Constitutional Court pointed out that, even if the phase of appeal follows a trial where the accused was present, the presence of the accused is still very important at appeal, because the court is mandated to take – also *ex officio* – new decisions or decisions which were missed previously.[102] In this case, the Constitutional Court referred[103] to its constant jurisprudence, namely that the open character of a penal procedure can be limited according to the dispositions of the Covenant and the Convention, for example, on moral grounds or to preserve public order, security of the state, state secrets or the privacy of individuals.[104]

Neither can fair trial requirements be refused in civil law litigation, even if the merits are linked to bank secrets. In the given case, a top manager was blamed for professional misbehaviour and the authority overseeing financial institutions issued a warrant prohibiting his employment (as a top manager) at other financial or banking organs. In this case mixing aspects of civil law, labour law and penal law, the Constitutional Court reiterated its *dictum* pronounced in the previously cited case 39/1997 and emphasised that – in conformity with the Strasbourg jurisprudential line – the principle of equality of arms must not be limited to penal law procedures.[105] As to banking secrecy, the Constitutional Court pointed out that it cannot be invoked in litigation if knowledge of the content of the given document is necessary for a decision on the merits of a case.[106]

The proper title of the procedure is not determinant when implementing the access-to-justice principle. The Constitutional Court applied this principle also to the disciplinary procedures of notaries[107] and in this case it summarised its approach by stating that "according to the practice of the Constitutional Court, underlying the notions of 'court', 'established by law', 'independent' and 'impartial' special dogmatics are hidden".[108]

The disciplinary procedures of secret services also have to undergo judicial control with guarantees of a fair trial. That is why the exclusion of the legal

---

99. Case 63/1997 (XII.11.) AB, ABH 1997, p. 368.
100. European Court of Human Rights, judgment of 29 April 1988.
101. Case 63/1997 (XII.11.) AB, ABH 1997, p. 368.
102. Case 20/2005 (V.26.) AB, ABH 2005, p. 223.
103. Ibid., p. 222.
104. Case 58/1995 (IX. 15.) AB, ABH 1995, p. 293.
105. Case 15/2002 (III.29.) AB, ABH 2002, p. 118.
106. Case 15/2002 (III.29.) AB, ABH 2002, p. 120.
107. Case 32/2002 (VII.4.) AB, ABH 2001, pp. 160-161.
108. Ibid., p. 159.

counsel of an individual from the disciplinary procedure of his client would hamper the access to justice.[109] In this case, the Constitutional Court cited the case of *Engel v. the Netherlands*[110] from the jurisprudence of the European Court of Human Rights.[111]

When in a law adopted by parliament in order to combat football hooliganism, a special Permanent Court of Arbitration for Sports was established and enabled with – among other things – the competency to adjudicate the legality of banning certain individuals from attending matches, decided by the organisers of a sports event, the Constitutional Court reached the conclusion that here access to justice is not guaranteed in an adequate manner. Submission to the competency of a court of arbitration depends always on the consent of both parties. Judicial control of a specific anti-hooligan measure adopted by the stadium cannot be taken for granted because one can expect to encounter the objection of the stadium, author of the disputed measure.[112]

In a similar way, religious freedom cannot be interpreted in such a manner that the judiciary would be excluded from overseeing normal, civil or labour law litigation of churches. "It is a constitutional requirement that if a legal dispute based on the law of the state arises between a church and a person linked to it with a legal relationship, this litigation should be adjudged *in merito* by the courts of the state."[113]

As a summary, it is helpful to remember the thesis of the Constitutional Court that "the right to a fair trial is an absolute right and no other fundamental right or constitutional purpose can be confronted with it."[114]

5.4. Rights to legal remedy and the Constitutional Court

The scrupulous observance of the right to legal remedies was emphasised in a long series of cases. It is worth mentioning some of these cases to show the extent of the principle as well as the temptation in legislation to get rid of judicial supervision.

In order to enhance the protection of some natural geological formations of national interest, the law on the protection of the natural environment mandated the responsible minister to decide which springs, moorlands, caves, sumps, salt marshes, tumuli or historical earthworks should be put under national protection. As according to the law the minister only "makes public"

109. Case 8/2004 (III.25.) AB, ABH 2004, p. 156.
110. European Court of Human Rights, judgment of 8 July 1976.
111. Case 8/2004 (III.25.) AB, ABH 2004, p. 156.
112. Case 35/2002 (VII.19.) AB, ABH 2002, p. 212.
113. Case 32/2003 (VI.4.) AB, ABH 2003, p. 380.
114. Case 14/2004 (V.7.) AB, ABH 2004, p. 266.

these geographical points, the owners of the given properties were not entitled to sue the government for an error in the list. The Constitutional Court concluded that parliament had acted contrary to the constitution by not having granted adequate legal remedies in the designation of protected areas.[115]

The legal problems were the same as those of forests of higher value, where a forest for economic purposes could be reclassified as a forest under natural protection. However, this classification was made by the minister by regulations, that is, legal norms of general applicability, and not in individual decisions. While the Constitutional Court recognised *in abstracto* the constitutionality of the enlarged protection of the given forests, it arrived at a similar conclusion as in the previously cited matter: the legislative authority should complete the actual law through a procedure where each case was the object of an individual ministerial decision that could be sued before the judiciary.[116]

While the legality of the classification in general should not be contested, it should however be possible to challenge the classification of a given individual forest as deserving protection or to settle a dispute about the adequacy of the ministerial regulation and the international treaty or Community law documents for which the given regulation is supposed to be the norm of execution.[117]

In a case linked to aspects of the compulsory vaccination of children against epidemics like diphtheria, tetanus and pertussis, the Constitutional Court felt that the system lacked a legal remedy for parents who did not want to let their child be vaccinated. A simple review by medical authorities of the decision of the local doctor was not enough for the Constitutional Court:[118] it required an effective judicial check, which meant the court should pass its decision *a priori*, that is, before the vaccination was given.[119]

In penal matters, the Constitutional Court recalled that even the judges at Strasbourg[120] do not claim to assure the full right of cassation when the criminal case is of minor importance and simple.[121] A general right of appeal appears only in Protocol No. 7[122] of the European Convention on Human Rights. However, the *ex lege* denial of reopening the procedure in a case of minor importance, even if a manifest violation of procedural rules occurred

115. Case 53/2002 (XI. 28.) AB, ABH 2002, p. 327.
116. Case 33/2006 (VII.13.) AB, ABH 2006, p. 447.
117. Ibid., p. 462.
118. Case 39/2007 (VI.20.) AB, ABH 2007, pp. 502-503.
119. Ibid., pp. 502-503.
120. The Constitutional Court recalled the following judgments of the European Court of Human Rights: *Delcourt v. Belgium*, 17 January 1970; *Monnel and Morris v. the United Kingdom*, 2 March 1987; *Campbell v. the United Kingdom*, 25 March 1992.
121. Case 49/1998 (XI.27.) AB, ABH 1998, p. 3383.
122. Article 2 of Additional Protocol No. 7.

(in the given case, the accused person was summoned to the tribunal without prior notification of the accusation) cannot be considered as constitutional.[123]

When the code of penal procedure recognised the possibility of the president of the court of appeal deciding whether to hear cases of minor offences alone (or in camera), or only after a public trial, the code was considered incompatible with the right to remedies and to a public trial.[124] Here too, a good number of jurisprudential cases were cited from the European Court of Human Rights[125] by the Constitutional Court.[126]

The Constitutional Court was also not satisfied that, for a minor offence, the local police had the right to order the custody of the offender for up to 72 hours in cases of *flagrante delicto* where the offence could also be punished by a short term of imprisonment. The Constitutional Court considered that it was not enough for the judge to pass a decision on the legality of the custody at the time of deciding the whole case. It pointed out that parliament was at fault in not legislating for a specific, prompt remedy vis-à-vis the custody, only later in the framework of the trial of the whole case before a tribunal.[127]

5.5. Decisions on European law and its status

Until now, the Constitutional Court has been very reluctant regarding this matter.

Even if there is a "European Union clause" in the Constitution,[128] it concerns much more the transfer of sovereignty than the status of EU law ("Community law") in the Hungarian legal system. Moreover, nothing is written in the act on the establishment and competencies of the Constitutional Court concerning European law: only its competencies vis-à-vis public international law are enumerated.[129] It is true, however, that this act was adopted in 1989, at the time of political regime change and the return to democracy, long before Hungary joined the European Union in 2004. Parliament has not amended the text since 1989.

In the so-called sugar quota case, a Community law regulation[130] was at stake. This was in the days before Hungary joined the EU (when the direct applicability of Community regulations could not be enforced in the Hungarian legal

---

123. Case 49/1998 (XI.27.) AB, ABH 1998, pp. 3379-3381.
124. Case 20/2005 (V.26.) AB, ABH 2005, pp. 230-231.
125. European Court of Human Rights: *Weber v. Switzerland*, 22 May 1990; *Rolf Gustafson v. Sweden*, 1 July 1997; *Helmers v. Sweden*, 29 October 1991; *Allan Jacobson v. Sweden*, 29 October 1991; *Meftah v. France*, 26 July 2002, etc.
126. Case 20/2005 (V.26.) AB, ABH 2005, pp. 212-213.
127. Case 3/2007 (II.13.) AB, ABH 2007, pp. 111-112.
128. Article 2/A of the Constitution.
129. Article 1 of Act XXXII of 1989 on the Constitutional Court.
130. Regulation 230/2004/CE.

system), which explains why the president of the state asked for an a priori review of the act passed by parliament before its promulgation. In its resolution, the Constitutional Court put special emphasis on the fact that the constitutional analysis of the norm, criticised for violating the non-retroactivity principle, concerned only a Hungarian act – and not the EU regulation.[131]

Later, the Constitutional Court recognised the *sui generis* nature of Community law in the case of Sportingbet (betting on the Internet),[132] but here the failure of the legislation to fulfil a commitment in the Treaty of Rome was at stake. According to the plaintiff, in this instance the constitutional article about the harmony between public international law and national law should be applied.[133] The Constitutional Court rejected this motion and refused its competency to adjudicate a legal dispute about the compatibility of a national legal norm and Community law.[134]

Generally, the conflict with European law emerged as the lack of implementation of a European law commitment, as, for example, in the case of the calculation of fees for night duty of medical staff,[135] where, *inter alia*, the improper execution of the directive 93/104/EC was emphasised by the plaintiff.[136] The Court, however, arrived at the conclusion that the given legal situation was already unconstitutional because a constitutional right should be regulated by law (that is, by parliament) and not by simple ministerial orders.[137] Thus, the Court was not obliged to examine the situation from the point of view of the satisfaction of the exigencies of Community law – which does not enter into its competency.[138] It was interesting to see that the given directive is presumably a directly applicable one – according to the jurisprudence of the Court of Justice of the European Communities[139] – that is, it should enjoy the same status as an act adopted by parliament. It was an important statement that primary community law and secondary community law are part of the Hungarian legal system.

The Constitutional Court followed this policy also when the compatibility of the Hungarian legislation on property limitations in falconry was challenged. The Court gave an overview of the international treaties (namely, the Washington Convention for the protection of endangered species, abbreviated

---

131. Case 17/2004 (V. 25.) AB, ABH 2004, p. 297.
132. Case 1053/E/2005, ABH 2006, p. 1828.
133. Article 7(1): "The legal system of the Republic of Hungary accepts the universally recognised rules and regulations of international law, and harmonises the internal laws and statutes of the country with the obligations assumed under international law."
134. Case 1053/E/2005, ABH 2006, p. 1830 (concurrent opinion of Judge Kovács).
135. Case 72/2006 (XII.15.) AB 2006, pp. 819-868.
136. Ibid., p. 861.
137. Ibid., pp. 844-845.
138. Ibid., p. 861.
139. Cases C-397/01-403/01, *Pfeiffer et al. vs. Deutsches Reutes Kreuz*, Kreisverband Waldshut eV, judgment of 5 October 2004, ECR I-8835, paragraph 120.

as CITES) and the related Community law rules[140] and it stated that the content of the Community law was manifestly different from the one which was alleged by the plaintiff. That is why the compatibility of the Hungarian law and Community law was not formally examined by the Court.

The conflict of Community law with basic constitutional principles could emerge in some aspects of co-operation in the context of the European Arrest Warrant[141] and its form contained in a treaty contracted between the European Union, Norway and Iceland signed on 28 June 2006 in Vienna. The head of state asked for an *a priori* constitutional review before the promulgation of the treaty – but in the meantime parliament amended the *nullum crimen sine lege* clause[142] of the constitution, taking into consideration the more efficacious co-operation in criminal matters planned by the Lisbon Treaty. The amended version of the constitution[143] will secure greater harmony between European penal law co-operation and the Hungarian constitutional background. Therefore a hypothetical judicial review of a Community act adopted in the context of the European arrest warrant seems to be actually out of the question – because of the constitutionally granted *a priori* habilitation.[144]

5.6. Conclusions

The Constitutional Court has paid special attention to the fact that access to justice and the right to judicial review should be secured. It has profited also from the jurisprudence of the European Court of Human Rights.

We can see that in the basic fields of legal practice this exigency of the rule of law is practically secured. However, there are still issues (like certain aspects of the protection of the natural environment or medical interventions) where the legislation still has to change some of the parameters if it is to promote a comprehensive system of checks and review exercised by the judiciary.

---

140. Council Directive 79/409/EEC of 2 April 1979, Council Directive 2006/105/EC of 20 November 2006.

141. Council Framework Decision 2002/584/JHA of 13 June 2002 on the European arrest warrant and the surrender procedures between member states.

142. Article 57(4): "No one shall be declared guilty and subjected to punishment for an offence that was not a criminal offence under Hungarian law at the time such offence was committed."

143. Article 57(4): "No one shall be declared guilty and subjected to punishment for an offence that was not a criminal offence under Hungarian law – or, for the purpose of promoting the principle of the mutual recognition of resolutions deriving from legal acts of the European Union without limiting the essential content of fundamental rights, according to the law of another state, partner in the creation of an area of justice, security and freedom – at the time such offence was committed."

144. See the commentary on this case in Péter Kovács, "A la recherche du bon chemin ... ou l'affaire du mandat d'arrêt européen devant la Cour constitutionnelle" in Jean-Denis Mouton (ed.), *La France, l'Europe et le Monde: Mélanges en l'honneur de Jean Charpentier*, Presses Universitaires de Nancy, 2008, pp. 349-365.

Chapter 6
National legal tradition – Romania

D. Dragos

6.1. The constitutional framework

In 1991, two years after the fall of the communist regime, Romania adopted a new Constitution which sought to establish, but fell short of explicitly declaring, the principle of separation of powers between the three branches of government. A clear statement of the principle of separation of powers had to wait until the constitutional reform of 2003.

In Romania, legislative power is exercised by Parliament (four-year terms), composed of two houses, the Senate and the Chamber of Deputies, which basically have the same responsibilities but in different areas. Drafts of laws are discussed first in the non-decisional chamber and then are adopted by the decisional chamber. Which House of Parliament is the decisional chamber for a given law depends on the category of law under consideration.

At the top of the executive branch is the President of the Republic and the Government, led by the prime minister. The president, elected directly by the citizens for a five-year term, nominates the prime minister to parliament, and then appoints the government. The president has no power to dismiss the government or dissolve parliament, except in very exceptional cases requiring a set of conditions that are very unlikely to ever be met.

In sum, the Romanian system of government is parliamentary, with a directly elected president. Parliament has authority over many independent agencies whose remits range from the regulation of specific areas (National Agency for Regulation of Energy Sector) to monitoring fair competition (Competition Council) or mediating in administrative disputes (the Ombudsman).

Judicial power is exercised by the courts – courts of first instance, tribunals, courts of appeal and the High Court of Cassation and Justice. From tribunals upwards, all courts have specialised sections (units of judges) for administrative and fiscal matters. In some cases, for reasons of internal organisation, these are combined with the civil or commercial sections. Based on special regulations, first-instance courts also hear administrative law cases, but these are judged alongside other cases, not separately as they are at the upper levels.

Judicial review of administrative decisions has a long tradition in Romania, but this practice has at times been challenged. Between 1864 and 1866, revolutionary forces established an institution modelled on the French Conseil d'Etat, with both consultative and jurisdictional powers. That lasted only two years, and then Romania adopted the Anglo-Saxon model of ordinary courts, which were competent in administrative matters as well. Special jurisdictions for fiscal matters and pensions have been established over time, reducing the competency of the ordinary courts.

From 1905 to 1910, the High Court of Cassation was entrusted with the power to review administrative decisions, through its specialised section for administrative matters. For a short time, between 1910 and 1912, this competency reverted to the ordinary courts, after which it was returned to the High Court's special section for administrative matters. For most of this time, though, the courts only had the right to grant compensation for damages caused by illegal resolutions, without annulling the resolution itself (a "private law" approach). After 1923 the constitution granted full powers of review to the ordinary courts, and in 1939 administrative courts were established with authority to review the decisions of local authorities.

Between 1948 and 1965, judicial review of administrative decisions was abolished, due to the communist idea that "the state can do no wrong because it is the expression of the will of the working class" and because "the administrative organs are subordinated to the Great National Assembly, which oversees their activity, so there is no need for judicial review". From 1965 to 1990, judicial review was reinstated. In 1967 the practice was regulated in clear terms, but few cases were brought before the ordinary courts on the basis of these regulations, owing to the control of the communist state.

One of the first laws adopted by the new Romanian Parliament after the 1989 regime change, even before the constitution was brought to a vote, was the Law on Judicial Review of Administrative Resolutions No. 29/1990. Inspired by its 1925 and 1967 predecessors, this law had the advantage of greater effectiveness.

As was to be expected, the adoption of a new constitution in 1991 brought changes in the application of Law 29/1990, which has since been interpreted according to the principles underlying the Fundamental Law. For instance, judicial review was applied to administrative decrees issued by any public authority, not only by administrative authorities (Decision 97/1997 of the Constitutional Court).[145] Competency for review remained at the level of ordinary courts, within which sections (units of judges) were established to deal with administrative law cases. In the 2003 constitutional revision, the provisions on judicial review were amended: the action of an aggrieved person was complemented by an action based on legitimate interest (Article 52 of the constitution).

---

145. Decision published in the *Official Monitor*, No. 210/1997.

Because the 1990 law was outdated and needed reform, in 2004 a new law came into force, Law No. 554/2004. It was amended in 2005, 2007 and 2008, on account of EC laws and recommendations, but also as a result of decisions of the Constitutional Court.

Romania's political model is one of decentralisation combined with deconcentration, within a unitary state. The principle of autonomy of local communities is stated in the constitution, but the decentralisation process is still under way. In recent years, local public administration has been faced with challenges arising from the decentralisation of powers in the absence of the financial means to exercise them, and also the lack of any ability at local level to make use of the autonomy provided by law.

6.2. Government and public administration

According to the constitution, Romanian public administration is structured in a three-tier system of government: central, county and local.

The government, consisting of the prime minister, ministers and other members established by law, has a duty to ensure implementation of the domestic and foreign policy of the country and exercise general management of public administration. Ministries oversee the main areas of public policy, and there are also specialised agencies, subordinate to the government or to one of the ministries. These agencies under government control are designed differently from the autonomous (independent) central agencies, which are organised under the supervision of parliament (Court of Auditors, Legislative Council, National Council for Audiovisual Matters, Competition Council, the Ombudsman, etc.) because they are not subordinate in any way to the government. Also, every ministry has territorial units in the counties (deconcentrated territorial agencies) which perform the tasks of the ministry in that area, bringing it closer to citizens. The attributions of these territorial units are subject to decentralisation, as their transfer to the counties or local communities is under consideration.

The state is divided geographically into counties, made up of communes, towns and cities (larger towns). In 1998, the grouping of several counties led to the formation of eight development regions to provide integrated management of European funds and access to international financing, and also to lay the groundwork for the time when Romania would be able to send representatives to the Committee of the Regions of the European Union. Nevertheless, the regions are not "administrative territorial units" and they are not legal entities, like the counties, cities and communes.

The role of the county level of government is to co-ordinate the work of local public authorities in projects of common interest and in the provision of public services. The county is a territorial unit, a public law entity, formed by communes, towns and cities. It has local autonomy and is run by a county council with 31 to 37 members elected directly by the inhabitants, depending on the population of the county. The executive body of the county is the president of the county council, elected directly in a single round of elections. This position is similar, in terms of authority, to that of a mayor.

Of French inspiration, there is also a representative of central government at county level, the prefect, who ensures that the administrative activity of mayors, local councils and county councils is carried out according to the law and who co-ordinates the administrative units of ministries in the area. The prefect has no power to annul an unlawful resolution of a local authority, but can challenge the resolution before a court.

Until recently the prefect was a political appointee of the central government, but significant changes have been made to this position, which should now be allocated to a high-ranking civil servant who theoretically has a non-political status. The de-politicisation of this office is only theoretical so far because the persons currently in these positions were members of political parties who were appointed prefects before the law requiring their non-political status was enacted. Consequently, they resigned from the party, took an examination and were re-appointed as non-political civil servants. In fact, their informal connection with the party is still a reality. In order to make the position fully non-political, the prefects should have been appointed from a pool of professionals, constituted before the appointment was made, and on a competitive basis.

Under the principle of local autonomy, the local level of government should bring public authorities close to the people. At this level there are communes, towns and cities. These are all public legal entities and the generic term for them is "territorial administrative units". The communes are composed of villages, but only the commune is a territorial unit with legal personality. Every city, town or commune has a mayor and a local council (with 9 to 31 members), both elected directly by the citizens "at large" – meaning the whole area as a single unit, not divided into constituencies. The councillors are elected from a block list of candidates; so, from each party's list, one or several candidates will be elected to the council, in proportion to the votes received in the election by proportional representation (PR). In the past, various civil society groups and organisations have drafted proposals for a nominal electoral system (electing the members of the council as individual candidates, representing a sub-unit of the city/town/commune, or at least on an "open list", not as part of a blocked list), but these have failed to be adopted because a political consensus blocked these measures from being discussed in parliament. Another issue is the large number of council members, which makes the decision process quite difficult and full of political compromises.

The current system has been criticised because it protects the members of local councils from being held accountable to the electors by being re-elected or not. The need to reform this system has been brought to the fore by several instances where friction with the local council impeded mayors from acting and fulfilling their electoral promises. On the other hand, several mayors blamed their own inaction on the local councils' lack of co-operation, thus hiding their own incompetence. It should be noted that the local council has the final decision on most local matters, with the mayor as the initiator and authority that implements the decision. The members of the council also have the right to propose legislation, so the mayor can theoretically be ignored in the process. The mayor's party does not necessarily have a majority in the local council, as is the case in France, for instance. In this context, a major criticism of the system is that the decision-making process is quite slow and full of compromises. In addition, if some villages in a commune do not have proper proportional representation in the local council, this encourages those villages to go it alone and form new communes, thus deepening the fragmentation of the area and dissipating its administrative capacity.

Apart from traditional public bodies, private persons can also act as public authorities when the law or an administrative resolution authorises them to use public power. They are thus associated with public authorities, and their resolutions can be challenged in administrative contentious proceedings. The leading cases in this matter involved the Bar Association (Decision No. 450/1997 of the former Supreme Court of Justice, Administrative Contentious Section) and private universities (Decision 1541/1996 of the former Supreme Court of Justice, Administrative Contentious Section).

6.3. Judicial review of government and administration

6.3.1. Judicial independence from the executive

In Romania, the independence of the judiciary from the executive branch is established in the Constitution and guaranteed by the independence of judges. According to the Fundamental Law, judges are appointed by the President of the Republic on nomination by the Supreme Council of Magistrates – an independent body under the authority of parliament, composed of judges, public prosecutors, members of civil society, the Ministry of Justice, the Chief Prosecutor and the President of the High Court of Cassation and Justice. Judicial review of administrative decisions is carried out by the ordinary courts, within which there are specialised units of judges for administrative law matters.

The revised constitution prohibits rulings of administrative bodies from being considered definitive and disqualifies any action which prevents access to courts. Thus, Article 21(4) of the constitution provides that "administrative special jurisdiction is optional and free of charge". The provision was adopted

after many years of long legal cases, dragged out by fiscal authorities, which led to decisions of the European Court of Human Rights condemning Romania for not ensuring access to an independent court. The over-long proceedings were accompanied by the obligation to pay the amounts stipulated in the appealed decision, until finalisation of the procedure, which could take up to three or four years. Since 2003, therefore, all jurisdictions that usually resolve administrative disputes at the administrative level, performed by administrative bodies following a quasi-judicial procedure, are constitutional only if they are free of charge, optional and do not prevent in the end the aggrieved person's access to the justice offered by courts.

Of the leading cases in this matter, Decision No. 34/1993 of the Constitutional Court[146] is worth special mention, as the decision interpreted the "definitive" character of a jurisdictional procedure expressly stated by the fiscal laws, as being definitive only at administrative level, thus opening up the right to access the courts for review.

The application of the principle of separation of powers is expressed very well by the interdiction for courts to reinstate administrative resolutions annulled as a result of judicial review. This practice, based on the express provisions of the Judicial Review Law (Article 18), was very well established in Romanian administrative law even before the new law came into effect (Decision 692/1994 of the former Supreme Court of Justice, Administrative Contentious Section).

6.3.2. The scope of judicial review

6.3.2.1. Political and security questions

In Romania, administrative resolutions or acts in general are subject to review by the ordinary courts, with this task allocated to groups of judges who are specialists in administrative and fiscal contentious proceedings. The basic rule for the competency of the courts is that administrative law sections of the tribunals deal with resolutions issued by local authorities (county or commune/town/city), whereas the resolutions issued by central authorities are dealt with by the administrative law sections of the courts of appeal. Any appeal[147] against a decision of a tribunal is lodged at the Court of Appeal, and the appeal against decisions of the courts of appeal is lodged at the High Court of Cassation and Justice, which also has a special section for administrative and fiscal contentious proceedings. Administrative resolutions are taken to mean only normative resolutions, in the sense that they contain norms of law, because non-normative resolutions (recommendations or preparatory resolutions) are analysed by the courts only indirectly, when they serve as

---

146. Decision published in the *Official Monitor*, No. 14 (1993).
147. This is called "recourse" in Romanian, because we have also "appeal" as a first appeal procedure, in civil, commercial and criminal cases.

the basis for issuing a normative resolution. The terminology is different in Romanian administrative law: by "normative" resolution we understand a general act, as opposed to an individual act.

Review of government resolutions

The government issues two types of administrative resolutions: decisions (general or individual) and ordinances (mostly general). The constitution permits ordinances only as an exception, because they have the power of laws enacted by parliament. Ordinances are issued on the basis of an express delegation by parliament, or in exceptional and urgent situations. Nevertheless, the practice of issuing ordinances is widely used by all governments, often not accompanied by the underlying justification. The ordinances are then discussed by parliament, which can confirm them by law or reject them.

The review of decisions issued by the government is granted to the courts of appeal with recourse to the High Court of Cassation and Justice. There is no time limit for lodging the action against general decisions, whereas individual decisions must be contested within six months from their notification and within one year from their issuance.

The regulation (Article 9 of Law No. 554/2004) on challenging government ordinances is controversial in that a challenge normally can be made only through the exception on unconstitutionality, because ordinances can modify a law passed by parliament. The exception can be raised by parties only within an existing proceeding, not directly to the Constitutional Court, and the judge has to agree before the exception can be sent to the Constitutional Court. Only the Ombudsman can directly challenge a law or government ordinance in the Constitutional Court. In this context, the Judicial Review Law of 2004, based on the texts of the constitution revised in 2003 (Article 126), instituted a procedure to compensate those who were aggrieved by ordinances declared unconstitutional by the Constitutional Court, but also granted a right to start an action in compensation, with the purpose of giving the plaintiff the opportunity to invoke the exception of unconstitutionality. Thus, the action in compensation caused by an ordinance can be filed together with an exception of unconstitutionality. If the judge considers the exception admissible, the Constitutional Court will be asked to review the constitutionality of the ordinance; if the ordinance is declared unconstitutional, the judge will continue the proceeding, considering compensatory action.

This interpretation of the text was not, however, what the legislators had intended; rather, it was what the Constitutional Court inferred from the text. The original intention was to institute a direct action on unconstitutionality against ordinances. Reacting to this interpretation, the court considered correctly that: a) an ordinance cannot be "illegal" just because it can modify laws, so this cannot be the scope of an action in administrative contentious proceedings, and b) the action in court cannot have as its scope the unconstitutionality of the ordinance, because that is exclusively a procedure triggered by an exception invoked by the judge. The constitution itself excludes ordinances from direct oversight by the courts (Article 126). Consequently, the Constitutional Court stated in Decision No. 660/2007 that Article 9 of Law No. 554/2004 is unconstitutional if interpreted as anything other than granting a right to action for compensation, or for annulment of the subsequent resolutions, and the unconstitutionality of the ordinances can be verified only on an exception raised in such a proceeding.

Exceptions

Judicial review of administrative resolutions in Romania is not absolute. The exceptions are provided by the constitution itself in Article 126: they are actions issued on public authorities' relations with parliament and military acts involving matters of command.

The first category of exception can be based on what the doctrine calls "the theory of acts of government" – resolutions not reviewable by the courts because of their nature (governmental as opposed to administrative) or because the authorities involved in their issuance cannot be subjected to the administrative courts' jurisdiction (parliament, foreign states).

In this context, it is considered that resolutions of parliament excluded from direct review as discussed above include resolutions of a political nature issued by the president (messages, proposal for a referendum, proposal for validation of the prime minister, etc.) and resolutions of the government (ordinances) issued on the basis of a delegated power coming from parliament.

Military acts are excluded from review only if they are of a command nature, not if they are of an economic (military purchasing) or a human resources nature – like decisions to put a soldier on reserve status.

Even in cases when direct review is prohibited, those affected by such resolutions can go to the civil court and file for damages.

The Law on Judicial Review No. 554/2004 complemented these two exceptions with many others: resolutions for which another procedure is expressly regulated; resolutions enacted in exceptional situations (state of war, state of emergency); resolutions regarding national security and public safety; resolutions issued in case of calamities, epidemics and epizootics. These exceptions would be unconstitutional if they were real, because they would restrict the right to judicial review provided by the constitution far beyond what the constitution itself states. No exception of unconstitutionality with this object has been invoked to date, mainly because none of the above-mentioned circumstances has occurred. On the other hand, these resolutions can still be challenged as an "excess of power", defined by the law as a breach of the law by excessive exercise of discretion. It can be observed that this definition is basically that of illegality. So, even though the law tries to exclude these resolutions from judicial review, it is nevertheless possible. In addition, going to court for compensation for such resolutions is always a possibility.

The exceptions provided by the judicial review law are not new in Romanian administrative law. They are not a response to the new challenges of the modern world, such as terrorism and epidemics, since they were regulated before in Romanian legislation, so there exists a kind of "tradition" of having them in the law. The doctrine, though, considers that such exceptions have no real use, because in all situations described in the law there are special regulations that resolve the problem of judicial review, either by establishing special procedures or by making reference to the general procedure. In any case, access to justice cannot be impeded by laws written in compliance with the constitution.

For instance, according to Law No. 132/1997 on requisitions for public interest, in exceptional cases, competent public authorities can mandate other public institutions, companies and individuals to temporarily cede the necessary goods and facilities to the national army forces, when a state of war or emergency is instituted or when disasters occur. Requisition can be ordered by the president by decree, or by governmental decision, in case of grave danger or catastrophe.

Resolutions referring to the internal and external security of the state are enacted according to Law 51/1991 by the Supreme National Council for defending the country, which thereby co-ordinates several ministries and agencies: the Ministry of Defence, Ministry of Internal Affairs, Ministry of Justice, Romanian Intelligence Service and the Romanian External Intelligence Service.

Finally, acts issued for the control of public meetings are regulated by Law No. 60/1991 and those regarding re-establishment of public order by Law No. 61/1991. In these cases, the mayor and the prefect can issue administrative acts, and police officers or the gendarmerie have the authority to intervene based on these acts. The mayor can decide to forbid a public meeting, while the prefect can approve the use of force if a public meeting becomes violent.

According to the Law on Judicial Review, these types of act can be challenged for "excess of power", defined similarly to illegality, so they can be challenged in court.

6.3.2.2. Administrative resolutions (acts)

Judicial review can only apply to administrative resolutions that have the nature of decisions (expressions of public power that produce legal effects).

This condition is meant to preclude actions against administrative operations, which may be:

- interpretative resolutions (circulars, directives, guidelines), which are usually considered not to produce legal effects – when they produce legal effects, review is possible because they become substantive administrative resolutions;

- procedural tools necessary for adopting or issuing administrative resolutions (consultations, proposals), which can be challenged only together with the resolution they serve;

- purely informative resolutions and declaratory resolutions, which have the role of acknowledging a fact, without any addition to the effects associated by the law to that fact – evidently, such resolutions are reviewable regarding their content and the reality of facts established, but mostly this is done by the civil sections of the courts, not by the administrative ones.

All administrative resolutions, whether general or individual, are reviewable by the courts. The difference lies in the deadline for taking them to court: no time limit for general resolutions; within six months from notification for individual resolutions and administrative contracts.

6.3.3. Access to the courts

6.3.3.1. Citizens' standing to sue

Romanian legislation allows both general and individual decisions to be challenged in courts, by every person who has standing to sue. Before the new law came into effect in 2004, there were debates about the right to directly challenge a general decision, but now the legislation is clearer on that issue.

When discussing *locus standi*, three aspects have to be considered: who are the possible plaintiffs, who has standing in relation to a particular decision, and who can act in the name of such plaintiffs. Romanian law categorises plaintiffs as individual or legal persons, public authorities with special standing and "interested social organs". The later category basically overlaps with the "private legal person" category, so there is no need to dwell on that group. The other categories deserve more consideration.

First, individuals (citizens or non-citizens) have standing in judicial review, when their rights or "legitimate interests" are aggrieved by an administrative decision. Romanian law treats subjective right and legitimate interest as equivalents, a doctrine that has been criticised because they should have different effects when invoked in the framework of judicial review.

Legal persons can challenge public decisions, upon receiving legal personality. The jurisprudence does however allow an exception for associations and foundations, which can exercise the right to review even before they are legally established if the scope of the review is related to their establishment as legal persons.

Public persons can also be plaintiffs. A distinction has to be made, in this case, between public persons and public authorities, because the jurisprudence has been confronted with actions of local councils against a mayor in the same municipality, or the other way around. Such standing is not acceptable, because those public authorities, even though their resolutions can be challenged separately, represent the same legal person, the commune/town/city. Only the mayor can act in the name of the municipality, but not against another body of the same municipality.

As public authorities, on the other hand, the mayor's resolutions and those of the city council can be challenged separately. When the action is also for compensation, the municipality has to be involved, because it manages the local budget.

Romanian law provides for special standing in the case of some public authorities. According to the Law on Judicial Review No. 554/2004, the Romanian Ombudsman, upon exhausting its own mediation procedure, has the power to go to court in the name of the applicant (petitioner) if the Ombudsman feels that the rights of the petitioner can be defended better in this way. Upon filing the action, the petitioner is asked by the judge if he/she wants to assume the legal action and continue the process; if the petitioner does not wish to continue the litigation, the action is considered dropped. The administrative law doctrine has criticised this legal provision, which transforms the Ombudsman into a court lawyer, paid from public money, who defends citizens, distorting thus the nature of the institution, that of a mediator between citizens and administration. Luckily, the Ombudsman now holding the office has declared the provision absurd and promised never to apply it, and never has to date. Nevertheless the provision does exist, and there are voices, even from the office of the Ombudsman, calling for its use in the future.

In the same fashion, the law empowers the prosecutor's office, which can also act in the name of the plaintiff and challenge a public decision. In this case, the provision poses a greater risk, because there are many prosecutors in the system, whereas there is only one Ombudsman, so the likelihood that the procedure will be used is higher. Prosecutors should not act as lawyers free of charge to private parties, when those parties are able to pursue litigation by themselves.

Finally, some public authorities can exercise a special action to review an administrative resolution issued by certain public authorities or in certain matters. This is the case with actions by a prefect against administrative decisions of local authorities (mayors, presidents of county councils, local and county councils) and proceedings lodged by the National Agency for Public Servants against any public body on any subject affecting public servants (for example, selection, appointment, dismissal). It is a public interest (objective) action, based on the general need for the public administration to act lawfully.

These plaintiffs also have standing for different types of action. Whereas individuals and legal persons can lodge an action of full jurisdiction, asking for annulment of the resolution, modification of the resolution, action by the public body or compensation for damages, the prefect and the National Agency of Public Servants can lodge only annulment actions (similar with the *recours pour excès de pouvoir* in French law).

Although a deadline exists for challenging individual decisions (six months from the date of notification, maximum one year from the date of issuance), the law states that the exception of illegality can be invoked at any time, even for resolutions issued before 2005, when the new law came into force. The exception of illegality can be raised in any proceeding and empowers the judge to disregard the resolution in question, as being unlawful, but without annulling it. For individual resolutions, though, the effect is similar to annulling the resolution, which is why in comparative law this institution is mostly limited to general (normative) decisions. Strong criticism was made against this provision, because in this way the deadlines for challenging individual decisions are useless. The exception of illegality should be admissible as long as the time limits for directly challenging the resolution have not expired.

Recently, the High Court of Cassation and Justice took the matter into its own hands, deciding not to apply the provision in question, by invoking principles of juridical security promoted by the European Court of Justice and by the European Court of Human Rights. This was the first time Romanian jurisprudence had struck down a provision of national law based on European principles of law, without any European legal instrument (directive, regulation or decision) being analysed during the process.

Thus, Decision No. 2547/2008 "broke the ice", and other decisions followed based on the same reasoning (Decision No. 2786/2008, Decision No. 2885/2008). Next, a plenary session of the judges of the High Court of Cassation and Justice, Administrative and Fiscal Contentious Section, established that the line followed in these decisions was endorsed by the High Court.

Two arguments were used to justify the High Court's refusal to apply Article 4(1) of the Law on Judicial Review.

The first argument was derived from the European Convention on Human Rights, which establishes the right to due process and the principle of legal certainty (European Court of Human Rights, Decision 6/2007 *Beian v. Romania*), in the sense that decisions of the courts should be challenged within a time limit and not be left for review for an indefinite time (European Court of Human Rights, Decision 28/1999 *Brumarescu v. Romania*). Based on this argument, and taking into account that the national judge is the first judge of the Convention and has the obligation to ensure its pre-eminence above any national provision, without waiting for the latter's abrogation (Decision 2/2007 *Dumitru Popescu v. Romania*), the Romanian Supreme Court concluded that definitive administrative resolutions should be treated as irrevocable court decisions, and the principle of legal certainty, even though not regulated in our legislation, should apply to Romanian administrative law as well. Two counter-arguments to this reasoning can be mentioned: a) the principles of law can be used to interpret the law, not to strike down express, clear provisions of the law; b) European Court of Human Rights principles of law can be used in national law cases, but in this case there was no human rights issue. Rather, it was a question of regular administrative law (delimitation of public domain).

The second argument used to justify the refusal was derived from European Community principles of legal certainty, upheld by the European Court of Justice (ECJ):[148] "It is for the national court to ensure the full application of Community law by setting aside or, in so far as necessary, interpreting a national rule ... which prevents such application. The national court may apply the Community law principles of legal certainty and the protection of legitimate expectations when assessing the conduct of both the recipient of the amounts lost and the administrative authority". Also, in the context of applying the Community Law, the exception of illegality is admissible only as long as the direct action is admissible, and the party should accept that expiration of the deadline means the decision is definitive.[149]

Again, it is clear that the European principles applied by the Court to make a legal text inapplicable were invoked in a case where no European legal instrument was to be interpreted and applied in concurrence with the national law – it was an "all national" case. Nevertheless, the initiative of the High Court shows a commitment to European principles of administrative law and a willingness to go forward in shaping national administrative law practice in accordance with such principles, which is commendable.

In the context of the issue of the standing to sue, mention should be made of internal administrative appeals, which serve to prevent actions being taken to court in cases where the litigation can be resolved at administrative level. Traditionally, in Romanian law, the exhaustion of administrative appeals before going to court was mandatory. The new judicial law of 2004 keeps the mandatory nature of internal administrative appeals, but renders them ineffective by tacking on additional provisions. Thus, according to Article 1, last paragraph, of Law No. 554/2004, if an administrative decision cannot be

---

148. ECJ decisions *Netherlands v. Vereniging Nationaal Overlegorgaan Sociale Werkvoorziening* (C-383/06), *Gemeente Rotterdam v. Minister van Sociale Zaken en Werkgelegenheid* (C-384/06), *Sociaal Economische Samenwerking West-Brabant v. Algemene Directie voor de Arbeidsvoorziening* (C-385/06).
149. ECJ Decisions *Universitat Hamburg* (C-216/82 pt 5), *Eurotunnel and others* (C-408/95 pt 26), *Banks* (C-390/98 pt 109).

revoked any more by the public authority because it "entered the civil circuit", the public authority wanting to revoke its decision has only one option: to go to court itself, asking for an annulment of its own decision. Oddly enough, this provision was justified by the fact that public authorities could not be trusted to revoke their own decisions in the transition period. Apart from the justification, which cannot be accepted, the major problem of the text is that it makes any revocation of administrative resolutions virtually impossible, because they "enter the civil circuit" (in the sense that they produce legal effects) right after notification or publication, so from this moment on they become irrevocable. In this way, an important institution of administrative law, the revocation of administrative resolutions, the essence and scope of the internal administrative appeals procedure, has been ruined.

Finally, in this survey of Romanian judicial review, we may mention a special revision procedure, introduced in 2007, on the basis of non-observance of the priority of EC law. After exhausting the procedure to appeal against a judge's decision, the definitive solution of the court can be challenged by revision (an extraordinary appeal procedure). Again, the reasoning for such a provision is at least debatable, because it entails the assumption that the first judge and the appeal judge did not (or were unable to) consider the EC law when assessing the lawfulness of the administrative decision, which is profoundly wrong. On the other hand, EC law and ECJ jurisprudence do not force national jurisdictions to introduce and regulate new stages of appeal, but simply insist on the proper observance and effectiveness of EC law, using the mechanisms of the national law. The autonomy of national mechanisms in assuring the priority of EC law – as long as they do not limit the effective implementation of EC law compared with national law (the equivalence principle) and do not make the effective exercise of rights based on EC law impossible in practice (the principle of practical possibility) – is based on several cases judged by the ECJ.[150] New procedural tools (remedies) imposed by the European Court of Human Rights jurisprudence on national courts have the scope of assuring the effectiveness of EC law when national systems do not offer such effectiveness or it is insufficient.[151]

Analysis shows that Romanian judicial review law offers the same protection against unlawful administrative resolutions to individuals and legal persons, regardless of whether national law or EC law was breached. The new revision procedure is thus just another appeals procedure, because it does not regulate "new remedies" for unlawful administrative resolutions when EC law is breached. In conclusion, it is acceptable as a second-tier appeal procedure,

---

150. Case 33/76, *Rewe-Zentralfinanz eG and Rewe-Zentral AG v. Landwirtskammer fur das Saarland* [1976] ECR 1989; Case 8/77, *Sagulo, Brenca and Bakhouche* [1977] ECR 1495; Case 14/83, *Von Colson and Kamman v. Land Nordrhein-Westfalen* [1984] ECR 1891.
151. Frankovich jurisprudence: Case C-6 and 9/90, *Frankovich and Bonifaci v. Italy* [1991] ECR I-5357.

but it cannot be justified as being the "Europeanisation" of judicial review procedure or as necessary from this point of view.

6.3.3.2. Public interest litigation

Until 2004, public interest litigation was not possible, unless expressly provided by law. One of the few cases where such action was admissible was the power exercised by the prefect, who could challenge in court unlawful decisions of local public bodies.

Though not clearly formulated, the provision of Article 1 of the Law on Judicial Review from 2004 introduced *actio popularis*, in the sense that any individual or legal person, whether private or public, could go to court and challenge a decision on the basis of the public interest. Under an amendment introduced in 2007, this was complemented by a specific provision, according to which private persons (individuals or legal entities) can invoke the violation of public interest only when it is a consequence of the violation of their private interest (subjective right).

There is still debate over the powers of the judge in such cases. Can the action exercised by private parties both on the basis of subjective right and public interest still continue to be judged *ex officio* if the judge finds that no right has been aggrieved? If the response is affirmative, the *actio popularis* could still be in place. If the answer is no, which is the well-reasoned interpretation, the *actio popularis* is confined to public bodies, which can still exercise it without any conditionality.

Individuals and groups of individuals, even with no legal personality, have equal standing when the group upholds the same rights and interests. The same can be said about NGOs, associations and foundations that invoke the rights of private persons or the public interest. They can go to court from the date of their creation, even before receiving legal status, if their mere existence is at stake. When they invoke other persons' right of public interest, they have to be already established legal persons in order to have standing.

References

Albu, E., "Contributia practicii judecatoresti la solutionarea unor aspecte de drept substantial in material exceptiei de nelegalitate" [Contributions of jurisprudence on the exception of illegality], *Revista de Drept Commercial* [Review of Commercial Law], Vol. 16, No. 9 (pt I) and 10 (pt II), 2006.

Auby, J. B., "Administrative law in France" in R. Serdeen and F. Stroink (eds), *Administrative law of the European Union, its member states and the United States*, Intersentia, Antwerp, 2002.

Barsan, G., and Georgescu, B., *Legea contenciosului administrativ adnotata* [Law on judicial review annotated], C.H. Beck, Bucharest, 2007.

Dragos, D. C., "Noua lege a administratiei publice locale" [The new law on local public administration], *Dreptul* [Law Review], No. 10, 2001.

Dragos, D. C., "Modele de justitie administrativa: aspecte de drept comparat" [Models of administrative justice: a comparative approach], *Revista Transilvana de Stiinte Administrative* [Transylvanian Review of Administrative Sciences], No. 2, 2002.

Dragos, D. C., "Consideraţii privind noua lege a contenciosului administrativ" [Reflections on the new law on judicial review of administrative decisions], *Pandectele Romane*, special issue, 2005.

Dragos, D. C., *Drept administrativ* [Administrative law], Accent, Cluj Napoca, 2005.

Dragos, D. C., *Legea contenciosului administrativ: comentarii si explicatii* [Law on judicial review annotated and commented], C.H. Beck, Bucharest, 2005.

Dragos, D. C., and Neamtu, B., "Reforming local public administration in Romania: trends and obstacles", *International Review of Administrative Sciences*, No. 40, December 2007.

Iorgovan, A., *Tratat de drept administrativ* [Treatise of administrative law], C.H. Beck, Bucharest, 2007.

Iorgovan, A., and Serban, F., "Despre actele de comandament cu caracter militar" [Regarding military acts of a command nature] in *Revista de Drept Public* [Public Law Review], Nos. 1-2, 1997.

Petrescu, R. N., *Drept administrativ* [Administrative law], Accent, Cluj Napoca, 2007.

Popescu, C.-L., "Notă aprobativă la decizia nr. 692/1994 a Curţii Supreme de Justiţie, secţia de contencios administrativa" [Comment on Decision 692/1994 of the Supreme Court of Justice], *Dreptul* [Law Review], No. 12, 1995, p. 70.

Tofan, D., *Drept administrativ* [Administrative law], C.H. Beck, Bucharest, 2007.

Chapter 7
National legal tradition – Spain

P. Acosta

7.1. The constitutional framework

In modern democratic countries, the constitution establishes the structure and functions of the state and the basic principles that rule the relationship between power and the citizens. In the Spanish Constitution, this includes a catalogue of inviolable civil rights, but goes further: Article 9.2 states that it is the responsibility of public authorities to promote conditions that ensure real and effective freedom and equality of individuals and of the groups to which they belong, to remove obstacles preventing or hindering their full enjoyment and to facilitate the participation of all citizens in political, economic, cultural and social life.

This means that the state is not superior to individuals but is at their service. The state and the law are human creations that cannot subjugate their creator. National sovereignty belongs to the Spanish people, from whom all state powers emanate (Article 1.2, Spanish Constitution). Our democracy has undergone a long evolutionary process in which infinitely more freedoms have been gained than have been given up. The state holds certain powers over individuals, but only to enforce the law in pursuit of the general interest. Arbitrary action by public powers and officers is contrary to the Spanish legal system. Public powers do not have freedom to act as they please; they are obliged to act according to the constitution, the law and legal procedures.

This is the framework of the current separation of powers in Spain, which follows the classic executive-legislative-judicial scheme, with some unique features arising from the peculiar relationship between the central state and the regions in this country.

It is well known that Montesquieu developed the theory of the division of powers as a technique to protect freedom. If state powers are concentrated in a single individual or body, who would be able to control their exercise? If different powers are separated in a structured design, and reciprocal control mechanisms are established, arbitrariness will be deterred, favouring freedom.

In Spain, state powers are rooted in the sovereignty of the people (Article 1.2 of the constitution); parliament exercises legislative power by elaborating the law in the name of the people (Article 66.1); government holds executive power (Article 97); and judges and courts are independent. This design also contains a system of control, including:

- the supremacy of law (Article 9.3);
- democratic election of representatives (Article 68.1);
- accountability of all state power holders (Article 9.3);
- accountable of government for its political action, before Congress (Article 108);
- public administrations all required to act in full subordination to the law (Article 103.1);
- courts that check the power to issue regulations, ensuring the rule of law prevails in administrative action and that the latter is subordinated to ends that justify it.

There is a separation of powers rather than a division, because there are some zones of intersection or grey areas:

- government has the power to pass acts under very specific circumstances (thus assuming to some extent the legislative power);
- constitutional bodies engage in some administrative action (disciplinary action over their personnel, contracts of purchase and employment, management of civil servants, etc.).

These activities are subject to the same judicial control as public administration.

A replicated legislative-executive-judicial model can be found in each region. Spain is neither a centralised nor a federal state. It is halfway between the two models, taking elements from both. This peculiar system is the product of 20th-century Spanish history and the denial of civil rights during Franco's 40-year-long dictatorship. By setting up the so-called State of Autonomies, which conceded a high degree of self-government to the regions, the 1978 Spanish Constitution tried to solve a problem that had repeatedly arisen in Spanish history because of the variety of identities making up the national identity. The authors of the constitution designed a voluntary system so that the regions with historic precedents could have access to a statute of autonomy, assuming competences from the central state. Eventually, all the regions adopted such autonomy. The centralised state of Franco's regime was divided into 52 administrative divisions called provinces. Spain is now divided into 17 autonomous communities, seven of them covering a single province, plus two autonomous cities (Ceuta and Melilla).

Unity is the key factor in this system, at three complementary levels: political, legal and economic. The main difference between the Spanish system and a federal system is that in Spain sovereignty resides in the central state, not in the regions, which are part of the state, not states themselves. Autonomous communities are regional entities inserted into a single state. And the state has a predominant position over the regions. Political unity means that the regions do not have the power or the right to secede from the state. Legal unity is based on the uniqueness of the constitution, which is the chief law of the whole legal system. Every autonomous community also has a chief law, called its Statute of Autonomy, passed by the national parliament in the form of an organic law which requires an overall majority of the members of Congress in a final vote on the bill as a whole. Statutes of Autonomy are therefore subject to the constitution. There is also an economic unit, with most of the competencies in the hands of the central power.

A principle of solidarity applies to this system, trying to reduce differences in economic conditions among the regions through a compensation fund. Co-ordination, co-operation and collaboration are functional principles that guarantee the unity of this political design.

All autonomous communities have adopted in their Statute of Autonomy a power division model replicated from the state model including:

- a legislative assembly of representatives;
- a council of government;
- a regional superior court.

The Legislative Assembly in each region operates like a national parliament, but it has a single chamber instead of the two national chambers. It passes the autonomic laws and controls the political action of the regional government. Parliament members are elected through an equal, free, direct and secret vote, according to the demographic weight of the different lands in the region. Their term of mandate lasts four years.

The Council of Government exerts the executive powers in the region, exercising its legal competencies as well as the regulatory powers. The President of the Council is elected by the Legislative Assembly, and is accountable to it for all political decisions.

The Regional Superior Court (*Tribunal Superior de Justicia*) is the head of the judiciary in the Autonomous Community. It has the final word on those lawsuits where the main applicable law has been approved by the Legislative Assembly. Nevertheless, the Regional Superior Court is inserted into the state judicial power, and forms part of it.

7.2. Government and public administration

7.2.1. Constitutional regulation of the executive

The powers of the executive branch are regulated in Part IV of the Spanish Constitution. The government's primary mission is stated in Article 97, which contains the political and functional definition of this constitutional body:

> The Government shall conduct domestic and foreign policy, civil and military administration and the defence of the State. It exercises executive authority and the power of statutory regulations in accordance with the Constitution and the laws.

The constitutional provision has been developed by statutory Law 50/1997, named the Law of the Government.

7.2.1.1. The government as a political and organisational concept

Article 97 of the Spanish Constitution is a very basic rule that provides the concept of a government with a multi-dimensional projection. The government has an inward political projection, inside the country's borders (conducting domestic policy), and an outward projection (conducting foreign policy), towards other countries and international organisations and bodies. The government also has two different fields of action: political direction and executive functions. Therefore, the government is the main actor and leader in the political agenda, and its main instruments to achieve its goals are direction of the public administration and drafting the general budget of the state, later approved by parliament.

In a parliamentary monarchy such as Spain, the king is a separate institution from the executive. Although the king is the head of state, all his powers are more symbolic than effective, because his acts must always be countersigned by the President of the Government and, when appropriate, by the competent ministers. Without such countersignature they will not be valid. The persons countersigning the king's acts are accountable for them. Therefore, all the powers that in other legal systems are shared by the head of state, the prime minister and the cabinet here belong to the government, increasing its real powers.

The government is not only a political actor, but also the head of the civil and military administrations. As the government holds the executive power, it executes the rules, and it also has the ability to approve rules, which however are subordinate to parliamentary regulation and law. The Spanish Constitution thus grants the government the political leadership of public action in an abstract fashion, but also by giving it specific powers contained in the constitutional text.

The fact that a specific regulation is contained in the constitution is highly important and signifies that such regulations cannot be easily changed; indeed, they are practically immutable. The only way to change a constitutional regulation is to modify the constitution; and modification, as regulated by the constitution itself, is a convoluted process that includes the dissolution of parliament.

The Spanish Constitution is not only a political text, but also a law, which means that it is directly enforceable without further legal developments. All provisions contained in the constitutional text are consequently applicable. Additionally, the constitution is a law of laws, superior to every other law: it has a higher value, so no other law may contradict the constitution, and no other law can amend it.

Therefore, no constitutional provision concerning the government can be changed by regular law or governmental regulations; to do this, it is necessary and mandatory to amend the constitution.

7.2.1.2. What is government?

According to the constitution, there are certain essential members in the government: the president and the ministers. It is also possible to include one or more vice-presidents (which is usual practice) and other posts whose existence and functions are determined by law. The performance of a government job impedes the practice of any other public or private function, including any professional or business activity, under strict rules on incompatibility.

Technically speaking, the government is a collegiate entity formed by the president and his or her ministers when joined in council. The President of the Government is not a prime minister, in the sense that his or her position is not *primus inter pares*, but a position of pre-eminence, because the president has the power to direct the government and the action of every minister. The ministers are freely chosen by the president, although ministers and the president are formally nominated by the king.

Three main characteristics define the government as a board: the president's direction of the government, the joint responsibility of its members and the wide autonomy granted to each of the ministers in their own area. The decision-making process in the Council of Ministers is not meant to be public; its deliberations are secret. As a *collegium politicum*, every decision adopted by the council is attributed to the government as a whole. In spite of this, every member of the government has their own specific function and competency. In a horizontal split of political issues and matters, every department (*ministerio*) has its own pre-determined competencies. If an administrative body lacks competency when it acts, this causes the nullity of the action.

7.2.1.3. Government powers

As stated, the government enjoys executive power in abstract, but the constitutional text defines several of its powers and functions, which may be summarised as follows:
– endorsement of the Crown's action,
– rule-making powers;
– law-making initiative;
– co-operative participation with the legislature;
– directing operations of the civil and military administration, including state security forces and bodies;
– exceptional powers;
– appointments to certain constitutional bodies;

- budgetary powers;
- co-ordination of regional action.

The King of Spain is the head of state, but his powers are merely representative. All his actions that may in any way compromise the state must be previously approved and countersigned by a member of the government. The king is inviolable but, despite his immunity, he holds no executive powers; the source of executive power lies with the government.

The Spanish Constitution grants the executive its rule-making powers (*potestad reglamentaria* as stated by Article 97). This power is essential in the political agenda, but it is also strictly subject to the rule of law. The executive power makes rules, but is strictly subject to the provisions laid down by parliament. The executive develops law by making regulations (*decretos*) derived from or subordinate to statutory regulations created by parliament. This regulatory authority has a strong impact in the political and legal life of the community, because very often acts of the parliament have a general scope, whereas government regulations are much more specific and detailed.

The executive also co-operates in the law-making process by promoting bills in order to submit them to the Congress for approval. This faculty to propose laws is not to be underestimated in a system where the government, as a political branch of the executive, is a result of a parliamentary majority that will ultimately support governmental action. A big part of the electoral programme of the political party that wins the elections is developed through the submission of bills to the Congress.

Another way the executive and the Congress co-operate is by government approval of regulations that, without being law, have the same value or rank as a law approved by parliament. The constitution states that, in cases of extraordinary and urgent need, the government may issue temporary legislative provisions which shall take the form of decree laws. These rules are subject to formal and material limitations: such a decree may not affect the legal system of the basic state institutions, the rights, duties and freedoms of citizens contained in part 1 of the constitution, the system of self-governing communities or the general electoral law. These decrees also have a limited validity, since they must be immediately submitted for debate and voting by the entire Congress, which must be summoned for this purpose if not already in session, within 30 days of their promulgation. The Congress is required to adopt a specific decision on their ratification or repeal within the same period.

The co-operative participation by the executive may also take place through express delegation from the Congress. Government provisions containing delegated legislation bear the title of legislative decrees. Legislative delegation must be granted by means of an act of basic principles when its purpose is to draw up texts in sections, or by an ordinary act when it is a matter of consolidating several legal statutes into one. In these cases, the primary law-making power remains with the Congress, which considers that the collaboration of the government is needed to achieve a better result. Therefore, the legislative delegation must be expressly granted to the government for a defined matter with a fixed time limit for its exercise. The delegation shall expire when the government has made use of it through publication of the corresponding regulation. It may not be construed as having been granted implicitly or for an indeterminate period. Nor shall sub-delegation to authorities other than the government itself be authorised.

Acts of basic principles must define precisely the purpose and scope of legislative delegation, as well as the principles and criteria to be followed in its exercise. Authorisation to consolidate legal texts determines the legislative scope implicit in the delegation, specifying if it is restricted to the mere drafting of a single text or whether it includes regulating, clarifying and harmonising the legal statutes to be consolidated. Acts of delegation may provide for additional oversight devices in each case, without prejudice to the jurisdiction of the courts.

The government has a double nature: political and organisational. It enjoys the political powers stated in the constitution and, at the same time, heads the public administration. It is a political actor and exerts the power of leading the managing bodies of the state. The constitution states that the government conducts the operation of civil and military administration, meaning that the military is no longer an independent institution (as it was before 1978). All military and police bodies are part of the administration, strictly subject to the rule of law and disqualified from playing any political role whatsoever.

The government can also declare exceptional states of alarm, emergency or siege (martial law) with the powers and restrictions attached to each of them. The implications and limits of these states are clearly defined in an organic act dated 1981. No such declarations have ever taken place since the constitution was approved.

As a significant political actor, the government has sole access to several prominent positions, as it enjoys the power to propose to the king the appointment of the state's public prosecutor, after hearing the general judiciary council, as well as appointing two judges of the 12 members of the Constitutional Court.

By drafting the state budget to be approved by parliament, the government gains control over all political areas involving budgetary expenses, which are the vast majority.

The central government also has predominance over the regional governments, because the constitution empowers it to compel them to fulfil their constitutional and legal obligations, in the terms stated in Article 155 of the constitution. The constitution also provides the central government with the legal capacity to appeal to the Constitutional Court against dispositions and resolutions adopted by organs belonging to the autonomous regions. The government also enjoys all other competencies and functions included in other statutory laws, especially Law 50/1997 of the Government.

The main functions of the president are to direct the government's action as a whole and to co-ordinate the action of all ministers. The president's specific prerogatives found in the constitutional text are the following:

- to lead the government's action;
- to appoint and dismiss members of the government;
- to co-ordinate ministers' action;
- to decide the organisation of a referendum, needing previous authorisation by the Congress;
- to ask the Congress for a vote of confidence in favour of his or her programme, or of a general policy statement;
- to propose, after deliberation by the Council of Ministers, on his or her sole responsibility, dissolution of the Congress, the Senate or the whole parliament, to be proclaimed by the king, the decree of dissolution setting the date for elections;
- to lodge at the Constitutional Court an appeal of unconstitutionality against acts and statutes having the force of an act.

7.2.1.4. Government and administration

The executive function resides in both the government and the administration, which are different but connected institutions. The government is a collective body chaired by its president that plays the political role in the executive function, assuming all political responsibilities. The government organises the resources of the public administration to achieve its political goals, in strict subjection to the constitution and law, always seeking the general interest.

The public administration is a bureaucratic structure which, despite being directed by the government, endures while governments change, thus assuring a certain degree of continuity in the operation of public institutions and the provision of public services to the citizenry. Some of its employees are civil servants, permanent workers who are unaffected by political changes, giving permanence and stability to the administrative structures and services.

This government-administration duality is related to the difference between political and administrative responsibilities; the former are demanded by the parliament, the latter are demanded by the ordinary courts.

7.2.1.5. Public administration: concept, principles and accountability

Whereas the government has a strong political nature in Spain, the public administration is conceived as a stable organisation that continues when political leadership changes. Public administration has been defined as the organisation of human and material resources directed by the government whose main aim is to satisfy general interest. In addition, the public administration is the essential organisational structure of the state, the management construction that embodies the state; the state itself is an abstract political idea that takes form through the public administration.

In accordance with the constitution's Article 103.1, the purpose of the public administration is to serve the general interest in a spirit of objectivity and to act in accordance with the principles of efficiency, hierarchy, decentralisation, deconcentration and co-ordination, in full subordination to the law.

There is not a single administration in Spain, but a plurality of administrations, because the Spanish state is territorially plural. The state general administration, autonomous communities, provinces, councils and other public entities exercise their competencies in their own territory. Some administrative entities have autonomy in fulfilling their goals. Nevertheless, the legal personality of the Spanish administration as an abstract, representing the state, is unique and single, comprising all administrative bodies.

The reason for the public administration to exist is not to serve the government, but to provide for the general interest from an objective and neutral position, always subject to the law (Article 103 of the Spanish Constitution). The administration manages all public funds and resources, and is the natural supplier of public services to the citizenry.

The key principle regulating public administrative activities is the rule of law, which means the supremacy of law. This rule, derived from the Spanish Constitution, embodies three concepts: the absolute predominance of regular law, so that the government has no arbitrary authority over the citizen; the equal subjection of all (including officials) to the ordinary law administered by the ordinary courts; and the fact that the citizen's personal freedoms as constitutionally formulated are directly applicable and protected by the ordinary courts.

The main consequence in the imposition of the rule of law is that the ordinary action of government and administration is subject to judicial review. When intervention by the courts is not applicable, parliament exerts its authority to review matters as they arise. There is no conflict between the two powers: parliament ensures political accountability and the judiciary determines the responsibilities and consequences for non-fulfilment of the law.

Public administration depends on the government, and here lies its connection with parliament, through the prime minister, who is elected by the Congress and stands responsible before it. Constitutional powers in Spain (legislative, executive and judiciary) are separated, but not disconnected. Article 66.2 of the Spanish Constitution declares that parliament controls government action.

Article 108 states that the government has a joint accountability, responding for its actions before the Congress.

The Congress may require political responsibility from the government by adopting a motion of censure with an overall majority of its members. The motion of censure must be proposed by at least one tenth of the members of Congress and shall include a candidate for the office of the presidency of the government. This tool to throw out the government must be handled with care because, if the motion of censure is not adopted by the Congress, its signatories may not submit another during the same session.

7.2.2. Types of public administration

Organisation implies the disposal of human, material and financial resources assembled together to perform certain functions and achieve defined aims. The state needs such organisation to accomplish its purposes as defined in the constitution and law.

The administrative organisation in Spain is based on the French model, designed by Napoleon from his military experience and theorised by Weber. It is called the bureaucratic model and it is based on the following basic principles: division of labour, so every organ and unit has its own competencies and functions; hierarchical in-line structure; uniformity of procedural rules; and professionalised personnel.

The operation of administrative organisation in Spain is strongly conditioned by three inputs: juridical, technical and political. First of all, the administrative structure is created by legal rules, because the constitution imposes the action principles, the acts of parliament define the essential aspects and other sub-law regulations describe the operational details. Secondly, the administrative organisation has no freedom to act whatsoever, and its operation is subject to the principles of efficacy, efficiency and proximity to the citizenry. Last but not least, the political agenda determines the administrative form and function.

Administrative organs are the functional units that constitute the administration. Although there is a plurality of organs, the administration has a single legal personality; the action taken by any organ is attributed to the administration as a whole. Thus a multiplicity of interlinked organs, every one of them performing its assigned duties, go to form the administration as a unique body.

The public administration has the power to configure its structure and function, to organise itself, as any other organisation. This is usually carried out through regulations and rules of procedure approved by the executive, although the main lines are regulated by constitution and the law.

The Spanish Constitution defines the main and primary organisational division, which is based on territory. Spain is divided into councils (about 8 000), provinces (50) and self-governed autonomous communities. The latter are the uniquely Spanish autonomous states that, adopting elements from the centralised state and the federal state, form a mixture of both. There are 17 autonomous communities in Spain, seven of them covering a single province, plus two autonomous cities (Ceuta and Melilla).

Councils, provinces and communities are the primary territorial-based political entities, which need to be complemented by other non-territorial entities more suitable to performing certain functions, like agencies, bars, chambers and other institutions. These entities are also subject to the same constitutional principles that guide all administrative activities, especially those related to the democratic operation of all public institutions.

Together with the territorial administrations, there are other specialised bodies also operating under the rule of law. These are the public institutions, a heterogeneous group of entities which share a mutual purpose: the fulfilment of public needs and interests. Professional bars, commerce chambers, agencies, public universities and others perform this function. They have in common not only a public aim, but also their creation by an act of parliament that defines their basic structure, competences and functions.

The Spanish Constitution thus defines a bureaucratic, decentralised model of administration, just as the Spanish state structure is politically decentralised. The different nature of its bodies enhances the significance of common principles, which are, as described in the constitutional text: efficacy, action by competency, hierarchy, decentralisation, deconcentration and co-ordination.

Efficacy is a natural principle in any organisation. Lack of efficacy becomes a liability of the government to be explained before the Congress. The result can be resignation of the individual responsible, or even disciplinary action when there is a failure to comply with due obligations.

Competency is defined as the set of faculties that the law provides for the organ to achieve its objectives. Competency defines the functional span and operational limits, sustaining an authority with faculties. It is the essential requirement for the validity of administrative action. It is constructed on the basis of a specific matter, a personal responsibility, a specific territory or a mixture of the three.

Hierarchy defines the distribution of competencies vertically, grading them in a pyramidal structure. Hierarchy implies the predominance of the upper organ over the lower. This predominance is based on specific powers: leading authority, based on due obedience, supervision and inspection faculties, and disciplinary powers.

Territorial decentralisation consists in creating independent public administrations in order to better serve the public interest. Spain covers a large territory, and decentralisation gets public services closer to the citizens.

Deconcentration is based on a break in the hierarchical, vertical distribution of authority over competencies; the upper organ makes a definitive cession of competencies in favour of the lower organ, which fully specialises in a specific subject. This is the origin of the regulatory agencies in Spain; deconcentration responds to a need of specialisation. Deconcentration and decentralisation are ways in which unitary states can disperse power from the centre.

Co-ordination is another basic principle of organisation. The functional specialisation of different organs and units makes co-ordination necessary, because the aim is shared. There is no possible efficacy without co-ordination.

All these principles are written into the Spanish Constitution, thus providing a common purpose to all bodies in the public administration: the satisfaction of the general interest. All administrative action of any public authority or administration is subject to judicial review, because political action must adhere to the political controls established in the constitution.

7.3. Judicial review of government and administration

7.3.1. Judicial independence from the executive

Judicial power in Spain is independent of all other powers and authorities. Its independence is established by the Spanish Constitution: Article 117 states that the members of the judiciary, judges and magistrates (justices) are not only independent, but also have fixity of tenure. Judges and magistrates may only be dismissed, suspended, transferred or retired on the grounds and subject to the safeguards provided for by law. These privileges of their position are counterbalanced by the responsibility they entail. Judges and magistrates are accountable for their acts. All their activity is absolutely subject to the rule of law, and free from any other influence.

The exercise of judicial authority in any kind of action, both in giving rulings and having judgments executed, is vested exclusively in the courts and tribunals as laid down by the law, in accordance with the rules of jurisdiction and procedure which may be established therein. Judges and courts must not exercise any powers other than those indicated in the Spanish Constitution and those which are expressly allocated to them by law as a guarantee of any right.

This special status is intended to satisfy the citizens and their fundamental right to obtain effective protection from the judges and the courts in the exercise of their rights and legitimate interests, and to enjoy the right to a fair trial with all the guarantees. Constitutional case law has determined that the impartiality of the judge is an additional feature of the full right to an unbiased judicial proceeding. In fact, this fundamental right is based on the impartiality of the judge.

Such impartiality has a double dimension: subjective, granting that the judge shall not have any improper relationship with the parties, and objective, imposing the condition that the judge shall not have any personal interest in the object of the judgment. The Spanish Constitutional Court has so stated in several decisions (Constitutional Court Decisions 155/2002 and 11/2000, among many others).

These constitutional rules have been developed in further legal provisions fixing all the conditions that make judicial independence possible. These conditions have also been described by the case law. Among these, the recruitment of judges is essential. Judges are selected and promoted through a competitive public examination based on objective parameters. Once they are selected, fixity of tenure applies, and they may only be dismissed, suspended, transferred or retired for objective reasons on the grounds of and subject to the safeguards provided for by the law. This means of selection protects the process from arbitrary decisions and influences, and ensures that the judges, once elected on their own personal merits, will do their job with impartiality.

Imposition of the rules that guarantee judicial impartiality corresponds to a constitutional body which is the "governing body" of members of the judiciary. This is the General Council of the Judicial Power (*Consejo General del Poder Judicial*), regulated by Organic Law 5/1985. It is composed of 20 members, 12 of them active judges and magistrates; it is not a court, but a government body that monitors all judicial activities in Spain.

Another dimension of the judicial independence of judges and magistrates is that, when exercising their jurisdictional functions, they are not bound by previous decisions by other judicial bodies. Possible inconsistencies in the judicial doctrine may be removed through a specific action (appeal for cassation), which has to be brought before the Supreme Court. The Constitutional Court has held that the constitutional guarantee of judicial independence allows lower judicial bodies to disagree with the Supreme Court's criteria (Constitutional Court Decision 130/2008).

This specific implementation of judicial independence, that permits different judicial solutions for similar cases, is applied to different premises: protection of the autonomy of judges acting in different jurisdictions (Constitutional Court Decision 70/1989); situations where the courts belong to the same jurisdictional order (Constitutional Court Decision 42/1993); even issues involving a specific court or judge (Constitutional Court Decision 3/1994). The different judicial bodies that may judge similar cases are not bound in any way whatsoever by the decision previously taken.

7.3.2. The scope of judicial review

7.3.2.1. Political and security questions

The current regulation of jurisdictional control over political actions of the government reverses the pre-constitutional situation. The 1956 Process Law (*Ley de la Jurisdicción Contencioso-Administrativa*) excluded "political acts of the Government" from judicial scrutiny. The reasoning behind this was the understanding that judges should rule on the compliance of administrative action to the law, but political issues should be kept beyond their reach. It is easy to conjecture that a non-democratic regime made wide use of this clause, extending the benefits of the exemption to other acts that, having an administrative nature, were unfairly excluded from judicial supervision.

The 1978 constitution put an end to this situation, as it assigned to the government the roles of political leadership, management of the public administration and the executive function, thus distinguishing between government and administration. Both could produce administrative acts, but only the former could promote political acts.

It took 20 years to pass a new administrative process law. During that time, there was strong debate among Spanish legal experts about judicial control over political acts of the government. Some experts understood that the new constitutional requirements justified plain judicial control over the action of all public powers; others underlined the difference between government and administration, and stressed that the constitutional attribution of political powers to the former, as a consequence of the division of powers, was beyond judicial control. Until 1998, the old pre-constitutional 1956 Process Law was applied in a conditional way by the courts. In every legal proceeding, the judges interpreted the 1956 law together with the constitution, admitting only an interpretation that agreed with constitutional rules and principles, ignoring incompatible applications.

This was the criterion adopted by the new 1998 Process Law, declaring that all administrative activity of any kind is subject to judicial scrutiny and announcing also that government acts without an administrative nature are also subject to review when the protection of human rights is concerned, when any regulated activity is involved and when the compensation of damages is to be decided (Article 2.a).

Therefore, there is a legal distinction over the double nature of the government's acts: on one hand, administrative acts and regulations are undoubtedly subject to judicial control; on the other hand, political or non-administrative acts are exempt from judicial scrutiny, save the limited control in three legal circumstances (human rights, regulated activity or damages compensation).

This theory was settled by the Supreme Court in an important issue involving the Spanish Intelligence Service (CESID). A magistrate demanded from the government the declassification of certain documents kept secret by the intelligence services that were needed for the resolution of a case. The Council of Ministers denied the claim in the name of the national security, after balancing the risks involved and taking a political decision believed to be beyond the reach of the judiciary. This resolution was challenged before the Supreme Court, who made an assessment of the two main principles concerned, national security versus the right to effective judicial protection, and decided on the declassification of several documents (Spanish Supreme Court Decision, 4 April 1997), denying the rest (Decision, 30 January 1998).

The Supreme Court has faced allegedly political decisions on several occasions: monetary decisions on economic policy (1984), the refusal of a regional government to give specific information to its parliament (1988), a request to the president for the remission of a law project to parliament (1990), dissolution of the chambers and a call for elections (1993), appointment of the state general prosecutor (1994) and a decree for legislative elections in a regional parliament (1997).

The Constitutional Court has also held that, under Article 97, not every action of the government must be open to review by administrative law. Governmental activity may have a purely political nature which is exempt from the control of the judicial power, as it entails some political purpose and function. The Constitutional Court has considered, for example, that the relationship of the government with other constitutional bodies and the normative initiative (the decision to send to parliament a law project) are political questions (Spanish Constitutional Court, Decisions 45/1990 and 196/1990).

7.3.2.2. Administrative resolutions

As stated above, parliamentary accountability is an expression of political control over the government's action. But this control is obviously insufficient for the purpose of submitting the executive power's actions to the law. The Spanish political system has gone through a profound evolution in the matter of civil rights, the 1978 constitution being the key to this process. Supervision powers of administrative courts extend not only over all public authorities (central, regional, local), but also over independent agencies and regulatory agencies developing public powers. The scope of administrative activity subject to judicial scrutiny has been widened to include regulatory provisions, administrative decisions and even inactivity.

The 1956 Process Law (*Ley de la Jurisdicción Contencioso-Administrativa*) permitted entities or associations representing collective or professional interests to challenge general normative provisions or regulations. The reason for this restriction was the understanding that general provisions, given their abstract nature, would not directly affect the interests of specific citizens. Individuals would be able to challenge the provision in an indirect way, when applied to a specific case. This restriction had been doubted by the Supreme Court as possibly unconstitutional (Decision dated 14 October 1981) and it was definitely abrogated in 1987 (Decisions dated 3 March, 18 and 21 April, and 1 July), declaring that, after the approval of the 1978 constitution, the challenge of a general regulatory provision would follow the same rule as the challenge of administrative resolutions: the legitimate interest of the plaintiff.

For the purpose of this chapter, the name of "administrative regulations" will be given to all legally binding, written regulations or by-laws announced with a general purpose by the public administration. The term "administrative resolutions" will be reserved for actions applying a regulation to specific facts. Resolutions are addressed to a particular citizen and contain a decision of a public power or body that influences his or her patrimony of rights and interests.

Administrative regulations are legal rules that are different from laws: regulations are announced by the executive power, whereas laws belong to parliament. This scheme converts the public administration into a rule maker, but it is a secondary-level rule maker, because sovereignty resides in the people, being held for them by parliament. Therefore, administrative regulations are secondary provisions, fully subject to the parliamentary provisions. The subjugation of administrative regulations to the law is absolute, following a principle of normative hierarchy, and the reason they exist is to develop and complement parliamentary provisions.

There are two ways of challenging administrative regulations before the administrative courts: direct challenge or indirect challenge. An administrative regulation may be challenged by the holders of affected rights or legitimate interests within two months after the announcement (publication in an official bulletin). After that term has finished, only an indirect challenge is possible, which means challenging the application of the regulation in a specific resolution, on the basis of the illegality of such a regulation. A direct challenge may lead to annulment of the regulation by the court; an indirect challenge may lead to annulment of the application activity and, if the court is competent, to annulment of the regulation. The judge who is competent to declare the annulment of the administrative decision, but incompetent to declare the annulment of the regulation, may address the issue to the competent court (*cuestión de ilegalidad*).

Administrative regulations must follow a strict procedure for their approval. When the corresponding rules are not followed, the regulation may be subject to annulment. A regulation may be also annulled when contrary to the constitution, to any parliamentary law or to other regulations of a higher degree.

Way to challenge before the administrative courts	Pretension	Possible reason
Direct challenge	Annulment of an administrative regulation	Regulation is against a parliamentary law or the constitution
Way to challenge before the administrative courts	**Pretension**	**Possible reason**
Indirect challenge	Annulment of an administrative action (and annulment of the administrative regulation, if petitioned for and if possible)	The administrative action is derived from an illegal regulation
	Annulment of an administrative action	The validity of the regulation is not doubted, but the act in and of itself is illegal (it was issued with no respect for the procedural rules)

All activity of the public administration is meant to fulfil the general interest. The 1956 Procedural Law permitted the challenge of formal administrative resolutions, or silence after a citizen's petition, ignoring other forms of administrative activity. The 1978 constitution made this idea obsolete; judges and courts review not only administrative resolutions, but also all administrative activity or inaction, whatever its form may be.

A traditional classification tries to differentiate the sectors of public administration activity according to its aim: law enforcement, promotional and public service. Law enforcement is understood in a broad sense: it includes actions of the armed police forces, but also the performance of any civil servant or administrative body applying mandatory rules (for instance, inspecting private activities). Promotional activity tries to accomplish public purposes through the voluntary co-operation of individuals and corporations (for example, subsidising activities). The management of public services seeks to satisfy basic needs of the population that have a universal character (all citizens in any territory of the state). The traditional system assumed that the judge had the power to review administrative action in any of these fields when the form of such an action was a resolution and the decision was taken after a regulated procedure. This concept kept part of the public activity outside judicial scope. Nowadays, all types of activity, even inaction, are subject to judicial scrutiny.

At this stage in the discussion it is important to point out that judicial scrutiny of public administration activity only takes place when formally requested by a citizen. The inquiring powers of Spanish judges and courts are not as broad as those of their Anglo-Saxon colleagues. This limitation has two consequences: illegal behaviour of the public administration will only be revealed if the affected party decides to fight it, and the courts usually act *ex post*, which sometimes means that the damage is already done when the court arrives at its decision.

The public administration may express its will in different ways: announcing a resolution, keeping silence, not acting or acting outside the boundaries of the law.

A resolution is a unilateral executive decision of a public administration or body entitled to take such a decision. This decision is binding, and it puts an end to the administrative procedure, whether it was initiated by the administration itself or in response to an individual's claim. Resolutions may be explicit or presumed. The explicit resolution is the normal way to end a procedure, because the General Procedure Rule (*Ley 30/1992, de Procedimiento Común, artículo 42*) states that resolving initiated procedures is mandatory, which means that the administration must put an end to any procedure once it is started, after following all legal prescriptions and stages. The general deadline for reaching a resolution is three months. But believing that this will always happen is not realistic, because sometimes administrative issues get lost in the bureaucratic seas.

This possibility – the absence of an explicit resolution – and its consequences are also considered in the General Procedure Rule. We call administrative silence the lack of resolution when resolution is due. Silence must not be confused with inaction; silence is more specific. Silence is produced when the deadline for resolution has ended, and it has two meanings: positive or negative. Positive administrative silence equals an explicit resolution, granting the petitioner the object of the claim. Negative administrative silence entitles the petitioner to challenge the denial, as if the claim had been explicitly refused. Administrative silence is a legal fiction, providing the absence of response with the same value as a specific resolution, its purpose being to guarantee that access to the courts is not diminished by the degree of administrative efficacy.

Administrative silence refers to a problem of procedural infraction, and inaction refers to undue administrative paralysis. Failure to act occurs when the administrative activity is due by law but the corresponding obligation is broken. For instance, some provision of public service is not working properly, and the competent body is not taking the appropriate action to fix the problem. Administrative failure to act is not mere inaction, because it means a breach of a law. The 1998 Procedural Law (Article 25.2) permits a challenge before a court of any administrative failure to act. Those who hold the right to be recipients of the administrative action have standing to sue. As a prerequisite, a claim must be addressed to the competent body, demanding the expected activity. If the claim is still unsatisfied after three months, access to the court is granted (Article 29.1).

Public administration must obey the law, but the Spanish Procedure Law also allows that there may be exceptions, and grants access to the courts to challenge those material activities (*vía de hecho*) not following the mandatory procedural laws or outside the boundaries of the law (such as undue occupation of private property). This provision tries to soften the formalistic nature of judicial scrutiny over the administration. In this case, no pre-litigation procedures are required.

7.3.3. Access to the courts

Access to the courts is an essential element of democracy. Through access to the courts, the rule of law becomes tangible. Courts play three basic roles: assisting the citizen in the free exercise of civil rights and liberties, controlling all public powers and declaring liability. Public law courts imply a balance of power: one state power (judicial) reviews how another power (executive) has applied rules made by the third power (legislative).

The Spanish Constitution, following the tradition in parliamentary democracies and the European Convention on Human Rights (Rome, 4 November 1950), states (Article 24) that everyone is entitled to a fair and public hearing within a reasonable time by an independent and impartial tribunal established by law. Consequently, the state holds the monopoly in resolving conflicts between parties, which must be exercised in an effective and expeditious way.

7.3.3.1. Citizens' standing to sue

Article 24 of the Spanish Constitution states that all persons have the right to obtain effective protection from judges and the courts in the exercise of their rights and legitimate interests, and in no case may there be a lack of defence. Likewise, all have the right to ordinary judgment as specified under the law; to defence and assistance by a lawyer; to be informed of the charges brought against them; to a public trial without undue delays and with full guarantees; to the use of evidence appropriate to their defence; not to make self-incriminating statements; to plead not guilty; and to be presumed innocent.

This basically means two things: all citizens have been granted access to the courts, and all of them have access under equal conditions. The 1978 Spanish Constitution thus guarantees everyone the right to obtain effective protection from judges and courts in the exercise of their rights and legitimate interests. Everyone has access to the courts, not only Spaniards, since Article 13 of the constitution makes nationals and immigrants equal in the possession of public freedoms and civil rights.

The executive is subject to judicial review in most of its actions; even political acts can be scrutinised by the judiciary when fundamental rights are involved. Any administrative activity other than plain political activity is subject to judicial review: administrative regulations, administrative decisions (in application of a law or regulation), presumed decisions (after authorities' silence), administrative inactivity and any other actions outside the bounds of the law.

Actions brought before an administrative court are primarily directed to the declaration of invalidity of an administrative activity, thus making it inapplicable. But the court's decision may go beyond the formal annulment of an administrative act or regulation, declaring the liability of the state, if the action is also directed to establish liability on the part of a public administration, thus gaining compensation for damage done, if any.

A plaintiff must satisfy two conditions to access courts in order to challenge public resolutions: legal capacity to sue and burden. The plaintiff must be entitled to sue, and the challenged administrative action or regulation must reduce the sphere of his or her individual rights and interests.

Otherwise, standing requirements are quite generous due to a broad understanding of what constitutes the fundamental right to an effective legal remedy. The rule is that full access to the courts by individuals and organisations is guaranteed whenever their rights and legitimate interests are in question. This access was not always so extensive. It was extended in three stages: the judiciary protection of individual rights and direct interests (from 1956 onwards), the protection of individual rights and legitimate expectations sustained by the pre-constitutional jurisprudence in case law, and the final introduction of the principle of legitimate expectations in the constitutional text (1978).

Judicial scrutiny based on public law underwent considerable development in Spain during the 1950s and 1960s, despite the country being a non-democratic military dictatorship, because the administrative courts had a technical profile. This generosity was not as real as it appeared in protecting citizens' rights, because the exclusion of political activity narrowed such protection. The rules applicable to judicial review ensured several limitations were maintained, for the sole purpose of restricting judicial scrutiny on certain matters. Nevertheless, the interpretation that the Supreme Court constructed of process law partially weakened the restrictions. The coming of the 1978 constitution, judicial interpretation of the principles of law and the approval of new administrative statutes made legal scrutiny of the executive's action evolve from the old formalistic parameters to the new constitutional framework.

Article 28.1.a of the 1956 Jurisdiction Law (now repealed) declared that standing to sue the administration corresponded to the directly affected right holder. In these cases, the plaintiff could ask the court for a declaration of his or her right and the restoration of the juridical situation affected by the administrative action. The strictness of this criterion was meant to be softened by an additional provision that permitted those whose direct interest would be affected by any administrative actions and normative provisions to demand from the courts the annulment of such actions and provisions.

But the concept of "direct interest" was, in its literal sense, quite inflexible, and this way to access the courts remained effective only for a few professional corporations, when challenging of administrative provisions was convenient for their corporate purposes. To avoid this difficulty, the courts interpreted the "direct interest" clause in a very broad way, a view seconded by most legal writers. The courts held the intention of the 1956 law provisions was to grant access to the courts to those whose fair interests could be damaged by the administrative action. As an example of this reasoning, the Supreme Court said, prior to the Constitution (Spanish Supreme Court Decision, 10 October 1976), that a restricted interpretation of the "direct interest" concept was not in agreement with the spirit of the 1956 procedural law, deeming appropriate the concurrence of a personal interest that would be fulfilled by the success of the claim contained in the lawsuit, providing the petitioner with a legal or material effective benefit. This court decision considers that access to the court must be also granted when persistence of the administrative action will damage the citizen's interests; it is not mandatory that such an interest is identified in a specified legal provision.

As several authors have pointed out, the 1956 law was an excellent statute from a technical point of view, and in fact it survived the coming of the constitution, lasting another 20 years. The key to this survival was not only the technical perfection of this law but, mainly, the fact that the courts made a progressive reading of it, adapting its provisions to the new constitutional framework.

In fact, the 1956 legal provisions concerning access to the courts were incompatible with the new fundamental right contained in Article 24 of the 1978 constitution:

> All persons have the right to obtain effective protection from the judges and the courts in the exercise of their rights and legitimate interests, and in no case may there be a lack of defence.

The constitution also states (Article 103) that public administration is fully subject to the law and to the principles of law, which must lead to comprehensive judicial scrutiny of any administrative activity, only excluding strictly political acts. The judiciary statute (*Ley Orgánica del Poder Judicial*, 1985) also submits all regulatory powers and administrative actions, including extra-legal actions and even inaction, to the legal scrutiny of the courts. In accordance with the new civil rights system, Article 106 of the Spanish Constitution defines the role of the judiciary as follows:

> The Courts shall check the power to issue regulations and ensure that the rule of law prevails in administrative action and that the latter is subordinated to the ends which justify it.

133

Thus, though it remained in the legal text, the concept of "direct interest" was fully replaced by the wider concept of "legitimate interest", more suited to the constitutional provisions. This was proclaimed by the Supreme Court in several decisions (for example 31 May 1995, 9 May 1994) and by the Constitutional Court, which declared (Decision 195/1992) that Article 24.1 of the Spanish Constitution, when granting all persons the right to obtain effective judicial protection of their interests and rights, imposes on judges and courts the obligation to interpret in a broad sense the procedural or adjective law rules, so access to the courts is not limited in the specific case of the "direct interest" clause.

The new Procedural Law issued in 1998 (*Ley 29/1998, de la Jursidicción Contencioso-Administrativa*) brought this discussion to an end, because its rule 19 grants the holders of "rights and legitimate interests" access to courts.

The principle of legitimate expectations was imported from German administrative law into the case law of the European Court of Justice. This principle was not present in Spanish public law tradition, but the Spanish courts made frequent use of it whenever a case bore some connection to European Community law (Craig and Tompkins 2006). This forced parliament to incorporate the protection of legitimate expectation into the law (see Section 3 of the Legal Regime of Public Administration Act).

For the purpose of this study, personal interests may be divided into three categories: simple interests, legitimate expectations and individual rights. Simple interest is the valid wish to obtain something related to human desires: affection, company, wealth or success. These goods are not directly protected by the law, even if they are substantial in human welfare. On the other end, an individual right is something protected by the law in favour of a specific individual, entitling the subject to require public activity in order to fulfil the right, which is attached to someone else's obligation. Legitimate expectations are something in between: they relate to something not as strongly guarded as an individual right, but still deserving the protection of the state. Legitimate expectations are not rights, in the sense that they lack specific law recognition in favour of a certain person, but they are also sustained by the law, in a less specific way.

Spanish law considers as an interested party not only the holder of an individual right, but also the person who has a legitimate expectation, individual or collective, of an objective that can be achieved or hindered by the activity of the public administration. Therefore, the standing to sue the state belongs not only to the holder of an individual right, but also to those who have legitimate expectations.

Access to the courts has been eased and broadened: first by the courts themselves, through case law, and second by the inclusion in the Spanish

Constitution (Article 24) of the term "legitimate interests" and the right to obtain effective protection.

The Spanish Constitutional Court has declared (Decision 119/2008 of 29 October 2008) that Article 24.1 of the constitution forces judges and courts to abide by a broad understanding of the formulae contained in the judicial process regulations related to citizens' access to the courts. The most favourable interpretation to access must be adopted, and restrictive interpretations of the access requirements are not permissible.

The Constitutional Court defines legitimate interest as the unique material link between the subject and the object of the claim, so that the claim's success will have an eventual positive impact, present or future, on the patrimony of the claimer.

7.3.3.2. Public interest litigation

Legitimate interests may be individual, or corporate and collective. In this latter case, an association, body or group might be entitled to access the court in order to ask for its protection. This is why Spanish Procedural Law (29/1998 Act) assigns the standing to sue in such cases to "public law corporations, associations, union trades, groups and entities that are affected by or legally entitled to protect collective rights and public legitimate interests". Therefore, public interest entities are entitled to appeal against administrative decisions and regulations that may affect groups or their members.

The option that an individual may have access to the courts in the defence of group interests has also been admitted by the Spanish Constitutional Court. In the renowned Violeta Friedman case (Spanish Constitutional Court Decision 214/1999), this woman demanded protection of the honour of the Jewish people, which she considered had been damaged by certain press publications. The ordinary courts denied such a claim, alleging that she lacked the ability to represent the whole Jewish people, and that she was not the individual subject of the press declarations, thus considering the inexistence of a legitimate interest. The Constitutional Court, defeating the opinion of the Supreme Court, decreed that, even if the standing to sue in the protection of a fundamental right corresponds to the affected individual, this fact does not exclude the chance that a member of an affected group may act in favour of the rest of its members. Because ethnic, social and religious groups may lack legal personality or status, to not admit the standing to sue of its members would leave the group defenceless. Since these kinds of groups do not have representative organs, the standing to sue may be attributed to the individual members under certain conditions. This is an example of the broad understanding of the requirements of the standing to sue in the Spanish legal system.

References

Craig, Paul and Tompkins, Adam, *The executive and public law: power and accountability in comparative perspective*, Oxford University Press, Oxford, 2006.

Galera, Susana, *Sistema Europeo de justicia administrativa*, Dykinson, Madrid, 2005.

García de Enterría, Eduardo and Fernández, Tomás Ramón, *Curso de derecho administrativo*, 2 vols., 14th edn, Civitas, Madrid, 2008.

González Pérez, Jesús, *Comentarios a la ley de la jurisdicción contencioso-administrativa*, Civitas Ediciones, Madrid, 2008.

Hague, Rod and Harrop, Martin, *Comparative government and politics: an introduction*, 7th edn, Palgrave MacMillan, Basingstoke, 2007.

Merino-Blanco, Elena, *Spanish law and legal system*, 2nd edn, Sweet & Maxwell, London, 2006.

Sarmiento, Daniel, "The executive and the law in Spain" in P. Craig and A. Tompkins (eds), *The executive and public law. power and accountability in comparative perspective*, Oxford University Press, 2006.

Chapter 8
National legal tradition – Sweden

G. Edelstam

8.1. The constitutional framework

The Swedish Constitution establishes that all public power comes from the people (Article 1:1 of the Instrument of the Form of Government Act or Regeringsformen, hereafter RF) and democracy is thus the constitutional foundation. The legislative, executive and judicial powers are the main public powers essential to the sovereign state. The Swedish Constitution does not contain any special rule concerning the separation of powers or the principal differences between these three divisions of sovereignty. Instead, jurisdiction and administration are dealt with together in one chapter and there is no special chapter on the courts. In addition, the legislative power of Parliament, exercised through acts of Parliament, and the legislative power of the government, based on ordinances, are set out in the same chapter.

The three parts of the sovereignty of the Government of Sweden will be explained, focusing mainly on the influence of the constitution on these powers.

8.1.1. Parliament (Riksdagen)

8.1.1.1. Nominations

The Riksdagen or Parliament is formed through direct elections and consists of a single chamber of 349 members. A Swedish citizen who has reached the age of 18 and who is currently domiciled within the country or who has always been domiciled there is entitled to vote. Only a party which receives at least 4 % of the votes cast throughout the entire country is entitled to share in the distribution of seats.

Members may not resign their seat without Parliament's consent and may be deprived of their seat only if they prove to be manifestly unfit by committing a criminal act. The decision in such cases shall be taken by a court of law.

8.1.1.2. Functions

Parliament appoints the prime Minister (RF 6: 2-4) and is entrusted with the power to control the country's finances, as it adopts the national budget. The main power of Parliament is of course legislative power. Legislation originating from Parliament can be constitutional legislation or ordinary acts of law.

The Swedish Constitution consists of the Instrument of Form of Government Act (RF), the Freedom of the Press Act, the Fundamental Law on Freedom of Expression and the Act of Succession. The term "constitution" has thus been defined in a purely formal way. It consists of these four laws of evolving content. There are, for example, procedural and penal law regulations in the Freedom of the Press Act, and it is possible to include new topics in the constitutional laws. Fundamental laws are enacted by means of two decisions of identical wording. The second decision may not be taken until nationwide elections for the Parliament have been held following the first decision, and the newly elected Riksdag has convened.

There is a special chapter (RF 2) in the constitution on fundamental rights and freedoms according to which every citizen shall be guaranteed certain rights and freedoms. From these rules it follows that provisions contradictory to these rules may not be adopted or may be adopted only by means of an act of law. This chapter on fundamental rights and freedoms was introduced with the new Instrument of the Form of Government Act in 1974, and some rights have been added later or given more specific content (such as the right to trade, to practise a profession, the welfare right to a free basic education and the property right). As, however, several of the fundamental rights and freedoms can be restricted through ordinary laws, their protection is not so strong (RF 2:12-14). The freedom of the press and media enjoys especially strong protection.[152]

Some areas can only be legislated through acts of law of the Parliament. This is the case with provisions related to personal status or the mutual personal and economic relations of private subjects (RF 8:2), provisions concerning the functions of the courts relevant to the administration of justice (RF 11:4), provisions concerning the relations between private subjects and public institutions which relate to obligations incumbent upon private subjects including those relating to criminal acts and the legal effects of such acts as well as provisions relating to taxes and requisitions and other such dispositions. Legislation on most other matters can be delegated to the government or sub-delegated to administrative authorities.

8.1.1.3. Judicial review

Sweden does not have a constitutional court and the possibilities for an individual to have a judicial review of law in an administrative court – about whether a decision taken by an administrative agency in accordance with

---

152. The fundamental rights of freedom of the press and public access to official documents have existed in the constitution since 1949. The regulation on the media is from 1992. There is an Act on Secrecy. The press may sometimes legally publish secret information under the Act on Secrecy, because the few instances in which a publisher can be prosecuted are regulated in the constitution and some secret issues may be published.

an act of Parliament is in accord with the constitution – are restricted when it concerns compliance with fundamental rights and freedoms. It has to be "obvious" that such a contradiction exists (RF 11:14).[153] Such contradictions are never obvious. It is easier to review issues of competence, which in general are obvious.

Review can only be done in connection with an appeal against an administrative decision. Normative review, meaning abstract control of a norm, is not possible in court unless it is in connection with an appeal against a decision.

Instead of review of a norm, constitutional control in connection with some legislation (RF 8:18) is meant to be done by a special Council on Legislation that includes justices of the Supreme Court and the Supreme Administrative Court. The council exists to pronounce an opinion on draft legislation. The council's scrutiny relates to legal but not political issues (RF 18:3). The government should obtain the opinion of the Council on Legislation on certain draft legislation before handing the draft over to Parliament, but it is not an obligation to follow the advice of the council in the draft.

8.1.1.4. Centralised/decentralised legislation

According to the constitution, legislation can be made through acts of Parliament but it can also be made through ordinances from the government or enactments by central administrative agencies, and to a limited degree by local government. At international level, it may be possible to hand over decision-making that involves law-making to the EU or to an international organisation.

Parliament

Legislation on the constitution is of course undertaken by Parliament, as is legislation that involves provisions relating to personal status or the mutual personal and economic relations of private subjects or provisions on relations between private subjects and the public institutions that relate to obligations incumbent on private subjects (RF 8:2, 3). There are some other issues that must be legislated by Parliament[154] but the rest can be delegated. Parliament is entitled to withdraw such delegation. One complicated issue is fees and taxes. Taxes must be decided by Parliament, because they involve obligations incumbent on private subjects, whereas fees can be decided by the government or local government. However, it is often debated whether, in fact, a fee is – or partly is – a tax.

---

153. There is a proposal for a new constitution according to which this prerequisite would be taken away.
154. RF 8:16, RF 3:12, RF 8:2 citizenship; RF 8:4, RF 9:12-14, RF 7:3, RF 8:6, RF 11:4 court procedure.

Government

Parliament may delegate[155] some of its legislative power to the government, which also has some legislative power of its own according to the constitution. The government might adopt, by means of a statutory instrument, provisions related to implementation of law and provisions that do not fall under fundamental law adopted by Parliament.

Central administrative authorities

When Parliament delegates some of its legislative power to the government, it may also give the government a competency to sub-delegate some of that legislative power.

Local government

Local government consists of county councils and municipalities, which handle different issues; they are not hierarchical. Parliament may delegate some legislative powers (on fees) to municipalities, or allow the government to do this (for example, on local law and order issues).

EU

Parliament may transfer a right of decision-making which does not affect the principles of the form of government within the framework of European Union co-operation. Such transfer presupposes protection of the rights and freedoms in the constitution (RF 10:5).

International organisations

A right of decision-making – including regulations, the use of national assets or the conclusion or denunciation of an international agreement or obligation – may be transferred, to a limited extent, to an international organisation for peaceful co-operation of which Sweden is a member, or to an international court of law (RF 10:5).

8.1.2. Government

8.1.2.1 Nominations

The prime minister appoints the other ministers. Only a person who has been a Swedish citizen for at least 10 years may be a minister.

8.1.2.2. Functions

The government holds executive power in accordance with legislation. The government governs the nation and is accountable to Parliament (RF 1:6). It

---

155. RF 8:7-12 and 13:6.

has some legislative power (RF 11) and it decides on appointments of officials. According to the constitution (RF 11:9), appointments to posts in courts of law or administrative authorities dependent on the government are made by the government or by a public authority designated by the government. It submits proposals for a national budget to Parliament (RF 9:7). It may exercise clemency remits or reduce a penal sanction or other legal effect of a criminal act, and remit or reduce any other similar intervention by a public authority concerning the person or property of a private subject (RF 11:13). It may to an extent approve an exception from a provision of a statutory instrument (RF 11:12).

Government offices exist to prepare government business, and responsibilities are allocated among the ministers. Government offices are a public authority with the prime minister as head of the authority, which takes decisions on numerous matters. The departments prepare the issues. The decisions are made by the government at meetings where the prime minister is the chairman and where at least five ministers must be present (RF 7:3-4). Ministers can in general not take decisions.

The preparation of government business of course involves many different issues. Of primary interest from an administrative law point of view are its legislative power, its decision-making power in relation to a citizen (the execution of power) and its power to appoint higher officials. It has legislative power as described above, either by delegation from Parliament or in some cases due to a constitutional rule (RF 8:13). As the highest public authority, it can also sometimes exercise public power through decision-making in relation to individuals. The government is an instance of appeal in certain administrative cases, but it can be the first instance in other cases – for example, some permits concerning highways and long-distance railways.[156] The possibility for the government to be an instance of appeal is not dealt with in the constitution. Instead, this possibility is stipulated in ordinary law.

8.1.2.3. Judicial review

Judicial review of the activities of the government can, according to the constitution, take place in the Supreme Court as a result of a review by the Committee on the Constitution if the case concerns the actions of a minister. Review of government decisions can take place in the Administrative Supreme Court, but this is according to an ordinary act of Parliament and will therefore be dealt with in section 8.2 below.

Review by the Committee on the Constitution and the Supreme Court

Parliament may – through its Committee on the Constitution – examine ministers' performance of their official duties and their handling of government

---

156. Environmental Law MB 17:1.

business. It may examine a specific decision or else the usual practice when the government handles a specific type or group of decisions. The examination can concern a legal or political responsibility. "Legal responsibility" implies that ministers or former ministers may be held accountable for any criminal act committed in the performance of their ministerial duties if they have grossly neglected their official duty thereby. A decision to institute criminal proceedings is taken by the Committee on the Constitution, and the case is tried before the Supreme Court. "Political responsibility" implies that Parliament may declare that a minister no longer enjoys its confidence. Such a declaration of no confidence requires the concurrence of more than half the total members of the Parliament.

8.1.2.4. Centralised/decentralised power

Different levels exist, according to the constitution, where public power can be exerted. Executive power of course mainly belongs to the government and its administrative agencies, but through legislation Parliament can hand over exercise of power in specific areas not only to the government and its administrative agencies but also to local government and to legal persons such as companies or to natural persons (RF 11:6).

Local government

Public executive power can be performed not only by the government and the public administrative authorities under the government, but also on a vertical level by local government. Sweden has two types of local government, the 21 county councils and the 290 municipalities. The county councils and the municipalities are not hierarchical as they handle different issues. County councils mainly handle hospitals and medical care, whereas the municipalities handle other local issues – for example, building and planning, social care and the nine-year compulsory schooling. Local governments are self-governing according to the constitution and according to the Act on Local Government. However, as mentioned, Parliament may entrust administrative functions to a local authority. There are several laws, like the Act on Social Services, by which Parliament establishes an obligation, especially for municipalities, to perform certain matters, along with the necessary executive powers.

Private legal entities

Administrative functions may be delegated to legal persons as well as to natural persons but, if the function involves the exercise of public power, delegation shall be made by virtue of law (RF 11:6).

International level

On an international level, some executive power might be exercised by the EU and by international organisations (RF 10:5).

8.1.3. The courts

The constitution has rather limited influence on legislation on administrative courts.[157] It states that the Supreme Court is the highest court of general jurisdiction, and the Supreme Administrative Court is the highest administrative court. The provisions on the functions of the courts relevant to administration of justice and the principal features of their organisation and procedure are not laid down in the constitution but in ordinary law. Their competencies are hardly mentioned in the constitution, which says (RF 11:2) that the provisions on functions of the courts relevant to the administration of justice, and the principal features of their organisation and court procedure, shall be laid down in acts of law from Parliament.

8.1.3.1. Functions

One way that the constitution bears on the judicial system is that public authorities may not determine how a court adjudicates.[158] The first chapter of the constitution (RF 1:2) stipulates that public power shall be exercised with respect for the equal worth of all and the liberty and dignity of the private person, which is the basis of legal procedure. But the right to a fair trial is never referred to and there are no constitutional controls on courts taking this requirement as a starting point. Sweden has no constitutional court and it can be difficult to have a constitutional review in a court. It must be "obvious" that an act of Parliament or ordinance is in contradiction to the constitution (RF 11:14).

Re-opening of closed cases and the restoration of lapsed time are granted by the Supreme Administrative Court for administrative law issues, but may also be granted by a lower administrative court, if so stipulated in the law.

There is very little on the functions of courts in the constitution. Their functions are laid down in the law on administrative courts and in special administrative laws. The procedure is laid down in the Administrative Court Procedure Act.

The administrative courts have mainly dealt with taxes and social care, but in the late 20th century many other matters were handed over to courts by administrative bodies. Since 2006, appeals against decisions that concern civil rights and duties must be taken to court and no longer to administrative agencies. Such government decisions can be taken to the Supreme Administrative Court. These possibilities have been stipulated in ordinary acts of Parliament

---

157. It has been proposed (SOU 2008:125) that judicial and executive powers be dealt with in different chapters of the constitution.

158. A special administrative body, the Domstolsverket (national court department/civil service), was set up in 1975 to lead and co-ordinate the courts, and there is a certain contradiction to the independence of the courts, though the department may not interfere in adjudications.

as a consequence of the influence of European law, especially Article 6 of the European Convention on Human Rights.

8.1.3.2. Nominations

The judges of administrative courts are appointed by the government, according to the constitution and the law on administrative courts.[159] The constitution also places some other checks on judges. Permanent, salaried judges can be removed from office if they have committed a crime or neglected their duties, and are therefore manifestly unfit to hold office, or if they have reached the age of retirement.

8.1.3.3. Centralised/decentralised judicial power

The constitution does not stipulate much on judicial powers, which are instead laid down in ordinary acts of Parliament. But the constitution stipulates the ombudsman institution (RF 12:6), which can institute criminal and disciplinary proceedings and has access to the records and other documents needed to form an opinion about the application of laws. The ombudsman plays an important role in the Swedish system, controlling the executive power in a way that is inexpensive for individuals.

The European Court and the European Court of Human Rights may also exercise jurisdiction. The constitution makes it possible to transfer powers by a decision of Parliament (RF 10:5).

8.2. Government and public administration

8.2.1. Constitutional regulation of the executive

The exercise of power can, according to the constitution, be handled by the government and its administrative authorities, but under the constitution power can also be exercised by local government and by private legal entities. This section deals primarily with the administration of the government and its national administration, but also deals with the possibility that executive power is used by local government or private legal entities.

8.2.2. Government and public administration

Administrative authorities under the government are independent bodies in relation to the state. The constitution (RF 11:7) does not permit the government to determine how an administrative authority shall decide in a particular case where it exercises public authority over a private subject or a local authority, or how it should apply the law.

---

159. Instead of offering such posts, it is proposed to set up an application procedure (SOU 2008:125).

The administrative authorities thus have no duty to obey the minister of the relevant department and, even though they are subordinate to the government and the ministers, the latter cannot interfere in the decision-making process in individual cases. This has a long tradition in Sweden and guarantees legal certainty when applying the law. The government offices are rather small from an international perspective. Their main function is to prepare and dispatch government decisions. The executive work is mainly performed by independent bodies.

The government may establish and abolish an administrative body under its governance, but Parliament decides the budget and legislation.

The government can govern the activity of national administrative authorities through ordinances and instructions. As mentioned, they may not interfere in decision-making in individual cases, but the government can appeal against – and thus may change – the outcome of some cases.

The government also appoints people to the top positions in administrative bodies.

8.2.3. Types of public administration

First, there is the national administration under the government. Then there is the specially regulated administration that is an obligation of local government. In addition, a private legal entity, such as a limited company, can be given responsibility for some administration. Neither private legal entities nor local governments are subordinate to the government, and the national administrative authorities that are subordinate to the government are still independent when making decisions in individual cases.

8.2.3.1. National administrative authorities

There are hundreds of widely varied administrative authorities under the government.

Public authorities under the government can be central or regional. However, local authorities have practically disappeared. Instead, local governments handle local issues according to acts of Parliament. The central administrative authorities can be superior to regional administrative authorities, and often govern the activity of the lower-level authorities through guidelines and supervision. Among other administrative bodies are business departments and universities; there are also some smaller decision-making bodies called "delegations", "boards" or "inspectorates" for different issues.

There is no exact definition of a central public administration, but the term generally includes the major national administrative authorities. These have the whole country as their area of activity and they are organised in a hierarchical way. Examples are the National Environmental Protection

Agency, the National Board of Health and Welfare, and the National Police Board.

8.2.3.2. Regional administrative authorities

County administrative boards handle national issues on a regional level. They also to an extent supervise local governments. County administrative boards are under the government in some matters and under national administrative authorities in other matters. Among other regional administrative bodies under a national administration are the police authorities, under the national Police Board. Regional administrative bodies are sometimes county-based, but another regional division can also be used.

Business departments can be considered as a special kind of organisation in between a civil service department and a company. They have been used as instruments when the state has engaged in infrastructure work for areas like the railways, the post and telecommunications. Today many of these business departments have been turned into limited companies – often owned by the state, sometimes owned privately – but there are still some civil service departments, such as the Civil Aviation Administration, the Maritime Administration and the Power Network Administration. Business departments are governed by public law, whereas company law applies to companies.

Universities and colleges are in general administrative bodies under the government, which appoints the rector, just as it appoints all other heads of administrative bodies. Colleges may be under a county council; two universities are handled by foundations.

8.2.3.3. Local government tasks and obligations

Administrative tasks of local government can be obligations under acts of Parliament, but local governments have self-governance within their area for issues of interest to the inhabitants. Although local governments in Sweden are self-governing, according to the constitution (RF 1:1) and the Local Government Act, they are in a way part of the state. The obligatory part of their tasks is very much the majority, because 80 % of what the local governments do is regulated by laws from Parliament. There is a transfer of money between local governments through the government.

There are two forms of local government in Sweden: the county councils that mainly handle the hospitals and medical care, and the municipalities that handle other issues such as social services. There are many laws of Parliament according to which the municipalities are expected to take care of administrative tasks. After the reform when the Local Governments Act was introduced, industrialisation, urbanisation and democratisation took place and this meant major changes for local governments. The social welfare state was mainly built up like this. The county councils were to handle the hospitals and the medical care and the municipalities were to handle other local matters such as social care. Between 1880 and 1980, local governments expanded and the regulation by Parliament of their activities increased. The administrative courts can oversee their decision-making according to parliamentary laws and the courts can alter such decisions. Thus local governments are, to an important extent, part of the state. The relation between the state and the municipalities has developed in a pragmatic way; they are seen as a part of the public sector and "Who does what?" is a question of expediency. The possibility of handing over administrative tasks to local governments exists as a constitutional rule. Without it, local governments would be self-governing and, if they were given responsibility for social welfare, there might be big differences in practice between different municipalities and between different county councils.

There is a transfer of money between the local governments through the government. Local governments, especially municipalities, handle many matters according to legislation from Parliament, so it is local politicians in local government assemblies and committees who see to it that these legal obligations are fulfilled. In local governments, a political assembly has the decision-making power, and an executive board is the central administrative body; there are also different boards for special issues.

8.2.3.4. Administrative functions handled by private legal entities

Administrative functions may be delegated to private legal entities like associations, foundations and companies, as well as to individuals; but, if the function involves the exercise of public power, this must be delegated by virtue of law according to the constitution.

The private legal entities can be companies owned by the state, for example the Swedish Motor-Vehicle Inspection Company. They can also be foundations established by the state, or associations where the state is an important member. It is also possible that a private legal entity that handles administrative tasks is not owned by the state.

8.2.4. Judicial review

With regard to the possibilities to review administrative decisions, the administrative courts can, in general, review resolutions from the national administrative authorities in individual cases. Of importance in this context is the control by the ombudsman. There is also review done by the Chancellor of Justice. Some possibilities exist for district courts to oversee administrative decisions if the individual claims damages according to civil law or if the prosecutor takes a penal law case concerning malpractice – where the official is accused – to court.

In some cases of the decisions of administrative bodies under the government, it is possible to appeal to higher administrative bodies and the government but, as a general rule, appeals are heard by administrative courts, and the court can then change the decision – that is, the court does not act as a cassation court. There are also boards that handle judicial matters.

The specially regulated activities of local government can be reviewed in the same way, except for review by the Chancellor as he is under the government.

There is also some review by private legal entities.

8.2.4.1. Judicial review of the government

The Supreme Administrative Court can review decisions taken by the government, according to a law on special judicial review of the decisions of government, if the decision concerns the civil rights and duties of a person. The law was introduced as a consequence of the European Convention on Human Rights ("the Convention"). Questions of law and of fact can be reviewed, and the decision can be rescinded.

8.2.4.2. Judicial review of national administrative authorities

Review by the administrative courts

The administrative courts are, according to the law on administrative courts, the court of first instance (Länsrätten), the Court of Appeal (Kammarrätten) and the Supreme Administrative Court (Regeringsrätten). There are special administrative courts for appeals in patent matters, and the Market Court handles some administrative law matters as well as civil law matters. There are also (since 2006) courts for migration matters: the Migration Court and the Migration Supreme Court. Some of the administrative courts of first instance act as migration courts and the Administrative Court of Appeal in Stockholm is the Migration Supreme Court.

The administrative courts can handle cases from administrative agencies. As a general rule in ordinary administrative procedural law, such cases can be appealed – under the Förvaltningslagen (Administrative Procedure Act, hereafter FL) – to the administrative court of first instance and then perhaps, depending on whether leave to appeal is necessary or not, to the Court of Appeal (FL 22a).

Judicial review of the national administrative authorities used to be possible mainly for taxes and social matters, but the administrative courts are, as a consequence of Article 6 of the Convention, able to adjudicate in administrative law cases. The main rule is that administrative decisions by administrative agencies of first instance should be appealed to the administrative court of first instance. This rule (FL 22a) was introduced in 1998. Before that, the main rule was that administrative decisions had to be appealed to higher administrative bodies and the highest level was the government. However, many special administrative laws stipulate that the appeal shall be made to a higher administrative body. Cases that are appealed to higher administrative bodies can, in general, be taken to the government as the highest administrative body. In such cases it can be possible to take the decision of the government to the Administrative Supreme Court under the mentioned law on special judicial review. This is possible if the case concerns the civil rights and obligations of all persons under Article 6 of the Convention. The Supreme Administrative Court can rescind the decision of the government.

These two possibilities of taking administrative cases to administrative courts were introduced in the Swedish legal system due the Convention's doctrine about the scope of the Swedish engagements regarding Article 6 of the Convention. The possibility of taking an administrative decision to the Administrative Supreme Court had been introduced in 1988, when it concerned all administrative decisions that could not otherwise be taken to court. The government could also be taken to the Supreme Administrative Court (for a couple of years the Administrative Court of Appeal also had this function in some cases), but with the introduction of the above-mentioned main rule in 1998 there were increased possibilities to take an administrative decision to an administrative court. The special review whereby administrative decisions could be taken to court has been reserved for decisions made by the government.

The right to have a case tried by the Supreme Court or the Supreme Administrative Court may be restricted in law, and in fact usually is. Leave to appeal is needed according to ordinary procedural law. According to ordinary acts of law, leave to appeal is often needed also for an appeal to the Court of Appeal.

Review by the Parliamentary Ombudsmen

The Parliamentary Ombudsmen, or Ombudsmen of Justice (JO), are according to the Swedish Constitution (12:6) appointed by the Swedish Parliament to supervise the application of laws and other statutes under terms of reference drawn up by Parliament. They ensure that public authorities and their staff comply with the laws and other statutes governing their actions and fulfil their obligations in all respects. The ombudsmen exercise this supervision by evaluating and investigating complaints from the general public, by inspecting the various authorities and by conducting other forms of inquiry that they initiate themselves. Those supervised by the ombudsmen are state and municipal authorities, officials and other employees of these authorities, and other individuals whose employment or assignment involves the exercise of public authority. The ombudsmen's inquiries are based on complaints from the general public, cases initiated by the ombudsmen themselves and on observations made during the course of inspections.

Every year the Parliamentary Ombudsmen receive almost 6 000 complaints of various kinds. Most of their work consists of dealing with complaints. Each ombudsman has a direct individual responsibility to Parliament for his or her actions. The Annual Report – which is one of the official publications of the Swedish Parliament – is submitted to the Standing Committee on the Constitution, which then draws up its own written report and notifies Parliament. The ombudsmen do not have sanctions at their disposal. According to the constitution (RF 12:6), an ombudsman may institute criminal and disciplinary proceedings in cases indicated in the Act of Laws drawn up by Parliament. If it is discovered that a public authority has applied the law erroneously, the most extreme recourse that the law allows an ombudsman is to act as a special prosecutor and bring charges against the official for malfeasance or some other irregularity. This very rarely happens, but the mere awareness of this possibility is considered to be important for the ombudsmen's authority.

Review by the Chancellor of Justice

The Chancellor of Justice (JK), a post established in 1713, is a non-political civil servant appointed by the government, performing duties from a strictly legal point of view. The Chancellor of Justice acts as the government's ombudsman in supervising the authorities and civil servants, and takes action in cases of abuse, performing supervision in much the same way as the Parliamentary Ombudsman; but since 1998 the JK performs more overall supervision directed to discovering faults in the system.

The JK is also the representative of the state in trials and other legal disputes. The JK receives complaints and claims for damages directed to the state, and decides financial compensation for such damages. This activity concerns damages due to wrongful decisions by the administrative agencies (such cases can also be taken to ordinary courts – see below), but also compensation to persons who have been wrongfully imprisoned. The JK also acts as the guardian of privacy in different fields, and has overall supervision of the legal profession. Another part of the work is to be counsellor to the government in legal matters.

Review by the district court

Ordinary district courts can in some cases control the executive power. The administrative courts cannot be controlled by Parliament or the government, because the courts are autonomous. The courts for general jurisdiction also have some possibilities to oversee the administrative authorities. If an official has committed a crime called "malpractice" in connection to decision-making power or if a wrongful decision has caused damages, the district court might review the decision in order to make an adjudication concerning the malpractice or the damages.

Cases on damages where the state is taken to court due to a wrongful decision which involves damages to an individual can also be taken to ordinary district courts, and the court must then first find out whether the decision was wrongful or not.

Boards

For some administrative cases, there are special boards as the last instance of appeal instead of a court – for example, the board of appeal for university colleges. Such boards are not formally courts, and perhaps cannot be regarded as equivalent to courts. There are cases where they have been accepted as equivalent to courts, but there are also cases where they have not been accepted as equivalent to courts.

8.2.4.3. Judicial review of local government

Decisions by local government, primarily the municipalities, can (as far as obligatory tasks assigned in acts of law are concerned) be reviewed by administrative courts in the same way as administrative authorities under the government – that is, an individual can appeal against such a decision by a local government body to the administrative court. The case can be scrutinised by the Parliamentary Ombudsman and it can be taken to a district court, if the individual claims damages or if the official (or politician of the Assembly or Board) that took the decision is prosecuted for malpractice. The legal chancellor cannot review a decision of local government in individual cases.

If the case instead concerns a decision that has been taken by a local government body in accordance with the self-governance of local government, the adjudication in the administrative court can only concern the legality of the decision, and the administrative court thus act only as a cassation court in such cases.

8.2.4.4. Judicial control of private entities that exercise public power

Supervision by the Parliamentary Ombudsmen and by the Legal Chancellor of the government is possible, and the person who is responsible for the exercise of public power can be prosecuted for malpractice. The state may be sued for compensation due to wrongful acting by a private entity when exercising public power.

8.3. Judicial review of government and administration

8.3.1. Judicial independence from the executive

Sweden has a long tradition of administrative decision-making without any court interference. It has been difficult to take an administrative case to court and the Supreme Administrative Court (its title is "the court of the government" in a direct translation), established in 1909, was very closely connected to the government during its first 60 years of existence. The Administrative Court of first instance was established in 1971 and the Administrative Court of Appeal – which had existed since the 17th century but with other functions – became a court of appeal at the same time.

8.3.1.1. Independence of the courts

The judicial independence of the courts was laid down in the constitution from 1974 onwards. According to the constitution (RF 11:2), no public authority may determine how a court of law shall adjudicate an individual case or otherwise apply a rule of law in a particular case. This, together with the constitutional rule (RF 11:5) that a judge may not be removed from office, guarantees independence from the executive branch.

8.3.1.2. Ordinances and preparatory works

The executive branch influences the courts through governmental ordinances and also regulations from the central administrative authorities. Many administrative laws are framework laws, so decrees and regulations can play an important role in interpreting the law. Also important is the preparatory work done before and while a law is being drafted. This is often done by a parliamentary committee but also by the government.

Preparatory legislative work starts with the government appointing a committee. This prepares a report following the direction given by the government. The report is published in *SOU* ("The public investigations of the state"), which is sent to different administrative bodies, courts and institutions that are asked to give their views on the report. The government then revises the proposal and this version is published in *Reg. Prop.* ("Proposal from the government") and submitted to Parliament. A legal council (purely advisory) with jurists from the Supreme Court checks the proposed law from a legal-technical point of view before Parliament takes its decision.

The courts are bound to follow the law, but also ordinances and other regulations that are in accordance with the law. The preparatory works are often referred to by the courts when applying the law and thus play an important role in interpreting the law. However, the government cannot directly interfere in a particular case that a court is handling.

8.3.2. The scope of judicial review

8.3.2.1. Governmental resolutions

It can be difficult to separate political issues from other legal issues, but some issues must be taken to the government. However, the resolutions of the government can in some cases be taken to court. The Administrative Supreme Court is competent to review governmental decisions in a case – if it concerns civil rights or duties – according to a law on special judicial review of government decisions in individual cases. The review can concern questions of law as well as questions of fact. The Administrative Supreme Court can in such a case only rescind the decision of the government.

The court cannot review separately a purely normative decision by the government, that is, a decision to issue a certain ordinance. Only the types of decision mentioned above in individual cases can be reviewed by the court, and it is thus only possible to review norms from the government if there is an individual case in which a decree from the government is said to be in contradiction to an act of Parliament.

8.3.2.2. Administrative resolutions

Instance

Administrative resolutions are generally taken to the administrative court of first instance, but this stipulation in the FL is secondary to other considerations. Special administrative laws can contain provisions by which the case must be taken to a higher administrative body. It is also possible for a special regulation to prohibit appeals against the administrative resolution.

Where administrative matters are obligations for local governments, their resolutions can be taken to the administrative courts in the same way as a resolution by a national administrative authority.

The regulations concerning possibilities to appeal administrative resolutions are rather complicated as there are many different solutions. The possibility exists as a secondary rule in the administrative act but there might be another stipulation in a special regulation which, in such a case, is primary to the stipulation in the FL. It is however important to stress that the Administrative Procedure Act contains a stipulation (FL 3 §) according to which the provisions of appeals to the administrative court of first instance always shall apply if necessary in order to provide for everyone's right to a fair trial in the determination of their civil rights or obligations as laid down in Article 6.1 of the Convention. A court procedure is thus always possible in such cases.

Scope

The scope of judicial review in the administrative courts is not limited; the court can change decisions of an administrative agency, including decisions by state agencies.

This is the case also for the many decisions by local government (that is, municipalities) acting under special regulations based on an act of Parliament. It is generally possible to appeal against such decisions in individual cases to an administrative court, which can change the decision; there are thus no limits on such judicial review. Appeals are also possible against local government decisions made under their self-governing powers, but such decisions cannot be changed; they can only be rescinded by the court.

Leave to appeal

Under the FL, there is often a need for leave to appeal in order to take the case to the Court of Appeal, but leave to appeal is not needed under some special administrative regulations. Leave to appeal to the Court of Appeal is in general not needed if the resolution involves a more severe exercise of public power.

8.3.3. Access to the courts

8.3.3.1. Citizens' standing to sue

The individual may only challenge a public resolution if he or she is affected by the decision. In general, there is only one person concerned, namely the one that applied for a grant but did not get it, or the person who got some kind of unfavourable decision on his duties. Other people can rarely challenge the decision. It is possible in cases about building permits that the neighbours may appeal. The individuals concerned are only allowed to challenge a regulation in connection with a decision that concerns them.

The individual standing to sue has been expanded as a result of Articles 6 and 13 of the Convention. Cases that before could not be appealed can now be appealed. Of special importance is the third section in the Administrative Procedure Act, by which there is always a guarantee of access to justice in an administrative court in cases that concern civil rights and duties.

8.3.3.2. Public interest litigation

Group action – where a plaintiff brings an action as the representative of several persons with legal effects for them, though they are not parties to the case – has existed since 2002. A group action may be instituted as a private group action, an organisation action or a public group action. The purpose behind this law was to increase the possibilities for citizens to take cases to court with less economic risk; it is considered to have fulfilled this purpose, even though only ten cases have been taken to court. By 2008 only one had resulted in adjudication and four cases were still being tried.

References

The Swedish Constitution in English: www.regeringen.se

Instrument of Government Act: www.riksdagen.se/templates/R_Page____ 6307.aspx

Abbreviations:

RF = Regeringsformen (Instrument of Form of Government Act)

FL = Förvaltningslagen (Administrative Procedure Act)

MB = Miljöbalken (Environmental law)

Chapter 9
National legal tradition – United Kingdom

D. Nassimpian

9.1. The constitutional framework

> [A]ll constitutions contain elements that are autobiographical and correspondingly idio-syncratic … Different historical contexts have generated different preoccupations and priorities, and these in turn have led to quite different constitutional structures.[160]

The most commonly shared piece of knowledge about the idiosyncratic, unique style of the United Kingdom's Constitution is that, unlike most of its counterparts, it is unwritten.[161] That is not to say, however, that the UK does not have a constitution or that it lacks constitutional rules. Drawing a parallel with the framework of the European Union (pre-Constitutional Treaty, Lisbon, etc.), what we have instead of a single, founding text is a collection of key documents of varying degrees of formality; principle and precedent-shaping case law; and an assortment of constitutional conventions.

The main benefit of the UK's constitutional formation is often thought to be its flexibility, where the supremacy of each successive Parliament is determined by the ability to pass or repeal any legislation that it deems fit. As there are generally no special procedures for amending an act of Parliament, for example, this may allow rules to evolve and change in a more informal manner. Moreover, the absence of a codified constitution providing positive statements of the basic rules governing the formation of the state and the exercise of state actions has meant that the concept of the rule of law has assumed pivotal relevance in prescribing such parameters. Although the above statements reflect broadly accepted views on the UK Constitution, there certainly are various objections and qualifications.[162]

---

160. S. E. Finer, V. Bogdanor and B. Rudden, *Comparing Constitutions* (Oxford University Press, 1995), p. 7.

161. It is, however, worth noting that New Zealand also does not have a written constitution in the traditional, single-document form and neither does Israel.

162. For example, judgments like *Thoburn v. Sunderland County Council* [2003] QB 151 have marked a departure from the concept of absolute parliamentary sovereignty by strongly qualifying the principle of implied repeal when amending "constitutional statutes" such as the European Communities Act 1972. For discussion on the nature and evolution of the UK Constitution, see, *inter alia,* Finer, Bogdanor and Rudden, *Comparing Constitutions,* op. cit; V. Bogdanor, "Our new constitution", *Law Quarterly Review,* No. 120 (2004), 242-262; J. L. Jowell and D. Oliver, *The Changing Constitution* (Oxford University Press, 2004); A. Lyon, *A Constitutional History of the United Kingdom* (Routledge, 2003). For a strong thesis on the constitution's non-existence, see F. F. Ridley, "There is no British Constitution: a dangerous case of the emperor's clothes", *Parliamentary Affairs,* Vol. 41, No. 3 (1988), 340-361.

According to K. C. Where's suggested pointers on constitutional classifications,[163] it is commonly suggested[164] that the UK Constitution is:

– largely unwritten in character, though a considerable body of rules – including some of great constitutional significance – is codified in acts of Parliament;

– flexible in nature, as amendments and alterations can occur with relative ease;

– supreme, because the legislative powers of the governing body are unlimited, rather than subordinate to some higher authority as is the case in federal systems;

– unitary in structure, since it does not rely on a federal model of division of powers between central government and states/provinces, though recent acts of devolution in Wales, Scotland and Northern Ireland have sparked reclassification debates;

– mainly, though not absolutely, based on separated powers between the legislature, the executive and the judiciary;

– founded on a constitutional monarchy, where Queen Elizabeth II is currently the head of state and all acts of government are undertaken in the name of the Crown, even though – in reality – the monarch's role is largely symbolic.

Most importantly, as is the case in most modern democracies, the UK is also seen as being in a continuing state of constitutional change, having evolved in a "pragmatic and gradual manner over the centuries".[165] Some instances of particular importance include its accession to the European Communities (now the European Union or EU) in 1973, significant constitutional reforms brought forward by the Labour government since 1997 (such as Scottish and Welsh devolution, the gradual reform of the House of Lords and the April 1998 settlement in Northern Ireland leading to its new Assembly) and the coming into force of the Human Rights Act 1998 (hereafter HRA 1998).[166]

---

163. K. C. Where, *Modern Constitutions* (Oxford University Press, 1966).

164. See, for example, H. Barnett, *Constitutional and Administrative Law* (Cavendish, 2004), p. 14.

165. Ibid.

166. In the absence of a written Bill of Rights or its equivalent, enactment of the HRA 1998 meant that, for the first time, rights upheld in the European Court of Human Rights were incorporated in UK law through a rule of consistent statutory interpretation of domestic legislation. See, *inter alia*: R. Clayton, "The Human Rights Act six years on: where are we now?", *European Human Rights Law Review* (2007) 11; D. Hoffman and J. Rowe, *Human Rights in the UK: An Introduction to the HRA 1998* (Pearson, 2006); F. Klug, "Judicial deference under the Human Rights Act 1998", *European Human Rights Law Review* (2003) 2; D. Oliver, "Functions of a public nature under the Human Rights Act", *Public Law* (2004), 328-349; J. Wadham et al., *Blackstone's Guide to the Human Rights Act 1998* (Oxford University Press, 2007).

9.1.1. Sources

As mentioned, the United Kingdom's constitutional backbone is composed of several different sources, namely legislation, case law, constitutional conventions and other relevant obligations, such as those deriving from the EU, the European Convention on Human Rights and international law. It is worth noting a few points in relation to acts of parliament and constitutional conventions, given that their nature and status is of direct relevance to the availability of judicial review.

First, much like the foundational treaties of EC/EU law, there are a number of statutes that have played a catalytic role in the country's constitutional development and are thus often perceived as having a superior, constitutional status. In the words of Laws LJ in *Thoburn* (2003), a constitutional statute is one which "(a) conditions the legal relationship between citizen and state in some general, overarching manner, or (b) enlarges or diminishes the scope of what we would now regard as fundamental constitutional rights".[167] Although there is no definitive list of such statutes, Laws LJ cites,[168] *inter alia*, the Magna Carta, the 1688 Bill of Rights, the Union with Scotland Act 1706, the European Communities Act 1972, the Scotland Act 1998, the Government of Wales Act 1998 and the HRA 1998.

Constitutional conventions can be regarded as unwritten maxims of the constitution, reflecting the understandings and habits of practices that are considered to be binding on actors, even though they are not legally binding rules per se. Thus, the key difference between conventions and laws can be understood in terms of their enforceability, since legal rules are enforced by the courts and by presiding officers in parliament, whereas constitutional conventions are not. Still, courts may recognise such conventions in cases where they could provide useful background to a particular decision.[169] Some examples of important constitutional conventions include the granting of royal assent to all legislation by the monarch (which has not been refused since 1708); the creation of institutions such as the Cabinet and the Office of the Prime Minister, and the relations between them; and the concept and operation of ministerial responsibility, which often comes up as subject matter in judicial review.[170]

---

167. *Thoburn v. Sunderland City Council* [2003] QB 151, paragraph 62.
168. Ibid.
169. See, for example, *Carltona Ltd v. Commissioners for Works* [1943] 2 All ER 560 on the convention governing ministerial responsibility.
170. For a helpful overview of constitutional conventions, see N. Parpworth, *Constitutional Law and Administrative Law* (Oxford University Press, 2005), pp. 223-233. See also: M. Elliott, "Parliamentary sovereignty and the new constitutional order: legislative freedom, political reality and convention", *Legal Studies*, Vol. 22 (2002), 340-376; J. Jaconelli, "Do constitutional conventions bind?", *Cambridge Law Journal*, Vol. 64 (2005) No. 1, 149-176; C. Munro, "Laws and conventions distinguished", *Law Quarterly Review*, Vol. 91 (1975), 218-233; Lord Wilson, "The robustness of conventions in a time of modernisation and change", *Public Law* (2004), 407-420.

9.1.2. Separation of powers

Montesquieu's *L'Esprit des Lois* being the most potent exposition of the doctrine of separation of powers, it is inevitably relevant here. The rationale underlying the doctrine is to prevent the abuse of power by maintaining a separation between the three main functions and organs of government, namely the legislature, the executive and the judiciary. Although the three unquestionably overlap in the UK constitutional context, the current system does apply the doctrine to a certain degree, albeit not in a purist form.

9.1.2.1. Parliament

The Parliament of the United Kingdom of Great Britain and Northern Ireland ("Westminster") consists of the monarch, the House of Commons[171] (elected members) and the House of Lords[172] (appointed members). Westminster has jurisdiction to make laws that apply to the whole of the UK. Acts of Parliament are initially introduced in draft form as bills, which go through several stages in each House, including passing through appropriate Committees in the House of Lords. Once a bill has reached its final stage, royal assent needs to be granted in order for it to become law as mentioned, although the monarch does have a right of veto, as a matter of constitutional convention assent is ordinarily granted.[173] In addition to acts of Parliament (primary legislation), there is secondary or delegated legislation – most commonly in the form of statutory instruments (SI) – concerning changes or additions to the law made by ministers, local authorities and other public bodies under powers granted by an existing act. A key example can be seen in SIs implementing EU/EC law obligations.

Traditionally, the UK Parliament has been considered as the supreme legal authority in the country. Unlike most states, where the legislature is bound by constitutional restrictions in its mandate, Westminster is regarded as having (nearly) absolute sovereignty[174] over matters of law-making. In that respect, Blackstone's proverbial phrase "what Parliament doth, no power on earth can undo"[175] still remains pertinent to a considerable extent. Hence, judicial review is generally not available against acts of Parliament, as courts do not have the power to declare such laws invalid. As explained below, however, the impact of EU law, certain matters relating to devolved and reserved competencies and the HRA 1998 have brought about a discernible shift in this respect.

---

171. The official House of Commons website can be found at www.parliament.uk/commons/.
172. The official House of Lords website can be found at www.parliament.uk/lords/.
173. For an official account of the legislative process in the UK Parliament, see www.parliament.uk/about/how/laws.cfm.
174. The most cogent argument relating to the concept of parliamentary sovereignty in the UK is still found in the seminal work of A. V. Dicey, *Law of the Constitution* (1885).
175. Sir W. Blackstone, *Commentaries on the Laws of England* (1768 edition), p. 161.

Devolved legislative competencies

Scotland has a separate, hybrid legal system and court structure, and the establishment of the Scottish Parliament in 1999 brought about significant changes in the allocation of legislative competencies. With regard to Scotland, matters of administrative law in general – and judicial review in particular – are somewhat different from those under English law. The Scottish Parliament (Holyrood)[176] sitting in Edinburgh has extensive, devolved powers to enact primary legislation, but certain matters are reserved for Westminster under section 29 of the Scotland Act 1998, which clearly delimits Holyrood's legislative authority: any Scottish act deemed to affect the powers of the UK Parliament may be struck down. Correspondingly, there is a separate government branch now called the Scottish Government (previously the Scottish Executive).

Devolution for Northern Ireland has led to the creation of a separate Assembly (the Northern Ireland Assembly)[177] through the Northern Ireland Act 1998, which also has the power to enact primary legislation. As with the Scottish model, certain matters are considered excepted from its competency and thus reserved for Westminster under Schedule 2 of the 1998 Act. Northern Ireland also has its own Executive Committee.

Lastly, the Government of Wales Act 1998 established the National Assembly for Wales,[178] which has limited law-making powers confined to making delegated legislation. It has various committees; some of the presiding officers essentially form the Welsh Cabinet.

9.1.2.2. The executive

The branch of the state that is responsible for the formulation and execution of UK policy has the sovereign, Queen Elizabeth II, as its formal head, and (under her) the Prime Minister, the Cabinet and other ministers, who are mostly elected members of Parliament. Decisions are generally made by the Cabinet and carried out by government departments in the name of the Crown. Most of the executive's powers derive from Parliament, to which ministers are answerable for the conduct of their departments. There are also residual powers known as "the royal prerogative". Historically, these derived from the common law and were exercised personally by the monarch, though nowadays they are mostly granted by statute and relate to the legislative, executive or judicial functions of government. Some examples include the prerogative of mercy, the granting of the royal assent, the summoning and dissolution of Parliament and the grant of honours, as well as immunities of the Crown.

---

176. The official website of the Scottish Parliament is to be found at www.scottish.parliament.uk/.
177. The official website of the Northern Ireland Assembly can be found at www.niassembly.gov.uk/.
178. The official website of the National Assembly for Wales is at http://new.wales.gov.uk/splash.

9.1.2.3. The judiciary

The independence of the judiciary has always been of prime importance in the UK, even if there is some overlap with the legislature and the executive. Judges are officially appointed by the sovereign on the advice of the Lord Chancellor, and have security of tenure and remuneration (security against government action). The office of the Lord Chancellor has been considered a prime source of fusion between state functions; it was historically part of both the executive and the judiciary, while also involved in the legislative process. The Constitutional Reform Act 2005 significantly altered the role of the Lord Chancellor, whose functions in organising and appointing the judiciary have now been largely transferred to the Ministry of Justice; his role in the House of Lords has been devolved to the Lord Speaker. An independent Judicial Appointments Commission (JAC) has been established, and the Lord Chancellor may now only decide whether to accept or reject the JAC's recommendations.

The United Kingdom does not have a unified judicial system, since Scotland and Northern Ireland operate independently in most matters.[179] There are lower and senior criminal and civil courts and tribunals, including county and magistrates' courts, as well as the Court of Appeal, the Crown Court, the Privy Council and the House of Lords, up to now the highest appeal court in England and Wales for all cases, and in Scotland for civil law cases. Judicial review cases are heard in the Administrative Court division of the High Court, with the Court of Appeal and the House of Lords having appellate jurisdiction. In Scotland, such cases are heard by the Court of Session (Outer House), with appeals possible to the Inner House and finally the House of Lords. Once all the provisions of the Constitutional Reform Act 2005 come into force, the new Supreme Court is expected to reinforce the functional and physical separation of powers between Parliament (particularly the House of Lords) and the judiciary. Furthermore, the new Supreme Court will be a United Kingdom body, with jurisdiction over Scotland and Northern Ireland too.

9.1.3. Availability of judicial review

The availability of review of governmental and administrative actions has developed gradually in the United Kingdom, as has the body of administrative law itself. The historical reluctance to challenge the lawfulness of Acts of Parliament and the notion of the absolute authority of the monarch have been readjusted in view of the need for accountability of public bodies. Accordingly, the courts have built on their inherent supervisory jurisdiction in determining the lawfulness of the exercise of executive power, whether it is granted

---

179. Official information on the judiciary of England and Wales, including court structure, appeal routes and the new Supreme Court can be found at the relevant official website, www.judiciary.gov.uk. The Scottish equivalent can be found at www.scotcourts.gov.uk/.

through statute or by way of royal prerogative. Nonetheless, courts are still unable to review the lawfulness of an Act of Parliament, even though they have authority to exercise their jurisdiction in relation to delegated (that is, secondary) legislation.

A possible exception can be found in relation to the HRA 1998. The Act incorporates specified Convention rights into domestic law and section 3 provides that all UK legislation must be interpreted, as far as possible, in a way compatible with the European Convention on Human Rights: where this is not feasible, courts may issue a declaration of incompatibility under section 4(2) of the Act. Still, such declarations do not have the effect of actually striking down primary legislation and rely on government to amend the offending law in question. But, following the House of Lords' application of the European Court of Justice's judgment in *Factortame* (No. 2) in 1991,[180] it was also established that UK courts could disapply part of an act of Parliament for the purposes of granting interim relief, if the act was found to be in breach of duties under Community law. This effectively meant that in cases concerning directly effective EC law, courts could set aside primary legislation. It should also be noted that, under the Scotland Act 1998 and the Northern Ireland Act 1998, acts made by these assemblies are amenable to judicial review and may be held to be invalid by designated courts.

9.2. Government and public administration

The difficulty in mapping out the precise form of the United Kingdom's governmental model is closely linked to the absence of a codified constitution. The main characteristic of the country's government and public administration, however, is that both central and local government is carried out in the name of the Crown. The modern administrative state comprises, *inter alia*, the civil service, local authorities, public and quasi-public bodies, agencies and nationalised industries. The powers granted to servants of the Crown – such as ministers, civil servants and members of the armed forces – derive from primary and secondary legislation and from the royal prerogative. The government and public administration has three areas: central government (including the civil service); regional and devolved government; and local government.

Central and local government share responsibilities in carrying out public policy, and specific areas of duty are conferred directly on relevant ministers. At the same time, following major governmental reforms since the late 1970s, many public functions have been assigned to agencies or to the private sector. This has resulted in the creation of a number of agencies, such as the Prison Service, and certain services (such as highway construction or refuse

---

180. Case C-213/89, *R. v. Secretary of State for Transport, ex parte Factortame Ltd (No. 2)* [1990] ECR I-2433; and *R. v. Secretary of State for Transport, ex parte Factortame Ltd (No. 2)* [1991] 1 All ER 70.

removal) are now provided by privately owned companies. The latter pose some potentially serious effects on citizens' ability to sue providers directly, though delegating ministers may be held accountable.

Powers relating to central government are mostly granted through statute, or they may form part of the royal prerogative. Duties are executed through various bodies and departments, such as the Ministry of Defence or the Home Office, that are headed by a relevant Minister or Secretary of State. The nature, roles and organisation of such offices are gradually evolving, often met with changes in the delegation and execution of the duties involved. A recent example can be seen in the reform of the office of the Lord Chancellor. Largely independent agencies have also assumed an increasingly important role in carrying out policies decided by government, as have other non-departmental public bodies, such as regional development agencies.

Local government operates in subordination to central government and, apart from the devolved governments of Scotland, Wales and Northern Island (discussed above), consists of numerous local councils. The main statutory framework is the Local Government Act 1972, as amended, and the various devolution acts mentioned earlier. There are also a number of regional development agencies for England, all carrying out specified tasks and providing local services to citizens.

9.3. Judicial review of government and administration

The statutory provisions on judicial review in the United Kingdom are mainly found in Part 54 of the Civil Procedure Rules (CPR), section 31 of the Senior Courts Act 1981 (SCA, originally named the Supreme Court Act 1981) and section 6 of the HRA 1998. As the central adjudicative action in the realm of administrative law, judicial review oversees the exercise of executive power. As mentioned above, such powers may originate in primary legislation or in the prerogative, while they may also constitute subordinate powers given to individuals or bodies by statute.

The historical premise of judicial review in the United Kingdom is rooted in the notion of *ultra vires*, prescribing that authorities cannot abuse or act outside the powers granted to them. As seen in the landmark case of *R. v Electricity Commissioners* (1924),[181] in such an event, courts are authorised to intervene and award remedies to the aggrieved citizen. Through evolution and successive reforms, judicial review in the United Kingdom is no longer confined to incidents of strict *ultra vires*. Recognised substantive grounds for review now include the three main headings of illegality, irrationality and procedural impropriety – famously summarised by Lord Diplock in the

---

181. *R v. Electricity Commissioners* [1924] 1 KB 171.

GCHQ case[182] – but also incompatibility with EC/EU law or with obligations arising under the HRA 1998. Proportionality has been suggested as a further heading, though it is clear that the list of potentially available grounds for review is neither conclusive nor rigidly set.[183]

The clarification that judicial review is not, in fact, an appeal on the merits of a case but an exercise of the courts' limited supervisory jurisdiction, is of paramount importance.[184] As a result, judicial review in the United Kingdom is clearly distinguished from any potential appeal that may be available, for example, by statute. When this type of appellate system exists, it is likely that courts will request exhaustion of such routes,[185] although they still maintain the discretion to allow a judicial review after taking into account several factors.[186] The various remedies that may be awarded following a successful case are discretionary and they are prescribed by statute.[187] Hence, even when a court finds that a public body has acted wrongly, it is not obliged to grant the remedy sought by the applicant and it may decide not to grant any remedy.

9.3.1. Judicial independence from the executive

In view of the changes that have taken place in the organisation of the country's state administration, especially since the 1960s, the importance of the role of the courts in safeguarding the correct application of legislation by various public sector agencies has increased significantly. Judicial power is unquestionably limited given that the will of Parliament remains supreme, and so court decisions can be over-ridden by the legislature. The availability and effect of judicial review, however, ensures that the exercise of executive discretion cannot take place in an arbitrary manner. The leading case of *Padfield* (1968)[188] proves that, even when ministers have wide discretionary powers to make delegated legislation, these are not unlimited. Lord Upjohn's marked position in that judgment was that "the use of that adjective [unfettered],

---

182. *Council of Civil Service Unions & Others (GCHQ) v. Minister for the Civil Service* [1985] AC 374.
183. For useful discussions on grounds of review see: M. Elliot, "The ultra vires doctrine in a constitutional setting: still the central principle of administrative law", *Cambridge Law Journal* (1999), No. 1, 129-158; T. Hickman, "The courts and politics after the Human Rights Act: a comment", *Public Law* (2008), 84-100; P. Leyland and G. Anthony, *Textbook on Administrative Law* (Oxford University Press, 2005), chapters 10-16; Parpworth, *Constitutional Law and Administrative Law*, op. cit., chapter 13.
184. *R. v. Secretary of State for the Environment, ex p Hammersmith and Fulham London Borough Council* [1991] 1 AC 521; *Reid v. Secretary of State for Scotland* [1999] 2 AC 512.
185. *R. v. Ministry of Agriculture, Fisheries and Food, ex p Live Sheep Traders Ltd* [1995] COD 297.
186. *Re Waldron* [1986] QB 824.
187. The available remedies that a judicial review claimant may seek are a quashing order (formerly *certiorari*); prohibiting order (formerly prohibition); mandatory order (formerly *mandamus*); declaration; injunction; and damages. The relevant provisions can be found in s. 31 of the SCA 1981; Pt 54 of the CPR 1998; and s. 8 of the HRA 1998.
188. *Padfield v. Minister of Agriculture, Fisheries and Food* [1968] AC 997.

even in an Act of Parliament, can do nothing to unfetter the control which the judiciary have over the executive",[189] hence sending a clear message that cases of suspected abuse in the exercise of such discretion will fall under the courts' supervisory jurisdiction.

Inevitably, judicial independence from the executive branch is critical in ensuring a genuine separation of powers that will enable courts to carry out their vested tasks. The changes to the office of Lord Chancellor (mentioned above) were specifically directed at achieving a more efficiently transparent and independent framework for the judiciary, and section 3(1) of the Constitutional Reform Act 2005 introduced an express provision that "the Lord Chancellor, other Ministers of the Crown and all with the responsibility for matters relating to the judiciary or otherwise to the administration of justice must uphold the continued independence of the judiciary". The importance of such independence is also highlighted in case law. Lord Atkin's remark in *Liversidge v. Anderson* (1942)[190] – a case involving the relationship between the courts and the state, and in particular the assistance that the judiciary should give to the executive in times of national emergency – still holds strong: "I view with apprehension the attitude of judges who ... show themselves more executive minded than the executive."[191]

9.3.2. The scope of judicial review

The general rule covering which acts, decisions or even inaction may be challenged in a judicial review brings us back to acts of government or public bodies. The subject of the review must relate to actions of public bodies that have occurred in a justiciable context, and only where there is a live issue. Thus, the question of non-justiciability remains pertinent, because not all disputes involving a public body lend themselves to resolution by judicial review. Accordingly, not all bodies that are seemingly public will be amenable to such litigation; it depends on the relevant statutory provisions that may apply, but also following case law, judicial reviews can take place against public bodies in relation to the exercise of public functions. As a result, not every public body is subject to judicial review for every action. To this end, the setting of an absolute boundary between private law and public law matters and bodies has proved to be a challenging task. Withal, certain conclusions can be drawn and two useful guides are the "sources of powers" test and the functions test or effects doctrine.

The sources of powers approach suggests that a public law issue may be defined by reference to the fact that a body is a public authority, such as a local council or the police, for example. The effects doctrine looks at the types of

---

189. Ibid., at p. 1060.
190. *Liversidge v. Anderson* [1942] AC 206.
191. Ibid., at p. 244.

powers being exercised and whether their effect has public law consequences. The latter is often seen in licensing cases or in relation to bodies regulating a certain activity, suggesting that a seemingly private organisation could be carrying out functions that are governmental in nature. A key case in the area is *Datafin* (1983),[192] where an unincorporated association (the panel on take-overs and mergers) exercising no statutory or prerogative powers was deemed to be amendable to judicial review and was regarded as a public body due to nature of its functions. The outcome of this case has led to the creation of the so-called "*Datafin* 'but for' test", by which a body may be held to be public if it can be shown that, but for the fact it already existed, the government would have been likely to set up a public body to perform that same function. The courts have applied the test with some caution. Cases like *The Aga Khan* (1993),[193] *Wachmann* (1993)[194] and *YL* (2007)[195] show that the existence of wide-ranging powers of great concern to the public, or even the existence of a contractual link with a public authority, will not necessarily suffice to determine that a body or matter is susceptible to judicial review.

9.3.2.1. Political and security questions

Given the complexity of questions that courts are often faced with, particularly in widely publicised cases with a strong political or security element, it is not surprising that judges are sometimes essentially expected to act as "tamers of politicians' passions" and "custodians of civic virtue".[196] The tapping of phones by the Home Office[197] or a policy of the Ministry of Defence to discharge homosexuals from the armed forces[198] undoubtedly entail political choices, yet courts have confirmed their supervisory jurisdiction in relation to such events. In contrast, the granting of honours, the making of a Treaty, the appointment of ministers[199] or the government's decision to go to war[200] have traditionally been regarded as purely political matters. What these examples suggest is that, notwithstanding the public nature of the source of powers being exercised or of their effects, some matters deemed to be of a political (rather than justiciable) nature ultimately rest outside the ambit of court scrutiny.

---

192. *R. v. Panel on Take-overs and Mergers, ex p Datafin PLC* [1987] QB 815.
193. *R. v. Disciplinary Committee of the Jockey Club, ex p the Aga Khan* [1993] 1 WLR 909.
194. *R. v. Chief Rabbi, ex p Wachmann* [1993] 2 All ER 249.
195. *YL v. Birmingham City Council* [2007] 3 WLR 112.
196. D. Nicol, "Law and politics after the Human Rights Act", *Public Law* (2006) No. 4, 722-751, at 722.
197. *Malone v. the United Kingdom* (A/82) [1985] 7 EHRR 14.
198. *R. v. Ministry of Defence ex p Smith* [1996] QB 517.
199. Examples of such functions that should not fall under the courts' supervisory jurisdiction were clearly outlined by Lord Roskill in *Council of Civil Service Unions & Others (GCHQ) v. Minister for the Civil Service* [1985] AC 374, at p. 418.
200. *R. (on the application of Campaign for Nuclear Disarmament) v. Prime Minister* [2002] EWHC 2777 (Admin).

Whereas, in jurisdictions such as that of the United States, courts are able to employ the well-established "political question doctrine",[201] this has not been adopted in the United Kingdom in the same manner. Thus, it appears that most cases are decided on an individual basis, and it is arguable that instances of judicial deference and restraint may well be followed by spurts of judicial activism. Thus, the difficulty mainly lies in the lack of set rules, or even consistency, in determining which cases containing clear political overtones will be deemed non-justiciable. According to Leyland and Anthony, such instances are more likely to involve the exercise of ministerial discretion under the prerogative, where courts appear to employ their own ability to intervene "almost at will".[202] By reference to Simon Brown LJ's comments in *ex parte Smith*, they suggest that a good guide to the judiciary's developing attitude can be seen in his assertion that "only the rarest of cases would today be ruled strictly beyond the court's purview: that is only those involving national security where the court lacked the experience or materials to form a judgment on the issues".[203]

Assessing the scope and availability of judicial review for matters involving political and security questions, two parameters must be looked at: one is whether the subject matter is open to review, as discussed above; the other is the requirement of standing (*locus standi*, discussed below), which is a necessary precondition in getting permission to proceed to a judicial review. When addressing issues of greater political significance involving policy decisions, precedent suggests that it may be harder to establish the necessary individual concern. Furthermore, even in cases when permission is granted at the application stage, courts are still able to rule that the subject matter (or part of it) is, in the end, non-justiciable and/or that the applicant does not have sufficient standing.

A very interesting example is the recent, high-profile judgment in *Wheeler* (2008).[204] In that case, an individual was successful in obtaining permission for a judicial review questioning whether statements and assurances made by the Blair government on holding a referendum for the ratification of the EU Constitutional Treaty had created a legitimate expectation in relation to the ratification process for the Lisbon Treaty as well. The case was subsequently dismissed at the hearing stage, primarily on the factual examination of circumstances, but also due to the weakness of the substantive grounds raised (procedural impropriety resulting from breach of a legitimate expecta-

---

201. The doctrine was established in the case of *Luther v. Borden*, 48 U.S. 1 (1849), its main purpose being to distinguish the role of the federal judiciary from that of the legislature and the executive. It forms part of the broader concept of justiciability, aiming to prevent federal courts from dealing with questions on the conduct of foreign policy, the ratification of constitutional amendments and the organisation of each state's government.
202. Leyland and Anthony, *Textbook on Administrative Law*, op. cit., at pp. 444-445.
203. *R. v. Ministry of Defence ex p Smith* [1996] QB 517, at p. 539.
204. *R. (on the application of Wheeler) v. Prime Minister* [2008] EWHC 1409 (Admin).

tion). The court remained unconvinced that the situation at hand concerned a justiciable error of law. It concluded that, in view of the particular events and outcome of the process in question, the decision on the ratification of the Treaty of Lisbon rested with Parliament and not with the executive. At the same time, the judges clearly stated that the decision to ratify a Treaty should not be considered as altogether outside the scope of judicial review and that it would be best to assess the limits of reviewability on a case by case basis.[205]

Another apt illustration is the case of *Gentle v. The Prime Minister* (2007),[206] where the relatives of two deceased soldiers applied for a judicial review of the refusal of the government to hold an independent inquiry into the circumstances that led to the invasion of Iraq. The application was refused on grounds of non-justiciability. This was due to the fact that reviewing the government's decision would involve a consideration of international instruments (UN Security Council Resolutions 678 and 1441) and also a detailed examination of policy decisions in the areas of foreign affairs and defence, which were held to be the exclusive responsibility of the executive and not of the courts.

The issue of national security appears to be equally sensitive, if perhaps a little more settled, as the overall approach tends to be one of judicial restraint. Even though courts have been critical of the government in cases involving national security,[207] the prevailing judicial view is that in certain circumstances the sensitivity of a matter demands that executive discretion be left in the hands of a minister.[208] As seen in the case of *Hosenball* (1977),[209] the normal rules of natural justice may have to be modified if the security of the country itself is at stake. In all, public interest cases show that the courts will evaluate matters of national security and weigh them against private rights, this being an approach that has persisted even in view of the HRA 1998.[210] An equally authoritative insight can be found in *Rehman* (2001).[211] The House of Lords held that although the definition of national security was for their Lordships to decide as a matter of law, the consideration and determination of what was in the interests of national security was a matter of judgment and policy best left to the Secretary of State.

9.3.3. Access to the courts

Judicial reviews are heard at the Administrative Court, after written applications – that take place *inter partes* – gain permission, usually from a single

---

205. Ibid., at paragraph 55.
206. *R. (on the application of Gentle) v. Prime Minister* [2007] QB 689.
207. See, for example, *A & Ors v. Home Secretary* [2004] UKHL 56.
208. Leyland and Anthony, *Textbook on Administrative Law*, op. cit., at pp. 365-368.
209. *R. v. Secretary of State for Home Affairs, ex p Hosenball* [1977] 3 All ER 452.
210. See, for example, *Conway v. Rimmer* [1968] AC 910.
211. *Secretary of State for the Home Department v. Rehman* [2001] UKHL 47.

judge.[212] There is a general presumption that Parliament intends citizens to have access to the courts, and judicial construction of statutes has consistently upheld this basic human right.[213] Indeed precedent indicates that, when ministers adopt regulations that may discourage individuals from pursuing genuine claims, courts will find these to be contrary to Parliament's intention.[214] In addition to this overall position, the gradual relaxation in the courts' interpretation on standing, coupled with a marked increase in the number of judicial reviews in recent years, has sparked greater discussion of the two models of litigation: "open access" versus "closed access".

9.3.3.1. Citizens' standing and public interest litigation

Before obtaining permission to proceed to a judicial review, a claimant must be deemed to have sufficient interest in the matter that the application relates to (section 31.3 SCA 1981). The courts have wide discretion in deciding whether an applicant fulfils this requirement, and case law since the 1980s suggests a gradual relaxation in the application of this requirement. The "*Fleet Street Casuals*" case (1982)[215] marked liberalisation in the House of Lords' approach. Although the particular applicants were not successful in establishing they had *locus standi*, the judgment allowed the possibility for individuals and groups to challenge any governmental decision if sufficiency of interest could be confirmed. This was done in view of the need to control illegality in the field of public law, so as to safeguard the interests of all those who might be directly affected, even if the act or decision in question did not specifically relate to them. Wider debate followed this judgment, querying its potential effects on the emerging attitude of the courts vis-à-vis group and public interest actions. Were courts to assume a more activist stance on important policy decisions affecting the public or should a close examination of the sufficiency-of-interest requirement persist?

Ensuing judgments suggest that both approaches may be followed, depending on the particular factual circumstances of each case. Examples such as *Greenpeace (No. 2)*[216] and *ex p World Development Movement* (1995)[217] are representative of the courts' willingness to accept that certain organisations may well be entitled, and even be better placed, to initiate an action. Parameters

---

212. Official information on the process, fees and funding possibilities for judicial reviews can be found at HM Courts Services' website at www.hmcourts-service.gov.uk/cms/1220.htm.

213. See, for example, *Chester v. Bateson* [1920] KB 829.

214. A number of such cases are from immigration or asylum law litigation, for example *R. v. Secretary of State for Social Security, ex p Joint Council for the Welfare of Immigrants* [1996] 4 All ER 385.

215. *IRC v. National Federation of Self-Employed and Small Businesses Ltd* (also known as "*The Fleet Street Casuals*" case) [1982] AC 617.

216. *R. v. Secretary of State for the Environment, ex p Greenpeace Ltd (No. 2)* [1994] 4 All ER 329.

217. *R. v. Secretary of State for Foreign Affairs, ex p World Development Movement Ltd* [1995] 1 WLR 386.

such as expert knowledge, membership, activity in the particular field and the situation at hand, as well as the view that these organisations would be better-informed challengers, led to the decision that they did have standing. In contrast, *Rose Theatre Trust* (1990)[218] may be regarded as an exception to this general trend, albeit one that can be factually distinguished from the majority of the case law. The trust in question had been formed specifically in order to seek a judicial review, in the knowledge that no individual member would have standing. Following Schiemann J's assessment, it would be "absurd if two persons without such standing incorporated themselves into a company or trust, and thus gained standing". Thence, it was held that this case concerned a governmental decision in respect of which the ordinary citizen would not have sufficient interest to entitle him to challenge it.

The rules on standing in cases involving human rights can be seen in section 7 of the HRA 1998. They are in line with the Strasbourg case law "victim test" and were designed to prevent interventions by public interest groups. Nonetheless, courts appear to have been quite generous in their application of this test, with cases such as *Holub* (2001)[219] suggesting that some flexibility in interpretation is likely to continue.

Problems with this more liberalised approach to standing in class and group actions relate both to questions of the desirability (and suitability) of judicial activism in areas that are mainly matters of policy, and to the possible political motives of organisations supposedly acting in the public interest. Critics such as Harlow argue that judicial review is in danger of becoming a political tactic, and they urge a modification of the current approach in view of the possibility of judicial review becoming a free-for-all.[220]

References

Books

Barnett, H., *Constitutional law and administrative law*, 6th edn (Routledge-Cavendish, Oxford, 2008).

Craig, P., *Administrative law*, 6th edn, Sweet & Maxwell, 2008.

Leyland, P. and Anthony, G., *Textbook on administrative law*, 5th edn, Oxford University Press, 2005.

---

218. *R. v. Secretary of State for the Environment, ex p Rose Theatre Trust Ltd.* [1990] 1 QB 504.
219. *R. (on the application of Holub) v. Secretary of State for the Home Department* [2001] 1 WLR 1359. It was held that parents could be regarded as victims when complaining of a breach of their child's rights.
220. C. Harlow, "Public law and popular justice", *Modern Law Review* (2002), No. 1. See also J. Miles, "Standing under the Human Rights Act 1998: theories of rights enforcement and the nature of public law adjudication", *Cambridge Law Journal*, Vol. 59 (2000), 133.

Loveland, I., *Constitutional law, administrative law and human rights*, 4th edn, Oxford University Press, 2006.

Parpworth, N., *Constitutional law and administrative law*, 5th edn, Oxford University Press, Core Text Series, 2008.

Turpin, C. and Tompkins, A., *British government and the constitution*, 6th edn, Cambridge University Press, 2007.

Wade, H. W. R. and Forsyth, C. F., *Administrative law*, 9th edn, Oxford University Press, 2004.

Woolf, H., *De Smith, Woolf & Jowell's principles of judicial review*, Sweet & Maxwell, 1999.

Articles

Carss-Frisk, M., "Public authorities: the developing definition", *European Human Rights Law Review* (2002) No. 3, pp. 319-326.

Clayton, R., "The Human Rights Act six years on: where are we now?", *European Human Rights Law Review* (2007), No. 11, pp. 11-26.

Elliott, M., "The ultra vires doctrine in a constitutional setting: still the central principle of administrative law", *Cambridge Law Journal*, Vol. 58 (1999), No. 1, pp. 129-158.

Fordham, M., "Judicial review: the new rules", *Public Law* (2001), No. 1, pp. 4-10.

Harlow, C., "Public law and popular justice", *Modern Law Review*, Vol. 65 (2002), No. 1, pp. 1-18.

Klug, F., "Judicial deference under the Human Rights Act 1998", *European Human Rights Law Review*, (2003), No. 2, pp. 125-133.

Leigh, I. D., "Taking rights proportionately: judicial review, the Human Rights Act and Strasbourg", *Public Law*, Vol. 47 (2002), pp. 265-287.

Lidbetter, A. W., "Judicial review and interested persons", *Law Quarterly Review*, Vol. 113 (1997), p. 40.

Woolf, H. [Lord], "The rule of law and a change in the constitution", *Cambridge Law Journal*, Vol. 63 (2004), pp. 317-330.

Chapter 10
European regional tradition – The Council of Europe

J. Ruiloba Albariño and S. Galera[221]

10.1. The constitutional framework

10.1.1. Introduction

Today we can affirm the unquestionable internationalisation and, in large measure, the Europeanisation of human rights.[222] In Europe, two systems of protection of human rights co-exist in different geographical areas. As we will show, the system established by the Council of Europe is pre-eminent because it is the older of the two and because it has been successful and efficient in protecting human rights. The signing of the Convention for the Protection of Human Rights and Fundamental Freedoms on 4 November 1950, setting up a Commission and a Court of Human Rights, marked the official beginning of the Council of Europe's commitment to human rights.

In the European Community, the protection of human rights long played a minor role since constitutional treaties were mainly focused on economic integration and did not mention human rights. This situation changed progressively as Community initiatives led first to the ratification by European members of the Convention for the Protection of Human Rights and later to dispositions in the European Union Treaty after its reform by the Amsterdam Treaty in 1997. Finally, in Nice in December 2000 the European Council issued the Charter of Fundamental Rights of the European Union.

There is also a third European sphere, the Organisation for Security and Co-operation in Europe (OSCE). Principle VII of the Helsinki Final Act is devoted to the respect for human rights and fundamental freedoms, and states that participating states will fulfil their obligations as set forth in international declarations and binding agreements. Later, within the framework of the OSCE, a supervisory mechanism was created to monitor compliance

---

221. J. Ruiloba wrote section 10.1 on the *Constitutional framework*; S. Galera wrote sections 10.2 on *Government and public administration* and 10.3 on *Judicial review of government and administration.*

222. The notion of "fundamental rights" is equivalent to "human rights" but it is only recently that the European Court of Human Rights has declared the rights contained in the Convention; see *Zana v. Turkey*, 25 November 1997, paragraph 55 and *Leyla Sahin v. Turkey*, 10 November 2005, paragraph 153.

with these obligations (Vienna, 1989) through the preparation of technical reports. Also created was a more specific mechanism for the protection of the rights of nationals (Moscow, 1991), which includes a commission of experts and a High Committee. Since 1990, co-operation between the OSCE and the Council of Europe has been promoted through the entry of new OSCE member states in the Council of Europe and the adoption in 1993 by the Parliamentary Assembly of a procedure to monitor compliance with the obligations acquired by new member states after their admission.

The Council of Europe is an intergovernmental organisation made up of 47 European states seeking to promote parliamentary democracy, rule of law and the protection of human rights. Its constituent act was the Statute of the Council of Europe, signed in London on 5 May 1949,[223] which defined the Organisation's objectives, its constituent bodies and the relations between these bodies.

In spite of the fact that the term "constitution" in a formal sense refers solely to states, at the very least it can be argued that, in a real sense, the Statute and other statutory texts are part of the Council of Europe's internal constitutional law. Thus, any state wishing to be a member of the Organisation must commit itself to some universally accepted texts, such as, for example, the Convention for the Protection of Human Rights.

The Organisation's aims, in the Statute's Preamble and Article 1a, are stated to be:

> the pursuit of peace based upon justice and international co-operation in their devotion to the spiritual and moral values which are the common heritage of their peoples and the true source of individual freedom, political liberty and the rule of law, principles which form the basis of all genuine democracy and in the interests of economic and social progress.

The programmatic section of the Preamble is set out in Article 1a:

> The aim of the Council of Europe is to achieve a greater unity between its members for the purpose of safeguarding and realising the ideals and principles which are their common heritage and facilitating their economic and social progress.

Article 3 of the Statute of the Council of Europe lists the preconditions for membership:

> Every member of the Council of Europe must accept the principles of the rule of law and of the enjoyment by all persons within its jurisdiction of human rights and fundamental freedoms, and collaborate sincerely and effectively in the realisation of the aim of the Council as specified in Chapter I.

Since they shared ideals and political traditions, the member states of the Council of Europe reaffirmed their commitment to the spiritual and moral values which are the common heritage of their peoples and the true source

---

223. The Statute was signed by 10 states: Belgium, Denmark, France, Ireland, Italy, Luxembourg, the Netherlands, Norway, Sweden, UK.

of individual freedom, political liberty and the rule of law – principles which form the basis of all genuine democracies.

The field of competency recognised by Article 1 of the Statute concerns the

> discussion of questions of common concern and by agreements and common action in economic, social, cultural, scientific, legal and administrative matters and in the maintenance and further realisation of human rights and fundamental freedoms.

More concretely, the issues of main concern to the Organisation are human rights, judicial co-operation, social issues and cultural and scientific co-operation. However, this same article explicitly excludes "matters relating to national defence". One last limitation appears in this same resolution stating:

> Participation in the Council of Europe shall not affect the collaboration of its members in the work of the United Nations and of other international organisations or unions to which they are parties.

The means given by the Statute to the Council of Europe to achieve its competencies correspond to the classic methods of international public law and are characteristic of a simple structure for interstate co-operation, which has nothing to do with the federalist thesis supported by the European movements meeting in the Hague Congress of 1948. Thus, as stated in Article 1 of the Statute, the Council of Europe accomplishes co-operation by means of international treaties duly ratified by the member states according to their respective constitutional requirements. So far, over 200 agreements have been signed, some open to any state, others only to member states. Likewise, its bodies adopt many recommendations and resolutions on various matters addressed to the member states which are not legally binding but which express the Organisation's point of view.

10.1.2. Organisation

The Council of Europe is organised according to the traditional division of powers that can only be put into practice in an international organisation. The Statute establishes an intergovernmental co-operation organisation hosting a classic intergovernmental organism. The Statute demonstrates states' sovereignty at the same time as it creates supranational elements, like a parliamentary assembly in which national delegates are not submitted to the instructions of their respective national rules, voting rules that allow the adoption of decisions by a majority (though some issues require unanimity) and a supranational court whose competency is limited to protecting human rights.

Executive power belongs to the Committee of Ministers, but with limited competencies since the recommendations it makes to member states are not compulsory. Likewise, the Committee of Ministers can encourage, but not force, member states to sign or ratify agreements negotiated internally by the Council of Europe. Its only real decision power lies in legally binding regulations on issues about organisation and internal affairs.

Legislative power resides in the Parliamentary Assembly, composed of representatives appointed by national parliaments. This has an advisory role, but it has progressively reinforced its autonomy and independence from the Committee of Ministers. The Parliamentary Assembly can approve its own agenda and discuss any political question related to competencies of the Council of Europe in order to make a recommendation to the Committee of Ministers. The public perception is that the assembly is an adequate forum where politicians can express their opinions. Since 1990, following the coming of democracy to central and eastern Europe, the enlarged assembly has seen its authority reinforced by being the most representative body of the entire European continent.

Judicial power is embodied by the European Court of Human Rights, a monitoring body instituted by the Convention for the Protection of Human Rights and amended by Protocol No. 11 on 11 May 1994. This court is charged with ensuring that the High Contracting Parties acknowledge that every person under their jurisdiction possesses the rights and freedoms established by Title I of the Convention.[224] To this end, the Court is granted full competency over all matters relating to the interpretation and application of the Convention and its protocols as stipulated by Articles 33, 34 and 47.[225]

The Statute establishes that the Council of Europe has two main bodies: the Committee of Ministers and the Parliamentary Assembly, which are served by a secretariat.[226]

The Committee of Ministers, the Organisation's decision-making body,[227] is mandated to

> consider the action required to further the aim of the Council of Europe, including the conclusion of conventions or agreements and the adoption by the governments of a common policy with regard to particular matters.[228]

The foreign ministers of the 47 member states[229] form the Committee of Ministers. This is a governmental body, where national approaches to problems facing European society can be discussed, and a collective forum, where Europe-wide responses to such challenges are formulated. In collaboration with the Parliamentary Assembly, it is the guardian of the Organisation's fundamental values, and it monitors member states' compliance with their undertakings. The Committee of Ministers operates on several levels. At their twice-yearly sessions, the ministers review European co-operation and matters of political concern. The ministers, or deputies acting on their behalf, conduct most of the day-to-day business of the Committee. They hold separate

---

224. Article 1 of the Convention.
225. Article 32 of the Convention.
226. Article 10 of the Statute.
227. Article 13 of the Statute.
228. Article 15 of the Statute.
229. Article 14 of the Statute.

meetings on human rights (execution of judgments) and the monitoring of commitments.

Article 15b of the Statute of the Council of Europe provides for the Committee of Ministers to make recommendations to member states on matters for which the Committee has agreed on "a common policy". Adoption of a recommendation requires a unanimous vote of all representatives present, but – to make the voting procedure more flexible – it has been decided by a "gentleman's agreement" not to apply the unanimity rule to recommendations; these are not binding on member states. The Statute also permits the Committee of Ministers to ask member governments "to inform it of the action taken by them" in regard to recommendations. Although records of the Committee of Ministers' sessions are confidential, a final communiqué is issued at the end of each meeting. The ministers may also issue one or more declarations.

The Parliamentary Assembly is the deliberative body of the Council of Europe. It is mandated to debate any matters within the scope of the Organisation and to present its conclusions, in the form of recommendations, to the Committee of Ministers.[230] The members and substitute members of the Assembly are appointed from their national or federal parliaments, where they also sit as parliamentarians.[231] Whereas in the Committee each member state has one vote, in the Assembly the number of votes (one per representative) is determined by the size of the country. The biggest national contingent has 18 representatives, the smallest two. There are over 636 representatives and substitutes in the Parliamentary Assembly, including 18 observers.[232]

The president, the 19 vice-presidents and the chairpersons of the political groups or their representatives make up the Bureau of the Parliamentary Assembly. The duties of the Bureau include the preparation of the Parliamentary Assembly's agenda, the referral of documents to committees, the organisation of day-to-day business and relations with other international bodies.[233]

The Parliamentary Assembly can adopt four types of text: recommendations, resolutions, opinions and orders. Recommendations contain proposals addressed to the Committee of Ministers, the implementation of which is beyond the competency of the Parliamentary Assembly, but within the

---

230. Article 22 of the Statute. In the initial draft of the Statute, there was a provision to create a Consultative Assembly in line with the British position, which was opposed to the creation of a constituent assembly. But in July 1974 the Permanent Commission of the Assembly decided to replace the original name by "Parliamentary Assembly", which better describes its function and composition.

231. Article 25 of the Statute.

232. The Council of Europe is genuinely pan-European, with 47 member states, one applicant country (Belarus, whose special guest status has been suspended due to its lack of respect for human rights and democratic principles) and five observer states: the Holy See, the United States, Canada, Japan, Mexico.

233. Article 28 of the Statute.

competency of national governments.[234] Resolutions embody decisions by the Parliamentary Assembly on questions of substance, which it is empowered to put into effect, or expressions of view, for which it alone is responsible.[235] Opinions are expressed by the Parliamentary Assembly on questions brought before it by the Committee of Ministers, such as the admission of new member states to the Council of Europe, and also on draft conventions, the budget and implementation of the Social Charter. Orders are generally instructions from the Parliamentary Assembly to one or more of its committees. An order concerns form, transmission, execution or procedure; it cannot deal with the substance of the matter.[236]

We can therefore conclude that the Council of Europe is an organisation of international co-operation that presents certain elements that differentiate it from classic intergovernmental organisations. The Parliamentary Assembly is made up of independent representatives of each of the national Parliaments and their voting rules, which, like the Committee of Ministers, are progressively changing to an adoption of resolutions by majority rather than unanimity, leaving this latter option for very important matters. On the other hand, the Committee of Ministers, though it preserves its power of decision, cannot ignore the opinion of the Assembly, to which it is obliged to respond. The constant evolution of the Organisation has opted to pursue a certain balance between the two institutions because the Assembly has learned to develop its own means of action to monitor member states, thus increasing its efficiency.

Although the state does not designate the Secretariat as a full body of the Council of Europe, it plays an essential role in defining the Organisation's politics. As established by Article 10 of the Statute, the Secretariat simply serves the Committee of Ministers and the Parliamentary Assembly. It is in fact the Parliamentary Assembly that appoints the Secretariat, following the recommendations of the Committee of Ministers.[237] The functions of this additional body are briefly defined in Chapter VI of the Statute[238] as well as in the Internal Rules and Regulations of the Assembly and Committee of Ministers. The Statute's authors did not wish to grant this body too much importance and wanted to limit its functions to the purely administrative field, following the example of the General Secretariat of the Society of Nations. However, the election by the Assembly of the third Secretariat helped to develop and reinforce its position at the heart of the Organisation by bestowing on it a certain political legitimacy.

---

234. Rule 23.1a, Rules of Procedure of the Assembly (Resolution 1202 (1999) adopted on 4 November 1999) with the subsequent modifications of the Rules of Procedure, 2008 Version.
235. Rule 23.1b.
236. Rule 23.1c.
237. Article 36b of the Statute.
238. Articles 36 and 37 of the Statute.

The Secretary-General plays an essential role in defining the general politics of the Organisation, partly because this position has been granted greater responsibilities and also because the people who have held this title have had very strong and dynamic personalities. The Secretary-General is the person who approves the Organisation's budget before sending it to the Committee of Ministers for their approval. The Secretary also ensures the correct administrative functioning of the Organisation and is present at all official sessions held by the Committee of Ministers (in voice though not in vote) and in the mixed Committee of the Parliamentary Assembly.

Within the framework of the Convention, the Secretariat plays two important roles. Its first role is related to the obligation of the member states to inform this body of any powers taken in case of war and/or any other dangers that threaten national security as well as the reasons behind this action.[239] The second basic role of this body is the power to request from any member state a precise explanation on how their national law is ensuring the effective implementation of any of the Convention's regulations.[240] This function will be further explained in another part of this survey.

10.1.3. Other bodies

There are other specialised bodies that aim to complement the role of the Council of Europe in specific areas. These bodies include the following.

10.1.3.1. The Congress of Local and Regional Powers

In 1957 the Conference of Local Powers was created to represent local and regional communities. On 15 October 1985 this body drew up what was known as the European Charter of Local Self-Government. The Conference then changed its name to the Congress of Local and Regional Powers and became a consultative body of the Council of Europe in matters that affect local and regional communities. It comprises two chambers: the Chamber of Local Authorities and the Chamber of Regions. Recently, due to the elective nature of its members and to increased regional participation in the Council of Europe's affairs, a new statutory resolution was adopted to increase the responsibilities of the Congress, granting it the authority to prepare the monitoring reports on local and regional democracies in the member states. This resolution also recognises the efforts of the Congress in the observation of regional and local elections as well as corroborating its co-operation with national associations that represent each collectivity and with the EU Committee of Regions.[241]

---

239. Article 15.3 of the Convention.
240. Article 52 of the Convention.
241. Statutory resolution CM/RES (2007).

10.1.3.2. The Commissioner for Human Rights

The idea behind creating this new institution was an initiative taken by the Heads of State and the Council of Europe during the 2nd Summit in October 1997. A resolution of the Committee of Ministers on 7 May 1999 established the role of the Commissioner and defined its scope.[242] This person is elected by the Parliamentary Assembly by a majority of votes from a list of three candidates presented by the Committee of Ministers.[243]

The Commissioner is a non-jurisdictional institution in charge of promoting education, awareness and respect for human rights under the terms established by the convention bodies of the Council of Europe. The Commissioner exercises his/her responsibilities without interfering with the competencies of the oversight bodies created by the European Convention and does not receive individual requests.[244] The objective of this position is mostly preventive, as it collaborates with the other institutions that comprise the Council of Europe. The Commissioner can draw up reports, recommendations and opinions on concrete matters or on bills, on his or her own initiative or on request of a national government. With the implementation of Protocol No. 14 of the Convention, the Commissioner can intercede as a third party in court matters because "in all matters pending in a court or superior court, the Commissioner for Human Rights will have the right to present written observations and take part in the hearings".

10.1.3.3. European Commission against Racism and Intolerance (ECRI)

This institution was created after the Vienna Summit of 1993 and was established by the Declaration drawn up on 9 October that year. On 14 June 2002, the Committee of Ministers adopted a statute by which this body was defined as an independent monitoring body specialising in all matters related to the fight against racism, intolerance, racial discrimination, xenophobia and anti-Semitism.[245]

In accordance with its statute, ECRI is in charge of examining the policies and legislation of member states in all matters pertaining to racism and similar matters. It is also in charge of making recommendations on these political issues. Within the framework of its statutory functions, ECRI exercises its rights and obligations by monitoring each of the states, by establishing recommendations on these political issues addressed to member states and by co-operation and communication with civil society.

---

242. Resolution 99(50) of 7 May 1999.
243. Article 9 of Resolution 99(50).
244. Article 1 of Resolution 99(50).
245. Resolution (2002)8.

10.1.3.4. Other specialised bodies

Apart from the treaties drawn up by the Council of Europe, there are additional partial agreements that do not correspond to that category but rather represent a particular form of co-operation between the member states of the Organisation. These agreements allow member states not to participate in a given activity carried out by other states. In accordance with a resolution adopted by the Committee of Ministers on 2 August 1951 and Statutory Resolution (93)28 on partial and extended agreements, there are two obligatory conditions to be met in order to reach a partial agreement: authorisation from the Committee of Ministers and a resolution (included in the Statute and adopted only by the states that wish to adhere to this new rule) establishing the agreement. The most important ones are the European Commission for Democracy through Law (the Venice Commission), the Council of Europe Development Bank (CEB), the Group of States against Corruption (GRECO), the European Audiovisual Observatory and the European Centre for Global Interdependence and Solidarity (North–South Centre).

10.1.4. The Convention for the Protection of Human Rights and Fundamental Freedoms of 4 November 1950

The "constitutionality block" of the Council of Europe does not end with the Statute and statutory resolutions[246] because those states that apply to join the Organisation commit themselves to signing or ratifying within a year several international treaties, such as the Convention for the Protection of Human Rights and the European Convention for the Prevention of Torture and Inhuman or Degrading Treatment or Punishment of 26 November 1987.

Therefore, these international treaties acquire the same binding judicial force as the Statute for the member states, since their membership of the Organisation is subject to their acceptance of these treaties. These changes came about in 1989 in response to the requests for membership from central and eastern European states that were just then sloughing off communist governments. These new requests forced the Parliamentary Assembly to have all states that wanted to join the Organisation ratify the Convention for the Protection of Human Rights and the European Convention for the Prevention

---

246. Statutory resolutions are texts created by the Committee of Ministers, aimed to adapt or complete one of the original statutes of 1949. Among others, the following statutory resolutions are included as annexes to the Statute: Resolution (2007)6 on the Congress of Local and Regional Powers; Resolution (2003)8 on the participation statute of non-governmental international organisations before the Council of Europe; and Resolution (2003)9 on the collaboration statute between the Council of Europe and national non-governmental organisations.

of Torture and Inhuman or Degrading Treatment or Punishment even though this condition is not included in the Statute.[247]

In 1994, the Parliamentary Assembly issued an opinion to the Committee of Ministers in which it listed a series of treaties that must be signed and ratified in order for new states to adhere to the Organisation. These treaties include those mentioned above, but also the European Social Charter, Protocol No. 6 of the Convention on the abolition of the death penalty, the convention which establishes the framework for the protection of national minorities, the European Charter of Local Self-Government and several conventions on criminal matters.

An obvious connection is established between respect for human rights and democratic systems as a result of this willingness to defend and promote the freedom and democracy mentioned in the Preamble of the Council of Europe's Statute and the mandate established in Article 3 for the recognition of the pre-eminence of law and the guarantee of human rights and fundamental liberties for all people under its jurisdiction. This idea is reinforced by the Convention for the Protection of Human Rights and Fundamental Freedoms as amended by Protocol No. 11, signed in Rome on 4 November 1950, which came into effect on 3 September 1953.[248] This agreement, which was the first multilateral treaty signed by the Council of Europe, establishes the statutory foundation required to achieve a closer union between its members on the basis of adhesion to a series of common ideals and political practices based on respect for fundamental freedoms and the pre-eminence of law.

This Convention, which has been ratified by all 47 member states of the Organisation, has become the signature feature of the Council of Europe.[249] It possesses a double dimension: institutional and legal, since it establishes a catalogue of rights and fundamental freedoms at the same time as it creates the jurisdictional framework required to ensure respect for the obligations taken on by the states that have ratified the Convention. The most immediate result was that, from that moment on, human rights fell within the scope of positive law establishing the European protection of human rights, which offered individuals legal control over their personal rights. Within its jurisdiction, the Court applies the Convention through an evolving and dynamic interpretation,

---

247. In this way, it would seem logical to include the Convention as the basic law of the Council of Europe by means of future statutory reforms.

248. Since the reform established by Protocol No. 11, the Convention has consisted of 59 articles divided into three Sections: Section I (Articles 2 to 18) Rights and freedoms; Section II (Articles 19 to 51) European Court of Human Rights; and Section III (Articles 52 to 59) Miscellaneous provisions.

249. After 1990, full acceptance of the Convention and its protection mechanism in its legal configuration became a political prerequisite to join the Council of Europe; thus all members now accept it in practice.

adapted to the changing conditions of today's society, by which the international responsibility of the member states[250] is constantly broadened.

It is only a compromise text, with all the difficulties that this entails. The main consequence is that it allows different states to adapt to these obligations progressively in order to solve and modify little by little any possible national reluctance or previous regulation. Since the system created by the Convention is not a consolidated system, it has foreseen an evolution of both the background regulations and the proceedings, by means of two legal techniques available to each of the states: amendment protocols and additional protocols. The first group implies a modification of the text of one of the regulations and requires unanimity on behalf of all the member states. The second group adds optional regulations that have their own independent identity with a limited amount of possible amendments that apply only to a certain number of states.[251]

Thus, implementation by member states has been progressive and each one has chosen its own pace with the ratification of the Convention, optional regulations, new additional protocols and possible reservations. This "changeable geometry" implies some inconvenience, since it can lead to a certain degree of incoherence when not all states agree to the same commitments. But the immense advantage of this way of proceeding is that it prevents delay in signing the Convention, since new commitments can be included in the future. As the Convention approaches its 60th year, there is now a certain harmony in the commitments taken on by states, which proves the success of this way of proceeding.[252]

The Convention has been successively modified and supplemented by 14 protocols, though the last one is not yet in force.[253] The amendment protocols, which depend on ratification by all member states before coming into force, are Protocols Nos. 3, 5, 8, 11 and 14.[254] The additional protocols, which

---

250. "Taking into account that the Convention is a live instrument that must be interpreted according to the conditions of modern-day life … certain acts, previously qualified as inhumane and degrading rather than as torture, could change this qualification in the future" – see *Selmouni v. France*, 29 July 1999, paragraph 101.

251. See Pettiti, L-E., Decaux, E., Imbert, P-H., *La Convention européenne des droits de l'homme. Commentaire article par article*, Economica, 1995, p. 20.

252. See Kiss, A., "La Convention européenne des droits de l'homme a-t-elle créé un ordre juridique autonome?", *Mélanges en Hommage à Louis Edmond Pettiti*, Brussels, Bruylant, 1998, pp. 493-505.

253. Having been ratified by three Council of Europe member states, Protocol 14bis entered into force on 1 October 2009.

254. Protocol No. 3, in force since 21 September 1970, Protocol No. 5, in force since 20 December 1971, and Protocol No. 8, in force since 1 January 1990, all refer to the modification of different regulations of the Convention; Protocol No. 11, in force since 1 November 1998, deals with reorganisation of the system of control foreseen by the Convention; and Protocol No. 14 refers to the control reform of the Convention but is not yet in force since ratification by the Russian Federation is still pending.

include rights not previously included in the Convention and bind only the states which have ratified them, are Protocols Nos. 1, 4, 6, 7, 12 and 13. Protocols Nos. 9 and 10 are also additional but do not have a fundamental nature since they do not add any new rights to the catalogue presented in the original document of the Convention. Protocol No. 9 refers only to the assertive legitimisation by the Court;[255] Protocol No. 10 refers to the voting majority required by the Committee of Minister in order to adopt a final and binding decision on matters pertaining to the violation of the Convention if that specific case has not been presented before the Court.[256] Finally, Protocol No. 2 attributes to the Court consultative jurisdiction so that the Committee of Ministers of the Council of Europe can formulate rulings on legal matters pertaining to interpretation of the Convention or its protocols.[257]

Article 1 of the Convention stipulates that the member states recognise for any citizen (not only nationals) under their jurisdiction the rights and freedoms recognised by Part I of the Convention. Consequently, the system foreseen by the Convention accomplishes a dimension that reaches far beyond Europe since it does not concentrate on the nationality of the claim – a characteristic of international responsibility – but on the jurisdiction of the member state on which that citizen depends.[258] The European Commission of Human Rights had already specifically recognised the objective nature of the Convention, when it declared that, in the elaboration of this document, the engaging states had not wanted to grant each other rights and obligations that helped them to reach their personal interests but instead had looked to respect the objectives and ideals of the Council of Europe as they are mentioned in the Statute, as well as to establish a certain public order of European democracies protecting the common heritage of political traditions, ideals, freedoms and the pre-eminence of law.

The Commission also concluded that the obligations agreed to by the states in the Convention were of an objective nature since they aim to protect the fundamental rights of people from the unjustified interference of their nations rather than create subjective rights and obligations between the member states. This objective nature is also evident in the control mechanisms applied in cases of inter-state appeals.[259] Furthermore, the Court has stressed the first ruling

---

255. This Protocol was in a hybrid state, because although its objective was to modify the text of the Convention introducing improvements in the foreseen proceedings, it would come into effect once it had received all ten of the required ratifications and therefore, the states who had not done so would be subject to the original established proceedings. See Decaux, E., op. cit. p. 21.
256. Protocol No. 9, in force since 1 January 1994, and Protocol No. 10, which has not yet come into effect since it has not been ratified by all the states.
257. In force since 21 September 1970, and abolished by Protocol No. 11.
258. *Loizidou v. Turkey*, "Preliminary objections", 18 December 1996, paragraphs 23 to 24 and *Ilaşcu and others v. Moldavia and Russia*, 8 July 2004. In this sense, see *Liber Amicorum J.A. Pastor Ridruejo*, UCM, Madrid, 2005, p. 219.
259. *Austria v. Italy*, Application No. 788/60, Decision of the Commission on admissibility, 11 January 1961, *Yearbook 4*, paragraphs 139 to 141.

derived from an inter-state appeal in which, as opposed to what happens with classic international treaties, the Convention goes beyond the usual framework of reciprocity between engaging states, establishing a series of objective obligations that, in accordance with the terms included in the Preamble, benefit from collective guarantees.[260] On this occasion, the European judge stressed the specificity of the Convention since it closely relates the objective nature of the regulation with the collective guarantee of its institutional expression.

The Convention is more than just a series of inter-state commitments since it guarantees that states, in the name of common and superior values, will protect the interests of their citizens at the same time as it creates objective obligations to be respected by the nations, not as a counterpart of the rights granted to member states, but as a series of commitments taken on with respect to the people. Its objective nature as an instrument of protection of human beings creates a common solidarity that is expressed in the establishment of a collective guarantee that characterises the Convention.[261] These characteristics evidence the unique character and constitutional dimension of the Convention as an international legal instrument of European public order.[262]

10.1.5. The European Court of Human Rights

The uniqueness of the Convention does not lie in the catalogue of protected rights, but in the creation of a supervisory mechanism that originally consisted of an investigation and conciliation body (the Commission), a political decision-making body (the Committee of Ministers) and a legal body (the European Court of Human Rights). These were all merged into one single body, following the entrance in force of Protocol No. 11, represented by the European Court of Human Rights.

From this starting point of consolidated jurisprudence, the Court has specified the real meaning of the Convention by formulating a series of principles that have developed simultaneously with the profound changes that have taken place in Europe since the 1950s. These principles evidence the evolving nature of the Convention, which was originally interpreted according to the classic principles of international law but is now considered a constitutional instrument of European public order.[263]

European Law frequently reminds us that the Convention has to be interpreted in the light of current circumstances,[264] and it will not cease to be

---

260. *Ireland v. the United Kingdom*, 18 January 1978, Series A, No. 25, paragraph 239.

261. *Berktay v. Turkey*, 1 June 2001, paragraph 151 and *Soering v. the UK*, 7 July 1989, paragraph 87.

262. *Loizidou v. Turkey*, paragraph 70.

263. Costa, J. P., "La Cour européenne des droits de l'homme: vers un ordre juridique européen", *Mélanges en hommage à Louis Edmond Pettiti*, Bruylant, Brussels, 1998.

264. *Airey v. Ireland*, 9 October 1979, paragraph 26.

influenced by the evolution of generally accepted regulations.[265] Therefore, each concept must be interpreted not in the literal sense of the Convention text, but according to the meaning established by democratic societies at the time of the matter being debated. The evolving interpretation is thus the correct one, not only because it adheres to the principle of development of rights but also because it is specified in the Preamble to the Convention and it pertains to constantly evolving social situations.[266] However, a European judge must not become involved in issues that affect the national politics of member states, since the judge's mission is to provide the legal text with its full meaning without varying its content.[267]

In this way the Court accepts that, although it must not willingly ignore a precedent without a valid reason, its first obligation is to guarantee the effectiveness of human rights through interpretation of the Convention, and it is therefore important to maintain a dynamic and evolving perspective on the different issues in order to re-evaluate the interpretation criteria and application of the Convention according to current social conditions.[268] Therefore, the Court adapts the Convention to social changes involving the rights of natural children, criminal repression of homosexuality, corporal punishment, transsexualism or the concept of family.[269] Since the Convention can only be interpreted by the European judge, it is the judge's responsibility to adapt it in line with changes in customs and mentalities in order to protect it from possible anachronisms and rid it of regulations that are no longer applicable.

We can clearly see the evolving nature of European jurisprudence, as it aims to ensure the rights guaranteed by the Convention, in the use of two techniques that can broaden the application of a right or extend its content: autonomous interpretation and positive duties.

The technique of autonomous interpretation is one of the basic interpretative principles used by the Court to remedy the imprecision of conventional terms as well as the lack of homogeneity of national rights, permitting a standard definition of state commitments. Many of the terms used in the Convention and additional protocols come from ideas taken from the legal systems of member states. If those terms were to be interpreted according to the relative reach and scope of each state, the level of protection offered by the Convention would be anything but uniform. To avoid this, all vague terms taken from different national systems that can lead to diverse interpretations are reinterpreted in

---

265. *Soering v. the UK*, paragraph 102; *Tyrer v. the UK*, 25 Apr 1978, paragraph 31 and *Loizidou v. the UK*, paragraph 71.
266. *Selmouni v. France*, 28 July 1999, paragraph 101.
267. *Johnston v. Ireland*, 18 Dec 1986, paragraph 77.
268. *Goodwin v. the United Kingdom*, 11 July 2002, paragraphs 74 to 75.
269. *Moldovan and others v. Romania*, 12 July 2005, paragraph 105; *Laskey, Jaggard and Brown v. the United Kingdom*, 19 February 1995, paragraph 36, and *E.B. v. France*, 22 January 2008, paragraph 96.

the European context by the Court. With this measure, the objective of the Court is to establish common ground for future constitutional human rights and to achieve a certain coherence with regard to a democratic society and the pre-eminence of law.

European judges have made use of this interpretation of the term "autonomous" in debates on rights, including property rights, freedom and safety rights, freedom of association rights, the principle of the legality of offences and sentences, and the right to respect for home and family life. Criminal matters[270] and civil rights and obligations[271] are clear examples of cases in which the law considers that, since these concepts are quite vague or misleading, they should be interpreted not according to national law but instead under the autonomous interpretation of the Convention and should thus be given a European sense to reinforce the effectiveness of the guaranteed rights.[272] In accordance with the jurisprudence of the Court, no disputes on fiscal matters, immigration and nationality issues, passport issuances, military service and patents would fall under Article 6. However, the previous regulation would apply to disputes on disciplinary measures and social content.

The principle of autonomous interpretations possesses two essential characteristics. First, it does not refer to the conditions in which the right can be exercised but to the applicability of the right. For example, the concepts "rights and obligations of a civil nature" and "accusations in criminal matters" would refer to the idea of the right to a fair trial, while the concept of "sentence" would refer to the principle of lawfulness of offences and sentences. Secondly, these concepts are interpreted differently than in internal law.[273] For example, in the *Engel* case, in accordance with Dutch law the sanctions were interpreted as "disciplinary" rather than "criminal". In these cases, the Court believes that if the nations could make discretionary interpretations of infractions as disciplinary rather than criminal, or could choose to prosecute the author of a mixed infraction under a disciplinary proceeding rather than a

---

270. *Engel and others v. the Netherlands*, 19 July 1974.

271. *Köning v. Germany*, 28 June 1978.

272. The Court must first ascertain whether there was a dispute over a "right" within the meaning of Article 6 paragraph 1 which can be said, at least on arguable grounds, to be recognised under domestic law. The dispute must be genuine and serious; it may relate not only to the actual existence of a right but also to its scope and the manner of its exercise, and the result of the proceedings must be directly decisive for the right in question. Finally, the right must be of a "civil" character (see, for example, *Zander v. Sweden*, 25 November 1993, Series A No. 279-B, paragraph 22). Article 6 paragraph 1 of the Convention is not aimed at creating new substantive rights without a legal basis in the contracting state, but at providing procedural protection of rights already recognised in domestic law (see, for example, *W. v. the United Kingdom*, 8 July 1987, Series A No. 121, paragraph 73). The term "right" must nevertheless be given an autonomous interpretation under Article 6 paragraph 1 of the Convention (see, for example, *König v. Germany*, 28 June 1978, Series A No. 27, paragraphs 88 to 89), *Posti and Rahko v. Finland*, 24 September 2002, paragraphs 50 to 51.

273. Sudre, F., *Droit européen et international des droits de l'homme*, 9th edn, PUF, 2008, p. 242.

criminal one, the fundamental clauses of Articles 6 and 7 would be completely subject to the nation's sovereign will. This posture would risk bringing about a solution that could be completely incompatible with the nature and object of the Convention.[274]

On the other hand, European law uses the positive duties technique to guarantee the full enjoyment of human rights. The concept of positive duty was developed and systematically incorporated into European jurisprudence in order to avoid a misunderstanding such as the one generated by the "International Covenant on Civil, Political, Economic, Social and Cultural Rights of the United Nations" of 1966. Traditionally, it was considered that civil and political rights required restraint from the state, whereas economic, social and cultural rights required a positive attitude from the state. However, this difference is refuted in practice, since many civil and political rights require the state's provision, such as happens with the right to a fair trial or the right to education. Conversely, certain rights included in the second category are of a mixed nature and require the adoption of certain measures by the state.

As the Court has reiterated, the Convention aims to protect concrete and effective rights rather than non-theoretical or imaginary rights.[275] It is therefore important to give individuals the opportunity to effectively exercise these rights, and also to demand that the state adopt positive and adequate measures to protect all the rights derived from the Convention.[276] The Court has recognised the possibility of applying the positive duties theory to all the different rights, making its scope global. Some examples include the right to education,[277] the right to home and family life[278] and the right to a fair trial.[279]

---

274. *Engel v. Pays-Bas*, paragraph 81. Following the jurisprudence of the European Court, the concept of " rights and obligations of a civil character" cannot be interpreted only by reference to the internal law of the defendant state. Repeatedly the Court has asserted the principle of "autonomy" related to this concept, in the sense of Article 6 paragraph 1 (see, among others, *König v. Germany*, 28 June 1978, series A No. 27, paragraphs 88 to 89, and *Baraona v. Portugal*, 8 July 1987, series A No. 122, paragraph 42). The Court affirms this jurisprudence, considering a different solution might lead to incompatible results with the object and purpose of the Convention (see, *mutatis mutandis*, dicta quoted before *König*, paragraph 88, and *Maaouia v. France* [GC], No. 39652/98, paragraph 34, CEDH 2000-X).

275. *Airey v. Ireland*, paragraph 26.

276. *López Ostra v. Spain*, 9 December 1994, paragraph 51.

277. *Affaire linguistique belge v. Belgium*, 23 July 1968, paragraph 3.

278. *Marckx v. Belgium*, 13 June 1979, paragraph 58.

279. The Court recalls the first sentence of Article 2, set among the main Articles of the Convention as it establishes the fundamental values of the democratic societies constituting the Council of Europe (*McCann and others v. the UK*, sentence of 27 Sep 1995, series A No. 324, paragraph 147), which requires the state not only to refrain from causing death "intentionally" but also to take the necessary measures to protect the life of people under its jurisdiction (see for instance *L.C.B. v. the UK*, sentence of 9 June 1998, Collection of *Sentences and Decisions* 1998-III, page 1403. These principles are also applied in the field of public health. The positive obligations involve the state setting up a regulatory framework forcing hospitals, public or private, to adopt certain measures, helping to protect the life of those who are ill. It is also about establishing an efficient, independent judiciary system that can establish the cause of death of a person who is

One of the most important functions of jurisprudence is to take significant cases and extract from them principles of a constitutional nature that later result in new rules in the European legal order. Despite the great increase in lawsuits before the Court, which have threatened to overwhelm and paralyse the system, some voices have suggested taking away the Court's repairing role and appointing it only with a constitutional role to arrive at decisions of principle that would generate European jurisprudence.

The Convention has thus created and developed a truly European legal order in human rights. The framework and material content of these regulations was progressively developed by the jurisprudence of the (old) Commission and Court. The Commission's statement describing the system established by the Convention as "a communitarian public order of European free democracies" was subsequently included by the court in an opinion issued on the reform of the monitoring mechanism, describing it as a "European Constitution of Human Rights".[280] The same idea appears in the *Loizidou* case in which the Court refers to the Convention as an "instrument of human beings", a "constitutional instrument of European public order" or a "European instrument of public order for the protection of human beings".[281]

The *Loizidou* case was in fact an important step forward in the consideration of the Convention as an instrument of a constitutional nature. The excessive specifications of the Convention had already been highlighted by the Commission when it abolished the principle of the reciprocity of the judicial order of human rights due to the objective nature of the duties derived from the Convention (p. 42). The Court also appealed to this principle when it declared in the *Ireland v. the UK* case that the Convention generates objective obligations in accordance with its Preamble that benefit from a recognised collective guarantee that, as established by Article I, applies to every person under the jurisdiction of the engaging states (p. 239).

The doctrine has several times established the similarities between the Convention and a constitutional instrument. Thus, Velu and Ergec speak of a "European constitution in matters of freedom"[282] and Sudre refers to a "true constitutional Charter of the Greater Europe".[283] Apart from what is stated in its Preamble, the object of the Convention is to lead to a more united front among members of the Council of Europe "by means of the protection

---

under the responsibility of a health professional, whether in the public or private sector, should the case arise, and oblige them to account for their actions (*Powell v. the UK* (dec.), No. 45305/99, CEDH 2000-V; *Calvelli and Ciglio*, sentence quoted before, paragraph 49).

280. Conseil de l'Europe, *Réforme du système de contrôle de la Convention européenne des droits de l'homme*, doc. H (92)14, p. 48.

281. *Loizidou*, paragraphs 72, 75 and 93.

282. Velu, J. and Ergec, R., *La Convention européenne des droits de l'homme*, Brussels, Bruylant, 1990, p. 53, No. 16.

283. Sudre, F., "L'Europe des droits de l'Homme", in *L'Europe et le droit*, Droits No. 14, 1991, p. 105.

and development of human rights and fundamental freedoms", thus helping to establish a series of common rights in European human rights issues.[284]

Nevertheless, the existence of a European public order does not mean that the Convention is a European *ius commune* of human rights. The Convention and its additional protocols of a legal nature establish a structure of legal regulations that do not constitute a common system of European human rights, due to the fragmentation and relativism that limit its scope. We must not forget that the European system of protecting human rights has been created by treaties, in which the consent of sovereign states determines their legal obligations in three ways: first, although the Convention has been ratified by all the states, not all of them are obliged by all the additional protocols that expand the list of rights and freedoms;[285] secondly, states can express reservations and make interpretation statements at the time of ratifying the Convention (and later any of its additional protocols) that exclude or interpret in a subjective way the obligations contracted by the member state; and, thirdly, the regulations of the Convention and the legal protocols allow limitation of their territorial scope.

Therefore, the Convention suffers from a certain degree of relativism and fragmentation that limits its scope, regardless of its undeniable constitutional dimension as a legal instrument that establishes a European public order of human rights. The true European *ius commune* of human rights will not exist until all the member states of the Council of Europe take part in the Convention and in all the additional legal protocols that have progressively expanded the catalogue of rights and freedoms.[286]

10.2. Government and public administration

The Court has expressly referred many times to "executive powers" and has delimited executive functions in relation to other public powers, especially judicial powers in order to preserve independence of the courts. In European Court of Human Rights case law, "government and public administration" are identified with the performance of certain public functions directly linked with discretionary powers, with the powers conferred by public law and, ultimately, with the state's sovereign power.

The recent use of the functional approach to characterise "government and public administration" should be stressed. Historically, and in consonance with national traditions, the nature of the law, public or private, governing the public entities was considered the decisive criterion in the resolutions

---

284. De Salvia, M., "L'élaboration d'un *jus commune* des droits de l'homme et des libertés fondamentales dans la perspective de l'unité européenne: l'œuvre accompli par la Commission et la Cour européenne de droits de l'homme" in *Protection des droits de l'homme: la dimension européenne – Mélanges en l'honneur de Gérard Wiarda*, Köln, Carl Heymans Verlag, 1988, pp. 555ff.
285. See *Soering v. the United Kingdom.*
286. Carrillo Salcedo, J. A., *El Convenio europeo de derechos humanos*, Tecnos, Madrid, 2003, p. 32.

of the Strasbourg Court. In fact, the Court used to apply the latter approach, gradually introducing functional considerations to the point of establishing a functional criterion as the general rule.[287] However, it is hard to distinguish between the two concepts, because of the breadth with which the concept "government" is interpreted and the indirect references to the concept of "public administration" which arise from decisions concerning government employees.

These resolutions have been based on two specific groups of case law: one determining what the word "government" means with respect to the admissibility of a complaint; the other deciding whether a dispute with civil servants or public employees falls within the scope of Article 6 of the Convention, the right to a fair trial. We briefly explain these criteria which, in general, shape the Court's approach to the concept of government.

The word "government", as regards matters dealt with here, appears in the expression "non-governmental organisation" which, along with "any person" and "groups of individuals", signifies a party that can present individual applications before the Court, according to Article 34 of the Convention. On the other hand, the previous Article 34 recognises "High Contracting Parties" as applicants in inter-state cases.

Many applications have been presented by public bodies trying to qualify as a "non-governmental organisation" under Article 34 and, by this route, gain access to the Judges in Strasbourg. The Court applies a functional criterion and, because these were public law bodies performing official duties, it declared inadmissible the applications presented by a city council (in spite of its statements of independence from the government), the General Council of an official economists' association (as a public-law corporation performing official duties assigned by the constitution and by statute) and a national railway company (because its board of directors were answerable to the government and it was regulated by public law).[288]

All these statements are based on a specific concept of "governmental organisations" in international law, by which this phrase "cannot be held to refer only to the Government or the central organs of the State. Where powers are distributed along decentralised lines, it refers to any national authority which exercises public functions."[289]

The Court's criterion for what should be considered "public administration" comes from the case law relating to disputes between public employees and

---

287. In this regard, and concerning public employees, governed by public or private law, the Courts underline that they, "in the current practice … perform equivalent or similar duties": European Court of Human Rights, judgment of 8 December 1999, case *Pellegrini v. France*, paragraph 59.
288. Decisions of the Commission 7 January 1991 (*M. Council v. Spain*), 28 June 1995 (*Consejo General de Colegios Oficiales de Economisatas de España v. Spain*), 8 Sep 1997 (*RENFE v. Spain*).
289. See Decision of the Court of 1 February 2001, *Mula Borough Council v. Spain.*

public (governmental) employers. Specifically the issue was whether or not the "right to a fair trial" in disputes of a "civil nature" should be applied in these cases. Initially, the Court fully accepted the distinction contained in many national laws between civil servants, submitted to a public law regimen, and employees governed by private law. This led the Court to hold that "disputes relating to the recruitment, careers and termination of service of civil servants are as a general rule outside the scope of Article 6 paragraph 1". This exclusion is explained by the existence of "some post in the public service with responsibilities affecting matters of general interest or entailing the exercise of public authority to which States are entitled to make appointments at their discretion".[290]

This general rule has its exceptions. Certain criteria do admit submission of "civil" disputes of public employees, even civil servants, to the check provided by Article 6.1. "According to other judgments, Article 6.1 applies where the claim in issue relates to a 'purely economic' right – such as payment of salary … or an 'essentially economic' one … and does not mainly call into question 'the authorities' discretionary powers'."[291]

However, the exact application of these criteria, and above all the aim of avoiding discriminatory situations, led the Judges in Strasbourg to adopt a new criterion in the well-known Pellegrini case. Since then, the Court has adopted a functional criterion based on the nature of the employees' duties and responsibilities, and it only excludes from the scope of Article 6.1 disputes which are raised by public servants whose

> duties typify the specific activities of the public service in so far as the latter is acting as the depositary of public authority responsible for protecting the general interests of the State or other public authorities … In practice, the Court will ascertain, in each case, whether the applicant's post entails – in the light of the nature of the duties and responsibilities appertaining to it – direct or indirect participation in the exercise of powers conferred by public law and duties designed to safeguard the general interests of the State or of other public authorities.[292]

10.3. Judicial review of government and administration

Submission of public activity to judicial control is either a rule-of-law requirement or a consequence of the right to a fair trial granted by the Convention, which however does not include any specific provision declaring the general

---

290. European Court of Human Rights, judgment of 17 March 1997, *Neigel v. France*, paragraphs 42, 43.
291. European Court of Human Rights, judgment of 8 December 1999, *Pellegrin v. France*, paragraph 59, referring to previous case law whose criteria were abandoned in this resolution.
292. See paragraph 66. This new functional approach was applied in European Court of Human Rights, 9 November 2006, *Stojakovic v. Austria*, paragraph 39.

submission of public powers to the law.[293] However, the Strasbourg Court has repeatedly referred to the tradition of the rule of law as an underlying principle when applying the right to a fair trial granted by Article 6.1 of the Convention ("In the determination of his civil rights and obligations ..., everyone is entitled to a fair ... hearing ... by an independent ... tribunal"). In 1975 it declared, "by reference to the principles of the rule of law and the avoidance of arbitrary power underlying much of the Convention, that the right of access to a court was an inherent aspect of the safeguards enshrined in Article 6".[294]

On the other hand, in states governed by the rule of law, the administration is subject to the law and supervision by the courts on the same basis as any individual and any citizens, in accordance with the principle of pre-eminence of the law.

The precedent considerations explain the fact that, although the Convention was not originally intended to apply to administrative proceedings, the Council of Europe has stated clear criteria on the standard of judicial review as it relates to public activities, both in its case law and in the acts adopted by the Council of Ministers. In particular, Rec(2004)20[295] of the Committee of Ministers on judicial review of administrative acts holds a pre-eminent place in European public law, notwithstanding its non-binding effect. This recommendation includes a cluster of common general rules taking into account the peculiarities of national law, and in some ways it codifies the Court's existing case law. Consequently, the unavoidable conclusion is that it represents the European standard on judicial review as required by the rule-of-law tradition.

Recommendation (2004)20 sets out five groups of principles on the scope of judicial review – access to it, the independence and impartiality of the courts, the right to a fair trial, the effectiveness of judicial review – and two essential concepts, "administrative act" and "judicial review":

– The phrase "administrative acts" includes:

- Legal acts (individual and normative) and physical acts of the administration taken in the exercise of public authority which may affect the rights or interests of natural or legal persons;

- Situations of refusal (or omission) to act in cases where the administrative authority is obligated to implement a procedure following a request,

– The phrase "judicial review" means the examination and determination by a tribunal of the lawfulness of an administrative act and the adoption of appropriate measures, with the exercise of review by a constitutional court.

---

293. Although the Statute of the Council of Europe (1949, Article 3) states that "Every member of the Council of Europe must accept the principles of the rule of law and of the enjoyment by all persons within its jurisdiction of human rights and fundamental freedoms".
294. European Court of Human Rights, judgment of 21 February 1975, *Golder v. UK*, paragraphs 28 to 36.
295. Adopted on 15 December 2004. Rec(2004)20 is reproduced in the Appendix to this work.

On the case law developed by Article 6.1 of the Convention, and related to what we are dealing with, some national particularities should be pointed out. In national systems, the submission of public powers to the law is commonly a constitutional requirement, as it is included in both the Constitution and the legislation that details the kinds of public activities submitted to judicial controls. The system at the Council of Europe reaches similar results, but it starts from different premises. The deciding factor in the European system is the alleged threat to a right granted by the Convention, whatever the threatening activity. On the other hand, submission of the threatening activity to judicial scrutiny is usually caused by the exercise of rights provided by Article 6.1 of the Convention. By this criterion, a wide range of national activities – legislative, executive and judicial – falls under the Court's jurisdiction. On judicial activities, it should be pointed out that it is not the function of the Court "to deal with errors of fact or law allegedly committed by a national court unless and in so far as they may have infringed rights and freedoms protected by the Convention".[296] Naturally, there are some exceptions to and many nuances in this general rule, first being the exceptions imposed by rule-of-law requirements, particularly the principle of separation of powers.

The principle of separation of powers legitimately excludes from judicial scrutiny the state's fundamental political decisions, separating the judiciary from the tasks of identifying objectives that serve the general interest and choosing the means to achieve them. A specific consequence of this general rule affects the right of access to a court with respect to some types of activity legitimately excluded from review by the courts, categories covered by the concept of "act of government" as used in comparative law and international law. Typical examples are the acts adopted in areas such as foreign affairs, national defence and general security. We refer to this doctrine below.

From another perspective, the actual submission of public activities to the tribunal's reviews requires the previous determination of what a "tribunal" or a "court" is in the sense of Article 6.1, that is, the previous definition of the kind of court that will protect the applicant's rights of a civil nature against unlawful public interference.

There is a huge volume of Strasbourg Court case law on the "independence" of the tribunal, which is also required by Article 6.1. In these resolutions, the Court has set limits for legislative and executive bodies, rules that must be observed in the judicial bodies themselves and specific requirements of the personal status of judges or the exercise of their functions.

However, beyond this case law there are other judgments helping to establish the essence of judicial functions – in the sense intended in Article 6 – that

---

296. European Court of Human Rights, judgment of 14 December 2006, *Markovic and others v. Italy*, paragraph 107, underlying the subsidiary role of the Court in Strasbourg with respect to national courts in implementing the Convention (paragraph 109).

is, "determining matters within its competence on the basis of rule of law and after proceedings conducted in a prescribed manner".[297] In one particular case, applying this perspective and considering that the scope of the review exercised in the applicant's case was not sufficient, the Court rejected the view that a Constitutional Court can be a "tribunal" under the meaning of Article 6.1 of the Convention.[298]

10.3.1. Judicial independence from the executive

Judicial independence, highly protected by the Court, precludes any interference influencing the judicial determination of a dispute. The concept is based on its double condition of being an essential of the rule-of-law tradition and a requirement imposed by the right to a fair trial in Article 6 of the Convention.[299] It protects judicial activity against alleged interference from executive and legislative bodies, and also excludes some specific behaviours in the judicial power itself. In order to establish whether a tribunal can be considered "independent", the Court reiterates that "regard must be had, *inter alia*, to the manner of appointment of its members and their term of office, the existence of guarantees against outside pressures and to the question whether the body presents an appearance of independence".[300] Rec(2004)20 submits the "independence and impartiality" of tribunals to the conditions stated in an earlier recommendation.[301]

In the Chevrol case,[302] the Court summarised its previous case law and described the content and requirements imposed by judicial independence in regard to executive bodies. A French legal provision was challenged because it obliged French courts to require the opinion of the Ministry of Foreign Affairs about a reciprocity clause in an international agreement. The French Government supported this regulation on the basis that foreign policy is a government prerogative, and assessment of the conduct of a foreign state was a more natural task for diplomatic authorities than for the courts. The Court in this judgment stated the following:

– First, what does the "court's independence" mean? In Strasbourg case law, "the court's independence from the parties and the executive means that, where it was dealing with a dispute that came within its jurisdic-

---

297. European Court of Human Rights, judgment, 9 November 2006, *Stojakovic v. Austria*, paragraph 46.
298. Ibid., paragraph 45, recalling previous similar statements.
299. European Court of Human Rights, judgment of 28 October 1999, *Zielinski and Pradak and Gonzalez and others v. France*.
300. European Court of Human Rights, judgment of 27 November 2008, *Miroshnik v. Ukraine*, paragraph 61.
301. R (1994) 12 of the Committee of Ministers on the independence, efficiency and role of judges.
302. Judgment given on 13 February 2003.

tion, it could not have the solution dictated to it by one of the parties or by a representative of the executive."[303]

– Second, "interpreting legal rules" is "one of the fundamental tasks of a court, which it cannot abandon without "mutilating" its judicial function. The Court admits that the external assessment could be suitable and convenient in order to determine whether or not, in a particular case, the treaty has been applied by the other contracting state. The courts may be required to consult with the Ministry of Foreign Affairs, which, by its very nature, will be likely to possess information about that state's application of the treaty.[304]

– Third, it clearly rejects the view that this opinion could be binding on the court, in that its decision could not be "solely" based on the opinion of administrative authorities. The Court considers that, in doing so, the "*Conseil d'Etat* considered itself to be bound by the opinion, thereby voluntarily depriving itself of the power to examine and take into account factual evidence that could have been crucial for the practical resolution of the dispute before it."[305]

– Fourth, consequently, an applicant's rights of defence granted under Article 6 of the Convention had been breached, in that he "cannot be considered to have had access to a tribunal which had, or had accepted, sufficient jurisdiction to examine all the factual and legal issues relevant to the determination of the dispute (see, among other authorities, *Terra Woningen B.V*).["][306]

In the area of relations with the executive power, the Court has also examined various cases relating to the independence of the military courts. In a recent case the Court declared the lack of independence of a military court in spite of there being guarantees of the independence of its judges provided, *inter alia*, by the manner of their appointment, the term of their office, their inviolability and the prohibition of interference with the administration of justice. However, there were some conditions which justified the applicant's doubts about its independence, such as the fact that the judges of the military courts were military personnel and thus they constituted a part of the staff of the Armed Forces subordinate to the Ministry of Defence, which was coincidentally the competent body to provide the judges of the military courts with appropriate flats or houses if they needed to improve their living conditions.[307]

On judicial independence from the legislative power also, there are often-repeated criteria, especially on new regulations liable to affect pending cases

---

303. Ibid., point 64.
304. Ibid., point 80.
305. Ibid., point 82.
306. Ibid., point 83.
307. See the previously cited case, *Miroshnik v. Ukrania*, paragraph 62.

before the courts. The Court has held that the rule-of-law principle and the notion of a fair trial preclude any interference by the legislature – unless on grounds of compelling general interest – with the administration of justice, if designed to influence judicial determination of a dispute.[308] Thus it declared that Article 6 had been breached because of the retroactive effect of legislative measures on proceedings that the applicants had initiated against the state to claim compensation for pecuniary and non-pecuniary damages.[309] The same conclusion was reached in a case relating to some employees in specialised institutions under state supervision.[310] Considering that they had been only partly remunerated according to the conditions of a collective agreement, they appealed to the courts. While most of their cases were still pending, a new law changing the conditions entered into force. The Court held unanimously that there had been a violation of Article 6.1.

In another similar case, the Court reached a different conclusion. The applicants brought proceedings against plans to build a dam that would result in three nature reserves and a number of small villages being flooded.[311] The national court partly allowed their application in September 1995 and ordered suspension of the work. Later (June 1996) the regional parliament passed a law which amended the rules applicable to conservation areas in nature reserves and, in the applicants' submission, effectively allowed work on the dam to continue. The Constitutional Court was asked to rule on a preliminary question by the applicant as to the constitutionality of certain provisions of the law, which were confirmed. As to the alleged interference by the legislature in the outcome of the dispute, the Court considered that, though enactment of the regional law had indisputably been unsupportive of the applicants' submissions, it could not be said to have been intended to circumvent the principle of the rule of law. The Court therefore held unanimously that there had been no violation of Article 6.1 on that account.

Finally, on the required independence within the judicial power itself, the Court found that there had not been an independent and impartial court in a case where a high court gave directions to the first-instance court in such a way that this latter court had little choice as to how to dispose of the case.[312] Nor is judicial independence respected when a judicial inspector having a decisive role in the functioning of the courts has a double link with the president of the court and the Minister of Justice.[313] Contrary to what occurred in the abovementioned cases, the Court held that Article 6 was not

308. See the already mentioned case *Zielinski and Prada and Gonzalez and Others v. France.*
309. *Draaon v. France* and *Maurice v. France.*
310. European Court of Human Rights, judgment of 9 January 2007, case *Arnolin and 24 others v. France.*
311. European Court of Human Rights, judgment of 27 April 2004, *Gorraiz Lizarraga and others v. Spain.*
312. European Court of Human Rights, judgment of 28 October 1999, *Brumarescu v. Romania.*
313. European Court of Human Rights, judgment of 26 July 2007, *Hirschhorn v. Romania.*

infringed by the mere fact that a member of the court in proceedings involving the applicant was at the material time a member of parliament. It could not find any indication that the judge's membership of a particular political party had had any connection with any of the parties in the case or with the substance of the case.[314]

10.3.2. The scope of judicial review. Political and security questions

The scope of judicial scrutiny of activities that cause breaches in the rights and liberties granted by the Convention is directly linked both to criteria attributing to the contracting parties the responsibility for these breaches and to criteria submitting specific categories of dispute – civil, criminal, administrative, social – to the Court's jurisdiction.

It is first worth recalling the Strasbourg Court's doctrine on "political questions" and "acts of government" which allows some types of public activity to be removed from judicial scrutiny, as required by the principle of separation of powers. The explanations for this are linked to Rec(2004)20, which specifies that it "does not prevent States from defining very limited exceptions established by law, for example certain acts in the field of foreign affairs, international agreements, defence or national security".

On the case-law criteria, the Court has confirmed its doctrine on this category of public activities in the Markovic case, which contains an interesting doctrinal summary of the issue, both in its ruling and in the main and joint dissenting opinions. The applicants' claim concerned deaths resulting from bombing of the radio station in Belgrade as part of NATO operations during the very complex Kosovo conflict. Determination of the merits of the claim would inevitably involve the national courts having to decide questions about the legality of the operation as a matter of international law, as well as reviewing the legitimacy of acts and decisions of the Italian Government in the exercise of its sovereign powers in the realm of foreign policy and the conduct of hostilities.

Exclusion from judicial review of public activities qualified as "acts of government" is bounded by some limits already stated by the Court. In the Fayed case, the Court found "it would not be consistent with the rule of law in a democratic society or with the basic principle underlying Article 6 paragraph 1" if a state could remove from the jurisdiction of the courts a whole range of civil claims, or confer immunities from civil liability on large groups or categories of persons without restraint or checks by the Convention

---

314. European Court of Human Rights, judgment of 22 June 2004, *Pabla Ky v. Finland*.

enforcement bodies.[315] As a general rule, "the scope of the exclusion clearly cannot extend beyond the bounds laid down in the legal rules that regulate and circumscribe the exercise of the relevant governmental attributions (act of government). The aforesaid legitimate aim cannot go beyond the scope of the discretion which the government authority is entitled to exercise within the limitations imposed by the law".[316]

10.3.2.1. Actions and omissions: the positive obligations

The general obligation assumed by the contracting parties to "secure to everyone within their jurisdiction the rights and freedoms" granted by the Convention (Article 1) has been interpreted in such a way that only a few very specific categories of public activities can be lawfully excluded from judicial control. In this way, the Court has declared that the state exercising its jurisdiction is able "to be held responsible for acts or omissions imputable to it which give rise to an allegation of the infringement of rights and freedoms set forth in the Convention".[317]

This insistent relation linking the public activity with its result – the infringement – explains the wide, non-formalistic conception of "administrative activities" described in Rec(2004)20, covering legal acts, both individual and normative, physical acts of the administration and refusals to act. This broad definition aims "to ensure judicial review of all administrative activities by the Administration". Consequently, the expression "administrative act (*acte de l'administration*)" is preferred to "administrative decision (*acte administrative*)" because this latter expression has very specific connotations in some legal systems, whereas the first "covers a wider area of activities conducted by administrations". Only acts or proceedings of Parliament in its legislative functions and those exceptions defined by the states in the framework of the "acts of governments" doctrine are specifically excluded from this definition.[318]

The Court's doctrine interpreting "actions and omissions" capable of breaching a right granted by the Convention is directly linked with the wide range of obligations that states have assumed to ensure its effectiveness. As a general rule, the state has assumed an obligation not to interfere in the exercise of rights by individuals. However, in some cases this negative obligation may not be enough and then there arise positive obligations making possible the exercise of these rights. This is the case with "right of access to a court". In

---

315. European Court of Human Rights, judgment of 21 September 1994, *Fayed v. UK*, paragraphs 49 to 50.
316. See dissenting opinion of Judge Zegrebelsky in *Markovic and others v. Italy*. This opinion, joined by six other judges, underlines the differences between political acts and acts of governments, and some interesting considerations about the "reason of state".
317. European Court of Human Rights, judgment of 8 July 2004, *Ilaşcu and others v. Moldova and Russia*, paragraph 311.
318. The quoted sentences are taken from Rec(2004)20, page 5.

the Airey case the applicant complained about the prohibitive cost of litigation in proceeding before the High Court. The Judges in Strasbourg considered that the option to appear in person before this court did not, in this case, give the applicant an effective right of access, underlining that "the fulfilment of a duty under the Convention on occasion necessitates some positive action on the part of the State",[319] and moreover that "Article 6.1 may sometimes compel the State to provide for the assistance of a lawyer when such assistance proves indispensable for an effective access to court either because legal representation is rendered compulsory ...".[320] Later, in a similar case, the Court found a violation of Article 6.1 based on lack of legal aid.[321]

Another right to which positive obligations have been repeatedly associated is that granted by Article 11, to demonstrations and peaceful assembly, where a negative conception of the state's obligation to provide has been declared insufficient: "genuine, effective freedom of peaceful assembly cannot be reduced to a mere duty on the part of the State not to interfere: a purely negative conception would not be compatible with the object and purpose of Article 11."[322] In general terms, the Ollinger case summarises the twofold obligations providing this right: "As regards the right to freedom of peaceful assembly as guaranteed by Article 11, the Court reiterates that it comprises negative and positive obligations on the part of the Contracting State. On the one hand, the State is compelled to abstain from interfering with that right, which also extends to a demonstration that may annoy or give offence to persons opposed to the ideas or claims that it is seeking to promote ... On the other hand, States may be required under Article 11 to take positive measures in order to protect a lawful demonstration against counter-demonstrations."[323]

It should be pointed out that the Strasbourg Court is reluctant to spell out a general theory on positive obligations ("the court does not have to develop a general theory of the positive obligations which may flow from the Convention")[324] or to specify the measures that authorities should take to comply with their obligations, though they "must verify that the measures actually taken were appropriate and sufficient"[325] in the case in question.

---

319. European Court of Human Rights, judgment of 9 October 1979, paragraph 24.
320. Ibid., paragraph 26.
321. European Court of Human Rights, judgment of 15 May 2005, *Steel and Morris v. UK*, paragraph 72; it had previously declared: "the question whether the provision of legal aid is necessary for a fair hearing must be determined on the basis of the particular facts and circumstances of each case" (paragraph 61).
322. European Court of Human Rights, judgment of 21 June 1988, *Platform "Ärzte für das Leben" v. Austria*, paragraph 32, where the applicants alleged insufficient police protection during a demonstration.
323. European Court of Human Rights, judgment of 29 June 2006, *Öllinger v. Austria*, paragraphs 35 to 37.
324. *Platform "Ärzte für das Leben"* case, paragraph 31.
325. *Ilaşcu and others* case, paragraph 334.

Finally, the question of who is able to impute to the state such activities and inactivities is also answered in a generous manner. The state could be liable by the acts of "persons acting in an official capacity" (Article 13 of the Convention) even "where its agents are acting *ultra vires* or contrary to instructions. Under the Convention, the state's authorities are strictly liable for the conduct of their subordinates; they are under a duty to impose their will and cannot shelter behind their inability to ensure that it is respected".[326] Furthermore, "the acquiescence or connivance of the authorities of a Contracting State in the acts of private individuals which violate the Convention rights of the other individuals within its jurisdiction may engage the State's responsibility under the Convention".[327]

10.3.2.2. The civil approach to administrative disputes

The right to a fair trial recognised in Article 6 of the Convention refers to "civil rights and obligations" and criminal charges against an individual.

The references to "civil rights and obligations" would eliminate from the application of Article 6 of the Convention the relation between individuals and governments, that is, those relations where typical public power prerogatives are involved. However, the word "civil" is an autonomous concept deriving from the Convention and, according to well-established case law, it cannot be interpreted solely by reference to the respondent state's domestic law. On the contrary, they have to be interpreted according to the Convention's object and purpose, and in the light of present-day conditions in democratic societies: "whether or not a right is to be regarded as civil within the meaning of that expression in the Convention must be determined by reference to the substantive content and effects of the right – and not its legal classification – under the domestic law of the State concerned".[328]

Working in such a way, the Court has extended the applicability of Article 6 to many relationships between citizens and governments, developed through proceedings which in the respondent state would come under public law. The following examples illustrate what disputes between individuals and governments the Court has so far held to be covered by the civil head of Article 6:[329]

> (a) proceedings on expropriation, planning decisions, building permits and, more generally, decisions which interfere with the use or enjoyment of property;[330]

---

326. Ibid., paragraph 319.
327. Ibid., paragraph 318.
328. European Court of Human Rights, judgment of 28 June 1978, *König v. Germany*, paragraph 89.
329. I follow the summary given in the dissenting opinion of Judge Lorenzen, joined by others, in the case *Ferrazzini v. Italy* (European Court of Human Rights, judgment of 12 July 2001). He states there is not a single concept about what is civil, but important elements identified from a huge doctrine produced on a case-by-case basis.
330. See, for example, *Sporrong Lönnroth v. Sweden*, judgment of 23 September 1982, Series A No. 52; *Ettl and Others v. Austria*, *Erkner and Hofauer v. Austria*, and *Poiss v. Austria*, judgments

(b) proceedings on a permit, licence or other act of a public authority, which forms a condition for the legality of a contract between private persons;[331]

(c) proceedings on the grant or revocation of a licence by a public authority which is required in order to carry out certain economic activities;[332]

(d) proceedings on the cancellation or suspension by a public authority of the right to practise a particular profession, etc;[333]

(e) proceedings on damages in administrative proceedings;[334]

(f) proceedings on the obligation to pay contributions to a public security scheme;[335]

(g) proceedings on disputes in the context of employment in the civil service, if "a purely economic right" was asserted (for instance, salary) and "administrative authorities' discretionary powers were not in issue".[336] But if "the economic aspect" was dependent on the prior finding of an unlawful act or based on the exercise of discretionary powers, Article 6 was held not to be applicable.[337]

From a formal perspective, not only administrative resolutions can threaten the liability of the state for breaches to the right of fair trial but this possibility is extended to other activities expressed in normative provision – even in a law passed by Parliament, or in non-statutory acts as Directives, Circulars or Instructions.[338]

Notwithstanding the broad interpretation of the term "civil", linking some classic public-law relations with Article 6, there are many situations where the Court has held this is not applicable to disputes between individuals and government.

In general terms, typical expressions of sovereign powers – such as foreign affairs, national defence and general security – are excluded from judicial scrutiny, as we have explained. Specifically, this approach affects the right

of 23 April 1987, Series A No. 117; *Håkansson and Sturesson v. Sweden*, judgment of 21 February 1990, Series A No. 171-A; and *Mats Jacobsson v. Sweden* and *Skärby v. Sweden*, judgments of 28 June 1990, Series A No. 180-A and B);

331. See, for example, *Ringeisen v. Austria*, judgment of 16 July 1971, Series A No. 13.

332. See, for example, *Benthem v. the Netherlands*, judgment of 23 October 1985, Series A No. 97; *Pudas v. Sweden*, judgment of 27 October 1987, Series A No. 125-A; *Tre Traktörer AB v. Sweden*, judgment of 7 July 1989, Series A No. 159; and *Fredin v. Sweden (No. 1)*, judgment of 18 February 1991, Series A No. 192.

333. See, for example, *König v. Germany*, judgment of 28 June 1978, Series A No. 27, and *Diennet v. France*, judgment of 26 Sep 1995, Series A No. 325.

334. See, for example, *Editions Périscope v. France*, judgment of 26 March 1992, Series A No. 234-B.

335. See, for example, *Feldbrugge v. the Netherlands*, judgment of 29 May 1986, Series A No. 99, and *Deumeland*, cited above.

336. See, for instance, *De Santa v. Italy*, judgment of 2 September 1997, *Reports of Judgments and Decisions* 1997-V.

337. See, for instance, *Spurio v. Italy*, judgment of 2 September 1997, *Reports* 1997-V. In this respect the case law of the Court later changed (see point 6 below, judgment of 8 December 1999 in *Pellegrin v. France*).

338. European Court of Human Rights, judgment of 25 March 1983, *Silver and others v. the UK*.

to stand for election;[339] decisions on entry, stay and deportation of aliens,[340] particularly political asylum or deportation[341] and extradition;[342] and public servants, whether established or under private contract, in posts involving "direct or indirect participation in the exercise of powers conferred by public law and duties designed to safeguard the general interest of the State or of other public authorities".[343]

10.3.3. Access to the courts

"Access to the courts", as part of the right to a fair trial provided in Article 6.1, is particularly protected by the system of the Convention "in view of the prominent place held in a democratic society by the right to a fair trial. It is central to the concept of a fair trial, in civil and criminal proceedings, that a litigant is not denied the opportunity to present his or her case effectively before the court".[344]

Recommendation (2004)20 establishes the following principle:[345]

> Judicial review should be available at least to natural and legal persons in respect of administrative acts that *directly affect their rights or interests*. Member states are encouraged to examine whether access to judicial review *should not also be opened* to associations or other persons and bodies empowered to protect collective or community interest.

From this wording there are two questions to be stressed: first, the capacity to bring court proceedings is directly linked to the existence of "rights and interests worthy of protection", considering these are adversely affected when the legal situation of the applicant is altered; second, the recommendation led governments to provide associations and bodies empowered to protect collective or community interests with access to the courts even "when no direct or particular interest are at issue",[346] with particular reference to environmental and consumers' associations.

Concerning the Strasbourg Court's case law, the outline of the right of access has been developed mainly around two sets of disputes: one delimits the personal characteristic of the applicant, having a strong link with the concept of "victim"; the other states the compatibility with the Convention of the national requirements ruling how access to the courts should be exercised.

---

339. *Pierre-Bloch v. France*, judgment of 21 October 1997, *Reports* 1997-VI, p. 2223.
340. *Maaouia v. France*, No. 39652/98, European Court of Human Rights, 5 October 2000.
341. *Maaouia v. France*.
342. European Court of Human Rights, judgment of 16 April 2002, *Peñafiel Salgado v. Spain.*
343. European Court of Human Rights, judgment of 8 December 1999, *Pellegrin v. France.*
344. European Court of Human Rights, judgment of 9 October 1979, *Airey v. Ireland*, paragraph 24.
345. Principle B, paragraph 2a. Italics added.
346. See Recommendation (2004)20, p. 8.

10.3.3.1. Citizens' standing to sue

Both signatories to the Convention and individuals have a broad basis for access to the Judges in Strasbourg in order to apply for its compliance. The requirements for citizens are in this system based on different premises from those generalised at national or Community level. Here, the regulation is focused on the condition of being a "victim" of a violation of a fundamental right, which is a different request from those referring an individual and direct interest or right, or a similar condition directly affecting an individual. Article 34 of the European Convention establishes that:

> The Court may receive applications from any person, non-governmental organisation or group of individuals claiming to be the victim of a violation by one of the High contracting Parties of the rights set forth in the Convention or the protocols thereto. The High contracting Parties undertake not to hinder in any way the effective exercise of this right.

The term "victim", like "civil", constitutes an autonomous concept which has to be interpreted, considering the aims of the Convention and beyond its meaning in domestic law. The Court puts the accent not on the specific characteristic of the applicant but on the effects of the alleged violation of his/her rights: "The Court points out that, in order to rely on Article 34 of the Convention, two conditions must be met: an applicant must fall into one of the categories of petitioners mentioned in Article 34, and he or she must be able to make out a case that he or she is the victim of a violation of the Convention. According to the Court's case law, the concept of 'victim' must be interpreted autonomously and irrespective of domestic concepts such as those concerning an interest or capacity to act. In addition, in order for an applicant to be able to claim to be a victim of a violation of the Convention, there must be a sufficiently direct link between the applicant and the harm which they consider they have sustained on account of the alleged violation".[347]

10.3.3.2. Public interest litigation

A generous consideration of this concept may be found in a case where the Court interpreted the national requirements imposed on foreign associations in general, and, particularly, two foreign associations complaining of defamation.[348] Their complaints and further appeals were dismissed on the grounds that they had not complied with the statutory procedure which all associations, both French and foreign, were required to follow to obtain capacity to take part in proceedings. The Court found that the national authorities, going beyond penalising the failure to comply with a simple formal step necessary to protect public order and third parties, had also imposed a restriction on the applicant association which infringed the essence of their right of access to court.

---

347. European Court of Human Rights, judgment of 27 April 2004, *Gorraiz Lizarraga and others v. Spain*, paragraph 34, quoting the previous case law.
348. European Court of Human Rights, judgment of 15 January 2009, *Ligue du Monde Islamique and Organisation Islamique Mondiale du Secours Islamique v. France*.

In contrast to this broad interpretation, the Court has taken a restrictive approach in order to enlarge the interpretation of "non-governmental association", going so far as to include in such a concept public bodies independent of government, recognising for them the right to bring an action before it. We have already mentioned the refusal to give the condition of "non-governmental association" to a city council, to a professional corporation and to a public company providing public services.[349]

From another perspective, the full rigour affirming the right of access does not preclude national requirements ruling its exercise. This right "is not, however, absolute and may be subject to restrictions, provided that these pursue a legitimate aim and are proportionate".[350] Naturally, the legality of these preconditions for enjoyment of the judicial guarantees stated in Article 6 is subordinate to compliance with the principles of the Convention. In *Z. and other v. the UK*, the Court established this condition of compatibility, stating that the right of the access to a court

> is not absolute, however. It may be subject to legitimate restrictions such as statutory limitation periods, security for costs orders, regulations concerning minors and persons of unsound mind .... Where the individual's access is limited either by operation of law or in fact, the Court will examine whether the limitation imposed impaired the essence of the right and, in particular, whether it pursued a legitimate aim and there was a reasonable relationship of proportionality between the means employed and the aim sought to be achieved ... If the restriction is compatible with these principles, no violation of Article 6 will arise.[351]

In examining this compatibility, the Court has created a very detailed doctrine identifying these kinds of procedural conditions,[352] distinguishing between two main kinds of requirement: "the distinction between substantive limitations and procedural bars determines the applicability and ... the scope of the guarantees under Article 6, which can, in principle, have no application to substantive limitations on the right existing under domestic law".[353] This doctrine is laid down over the previous one stating that "the Court may not create by the way of interpretation of Article 6.1 a substantive right which has no legal basis in the State concerned".[354]

According to this conceptual framework, the Court will set the specific national limit which is alleged inconsistent with the right granted in Article 6 in one or another category and from this deduce its admissibility. Thereby, in *Z. and*

---

349. See section 10.2 on Government and public administration.
350. European Court of Human Rights, judgment of 28 May 1985, *Ashingdame v. the UK*, paragraph 57.
351. European Court of Human Rights, judgment of 10 May 2001, *Z. and others v. the UK*, paragraph 93.
352. The European Court of Human Rights examines severely the "restrictions which are of a purely financial nature and which ... are completely unrelated to the merits of an appeal or its prospects of success" in the Court's judgment of 26 July 2005 *Pobbielski and PPU Polpure v. Poland*.
353. *Markovic* case, paragraph 94.
354. European Court of Human Rights, judgment of 19 October 2005, *Roche v. the UK*, paragraphs 116 to 117.

other v. the UK, the Court held that the category of "political act" could not be considered a "procedural bar" to the domestic courts' power to determine a substantive right, but was rather a limitation on that right.[355] However, this statement should be interpreted carefully, as it was preceded by the qualification of the activity in question as a "political act", a concept which is far from being clearly delimited. On the contrary, the need to distinguish between an "act of government" and "political acts" has been pointed out,[356] just as "the borderline between procedural restrictions and substantive limitations has frequently proved difficult to be drawn in practice".[357]

References

Alcaide Fernández, J., "Orden público y derecho internacional: desarrollo normativo y déficit institucional" in *Soberanía del Estado y Derecho internacional, Homenaje al Profesor Juan Antonio Carrillo Salcedo*, Sevilla, 2005, pp. 91-115.

Almqvist, J., "A human rights critique of European judicial review: counter-terrorism sanctions", *International and Comparative Law Quarterly*, Vol. 57, part 2 (April 2008), pp. 303-331.

Benoit-Rohmer, F. and Klebes, H., *Council of Europe law: towards a pan-European legal area*, Council of Europe Publishing, Strasbourg, 2005.

Berger, V., *Jurisprudence de la Cour Européenne des Droits de l'Homme*, 11th edn, Sirey, Paris, 2009.

Bonnefous, E., *L'Europe en face de son destin*, Éditions du Grand Siècle, PUF, Paris, 1952.

Brugmans, H., *L'idée européenne, 1920-1970*, Collège d'Europe, 1970.

Burban, J.-L., *Le Conseil de l'Europe*, in the series Que Sais-Je?, 3rd edn, PUF, Paris, 1996.

Cohen-Jonathan, G., and Flauss, J-F., *Le rayonnement international de la jurisprudence de la Cour européenne des droits de l'homme*, Bruylant, Brussels, 2005.

Costa, J. P., "La Cour européenne des droits de l'homme: vers un ordre juridique européen", *Mélanges en hommage à Louis Edmond Pettiti*, Bruylant, Brussels, 1998.

Costa, J. P., *L'accès direct à un tribunal spécialisé en matière de droit à l'égalité: l'urgence d'agir au Québec?* (Access to a specialised human rights tribunal: an urgent need to act in Quebec?), Colloquium organised by Le

---

355. European Court of Human Rights, judgment of 10 May 2001, *Z. and others v. the UK*, paragraph 93.
356. See dissenting opinion of Judge Zagrebelsky in the Markovic case.
357. See concurring opinion of Judge Bratza in the Markovic case.

Tribunal des droits de la personne et le Barreau du Québec, Cowansville, Québec: Yvon Blais, 2008, pp. 405-420.

Dalton, H., *High tide and after: memoirs, 1945-1960*, Frederick Muller, London, 1962.

Decaux, E., "Droit déclaratoire et droit programmatoire", *La protection des droits de l'homme et l'évolution du droit international*, Colloquium of Strasbourg, 1998, pp. 81-120.

Decaux, E., "Conseil de l'Europe: structures politiques et administratives", LexisNexis, *Jurisclasseur Europe Traité*, Fascicule 6100, May 2005.

Diez de Velasco, M., *Las Organizaciones Internacionales*, 15th edn, Tecnos, Madrid, 2008.

Harris, D., *The evolution of judicial review of administrative action in the light of the case law of the European Court of Human Rights*, Liber Amicorum Cançado Trindade, Fabris, 2005, pp. 401-415.

Huber, D., *Une déccennie pour l'histoire. Le Conseil de l'Europe, 1989-1999*, Conseil de l'Europe, Strasbourg, 1999.

Kiss, A., *Annuaire Français de Droit International*, Vol. I, Conseil de l'Europe, Strasbourg, 1955, pp. 425-454.

Kiss, A., "La contribution du Conseil de l'Europe au développement du Droit International public", *Mélanges offerts à Polys Modinos*, Pedone, Paris, 1968, pp. 61-70.

Kiss, A., "La Convention européenne des droits de l'homme a-t-elle créé un ordre juridique autonome?" *Mélanges en hommage à Louis Edmond Pettiti*, Brussels, Bruylant, 1998, pp. 493-505.

Martín-Retortillo, L., *La Europa de los derechos humanos*, Ed. CEPC, Madrid, 1998.

Massigli, R., *Une comédie des erreurs*, Plon, 1978.

Pettiti, L.-E., Decaux, E. and Imbert, P.-H., *La Convention européenne des droits de l'homme. Commentaire article par article*, Economica, 1995.

Remiro Brotóns, A., Andrés Sáenz de Santa María, P., Pérez-Prat Durbán, L. and Riquelme Cortado, R., *Los límites de Europa*, Academia Europea de Ciencias y Artes, Spain, 2008, pp. 269-275.

Renucci, J.-F., *Droit européen des droits de l'homme*, Librairie Général de Droit et de Jurisprudence (LGDJ), Paris, 2007.

Rodin, S., "Judicial review and separation of powers in Croatia in light of the German experience", *Journal of Constitutional Law in Eastern and Central Europe*, Vol. 4 (1997), No. 1, pp. 75-107.

Schneider, C. (ed.), "Le Conseil de l'Europe: acteur de la recomposition du territoire européen", *Cahiers de l'Espace Europe* (May 1997), No. 10.

Sudre, F., "L'Europe des droits de l'homme", *L'Europe et le Droit* (1991), No. 14, p. 105.

Sudre, F., *Droit européen et international des droits de l'homme*, 9th edn, PUF, 2008.

Taxil, B., "L'individu entre ordre européen et ordre international: y-a-t-il une spécificité du statut de l'individu en droit européen?", *Annuaire de Droit Européen, 2005*, Vol. III, 2008, pp. 155-182.

Velu, J. and Ergec, R., *La Convention européenne des droits de l'homme*, Bruylant, Brussels, No. 16, 1990, p. 53.

Wakefield, J., *The right to good administration*, Kluwer Law International, Leiden, 2007.

Part III
The European Union legal order

Notice

The recent entry into force of the Lisbon Treaty made an important structural amendment to the European Union legal order. The EU's long integration process had resulted in a structure based on three pillars. However, as of 2 December 2009, this three-fold structure no longer represents the EU's legal architecture. The first pillar was the European Community – created on the basis of the three older European Communities – a supranational structure with institutions empowered to create law directly binding for the member states. This supranational structure was supplemented by more international forms of co-operation that gave rise to the second – Foreign and Security Policy – and the third pillars – Judicial and Police Co-operation. This structure was introduced by the Maastricht Treaty (1992) and was amended by later ones – Amsterdam 1997 and Nice 2001 – which included some of the issues of the third pillar with the Community pillar. Finally, the Lisbon Treaty completes this trend. The Treaty includes the remaining issues from the third pillar in the common institutional framework – now named Justice, Freedom and Security, although, as an exception, it does provide a specific area for the Foreign and Security Policy – the former second pillar.

However, in this section there are frequent references to the old pillars. This is because both the case law and the academic analysis on these issues inevitably refer to the former structures which have been worked on for nearly 20 years. Notwithstanding, the references to the provisions currently in force are made to the new wording stated by the Lisbon Treaty (TEU for Treaty on the European Union and TFEU for the Treaty on the Functioning of the European Union) and, in some cases, we will indicate the correspondence of the old wording with the new one if necessary (that is, if the case law necessarily refers to the former Treaties).

Chapter 11
The EU's first pillar – Constitutional basis

S. Galera

11.1. The constitutional framework

Although the Community legal order is based on texts with the legal nature of international treaties, a constitutional order is affirmed, from a material point of view, by both Community case law and legal doctrine. Hence, while the European Court of Justice (ECJ) has declared treaties to be the "Community basic constitutional order",[358] some scholars consider that the "normative values of which the constitutional and political discourse is an expression"[359] are the basis of the current constitutional architecture in Europe. This position underlies an adapted concept of federalism that rejects its identification with any specific manifestation of the federal state, holding that current European federalism is the product of a set of constitutional norms "in most respects indistinguishable from that which you would find in advanced federal states".[360] From this point of view, the recent debate about the constitutionalisation of Europe which culminated in the Constitutional Treaty is perceived as an ambitious constitutional reform project rather than the making of a constitution.[361]

However, the debate is obviously still open. Even when the "Community constitutional order" is accepted as a reality, attention is immediately drawn to the peculiarities of its so-called *pouvoir constituent*, that is, the absence of a process of constitutional adoption following the classic constitutional order. Other critical voices focus specifically on the substantial differences in content from an orthodox constitutional charter.[362]

Notwithstanding these considerations, our point of departure here is the Community constitutional order, so we are going to describe briefly how this

---

358. ECJ 23 April 1986, Case 294/93, Les Verts, paragraph 23; recently, in ECJ 3 September 2008, Cases C-402/05 P and C-415/05 P, paragraph 21.
359. J. H. H. Weiler, "Federalism and constitutionalism: Europe's *sonderweg*", Jean Monnet Working Paper, New York University 10/2000, available in www.jeanmonnetprogram.org/papers/00/001001-01.html#P8_131.
360. Ibid., referring to the Dan Elazar view on federalism.
361. F. Schorkopf, "Constitutionalization or a constitution for the European Union?" in *The emerging constitutional law of the European Union. German and Polish perspectives*, ed. A. Bodnar, M. Kowalski, K. Raible and F. Schorkopf, Springer, Berlin, 2003, p. 4.
362. See R. Alonso García, *Las sentencias básicas del Tribunal de Justicia de las Comunidades Europeas*, 2nd edn, Madrid, CEC 2003, p. 28.

constitutional order shapes the division of powers among institutions and bodies and how the attributed powers are controlled under the constitutional tradition's requirements.

By working in this way, we confirm the aim that underlies the present study: we accept the fact that we are living in a challenging time in which a new legal order is currently forming. However, we do not attach any creationist theory to this. It is true that national legal tools now do not always work to solve the increasingly interdependent issues of concern to societies and their citizens, but this does not in any way mean that the legal tradition built up over centuries should be abandoned completely. We share the opinion that the constitutional question is not the main issue for Europeans: "The challenge before us is not to invent anything but to conserve the great democratic achievements of the European nation-state beyond its own limits"[363] on the understanding that what will be preserved are the essentials of our democratic and legal tradition.

The constitutional order is shaped by Treaties – the original Treaty and its successive amendments – which articulate an institutional framework distributing public powers and develop an autonomous system of creation of law.[364] Consistent with recognition of the rule-of-law tradition, the constitutional order includes the mechanisms that make possible the control of public activities: "The Community is based on the rule of law, inasmuch as neither its member states nor its institutions can avoid review of the conformity of their acts with the basic constitutional charter, the EC Treaty".[365] In this regard, Article 19 TEU confers exclusive jurisdiction on the European Court of Justice. Finally, this constitutional order grants the protection of fundamental rights, first recognised in a praetorian way, later by text, with a different legal value as well, in such a way that their respect is "a condition of the lawfulness of acts, and measures incompatible with respect for human rights are not acceptable in the Community".[366]

The division of power among Community institutions follows basically the classic three-fold division, with some peculiarities: there is a legislative power, attributed to the Council of Ministers and the European Parliament, with the participation of other bodies; there is an executive power, represented by the European Commission and its bureaucratic organisation; and there is a judicial power, attributed to the jurisdictional European bodies, which must check the legality of Community action.

---

363. J. Habermas, "Why Europe needs a constitution?" in *Developing a constitution for Europe*, ed. E. O. Eriksen, J. E. Fossum and A. J. Menéndez, Routledge, London, 2004, p. 21.
364. It was in the early period that the ECJ affirmed the autonomy of the Community legal order, pointing out its differences with the existing legal order of public international law (Van Gend en Loos, 1964).
365. ECJ 3 August 2008, paragraph 281.
366. ECJ 3 August 2008, paragraph 284.

A quick summary of the peculiarities of this institutional architecture is in order. First, in spite of the autonomy of institutions, the exercise of each of their public functions requires the concurrence of the member states. So, the legislative function is attributed neither only nor mainly to the legislative European body, the European Parliament, but is shared with a Community institution which represents the national interests, the Council. Executive power is attributed to the Commission; however, the public administration that depends on the Commission is not by itself able to deal with one of the main executive functions, namely the administrative implementation of Community law, where the public national administrations have a pre-eminent role. Finally, judicial functions are attributed to the judicial body, the Court of Justice of the European Union, which consists of three courts: the Court of Justice, the General Court (created in 1988) and the Civil Service Tribunal (created in 2004).

The body representing the political driving force in the European Union is the European Council. It is composed of the heads of state and government and the Commission, and has regular meetings, traditionally twice per year, after the six-month presidency. It was informally set up in 1975 and has had formal recognition in treaties through the Single European Act in 1986. Its traditional role has been to provide the European Union with the necessary impetus for its development and to define the general political guidelines, without enacting legislation by itself. The outcome of the European Council deliberations is recorded in conclusions published at the end of the meeting. The Lisbon Treaty introduces two main changes to the European Council. On one hand, the Treaty raises the Council to the category of institution, with important competencies concerning the functioning of the other institutions; on the other hand, it reinforces the Council's stability by providing a presidency for two and a half years.

Following the traditional scheme, the decision-making power in the European Community is shared between the Council of the EU and the European Parliament. The Council has been, up to now, the main decisional body, although the European Parliament has achieved an increased participation in the decisional process; they constitute the main source of secondary law, directives and regulations, -legislative acts after the Lisbon Treaty, which are adopted following the specific procedure provided by the Treaties. Both the Treaties and secondary provisions have primacy over national law and over each of the public national powers. An updated version of primacy stresses this principle which, "initially referred to in *Costa*, … in the words of another great French legal writer, defined that basic concept with respect to law as a whole. In the event of conflict, that principle stipulates that law takes precedence vis-à-vis the government and administrative authorities, the legislature and the judiciary".[367]

---

367. See Opinion of Advocate General Ruiz-Jarabo Colomer, 18 May 2006, Case C-232/05, paragraph 49, with reference to D. Simon, *Le système juridique communautaire*, 3rd edn, PUF, Paris, 2001, p. 410.

The Council of the European Union, also known as the Council of Ministers or, since the Lisbon Treaty, simply as the Council, represents the national interest before the institutional system. It is made up of one ministerial representative of each member state, its composition depending on the kind of policy that is going to be dealt with in the meeting, with up to nine different configurations. Each national representative has a different weight in the adoption of the final decision, as the Treaty allocates a different number of votes to each country according to territory and population criteria.

The Council is empowered by the Treaty with specific functions: jointly with the European Parliament, it has normative power, including approval of the budget; it enters into international agreements between the EU and other countries or international organisations; and it co-ordinates the broad economic policies of the member states. Furthermore, it defines and implements the EU's common foreign and security policy (former second pillar) following the guidelines set by the European Council, and it co-ordinates the actions of member states and adopts measures in the area of police and judicial co-operation in criminal matters (former third pillar).

The European Parliament represents the people of Europe. It has nearly 800 members elected directly by European citizens and organised in the assembly in political groups and not in national blocs.[368] The European Parliament has increasingly reinforced the democratic legitimacy of the European Union, on one hand, by the direct popular election of its members since 1979, and, on the other hand, by increasing participation in the decisional process, where the Council of Ministers used to have greater weight.

Besides the European Parliament's normative power – including the approval or rejection of the EU budget – its functions make possible the democratic supervision of Community institutions. In parallel with the national parliaments, it has to give its approval to the Commission as a whole, which has been nominated by the EU member state governments. The Commission is politically accountable to the parliament, which can pass a "motion of censure" calling for the Commission's resignation. The members of the parliament regularly ask the members either of the Commission or the Council about specific questions, which the Commission and Council are legally required to answer. According to the ECJ, "the European Parliament is at the same time the Community institution whose task is to exercise a political review of the activities of the Commission, and to a certain extent those of the Council".[369] The European Parliament engages in direct dialogue with European citizens, through its Petitions Committee and through the European Ombudsman, a body dependent on the parliament.

---

368. See Article 29.1 Parliament's regulation and CFI 2 Oct 2001, T-222/99.
369. See ECJ 22 May 1985, 13/83, *Parliament v. Council*, paragraph 18.

The European Commission follows very closely the functions which at the national level are attributed to governments. It has an executive power which represents the Community interest. It is a body with a high degree of independence from the member states in exercising its power, although it is the member states which appoint the President of the Commission. It has a commissioner from each member state.[370]

According to its executive nature, it has the power of normative initiative, that is, the power to initiate the decisional process by sending to the Council and the parliament proposals for future Community general provisions; it has a sort of *pouvoir réglementaire*, which means that it is able to adopt normative decisions developing the legal framework first adopted by the Council and the European Parliament; it has administrative faculties in order to implement Community law and to monitor the national fulfilment of obligations, the power to set up serious fines in this regard and the faculty to bring an action before the ECJ as well. Due to these functions, the Commission is known as the guardian of the treaties. In addition, it has the power to directly address individual resolutions ("decisions") to the citizens.

The judicial institution of the Community is the ECJ, which ensures both that EU legislation is interpreted and applied in the same way in all the member states and that the European institutions and member states act as Community law requires. It is made up of three judicial bodies: the Court of Justice, the Court of First Instance (since 1988) and the Civil Service Tribunal (since 2004). The Court of Justice, the highest judicial instance applying Community law, consists of 27 judges and eight Advocates General, who are responsible for presenting, with complete impartiality and independence, an "opinion" before the court adopts a judgment.

The ECJ develops its jurisdictional function in two ways, deciding on direct and indirect actions presented by it.[371] The main direct actions are: action for annulment (Article 263 TFEU) relating the legality of the normative provisions adopted by institutions; action for failure to fulfil an obligation (Article 259) against the member states; action for failure to act (Article 265); and action for damages (Article 340) against Community institutions. The indirect actions, one of the most important pieces in the system, are the references for a preliminary ruling presented by the national courts (Article 267). While

---

370. See ECJ 11 July 2006, C-432/04, where the court underlines the "independence" of commissioners as their main personal obligation, either from national interests or from particular ones.
371. The Treaty of Nice made the main change to European judicial institutions: the goal in the Nice reform was to reinforce the constitutional functions of the ECJ and its nature of highest judicial body and to attribute to the Court of First Instance the nature of general court of the EU; however, the transfer of competencies has not operated automatically, and the ECJ retains the normal functions of a court of instance. For a detailed explanation, see S. Soldevila Fragoso, "Justicia Europea: entre Niza y Lisboa", *Noticias de la Unión Europea* No. 291, April 2009, p. 41 and ff.

applying law in a national procedure, they submit questions incidentally to the Court of Justice about the interpretation or validity of a community provision.

The essential role that preliminary references play in assuring the uniform application of Community law places the national courts in a pre-eminent role as well. In fact, the national court is the "common judge of law", the body before which citizens normally appeal for the rights provided to them by Community law. This circumstance makes the obligation to provide wide access for citizens to the (national) courts especially rigorous, working as an essential piece of the whole Community system: the more private parties are enabled to act before the national courts, the greater are the chances Community law will be applied. It has been stressed that "in accordance with the principle of sincere co-operation ... national courts are required, so far as possible, to interpret and apply national procedural rules governing the exercise of rights of action in a way that enables natural and legal persons to challenge before the courts the legality of any decision or other national measure relative to the application to them of a Community act of general application, by pleading the invalidity of such an act".[372]

Both jurisdictional levels, national and Community, form a functional unity in a single procedural system: "The Treaty has established a complete system of legal remedies and procedures designed to ensure judicial review of the legality of acts of the institutions, and has entrusted such review to the Community courts. Under that system, where natural or legal persons cannot ... directly challenge Community measures of general application, they are able, depending on the case ... to do so before the national courts and ask them, since they have no jurisdiction themselves to declare those measures invalid ... to make a reference to the Court of Justice for a preliminary ruling on validity."[373]

The role of the ECJ in the European constitutional architecture has been consistently stressed by the academic literature. It is pertinent to point out two main elements in this construction. First, the respective fields of Community and national competency – that is, the distribution of public power which constitutes an essential part of the rule-of-law tradition – are ultimately delimited by case law interpreting the Treaties' provisions. In defining them, the ECJ does not make any sort of European federalism theory but specifically interprets the meaning of the relevant Treaty provisions attributing specific competencies.[374] Second, the constitutional architecture has set up (new) Community principles which are the foundation of the whole Community legal system, merging Community provisions into national laws: principles of direct effect and primacy, in the early days, and more recently the liability

372. ECJ 25.07.2002, C-50/00, *UPA v. Council*, paragraph 42.
373. Ibid., paragraph 40.
374. J. Mischo, "The contribution of the Court of Justice to the protection of the Federal Balance in the European Community" in D. O'Keeffe (ed.), *Judicial Review in European Union Law*, Kluwer Law International, The Hague, 2000.

the member states have to individuals for breaches of Community obligations have made a praetorian construction on which to build the legal architecture of the EU.[375]

In both cases, the ECJ has dealt with Community law by a method which goes beyond a literal or word-for-word interpretation. Initially the ECJ showed its preferences by finalist and systematic interpretative methods. Furthermore, the Court reinforces the "effect utile" of the Treaty provisions, making an evolutionary interpretation which allows their application taking into account the new needs appearing after they were established.[376] This creative praetorian construction is essential for the European integration process to go ahead, although it cannot avoid some criticism of this so-called "judicial activism".

Up to now, we have referred to the institutions and bodies corresponding to the classic three-fold view of public powers, that is, those which correspond to the legislative, executive and judicial power in the European institutional framework. However, the Treaties create other entities which should be briefly mentioned.

The Committee of the Regions (Article 300.1 and 3 TFEU) and the European Economic and Social Committee (Article 300.1 and 2 TFEU) are collegial bodies with representative and participative aims. The first, set up in 1994, is an advisory body composed of representatives of Europe's regional and local authorities; in the second, economic and social components of organised civil society have been represented since 1957. Both participate in the procedure of adoption of regulative measures on specific issues foreseen by the Treaties and they share a common organisational structure.[377] The Lisbon Treaty reinforces the position of the Committee of the Regions, as it provides for access to the European Court, but only for appeals related to observance of the principle of subsidiarity.

The European Court of Auditors examines the accounts of all revenue and expenditure of the Community and its dependent bodies, except those specifically excluded. It oversees implementation of the EU budget, particularly during the discharge procedure. Its review has been distinguished from those attributed to Community judicial bodies: "The court of auditors only has power to examine the legality of expenditure with reference to the budget and the secondary provision on which the expenditure is based (commonly called the basic measure). Its review is thus in any event distinct from that exercised by the Court of Justice, which concerns the legality of the basic measure".[378]

---

375. There is an overwhelming academic literature on this issue. Among many others, see J. Mischo above and, in the same volume, V. Constantinesco, "The ECJ as law-maker: *praeter aut contra legem?*"

376. In this regard, see G. Isaac and M. Blanquet, *Droit Communitaire General*, 8th edn, Dalloz, Paris, 2001, p. 174 and ff.

377. See CFI 1997 Case T-220/1995.

378. ECJ 23 Apr 86, Case C-294/83, Les Verts/Parliament, paragraph 28.

The European Ombudsman was created in 1994 by the Maastricht Treaty, and according to Article 228 TFEU and its statute it investigates complaints about maladministration in the institution and bodies of the EU. Only the European Court of Justice acting in its jurisdictional functions is not submitted to its investigative powers. According to its own definition, "maladministration occurs when a public body fails to act in accordance with a rule or principle which is binding upon it".[379]

The Ombudsman usually conducts inquiries on the basis of complaints but can also launch inquiries on his or her own initiative. If maladministration is such that it undermines the legality of the Community decision in question, the decision can be the object of an action of annulment under Article 263 TFEU as well. In such cases, these remedies are alternatives; that is, citizens must choose between presenting a complaint to the Ombudsman or an action of annulment before the ECJ.[380]

The European Central Bank (ECB) is the core of the economic and monetary institutional system in the EU. The national central banks (NCBs) of all the EU member states make up the European System of Central Banks or ESCB (Article 129 TFEU). It is worth pointing out the role of the Eurosystem inside the ECB as a smaller version of the ESCB from which countries that have not adopted the euro are excluded.

Among the tasks conferred by the Treaty, the ESCB is concerned with the definition and implementation of monetary policy for the eurozone and the conduct of foreign exchange operations (Article 127.2 TFEU). The ECB has legal personality, and it is empowered to make regulations having general application and to impose fines or periodic penalties for failure to comply with obligations under its regulations and decisions – Article 132 TFEU.

The independence of the ECB is strictly preserved by Treaty provisions and by the ECJ who stress that this independence seeks, "in essence, to shield the Bank from all political pressure in order to enable it effectively to pursue the objectives attributed to its tasks, through the independent exercise of the specific powers conferred on it for that purpose by the Treaty and the Statute. By contrast, recognition that the Bank has such independence does not have the consequence of separating it entirely from the European Community and exempting it from every rule of Community law. There are no grounds which *prima facie* preclude the Community legislature from adopting ... legislative measures capable of applying to the European Central Bank"[381] – and the same is true of submission to Community financial control managed by the Commission's bodies.

---

379. Definition adopted in his 1997 Annual Report and approved by the European Parliament in its resolution approving the Code of Good Behaviour.
380. CFI 10 April 2002, T-209/00.
381. ECJ 10 July 2003, Case C-11/00, *Commission v. ECB*, paragraphs 134 to 136.

From the ordinary functioning of Community institutions, some clashes occasionally arise that are explained by the fact that each institution defends the functions and powers attributed by the Treaty against alleged interference by the others. From the "constitutional perspective", the attribution of specific powers and functions to each Community institution by the Treaty is known as the "institutional balance" – a communitarised version of the principle of division of powers, enshrined in Article 13.2 TEU, according to which each institution is to act within the limits of the powers conferred upon it by the Treaty.[382] In this regard, some controversial situations arise from the actions brought by one institution against the others defending their own prerogatives, especially those relating to participation in legislative procedures. It is not unusual that this kind of dispute starts with a discussion about the legal basis on which a draft legislation is going to be adopted, since different articles require different legislative procedures where the institutions have different types of participation.[383] Although the Lisbon Treaty has simplified the normative procedures, there is not a single one yet: the ordinary legislative procedure (codecision, Articles 294 and ff. TFEU) puts Parliament on an equal footing with the Council, whereas in the special legislative procedures, which apply only in specific and sensitive cases, the Parliament has only a consultative role.

11.2. Government and public administration

We have referred to the European Commission as the Community government, since the Treaty awards it classic executive faculties: it has the power to initiate the decisional process by sending to the Council and Parliament its legislative proposals; it has a sort of *pouvoir réglementaire* as it takes measures implementing basic regulations adopted by the Council and the Parliament; and it has a general function of ensuring the due application of law by exercising its relevant specific powers given by treaties.

As a governmental body, the European Commission operates on the principle of collegial responsibility, which ensures it acts collectively in compliance with political guidelines laid down by its president. This means decisions are discussed collectively and all members have collective responsibility: the "College of Commissioners" is a collective decision-making body with a single voice. This principle has no impact on its power to authorise its members to adopt certain decisions in its name, especially procedural measures: this system of delegation does not divest the Commission of powers, because the Commission remains fully responsible for delegated decisions.[384]

---

382. Case 403/05, *Parliament v. Commission*, paragraph 49.
383. To illustrate this kind of dispute, see ECJ 22 May 1990, C-70/88, *European Parliament v. Council*, paragraphs 26 to 31.
384. ECJ 23 September 1986, Akzo/Commission, 5/85, paragraphs 35 and 36.

The Commission has its own services organised on the basis of a bureaucratic scheme. In addition to the 27 commissioners and their internal services, it has departments which do the groundwork for and implement actions approved by the Commission as a whole. In recent decades, certain bodies and agencies have been created to take over specific executive functions from the Commission's services, normally under their supervision.

Here we briefly describe these two pre-eminent elements of "government and public administration" at Community level: first, the European Commission, its functions and powers; second, the Commission's services conforming to an organisational structure and implementing Community law. However, this organisational perspective is not enough to cover all the executive action which is needed to implement Community law, so it is necessary to consider as well the functional perspective, where "public administration" must include the national administrative units whose participation is required when a Community provision is implemented. As we argue, the classic distinction between the two ways by which Community law is implemented – direct and indirect administration – is not valid any more, if it ever was.[385] If we consider a single procedure implementing a single Community provision, usually we find both Community and national administrative units participating at different times before the decision is adopted. This so-called mixed administration implements most Community provisions.

11.2.1. The European Commission

The European Commission represents the Community interest, and it assumes in general terms the executive function. In fact, as already mentioned, it takes part in the political body of the European Union, that is, the European Council. The Lisbon Treaty reinforces its political dimension, as one of its vice-presidents is to be nominated the High Representative of the Union for Foreign and Security Policy. This post is consistent with the (partial) communitarisation of the second pillar and is to be assisted by the European External Action Service (Article TEU), composed of members of the Council, the Commission and national foreign office services.

Up to the Lisbon Treaty's entry into force, the Commission had a two-fold normative power. It had its own power of decision as well as delegated normative powers conferred by the Council for the implementation of the rules laid down by the latter. This double source for normative powers was conferred by the original Article 155 EEC Treaty (later Article 211 EC Treaty) and

---

385. Some critical voices stressed some time ago that a clear distinction is not possible. See among the earliest works, S. Galera, *La aplicación administrativa del Derecho Comunitario. Administración Mixta. Tercera Vía de Aplicación*, Cívitas, Madrid 1998, and A. M. Moreno Molina, *La ejecución administrativa del Derecho comunitario. Régimen Europeo y español*, Marcial Pons-Univ. Carlos III, Madrid, 1998.

Article 145 EEC Treaty (later Article 202 EC Treaty).[386] In this framework, it was not possible to identify a distribution of the normative power which on the one hand gives the Council – jointly with the Parliament – power to adopt provisions with general application as a direct implementation of the Treaties, and on the other hand the Commission taking its regulatory developments on provisions with only specific measures. The ECJ has rejected the idea that this distribution constitutes a general rule: "The Commission is to have its own power of decision in the manner provided for in the Treaty. … The limits of the powers conferred on the Community by a specific provision of the Treaty are to be inferred not from a general principle, but from an interpretation of the particular wording of the provision in question … analysed in the light of its purpose and its place in the scheme of the Treaty".[387]

The rule establishing that the "Council shall … confer on the Commission … powers for the implementation of the rules which the Council lays down" (Article 202 EC Treaty) was interpreted as the Council being practically bound to do so: "Under the third indent of Article 202 EC, in order to ensure that the objectives set out in the Treaty are attained and in accordance with its provisions, the Council is to confer on the Commission, in the acts which the Council adopts, powers for the implementation of the rules which the Council lays down. The Council may impose certain requirements in respect of the exercise of those powers and may also reserve the right, in specific cases, to exercise directly implementing powers itself."[388] Whether the Council decides to reserve the right to exercise implementing powers, this exception should be properly explained "by reference to the nature and content of the basic instrument to be implemented".[389]

This important provision has been notably amended by the Lisbon Treaty: as usual, the Commission has the power to initiate the legislative procedure (Article 294 TFEU) ending in legislative acts (Article 289 TFEU). However, currently, all the Commission's normative power is delegated. According to Article 290 TFEU "a legislative act may delegate to the Commission the power to adopt non-legislative acts of general application to supplement or amend certain non-essential elements of the legislative act". The objectives, content, scope and duration of the delegation of power shall be explicitly defined in the legislative acts.

---

386. Former Article 211 EC stated that the Commission "shall … have its own power of decision … and exercise the powers conferred on it by the Council for the implementation of the rules laid down by the latter", meanwhile the former Article 202 EC stated that the Council "shall … confer on the Commission, in the acts which the Council adopts, powers for the implementation of the rules which the Council lays down".

387. ECJ 6 July 1982, *France and others v. Commission*, 188 to 190/80, paragraph 6.

388. ECJ 1 April 2008, *European Parliament and Denmark v. Commission*, C-14/05 and 295/06, paragraph 51.

389. ECJ 6 May 2008, *Parliament v. Council*, Case C-133/06, paragraph 47.

Another pre-eminent Commission empowerment is related to its function of "treaty guardian": It shall "ensure that the provisions of this Treaty and the measures taken by the institutions pursuant thereto are applied" (Article 17.1 TEU). This general function of ensuring the application of Community law needs specific further empowerments, either by treaties or by secondary law.[390] In this regard, the treaty confers on the Commission the power to bring an action before the ECJ against a member state that fails to fulfil its Community obligations (ex Article 258 TFEU). It also awards the power to direct member states to abolish or alter aid considered incompatible with the common market (ex Article 198 TFEU) even when a national court has declared the legality of this aid in a judgment with the authority of *res judicata*.[391] Finally, the basic Regulations on Competition Law empower the Commission to hand out serious fines to companies for breaches of the Competition Law.

11.2.2. Commission services and the decentralised bodies

From an organisational point of view, the Commission includes 40 directorates-general and specialised services: among them, the Secretariat-General of the European Commission supports the whole of the Commission, in particular the 27 commissioners. A new staff regulation has now entered into force, supporting a general programme of reform with the goal of creating a modern public administration based on the principles of efficiency, transparency and accountability.[392]

The functioning of this bureaucratic organisation follows very closely the continental model of public administration, with a highly empowered public body, and classic techniques of public management such as the hierarchy and delegation of powers. In managing its own staff, a Community body is "entitled to lay down a body of measures of an organisational nature, delegating powers to its own internal decision-making bodies … [although] such delegation of powers must comply with a number of conditions".[393] More specifically, officials can be "empowered to take in the name of the Commission and subject to its control clearly defined measures of management or administration" such as the delegation of authority to sign a decision.[394]

---

390. See ECJ 23 February 2006, C-171/05 P, where the Court denied a Commission general power to address sanctions for any breaches of Community law and underlined the need for a specific conferral of such power. For the distinction of the underlying legal concepts, see M. Baena del Alcázar, "Competencias, funciones y potestades en el ordenamiento jurídico español", *Estudios sobre la Constitución Española, Homenaje al prof. Gracía de Enterría*, Cívitas, 1991, Vol. III.
391. ECJ 18 July 2007, C-119/05, paragraphs 543 to 560.
392. The Commission's rules of procedure were published in OJL 308, 8 December 2000, and last modified by Decision 2005/960/CE (OJL 347, 30 Dec 2005). See also Governance Statement of the European Commission (30 May 2007) covering its internal functioning.
393. ECJ 26 May 2005, C-301/02, Tralli/ECB.
394. CFI 6 December 1994, T-450/93.

The bodies and agencies which form a decentralised Community administration were created in the 1970s. In the 1990s a second generation of agencies appeared, linked with finalisation of the internal market. From 2003, a third generation of Community bodies was born. This decentralised administration is made up of two types of body: the *executive agencies*, created by the Commission in accordance with a common general framework; and the *Community agencies*, provided with legal entity and created by a regulatory measure which establishes their legal statute as well.

The general framework for *executive agencies* is laid down in Council Regulation 58/2003, which ensures certain uniformity in the executive agencies, ruling in particular on essential aspects of their structure, task, operation, budget system, staff, supervision and responsibility. These agencies represent the outsourcing of certain management tasks as a way of achieving the goals of some programmes more effectively. Tasks that may be delegated include managing all or some phases in a given project, implementing the budget, gathering and processing information or preparing recommendations for the Commission. Tasks requiring discretionary powers in translating political choices into action may not be delegated.

Among these executive agencies, the European Anti-Fraud Office – OLAF in its French acronym – stands out because of the increasing role it performs. OLAF was created in 1999 by the Commission with responsibility to execute the Commission's functions in protecting the financial and economic interest of the Community,[395] and to fight against transnational organised crime, fraud and other activities prejudicial to the budget. Dependent on the Commission, its functional independence from Community institutions and the member states is provided by their statutes and granted by the ECJ. The European Court has expressly stated that Community entities and bodies like the European Central Bank[396] and the European Investment Bank[397] fall under the scope of OLAF's investigative powers.

In contrast to this harmonised model, *Community agencies* are characterised by their legal diversity. They have legal entity and are created by a regulatory provision of the Council, which establishes their tasks, functions and structure, and in general the legal statute of each of them. They follow a common organisational scheme, with a sort of management board where member states and Community institutions are represented.

Among existing Community agencies, two groups have been distinguished according to their task. The first group are data-collecting agencies, whose main role involves the gathering and provision of specialised information to the Commission and the member states but not the adoption of individual

---

395. By Articles 274 and 280 EC Treaty. OLAF was set up by Decision 1999/352 of 28 April 1999.
396. ECJ 10 July 2003, Case C-11/00, Commission/ECB.
397. ECJ 10 July 2003, Case C-15/00, Commission/EIB.

decisions; the second group, the regulatory agencies, implement Community regulations through individual decisions.[398] Other authors stress the representative composition of the collegial bodies forming part of their structures and, in functional terms, the collaborative framework by which technical or administrative tasks are dealt with, linking national authorities and supranational institutions.[399]

One further aspect of Community public administration should be mentioned: the rules applied by this organisation in relation to third parties. Here, two levels of Community rule can be distinguished. On one level are the procedural rights recognised mainly by the ECJ in its case law, especially when rights of defence are concerned. In other cases, the procedures set by Community law should be applied by the national authorities when implementing basic provisions of Community law. Such procedures, increasingly common, have an instrumental aim. Unlike national procedural rules, historically looking to balance citizens' rights with public power, Community procedural rules are much more concerned with efficiency of administrative action and implementing public policies.[400] Thus, this procedural system is balanced by the protection given to citizens by the ECJ in recognising their rights before the public power, which it limits.

However, both types of rules form a fragmentary body made up of pieces of normative provisions and case law requirements. There is no binding general code of procedure to be applied in administrative relations linking private parties with the European public administration.[401] However, it seems European institutions are working in that direction. The most outstanding example of such action would be the resolution adopted by the European Parliament, on the basis of the European Ombudsman's proposal, approving the Code of Good Administrative Behaviour, for application by officials of all Community institutions and bodies in their relations with the public. Up to now, this code has had no overall effect; only the Commission and a few Community bodies have declared they will be bound by it.[402]

---

398. E. Nieto-Garrido and I. Martin Delgado, *European Administrative Law in the Constitutional Treaty*, Hart Publishing, 2007, p. 155 and ff. In fact, they identify a third group coincidental with the executive agencies we referred to first. As an example of the first group, there is the European Environmental Agency and of the second one the Office for Internal Market Harmonisation.

399. E. Chiti, "Administrative proceedings involving European agencies", *Law and Contemporary Problems*, Vol. 68, No. 1, 2004, p. 219.

400. K. Kanska, "Towards administrative human rights in the EU: impact of the Charter of Fundamental Rights", *European Law Journal*, Vol. 10, No. 3, May 2004, p. 299.

401. And according to some respected opinions there is no need: see Harlow.

402. European Parliament Resolution of 6 September 2001. The Commission included the code as an Annex to its Rules of Procedure C(2000) 3614; it covered the European Environment Agency (EEA, OJL 216, 26 August 2000), European Foundation for the Improvement of Living and Working Conditions (Eurofound, OJL 316, 15 December 2000) and the European Investment Bank (EIB, OJC 317, 19 January 2001).

Furthermore, the European Charter of Fundamental Rights recognises the "right to good administration", which includes a list of citizen's guarantees with respect to the public administration already recognised by the ECJ.

This sort of administrative procedural patchwork is also evidenced in the so-called European Administrative Law, which is a broader concept also covering some other legal issues. We wish just to mention a very detailed description of the possible contents of this law, in order to stress the erroneous and ever more frequent tendency to identify Community Administrative Law with European Administrative Law. One can identify in European Administrative Law the following elements: 1. National Administrative Laws, on which European Administrative Law is based; 2. the Administrative Law of the European Community relating to the organisation and functioning of its institutions; 3. Community Administrative Law, made up of administrative law coming from Community policies; 4. Administrative Co-operation Law.[403]

11.2.3. Mixed administrative and transnational procedures

The Commission services, European agencies and similar bodies form, in general terms, the "Community administration", which belongs to the executive power and applies Community law. However, this is a realistic assertion only from an organic point of view, as it considers the Community administrative unities and bodies with executive functions. If, on the contrary, we want to refer to the body in charge of "Community administrative activity", that is, the body which implements Community policies, it is necessary to consider also "national public administration" because implementation of Community law is usually the duty of national administrative bodies. This perspective stresses the double role performed by national administrations: they can act either as national bodies or as a part of a supranational public body.[404]

In the past, a distinction was frequently made between direct and indirect administration as the two ways by which Community law was implemented: *direct administration* covering the exceptional issues directly implemented by the Commission service, and *indirect administration* referring to national implementation of Community law by the national administrative bodies under the principle of national autonomy. However, at the current stage of European integration, neither a two-fold model of administration nor a well-defined principle of national autonomy is fully comprehensive of the administrative activity required for the implementation of Community law.[405]

---

403. See E. Schmidt-Assman, *La Teoría General del Derecho Administrativo como sistema*, INAP-Marcial Pons, Madrid, 2003, p. 392 and ff.

404. M. Chiti, "Forms of European administrative action", *Law and Contemporary Problems*, Vol. 68, No. 1, 2004, p. 52.

405. Recently, M. Chiti has emphatically referred to the "disappearing system of indirect administration", op. cit., p. 51, and G. J. Della Cananea has underlined a current (European)

The principle of national procedural autonomy is a doctrine mainly adopted in relation to the application of Directives: According to Article 288 TFEU Treaty, the member states are bound to adopt all measures necessary to ensure the effectiveness of the directive, though they are free to choose the ways and means of implementing it. That is, the formal normative instrument – the procedures and authorities by which the directive is going to be implemented – is determined by the member states.

However, this autonomy has never been understood without nuances, and the way Community law is implemented has never been an issue about which Community institutions were not concerned. We have at least three reasons explaining why national procedural autonomy is currently hard to be recognised.

First of all, the European Court has pointed out that, ever since the early years, national autonomy has been in some ways subordinate. In implementing Community rules, the national authorities are to act in accordance with the procedural and substantive rules of their own national law so far as Community law, including its general principles, does not include common rules to that end.[406]

Secondly, even when there are no Community procedural provisions, the national procedures are applied under certain conditions imposed by the principles of effectiveness and equivalence. According to these principles, the detailed procedural and substantive rules laid down in national law must not render it virtually impossible or excessively difficult to implement Community rules, and national law must be applied in a manner which is not discriminatory compared to corresponding proceedings or procedures which concern purely domestic law.[407]

Finally, the most recent Community procedural provisions seriously impinge on national procedural autonomy, specifically those procedures by which Community law is applied in a functional unity connecting national authorities with Community services in the procedural stages preceding the administrative resolution formally adopted at the national level (*mixed administration*). Hence, national authorities can be connected not only with Community services but also with other national authorities. In such cases, when citizens ask for application of a Community provision before their national authorities, a single procedure is followed involving administrative authorities of different countries, which have to show their position before the initial authority

---

administrative power distinct from the initial model of European law making and national implementation, in "The European Union mixed proceedings", in *Law and Contemporary Problems*, Vol. 68, No. 1, 2004, p. 198.

406. ECJ 16 December 1976, Case 33/76, *Rewe*; more recently, ECJ 13 April 2000, Case C-292/97 *Karlsson and others*, paragraph 27.

407. ECJ 21 September 1983, joined cases 205/82 to 215/82, *Deutsche Milchkintor and Others*, paragraph 19, ECJ 7 January 2004, Case C-201/02, *Wells*.

adopts a final resolution. These Community procedures not only exclude national procedural rules being applied by the national authorities, but also reduce their decisional autonomy.

These procedures have been identified as *mixed or transnational procedures* and are easily found in the field of Community customs law, environmental law or, more recently, in technological and pharmaceutical issues. They merge into a single procedure the collaboration among the authorities whose territories are concerned by the activity under authorisation, for example, waste transportation or new pharmaceutical products in the entire European market, and are consistent with and a consequence of the functioning of a single European territory for economic purposes.

It is not easy to systematise the great procedural variety in a single outline, so it is worth referring to the first attempts to do this. Focusing on the level where a procedure ends with an administrative resolution, two general types of mixed administrative proceeding have been distinguished:[408] top-down proceedings, which start with a decision made by the European authorities and end with a measure taken by national authorities; and bottom-up proceedings, where the initial decision in the administrative sequence is made at national level and the final decision rests with the European administration.

From another point of view, paying attention to the links between the Commission phase and the national phase of mixed proceedings and, specifically, the strength of the Commission's intervention in the administrative resolution-making process, up to six different procedures have been distinguished.[409] A common element in all of them, however, is the structural link between the administrative authorities, which leads to difficulty in keeping the Community stage of a proceeding distinct from the national one[410] – on the understanding that such links could be established not only between the Commission and the national authorities but also between different national authorities.

Beyond this formal co-operative model, another kind of activity has been pointed out, referring to transnational "networks" of public powers, where private parties take part as well. With different profiles, the European Agencies have a pre-eminent role in this kind of administrative activity, being empowered sometimes just to guide the activity of the participants on a non-compulsory basis, at other times producing forms of hierarchical ordering through real co-ordination and planning powers.[411]

---

408. G. J. Della Cananea, "The EU's mixed administrative proceedings", op. cit., p. 99 and ff.
409. S. Cassese, "European Administrative Proceedings", *Law and Contemporary Problems*, Vol. 68, No. 1, 2004, pp. 26 and ff.
410. Ibid., p. 24.
411. E. Chiti, *Administrative proceedings involving European agencies*, op. cit., pp. 232, 233.

From these new forms by which administrative activity is carried out arise interesting questions on the traditional doctrine of administrative law. There is already an elaborated doctrine of European Administrative Law which, though its content varies, generally assumes loss of nationality as a premise of current administrative law.[412]

The most important issue that arises is the position of private parties in these kinds of mixed proceeding, particularly their ability to challenge decisions of foreign authorities with a positive effect on final resolutions affecting such parties. Neither the national rules stating the standing to sue nor the national requirements in basic procedural rules – for example, access to the documents or the key distinction between procedural and final acts – are adapted to these new situations.[413]

The earliest ECJ case law was reluctant to recognise the functional unity of such procedures and the corresponding displacement of real decisional power.[414] At that time, the ECJ insistently held to the principle of national autonomy, refusing to admit the effective incidence of Commission participation in a single procedure ending in a national resolution. The consequence of this position was the difficulty to identify the right judicial body to challenge a resolution or the right authority to sue for responsibility for damages. However, judicial attitudes have begun to change in this regard. Recent European judgments recognise that the Commission's participation has an impact on the national resolution, implicitly accepting the structural unity of the proceedings and the right of interested parties to take part in the Commission phase of the proceeding.[415] This is, however, a very limited remedy, as it is only applied to procedures linking the Commission with the national authorities, and leaves out of its scope the (frequent) situations involving various national authorities.

11.3. Judicial review of government and administration

It was in 1986 that the European Court of Justice first referred to the legal order formed by the Community Treaties as the "constitutional charter", the central idea of this "charter" being the submission of (European) public power

---

412. Among the earliest works should be mentioned J. Schwarze, *European Administrative Law* (Sweet & Maxwell, London 2006) and S. González-Varas, *Derecho Administrativo Europeo*, Instituto Andaluz Administración Pública, Sevilla 2000, updating the debate in J. Ziller (ed.), *What's new in European administrative law?*, EUI Working Paper Law, No. 2005/10.

413. M. Chiti, "Forms of European administrative action", op. cit., p. 56.

414. I reported this case law in my work *La aplicación administrativa*, op. cit. pp. 33 and ff., among the most significant judgments being those in cases C-422/1992, C-121/1991, 175/1984 and T-492/1993.

415. G. J. Della Cananea, "The European Union's mixed administrative proceedings", op. cit., p. 211, referring to Cases T-346/94 and 32/95.

to judicial review as imposed by the rule-of-law tradition.[416] Earlier the Court had recognised the right to a fair trial as a common principle of Community law, directly connected with judicial review requirements.

In 2008, the Court reiterated this doctrine: "The Community is based on the rule of law, inasmuch as neither its member states nor its institutions can avoid review of the conformity of their acts with the basic constitutional charter, the EC Treaty, which established a complete system of legal remedies and procedures designed to enable the Court of Justice to review the legality of acts of the institutions."[417]

Being an essential of the Community, this section describes how Community law states the requirements through which either the submission of public power to the law or the right to challenge their activity by the citizens are effective. We focus on how these two mechanisms are to operate and analyse them following a common outline that reveals the criteria for the independence of courts, the kind of Community measures that can be the subject of a Community action and citizens' access to the ECJ.

11.3.1. Judicial independence from the executive

Judicial independence is a two-fold issue in Community law. On one hand, it is applied to the members of Community judicial bodies, and, on the other hand, Community case law has developed its own concept of this issue which is applied to European courts and to national ones. In fact, this doctrine has been shaped in great part when the European court has had to identify a national body equivalent to a judicial court, stressing its independence as an essential feature.

Both the Treaties and the text governing procedures require "independence" as one of the main conditions that members of the Community courts should fulfil. Article 254 TFEU establishes that "the Judges and Advocates-General of the Court of Justice should be chosen from persons whose independence is beyond doubt". The Statute of the Court of Justice imposes on the judges an "oath to perform their duties impartially" and confidentially, and establishes a specific procedure to deprive a judge of office in the event he or she no longer fulfils the requisite condition or does not meet the obligations arising from the office.[418]

In Community case law, judicial independence has been recognised as part of the "right to a fair trial" and different faculties have been deduced from it depending on the varied situations to which it has been applied. In general

---

416. ECJ 23 April 1986, Case 294/83, *Les Verts.*
417. ECJ 3 September 2008, Cases C-402/05 and C-415/05 P, *Al Barakaat et al.*
418. Articles 2 and 6, respectively, relating to the judges of the ECJ, and Article 47 extending these requirements to the members of the CFI.

terms, the ECJ, with specific reference to the Strasbourg Court's case law, states that:

- "the general principle of Community Law under which every person has a right to a fair trial, inspired by Article 6 of the ECHR, comprises the right to a tribunal that is independent of the executive power";[419]

- the CFI, on the basis of Article 6 ECHR, declares that the "right of every person to a fair hearing by an independent tribunal means, *inter alia*, that both national and Community courts must be free to apply their own rules of procedure concerning the powers of the judge, the conduct of the proceedings in general and the confidentiality of the documents on the file in particular";[420]

- "independence" is one of the required characteristics that determines whether a national body is a "court or a tribunal" empowered to refer a preliminary ruling to the ECJ: "the Court takes account of a number of factors, such as whether the body is established by law, whether it is permanent, whether its jurisdiction is compulsory, whether its procedure is inter partes, whether it applies rules of law and whether it is independent".[421] Consequently, a national regulation that omits sufficient safeguards for dismissal or termination of the members' appointment "does not appear to constitute an effective safeguard against undue intervention or pressure from the executive"[422] on the members of the national body.

11.3.2. The scope of judicial review

This section aims to describe which kind of public activities are under the competency of the ECJ for verification of their compliance with Community law. Following the common outline of this work, we distinguish between activities – administrative and normative – and omissions, at both Community and national levels, where the public activity applying Community law is developed, indicating for each the specific way by which they should be challenged before the ECJ. First it is helpful to make a clear theoretical distinction between "Community" and "non-Community" activity among those coming from the European Union, as they follow very different rules when under

---

419. Case C-185/95 P *Baustahlgewebe* 1998, paragraphs 20, 21; this criterion was repeated in ECJ 11 January 2000, C-174/98 P and C-189/98 P, paragraph 17, which pointed out some limits to this general statement.

420. See CFI resolution 19 March 1998, Case T-83/96, paragraph 47, and ECJ 11 January 2000 *Gerard van der Wal*, paragraph 14.

421. ECJ 31 May 2005, C-53/03, paragraph 29; I omit references to previous case law for easier reading.

422. Ibid., paragraph 31, citing Case 103/97, 1999, paragraph 21. In contrast, the Spanish Tribunales Economico-Administrativos, though functionally dependent on the Finance Minister, has been recognised as a "judicial body" able to refer preliminary rulings to the ECJ (C-110/98 to C-147/98, *Gabalfrisa* judgment 2000, paragraphs 39 and 40).

judicial review and it is not always easy to distinguish Community and non-Community activities in practice.

11.3.2.1. Community and other EU measures

After successive Treaties, the European Union was shaped around the so-called three pillars: the European Community, as the legacy of the three original communities, and the two inter-governmental pillars. These inter-governmental pillars were dealt with outside the common institutional structure, but they brought towards the European Community issues of common interests which still remained within the states' sovereignty. Although the Lisbon Treaty changes this framework, it is worth considering the differences among the former three pillars, and their correspondent legal ramifications, as far as these last are still in force, and consequently providing a legal basis for future normative developments. There is a clear and didactic description in a General Advocate's Opinion:[423]

> The European Union, which embodies a new stage in the process of creating an ever-closer link between the peoples of Europe, is based on the Communities, supplemented by the policies and with the forms of co-operation established in the Treaty on European Union itself (Article 1). Accordingly, there are three distinct pillars:
>
> – the first, or "Community", pillar;
>
> – the second pillar, covering common foreign and security policy (Title V);
>
> – the third pillar, concerning police and judicial co-operation in criminal matters (Title VI).
>
> The latter aims, without prejudice to the powers of the European Community, to provide citizens with a high level of safety within an area of freedom, security and justice, by means of common action among the member states in the fields in question, in order to prevent and combat crime, through the approximation, where necessary, of national rules on criminal matters, in accordance with the provisions of Article 31(e) EU (Article 29 EU).
>
> Judicial co-operation includes the progressive adoption of measures establishing minimum rules relating to the constituent elements of offences and to penalties in the fields of organised crime, terrorism and illicit drug trafficking (Article 31(1)(e) EU).

With respect to the first (Community) pillar, the main provisions – Directives, Regulations and Decisions – are adopted autonomously by the Community institutions, whereas for the other pillars there were "common positions, joint actions and international agreements" (second) and "common positions, framework decisions and decisions" (third), the main tools created to provide an approximation to national provisions. This is not the right place to examine the differences between these different acts, but we can point out the general submission to the ECJ's jurisdiction of measures adopted in the framework of the Community pillar, whereas the rest are subject to a limited (former third pillar) or null (former second pillar) judicial scrutiny. It is in the Treaty itself where this jurisdictional immunity is stated.

---

423. Delivered on 26 May 2005 by Mr Ruiz-Jarabo Colomer, Case C-176/03, paragraphs 12 and ff.

It is not always easy to classify a measure correctly, since it could be understood as implementing different provisions of the Treaties. Such difficulties can arise in various ECJ judgments, usually ruling on disputes between institutions claiming a different legal basis for the same measure. The correct ruling is not as meaningful as determining whether it can be submitted to judicial review. Three types of case are relevant here.

First is a framework decision, entailing harmonisation of the criminal laws of member states, in particular harmonising the constituent elements of various criminal offences related to harming the environment. In its judgment, the Court pointed out its previous case law stating that:

> as a general rule, neither criminal law nor the rules of criminal procedure fall within the Community's competence ... However, the last-mentioned finding does not prevent the Community legislature when the application of effective, proportionate and dissuasive criminal penalties by the competent national authorities is an essential measure for combating serious environmental offences, from taking measures which relate to the criminal law of the member states which it considers necessary in order to ensure that the rules which it lays down on environmental protection are fully effective.[424]

In this particular case, the Court finally annulled the framework decision because, since its aim and content were the protection of the environment, it "could have been properly adopted on the basis of Article 175 EC",[425] that is, a Community act.

A further implementation of this criterion and the above-mentioned judgment was made in case C-440/05,[426] which was about a framework decision strengthening the criminal-law framework to improve enforcement of the law on ship-source pollution, requiring member states to apply criminal penalties to certain forms of conduct.

This debate has partially lost its meaning as far as the Lisbon Treaty keeping police and criminal co-operation under the Community's institutional framework. However, in the case of the second pillar, common foreign and security policy (CFSP), notwithstanding having lost its inter-governmental nature, the Community institutions are not empowered to adopt legal acts under the common legislative procedure. Consequently, it is worth taking into account the case law criteria delimiting the CFSP measures from the community ones. One of these is particularly relevant since, without calling into question the lack of jurisdiction to rule on the legality of a measure falling within the CFSP, the Court affirmed its competency in some situations to consider an action for annulment brought against a CFSP act. That happens when the question is whether a measure adopted in the framework of the second pillar having legal effects does not fall under the scope of a "Community policy" or, in its

---

424. ECJ 13 September 2005, C-176/03, *Commission v. Council*, paragraphs 47 and 48.
425. Ibid., paragraph 51. Article 175 EC stated the legislative procedure for environmental community measures; it is currently stated in Article 192 TFEU.
426. ECJ 23 October 2007.

own words, does "not encroach upon the powers conferred by the EC Treaty on the Community".[427] Having interpreted the content of the CFSP measure and having stressed the pre-eminence of Community measures over those of the CFSP ("the Union cannot have recourse to a legal basis falling within the CFSP in order to adopt provisions which also fall within a competence conferred by the EC Treaty on the Community"),[428] in the end the Court annulled the challenged decision.

Chapters 12 and 13 consider the second and third pillars in more detail.

11.3.2.2. Community acts

Concerning the activities of Community institutions, we have already noted the Court's emphasis in the *Les Verts* case that it is a general consequence of the rule of law that Community institutions cannot "avoid a review of the question whether the measures adopted by them are in conformity with the basic constitutional charter, the Treaty". From this broad statement it could be initially inferred that measures with a normative nature and general effects and those only including administrative resolutions could be equally the subject of an action of annulment.

However, the question about which "Community measures" can be the subject of an action of annulment needs additional explanation. The rules governing this action have been successively amended to reflect the institutional reforms relating to the decisional procedure and to the emergence of new institutions and bodies. In Article 263 TFEU currently, the action of annulment refers to the

> acts adopted jointly by the European Parliament and the Council; acts of the Council, of the Commission and of the ECB, other than recommendations and opinions, and acts of the European Parliament intended to produce legal effects vis-à-vis third parties.

In addition, natural or legal persons can bring such an action against "decisions addressed to them or to other persons, which, although in the form of a regulation, are of concern to them directly and individually". The Lisbon Treaty adds the possibility for individuals to bring action "against a regulatory act which is of direct concern to them and does not entail implementing measures".[429]

This general action to shape the legality of Community activity is initially understood from a non-formalistic perspective, considering that "an action for annulment must be available in the case of all measures adopted by the

---

427. ECJ 20 May 2008, C-91/05, *Commission v. Council*, paragraphs 33 and 34.
428. Paragraphs 76 and 77, interpreting Article 47 EU which precludes the Union from adopting, on the basis of the EU, a measure which could properly be adopted on the basis of the EC Treaty.
429. This possibility was advanced in the CFI 3 May 2002, Case T-177/01, *Jego-Quere*; this judgment was later annulled by the ECJ (1 April 2004, Case C-263/02) considering the action could not be admitted due to the lack of (this) legal basis in the Treaties.

institutions, whatever their nature or form, which are intended to have legal effects".[430]

From the huge volume of case law, it is possible to identify the deciding factor on the admissibility of an action of annulment against the acts of Community institutions as "measures producing binding legal effects of a nature such as to affect the interests of the applicant by bringing about a distinct change in his legal position".[431]

Following this general assertion, some categories are excluded from this action, some of them coincidental with national ones. This is the case for *confirmatory acts*: "It is settled case law that a decision which merely confirms a previous decision is not open to challenge and that any action directed against such a decision is accordingly inadmissible".[432] The Court considers that a "decision is merely confirmatory of a previous decision" if:

> it contains no new factor as compared with the previous measure and was not preceded by a re-examination of the circumstances of the person to whom that previous measure was addressed.[433]

The same occurs with *non-final acts*, a category whose review is subject to very restrictive conditions: "Measures of a purely preparatory character may not themselves be the subject of an application for a declaration that they are void".[434] This criterion is also applied in the framework of mixed or trans-national administrative proceedings, which link activities of the Community and national administrative bodies in a single procedure:

> In the case of acts or decisions adopted by a procedure involving several stages, in particu-lar where they are the culmination of an internal procedure, only measures definitively establishing the position of the institution on the conclusion of that procedure, and not provisional measures intended to pave the way for the final decision, may be the subject of an action for annulment.[435]

Conversely, the Court has admitted an action of annulment brought against an interpretative communication from the Commission specifying how to apply a Directive's provisions on financial transparency. Because the communication stated new obligations for member states – annual reports and specific data to be transmitted, among others – the Court considered it "constitutes an act intended to have legal effects of its own".[436]

---

430. See the judgment in Case 22/70, *Commission v. Council* [1971].
431. ECJ 11 November 1981, Case 60/81, IBM/Commission, among many others.
432. Order of the CFI 9 June 2005, T-265/03, Helm Düngemittel/Commission, paragraph 62 referring to previous case law.
433. CFI 15 October 1997, T-331/94, paragraph 4.
434. ECJ 11 November 1981, Case 60/81, IBM/Commission.
435. Order of the President of the Court of First Instance of 5 July 2001, *Asahi Vet SA v. Commission*, Case T-55/01 R, paragraph 62.
436. ECJ 16 June 1993, C-325/91, France/Commission, paragraphs 20 to 23.

It should also be considered whether or not an action of annulment could be brought against measures taken by Community bodies and agencies about which the Treaties used to remain silent. There is not a single rule in this regard. In fact, there are three possible situations governed by the acts setting up these bodies.[437] First, the Court of Justice is competent to act on proceedings instituted against the Agency;[438] secondly, any act of the agency may be referred to the Commission with a view to verification of its legality, and the Commission's decision can then be the subject of proceedings for annulment;[439] thirdly, the act is silent on verification of the legality of acts of the agency.[440] The Lisbon Treaty introduces a (new?) provision in Article 263 TFEU, which refers to the possibility of action against the bodies, offices and agencies of the Union as long as it is provided for in their corresponding constituent Act.

Unlawful omissions by Community institutions can also be challenged before the ECJ by means of an "action for failure to act", which is governed by Article 265 TFEU.[441] This action is open to natural and legal persons who, according to settled case law, may bring such proceedings "for a declaration that an institution has declined, in breach of the Treaty, to adopt decisions of which those persons are the potential addressees or which they could challenge in annulment proceedings".[442] Formally, this action must be preceded by a formal notice calling on the defendant institution to act, making clear what decision should have been taken under Community law.

There is an interesting point related to this action, since it is connected with another procedural route, the action for infringements against member states. As we will see, this action is only provided for the Commission and member states, not for individuals. If they consider a member state could be brought before the ECJ, the only way for them is to address a petition to the Commission, which is not bound by it. That is, the Commission has discretion to decide whether or not to bring an action against the member state after an individual has so petitioned, and its refusal to do so cannot be challenged by means of an action for failure to act. In this regard, "the Court has consistently held that natural and legal persons have no right … to obtain a declaration

---

437. See WD 08 and WD 09 ("Right of appeal against agencies created by secondary legislation"), Discussion Circle I ("Court of Justice"), on the web page of the Secretariat of the European Convention (european-convention.eu.int). See also E. Nieto and I. Martin, op. cit., p. 122 and ff.
438. European Monitoring Centre on Racism and Xenophobia.
439. European Agency for Safety and Health at Work.
440. European Maritime Safety Agency.
441. "Should the European Parliament, the Council or the Commission, in infringement of this Treaty, fail to act, the Member States and the other institutions of the Community may bring an action before the Court of Justice to have the infringement established. … Any natural or legal person may, under the conditions laid down in the preceding paragraphs, complain to the Court of Justice that an institution of the Community has failed to address to that person any act other than a recommendation or an opinion".
442. Order CFI 14 July 1994, Case T-13/94, paragraphs 13 and 14.

that the Commission has failed to initiate a procedure for infringement of the Treaty".[443]

The legality of Community activity can be challenged also indirectly, by a co-operative tool linking national courts with the Community jurisdiction. In the framework of a national proceeding, the national judge asks the ECJ for an interpretation of a specific Community measure or for a statement on its validity, because the ECJ is the only competent body to decide the matter. This is the preliminary ruling, a fundamental mechanism of European Union law aimed at enabling national courts to ensure uniform interpretation and application of its law in all member states.[444]

Any court may refer to the ECJ a question that it considers necessary to resolve a dispute brought before it. However, courts or tribunals for whose decisions there is no judicial remedy under national law must, as a rule, refer such a question to the Court, unless the Court has already ruled on the point (and there is no new context that raises any serious doubt whether the case law may be applied) or the correct interpretation of the rule of Community law is obvious. These two exceptions to the obligation of courts of last instance to refer a question arose from the *acte claire* doctrine, first established by the Da Costa (1963) case to prevent overloading the ECJ with questions whose interpretations are obvious or already stated. The Court later extended the scope of these exceptions (CILFIT) and, according to some authoritative opinions, some high national courts have exceeded the rational use of this possibility, referring to these theories to avoid questions even when doubtless they needed to ask the ECJ.[445]

Another highly controversial aspect is that related to interim measures: if a national court has serious doubts about the validity of a Community act on which a national measure is based, it may exceptionally suspend application of that measure temporarily or grant other interim relief with respect to it. There have arisen serious objections, even of a constitutional nature, to this rule, whose rigorous application can determine the provisional deprivation of the effects of national general provisions even if they are in the form of law passed by Parliament.[446]

The preliminary ruling in Article 267 of the TFEU has a particular version when it refers to specific fields of activity. It is the urgent preliminary ruling

---

443. Order CFI 10 Jul 2001, Case T-191/00, *Werner Edlinger v. Commission*, paragraph 7.
444. See ECJ's "Information Note on references from national courts for a preliminary ruling", OJC 143, 11 June 2005.
445. See Opinion of General Advocate Ruiz Jarabo in Case C-461/03, particularly paragraphs 47 to 53.
446. E. García de Enterria, *La batalla por las medidas cautelares Derecho comunitario europeo y proceso Contencioso-Administrativo español*, Cívitas, Madrid, 2006.

added by the Amsterdam Treaty[447] which applies only in the area of freedom, security and justice – covering policies on border checks, asylum and immigration (Articles 77 to 80 TEU), judicial co-operation in civil matters (Article 81 TEU), judicial co-operation in criminal matters (Articles 82 to 86 TEU) and police co-operation (Articles 87 and 88 TEU). The main difference between both is that the urgent procedure simplifies the various stages of proceedings before the Court, with its application entailing significant constraints on the Court and on the parties and other interested persons taking part in the procedure, particularly the member states.[448]

Finally, damages caused by illegal activities are also ruled by Community law. On non-contractual liability, Article 340 TFEU states that "the Community shall, in accordance with the general principle common to the law of the member states, make good any damage caused by its institutions or by its servants in the performance of their duties". Settled case law has delimited the conditions which should be satisfied for the liability to be admitted: the Community conduct complained of must be illegal; actual damage must have occurred; and there must be a causal link between the illegal conduct and the damage alleged. These three conditions must be concurrent cumulatively so that, if any one is lacking, the action must be dismissed in its entirety.[449] With regard to the first of these conditions, the case law requires demonstration of a sufficiently serious breach of a law intended to confer rights on individuals, having declared that "a breach of Community law is sufficiently serious if the Community institution concerned manifestly and gravely disregarded the limits on its discretion".[450]

These proceedings are subject to some limits, one of which is initiating the action within five years of the occurrence of the event motivating such legal action. However, there is a different rule in cases where the liability of the Community arises from a legislative measure. In such an event, "that period of limitation does not begin until the damaging effects of that measure have arisen and, therefore, until the time at which the persons concerned were bound to have suffered certain damage".[451]

In the specific cases of "co-operative procedures" linking the Commission with national authorities, which implement Community provisions, the general rule is that Community liability is not admitted even when the national authorities cannot set aside the Commission's criteria while they finally adopt a (national) resolution. In such cases, the Court defers to the national

---

447. See ECJ's "Information Note on References from national courts for a preliminary ruling" (OJ C 297 5 December 2009), whose Part II is devoted to the Urgent Preliminary Ruling.
448. The procedure is governed by Article 23a of the Protocol on the Statute of the Court of Justice and Article 104b of its Rules of Procedure.
449. Case C-146/91, *KYDEP v. Council and Commission* [1994] ECR I-4199, paragraphs 19 and 81.
450. CFI 26 June 2008, Case T-94/98, *Alferink and Others v. Commission*, paragraph 62.
451. Case C-282/05 P *Holcim (Deutschland) v. Commission* [2007] ECR I-2941, paragraph 29).

jurisdictions the control of the (formally) national administrative action.[452] This criterion has the merit of critical opinions focused on the very few cases stating Community liability.[453] Far from being palliated, this lack has been reinforced, since these co-operative procedures have substantially increased in recent decades. Also, the Commission is not now the only co-operative body: decentralised bodies and agencies created for these purposes co-operate with national authorities in a single procedure which we referred to above in the section on transnational procedures and mixed administrative action. Recent case law has decided cases where national authorities worked closely with Community bodies such as the European Food Safety Authority[454] and the European Agency for the Evaluation of Medicinal Products.[455]

Finally, it has to be pointed out that there is a limited judicial scrutiny on national actions implementing some of the measures adopted in the framework of the Liberty space. Notwithstanding that this field is, in the aftermath of the Lisbon Treaty, a Community issue and consequently fully included in the Community institutional structure, it seems to retain some traces of its former Third Pillar nature. That is, Article 276 TFEU states that, regarding the provisions on judicial co-operation in criminal matters and on police co-operation, "the Court of Justice of the European Union shall have no jurisdiction to review the validity or proportionality of operations carried out by the police or other law-enforcement services of a Member State or the exercise of the responsibilities incumbent upon Member States with regard to the maintenance of law and order and the safeguarding of internal security".

11.3.2.3. National acts

Compliance with Community law on national activities is verified either at Community or national level, depending on the applicant. At Community level, the ECJ has jurisdiction to take cognisance of an application brought by the Commission or by the member states against the alleged infringement attributed to a member state (Articles 259 and 260 TFEU, action for failure to fulfil an obligation).

However, direct access to the ECJ to challenge such national infringements is not provided for individuals: "No provision in the EEC Treaty provides for the possibility for a natural or legal person to bring before the Court an action

---

452. See, among many others, ECJ 27 March 1980, Case 133/79, *Sucrimez v. Commission* and ECJ 10 June 1982, Case 217/81, *Interagra v. Commission*.

453. F. Fines, *Etude de la Responsabilité Extracontractuelle de la Communauté Economique Europeenne*, Librairie Générale de Droit et Jurisprudence, Paris, 1998.

454. Order CFI 17 June 2008, Case T-397/06, *Dow AgroSciences v. European Safety Authority*, related to the Agency's assessment of an active substance before being placed on the market. On the same date, an Order dismissed an action in a similar case on identical grounds (T-312/06, FMC Chemical SPRL).

455. CFI 18 December 2003, Case T-326/99, *Nancy Fern Olivieri v. Commission and European Agency for the Evaluation of Medicinal Products*.

directed against a Member State".[456] If an individual looks for an infringement to be declared, he or she can complain before the Commission against the member state, but finally it will be the Commission which decides to bring an action before the ECJ. We have already pointed out that the Commission is not bound by the individual's petition to bring an action and that the refusal to do so cannot be the subject of an action of omission.

The usual way for individuals to claim against unlawful implementation – normative or administrative – of Community law is to bring an action before the national courts. In the framework of these national proceedings, the preliminary ruling will help the national judge to state the possible infringements. It is not for the ECJ to state whether or not there is an infringement of Community law, but simply to interpret the scope of the Community provision which is applied by the challenged national measure. However, the border between the corresponding judicial functions is not always easy to perceive, as is clearly shown by the following opinion:[457]

> From the very first references the Court has emphasised that its jurisdiction under Article 177 of the Treaty is limited to the interpretation of the rules of Community law, and that it has no jurisdiction with respect to the facts of cases ... The facts (and the relevant rules of national law) must be established by the referring court, and it is that court which decides the case by applying, to the extent necessary, the interpretation which this Court has given to the relevant rules of Community law.
>
> However, the Court's approach to that distinction is pragmatic; it is not characterised by excessive formalism. Frequently, for example, a national court asks the Court whether a particular rule of national law is compatible with Community law, a question which the Court cannot answer as such, but which it will normally reformulate as a question of interpretation of Community law ... That practice is guided by the principle that the Court should assist the referring court as much as possible, by giving a reply which will enable that court to give judgment. Further, the Court's insistence, especially in recent years, on the national court's duty to inform it of the legal and factual context of the case referred ... is doubtless inspired by the same principle. It is not the Court's task to deliver preliminary rulings containing only abstract interpretations of Community law rules, which may be of little use for the resolution of the actual dispute .... It is rather the Court's task to give an interpretation which is tailored to the needs of the referring court.

Finally, it has to be pointed out that there is a limited judicial scrutiny on national actions implementing some of the measures adopted in the framework of the Liberty space. Notwithstanding that this field is, in the aftermath of the Lisbon Treaty, a Community issue and consequently fully included in the Community institutional structure, it seems to retain some traces of its former Third Pillar nature. That is, Article 276 TFEU states that, regarding the provisions on judicial co-operation in criminal matters and on police co-operation, "the Court of Justice of the European Union shall have no jurisdiction to review the validity or proportionality of operations carried

---

456. Order ECJ 27 September 1991, Case C-285/90, Tsitouras.
457. See Opinion delivered on 10 July 1997 by Advocate General Mr Jacobs on Case C-338/95, paragraphs 12 and 13. Former Article 177 EEC Treaty is now Article 267 TFEU.

out by the police or other law-enforcement services of a Member State or the exercise of the responsibilities incumbent upon Member States with regard to the maintenance of law and order and the safeguarding of internal security".

11.3.3. Access to the courts

In general, access to the courts has been increasingly reinforced by ECJ case law, which recognised the right to a fair trial first as a general principle of Community law and in later statements as a fundamental right protected by the Community legal order.[458]

However, the access to the ECJ provided for individual, legal and natural persons is a highly controversial issue which has been repeatedly reported by the most authoritative opinions. The only direct access for individuals to the ECJ is set within the framework of the action of annulment by the fourth paragraph of Article 263 TFEU, requiring of the applicant "direct and individual" affectation by the contested measures – which is hard to comply with in the case of measures having general effects. Furthermore, the ECJ interpreted "direct"[459]and "individual"[460] to mean that it "cannot have the effect of setting aside the condition in question, expressly laid down in the Treaty",[461] rejecting the wider interpretation the General Advocate had asked for.

On the access to the ECJ for associations, NGOs and similar legal persons, the Court applies these requirements cumulatively, leading to a restrictive result and a very different understanding of such entities at national and Community levels. Generally,

> an association formed to further the collective interests of a category of persons cannot be considered to be individually concerned ... by a measure affecting the general interest of that category.[462]

However, an action of annulment brought by these entities can be admitted under special circumstances, such as the role played by the association in a procedure which led to the adoption of the contested measures. For example,

458. For a clear view on these developments, see C. Harlow, "Access to Justice as a human right. The European Convention and the European Union", and D. Spielmann, "Human Rights Case Law in the Strasbourg and Luxembourg Courts: conflicts, inconsistencies and complementarities", both works in *The EU and Human Rights*, ed. P. Alston, M. Bustelo and J. Heenan, Oxford University Press, 1999. Also, the European Court of Human Rights 30 Jun 2006, *Bosphorous Hava v. Ireland*, reports in paragraph 73 the Luxembourg's case law on this field.

459. Effects on the applicant are directly caused by the contested measure, excluding any further implementation decision. See Opinion of General Advocate Van Gerven, Case C-213/91, paragraph 20.

460. The persons should be affected by the measure "by reason of certain attributes peculiar to them or by reason of factual circumstances in which they are distinguished from all other persons". See ECJ 15 Jun 1963, Case 25/62, *Plauman v. Commission*, among many others.

461. ECJ, 25 Jul 2002, Case C-50/00, paragraphs 44 to 45.

462. Order in *Greenpeace and Others v. Commission*, paragraph 59 upheld by the ECJ in its judgment in *Greenpeace Council and Others v. Commission*.

the admission has been adopted when the applicant association was entitled both to negotiate and conclude a tax agreement with the Commission having effects for the represented sector[463] and to play a pre-eminent role in restructuring the represented sector by establishing and adapting with the Commission the constraint on state aid in that sector.[464] Conversely, the argued "special circumstances" were not enough to break the general rule of inadmissibility when the applicant association was only requested by its national ministry to attend a few meetings in order to exchange information and to define, with other participants, a common course of conduct vis-à-vis the Commission.[465]

The opinion of General Advocate Mr Jacobs in the famous UPA case highlights, among many other interesting points, the lack of compatibility of the case law on *locus standi* with the principle of effective judicial protection in general, and in particular the serious delays and problems in the interim that lead to other disadvantages.[466] Similar analysis can be found on the preparatory works of the Constitutional Treaty, when some representatives of the Community institutions aired coincidental opinions. In this regard, it is worth recalling the contribution of Judge Mr Vassilios Skouris, referring to "possible improvement in judicial protection",[467] and rejecting the idea that the effect of increasing "the number of cases brought before the Court" could be considered a "criterion for determining whether to change these rules". In a similar vein is the final report of Mr A. Vitorino, Commissioner of Justice Issues, referring to the different proposals at the discussion circle on the Court of Justice.[468]

I began the previous paragraph by underlining the improvements in recognition of the right of access provided by the Community legal order, which could apparently be inconsistent with previous considerations. There is no such inconsistency. As it happens, it has been widely pointed out that the obligation to provide broad access to the courts has been addressed much more to national jurisdictions than it has been to the European jurisdiction. This imbalance could be explained on the basis of the efficacy and due application of Community law. In the absence of a centralised administration applying Community law, its effectiveness resides to a large extent in national courts, requiring wide access for individuals to the courts in order to ask for rights provided by Community law. From this perspective we can state that the more that citizens are able to go before the national courts, the more national law and measures implementing Community law will be under judicial scrutiny. In these circumstances, "the right of access to justice receives implicit rec-

---

463. Order ECJ 3 May 1985, Cases 67 to 70/85, *Van der Kooy and others v. Commission.*
464. Order ECJ 17 Jan 1990, Case 313/90, *CIRFS and others v. Commission.*
465. CFI 11 Feb 1999, Case T-86/96, *ADL and HLF v. Commission.*
466. See his opinion delivered on 21 March 2002, in toto.
467. Currently, President of the ECJ: its hearing, "representing his own view, not the official position of the institution" can be found in Working Document 19, Working Group II, 11 September 2002, available at www.european-convention.int.
468. Working Document 08, Circle I, available at www.european-convention.int.

ognition inside the doctrine of 'direct effect' … indeed, it is fair to describe direct effect as premised on a right of access to justices".[469] In my opinion, this is the right way to understand the important doctrine about interim reliefs, and specifically the provisional suspension of a parliamentary measure by a national judge.

The official position mitigating the gaps in access to the ECJ provided for individuals is the one that presents, for these effects, the preliminary ruling as a complementary tool of the action for annulment.[470] The narrow access for individuals to the ECJ to bring an action of annulment is balanced by the (necessarily) wide access to the national courts from which they can indirectly access the ECJ through the preliminary ruling. However, as will appear in the last part of this work, the procedural characteristics and the parties' faculties are so different that the alleged mitigation can hardly be accepted.

References

Alonso García, R., *Las sentencias básicas del Tribunal de Justicia de las Comunidades Europeas*, 2nd edn, CEC, Madrid, 2003.

Bacigalupo Sagesse, M., *La justicia comunitaria*, Marcial Pons, Madrid, 1995.

Baena del Alcázar, M., "Competencias, funciones y potestades en el ordenamiento jurídico español", *Estudios sobre la Constitución Española: homenaje al prof. Gracía de Enterría*, Vol. III, Cívitas 1991.

Cassese, S., "European administrative proceedings", *Law and Contemporary Problems*, Vol. 68 (2004), No. 1.

Chiti, E., "Administrative proceedings involving European agencies", *Law and Contemporary Problems*, Vol. 68 (2004), No. 1.

Chiti, M., "Forms of European administrative action", *Law and Contemporary Problems*, Vol. 68 (2004), No. 1.

Constantinesco, V., "The ECJ as law-maker: praeter aut contra legem?" in D. O'Keeffe (ed.), *Judicial review in European Union law*, Kluwer Law International, The Hague, 2000.

Della Cananea, G.J. "The European Union mixed proceedings", *Law and Contemporary Problems*, Vol. 68 (2004), No. 1.

Fines, F., *Etude de la responsabilité extracontractuelle de la Communauté Economique Européenne*, Librarie General de Droit et Jurisprudence (LGDJ), Paris, 1998.

---

469. C. Harlow, "Access to Justice", op. cit., p. 191.
470. ECJ, Case C-294/83, Les Verts, paragraph 23.

Galera Rodrigo, S., *La aplicación administrativa del derecho comunitario: administración mixta, tercera vía de aplicación*, Cívitas, Madrid, 1998.

Galera Rodrigo, S., *Sistema Europeo de justicia administrativa*, Dykinson, Madrid, 2005.

García de Enterría, E., *La batalla por las medidas cautelares: derecho comunitario europeo y proceso contencioso-administrativo español*, Cívitas, Madrid, 2006. Gil Ibáñez, A., *El control y la ejecución del Derecho comunitario. El papel de las Administraciones nacionales y europea*, Instituto Nacional de Administración Pública, Madrid, 2000.

González-Varas Ibáñez, S., *Derecho administrativo europeo*, Instituto Andaluz Administración Pública, Sevilla, 2000.

Habermas, J., "Why Europe needs a constitution?" in E. O. Eriksen, J. E. Fossum and A. J. Menéndez (eds), *Developing a constitution for Europe*, Routledge, London, 2004.

Harlow, C., "Access to justice as a human right. The European Convention and the European Union" in P. Alston, M. Bustelo and J. Heenan (eds), *The EU and human rights*, Oxford University Press, Oxford, 1999.

Isaac, G. and Blanquet, M., *Droit communautaire général*, 8th edn, Dalloz, Paris, 2001.

Jansen, O., and Langbroek, P. (eds.), Defence Rights during Administrative Investigations, Intersentia, Antwerp 2007.

Kanska, K., "Towards administrative human rights in the EU. Impact of the Charter of Fundamental Rights", *European Law Journal*, Vol. 10, No. 3 (May 2004).

Mischo, J., "The contribution of the Court of Justice to the protection of the federal balance in the European Community" in D. O'Keeffe and A. Bavasso (eds), *Judicial review in European Union law*, Kluwer Law International, Leiden, 2000.

Moreno Molina, A. M., *La ejecución administrativa del Derecho comunitario. Régimen Europeo y español*, Marcial Pons-Univ. Carlos III, Madrid, 1998.

Nieto-Garrido, E. and Martin Delgado, I., *European administrative law in the constitutional treaty*, Hart Publishing, Oxford, 2007.

Ordeñez Solís, D., "Derecho, administración e integración de España en la Unión Europea bajo el prisma del Consejo de Estado", in *Civitas. Revista española de derecho europeo*, No. 27, 2008.

Ruiz-Jarabo Colomer, D., "El Tribunal de Justicia de la Unión Europea en el Tratado de Lisboa" in *Noticias de la Union Europea* (April 2009), No. 291.

Schmidt-Assman, E., *La Teoría General del Derecho Administrativo como sistema*, INAP-Marcial Pons, Madrid, 2003.

Schorkopf, F., "Constitutionalization or a constitution for the European Union?" in A. Bodnar, M. Kowalski, K. Raible and F. Schorkopf (eds), *The emerging constitutional law of the European Union: German and Polish perspectives*, Springer, Berlin, 2003.

Schwarze, J., *European administrative law*, Sweet & Maxwell, London, 2006.

Soldevila Fragoso, S., "Justicia Europea: entre Niza y Lisboa", *Noticias de la Union Europea* (April 2009), No. 291.

Spielmann, D., "Human rights case law in the Strasbourg and Luxembourg courts: conflicts, inconsistencies and complementarities" in P. Alston, M. Bustelo and J. Heenan (eds), *The EU and human rights*, Oxford University Press, Oxford, 1999.

Weiler, J. H. H., "Federalism and constitutionalism: Europe's sonderweg", Jean Monnet Working Paper, New York University 10/2000, available at www.jeanmonnetprogram.org/papers/00/001001-01.html#P8_131.

Ziller, J. (ed.), *What's new in European administrative law?*, EUI Working Paper Law, No. 2005/10.

Abbreviations

EEC Treaty: Treaty of Rome 1957 establishing the European Economic Community

EC Treaty: Treaty of the European Community, after amendments introduced in 1991 by the Maastrich Treaty in the former three Communities (EEC, ECCS and EURATOM)

TEU: Treaty of the European Union, after amendments introduced in 2007 by the Lisbon Treaty (in force since December 2009).

TFEU: Treaty of Functioning of the European Union, after amendments introduced by the Lisbon Treaty.

CFSP: Common Foreign and Security Policy (former second pillar).

ECJ: European Court of Justice

CFI: Court of First Instance.

Chapter 12
The EU's second pillar – Foreign and security policy

F. Jiménez García

12.1. The test of equivalent protection

Before the Lisbon Treaty, both the European Union's Common Foreign and Security Policy and the EU Police and Judicial Co-operation in Criminal Matters followed an intergovernmental structure that adopted decisions freely, without limitation by parliaments, and judicial review over such adopted acts was restricted or non-existent. Thus the European Council[471] and the Council of the Union[472] ("the Councils") were the principal organs of these pillars of co-operation. These bodies' political and international nature implied a democratic deficit and a judicial deficit created by the founding treaties. With regard to effective judicial protection, it was (and is) a matter of controversy whether these pillars of co-operation did in fact pass the test of "equivalent protection" which the European Court of Human Rights demanded of the European Council in the *Bosphorus* case,[473] specifically when the Councils adopt acts that concern the rights and freedoms of individuals.

In agreement with the European Court of Human Rights' *Bosphorus* judgment, repeated in the decision on admissibility of 2 May 2007 in *Behrami and Behrami v. France and Saramati v. France, Germany and Norway*, although the European Convention on Human Rights did not prohibit a state from transferring sovereign power to an international organisation in order to pursue co-operation in certain fields of activity, the state remained responsible under Article 1 of the Convention for all acts and omissions of its organs,

---

471. In accordance with Article 4 EU Treaty of Nice, the European Council brings together the heads of state or government of the member states and the President of the Commission. They are assisted by the ministers for foreign affairs of the member states and a member of the Commission. The European Council meets at least twice a year, under the chairmanship of the head of state or government of the member state which holds the presidency of the Council. The European Council provides the Union with the necessary impetus for its development and defines the general political guidelines thereof. Similarly, Article 15 EU Treaty of Lisbon introduces the presence of President of the European Council.
472. In accordance with Article 203 of the Treaty establishing the European Community, similar to Article 16 EU Treaty of Lisbon, the Council consists of a representative of each member state at ministerial level, authorised to commit the government of that member state.
473. European Court of Human Rights (Grand Chamber), *Bosphorus Hava Yollari Turizm ve Ticaret Anonim Şirketi v. Ireland*, Application No. 45036/98, judgment of 30 June 2005, paragraphs 155 to 165.

regardless of whether they were a consequence of the necessity to comply with international legal obligations, Article 1 making no distinction as to the rule or measure concerned and not excluding any part of a state's "jurisdiction" from scrutiny under the Convention. The Court went on, however, to hold that where such state action was taken in compliance with international legal obligations flowing from its membership of an international organisation and where the relevant organisation protected fundamental rights in a manner which could be considered at least equivalent to that which the Convention provides, a presumption arose that the state had not departed from the requirements of the Convention. Such presumption could be rebutted if, in the circumstances of a particular case, it was considered that the protection of Convention rights was manifestly deficient: in such a case, the interest of international co-operation would be outweighed by the Convention's role as a "constitutional instrument of European public order" in the field of human rights.[474]

On the other hand, with regard to Community acts executing international obligations created by acts of the intergovernmental pillars, particularly of the CFSP, the Court of Justice of the European Communities repeated in its judgment on the case of *Kadi v. Council* (2008) three basic principles of the Law of the European Union arising from Article 6 EU Treaty. First, the Community (and, by extension, the European Union) is based on the rule of law, inasmuch as neither its Member States nor its institutions can avoid review of the conformity of their acts with the basic constitutional charter, the EC Treaty. Second, an international agreement cannot affect the allocation of powers fixed by the treaties or, consequently, the autonomy of the Community legal system, observance of which is ensured by the Court. Finally, the fundamental rights form an integral part of the general principles of law whose observance is a condition of the lawfulness of Community and Union acts.

For that purpose and in conformity with Article 6 of the EU Treaty, the Court draws inspiration from the constitutional traditions common to Member States and from the guidelines supplied by international instruments for the protection of human rights on which the Member States have collaborated or to which they are signatories. In that regard, the Convention has special significance. It follows from all these considerations that the obligations imposed by an international agreement and the legal instruments of these intergovernmental pillars cannot have the effect of prejudicing the constitutional principles of the EU Treaty, which include the principle that all acts of the Community and of the Union must respect fundamental rights.[475]

---

474. See European Court of Human Rights (Grand Chamber), Decision as to admissibility, 2 May 2007, in *Behrami and Behrami v. France and Saramati v. France, Germany and Norway*, paragraph 145.
475. See CJEC, *Kadi v. Council of the European Union and Commission of the European Communities*, Joined Cases C-402/05 P and C-415/05 P, judgment of the Court (Grand Chamber),

Since the intergovernmental pillars obey a constitutional and institutional configuration different from that of the integration of the Community, having a potential impact in sensitive areas and jurisdictional guarantees, it is necessary to defend strict observance of dispositions against any extension of the bridge between these governmental pillars and articles of the EC Treaty other than those with which they explicitly create a link. Otherwise imbalances would occur to the detriment of other international entities or, in certain cases, to the national authorities, including judicial and constitutional bodies, of the member states. The intergovernmental nature of these pillars demands that their normative and sanctioning capacity should not overflow into areas of integration that determine, limit or create individual rights and freedoms or affect democratic citizenship, since such goals, in the constitutional tradition, can only be reached by means of scrupulous respect for democratic principles, the rule of law and the guarantee (including judicial guarantee) of fundamental rights.

In this respect, the Court of First Instance and the Court of Justice of the European Communities, referring to application of the clause of flexibility in Article 308 of the EC Treaty, consider that

> the co-existence of Union and Community as integrated but separate legal orders, and the constitutional architecture of the pillars, as intended by the framers of the Treaties now in force, authorise neither the institutions nor the member states to rely on the "flexibility clause" of Article 308 EC in order to mitigate the fact that the Community lacks the competence necessary for achievement of one of the Union's objectives. To decide otherwise would amount, in the end, to making that provision applicable to all measures falling within the CFSP and within police and judicial co-operation in criminal matters (PJC), so that the Community could always take action to attain the objectives of those policies. Such an outcome would deprive many provisions of the Treaty on European Union of their due ambit and would be inconsistent with the introduction of instruments specific to the CFSP (common strategies, joint actions, common positions) and to the PJC (common positions, decisions, framework decisions).[476]

The Lisbon Treaty abolishes the "pillar structure" of EU legislation although without substantial changes in the field of foreign and security policy. Nevertheless, matters which were previously dealt with under the third pillar, such as judicial co-operation in criminal matters and police co-operation, will be treated under the same kind of rules as those of the single market. Consequently, EU and national measures in these areas will be subject to the judicial review of the Court of Justice. However, Article 10 of Protocol 36 on transitional provisions concerning acts adopted on the basis of Titles V and VI of the Treaty on European Union prior to the entry into force of the Treaty of Lisbon provides that: i) the legal effects of the acts of the institutions,

---

3 September 2008, paragraphs 281 to 285.

476. See *Kadi v. Council of the European Union and Commission of the European Communities,* Case T-315/01, judgment of the Court of First Instance, 21 September 2005, paragraph 120; Cases C-402/05 P and C-415/05 P, judgment of the Court (Grand Chamber), 3 September 2008, paragraph 202.

bodies, offices and agencies of the Union adopted on the basis of the Treaty on European Union prior to the entry into force of the Treaty of Lisbon shall be preserved until those acts are repealed, annulled or amended in implementation of the Treaties (the same shall apply to agreements concluded between member states on the basis of the Treaty on European Union); ii) the full powers of the Court of Justice and the Commission become applicable to the existing "acquis" of the third pillar legislation five years after entry into force of the Treaty of Lisbon, that is, 1 December 2014.

12.2. The constitutional framework

One of the objectives of the EU is to assert its identity on the international scene, in particular by action on a common foreign and security policy including the progressive framing of a common defence policy, which might lead to a common defence. If the Common Foreign and Security Policy (CFSP) tries to unify the voice of the EU on the international scene, the European security and defence policy (ESDP) aims to allow the Union to develop its civilian and military capacities for crisis management and conflict prevention at the international level, thus helping to maintain peace and international security, in accordance with the United Nations Charter. The definition and execution of such objectives correspond to the European Council and the Council of the European Union through the following legal instruments, treated below: common strategies, joint action, common positions and international agreements.

For almost 40 years of European construction, the very expression "common foreign policy" found no place in the Treaties. From October 1970 the member states of the European Community co-operated and tried to consult one another on major international policy problems, but this was at the intergovernmental level in the context of "European political co-operation". In 1986, the Single European Act formalised this intergovernmental co-operation without changing its nature or methods of operation. The change came at Maastricht where, for the first time, member states incorporated into the treaty the objective of a "common foreign policy". Since the treaty's entry into force on 1 November 1993, the European Union as such can make its voice heard on the international stage and express its position on armed conflicts, human rights and any other subject linked to the fundamental principles and common values which form the basis of the European Union and which it is committed to defend.

Provisions on the CFSP were revised by the Amsterdam Treaty, which came into force in 1999. An important decision, improving the effectiveness and profile of the Union's foreign policy, was the appointment of a High Representative for the CFSP. New objectives were included in the Treaty on European Union, relating to humanitarian, rescue and peacekeeping operations and the use of combat forces in crisis management, including peacemaking operations (known as "Petersberg tasks"). In addition to these civilian and military crisis management operations, the ESDP includes a conflict-prevention component. The Political and Security Committee (PSC), the EU Military Committee (EUMC) and EU Military Staff (EUMS) are the permanent political and military structures responsible for an autonomous, operational EU defence policy.

The Treaty of Nice came into force on 1 February 2003. Its new CFSP provisions notably increased the areas falling under qualified majority voting, enhanced the role of the Political and Security Committee in crisis management operations and introduced the possibility, under certain conditions, of establishing closer co-operation in the CFSP field for implementation of joint actions and common positions. This closer co-operation may not be used for matters with military or defence implications.

Finally, Chapter 2 of Title V of the Lisbon Treaty on the European Union, adopted on 17 December 2007, relates to "Specific Provisions on the Common Foreign and Security Policy". Article 24.2 establishes that "within the framework of the principles and objectives of its external action, the Union shall conduct, define and implement a common foreign and security policy, based on the development of mutual political solidarity among Member States, the identification of questions of general interest and the achievement of an ever-increasing degree of convergence of Member States' actions", whereas point 3 says that "the Member States shall support the Union's external and security policy actively and unreservedly in a spirit of loyalty and mutual solidarity and shall comply with the Union's action in this area".

Likewise, the Lisbon Treaty (Article 21.1) maintains that

> the Union's action on the international scene shall be guided by the principles which have inspired its own creation, development and enlargement, and which it seeks to advance in the wider world: democracy, the rule of law, the universality and indivisibility of human rights and fundamental freedoms, respect for human dignity, the principles of equality and solidarity, and respect for the principles of the United Nations Charter and international law.

12.3. Organs of government in the framework of the CFSP

The European Council and the Council of the Union are the decisive and decision-making organs in the construction and functioning of this pillar, without the active participation of the Commission or the European Parliament. Other organs and agencies accentuate the intergovernmental character of this pillar.

The first of these is the High Representative for the Union for Foreign Affairs and Security Policy (HR), who under the Treaty of Lisbon is named by a qualified majority of the European Council with the agreement of the President of the Commission. The High Representative shall conduct the Union's common foreign and security policy. He shall contribute by his proposals to the development of that policy, which he shall carry out as mandated by the Council. The same shall apply to the common security and defence policy. Moreover, he shall represent the Union for matters relating to the common foreign and security policy, shall conduct political dialogue with third parties on the Union's behalf and shall express the Union's position in international organisations and at international conferences. The Council may, on a proposal from the High Representative of the Union, appoint a special representative with a mandate in relation to particular policy issues. The special representative shall carry out his mandate under the authority of the High Representative (Article 33 EU Treaty). The EU Treaty of Lisbon also provides that the High Representative of the Union for Foreign Affairs and Security Policy, who shall chair the Foreign Affairs Council and shall be one of the Vice-Presidents of the Commission elected by the European Parliament, shall be assisted by a European External Action Service. This service shall work in co-operation with the diplomatic services of the member states and shall comprise officials from relevant departments of the General Secretariat of the Council and of the Commission as well as staff seconded from national diplomatic services of the member states. The organisation and functioning of the European External Action Service shall be established by a decision of the Council. The Council shall act on a proposal from the High Representative after consulting the European Parliament and after obtaining the consent of the Commission.

In conformity with Article 38 of the EU Treaty, a Political and Security Committee (PSC) monitors the international situation in the areas covered by the CFSP and helps to define policies by delivering opinions to the Council at the request of the Council or of the High Representative of the Union for Foreign Affairs and Security Policy or on its own initiative. The PSC also monitors implementation of agreed policies, without prejudice to the responsibility of the Presidency and Commission. This Committee exercises, under the responsibility of the Council and of the High Representative, political control and strategic direction of crisis management operations. The Council may authorise the PSC, for the purpose and duration of a crisis management operation, as determined by the Council, to take the relevant decisions on political control and strategic direction of the operation. The PSC is made up of the political directors of the member states' foreign ministries.

Though the Council, whose preparatory work is carried out by the Committee of Permanent Representatives (Coreper), and the Commission alone have powers to take legally binding decisions, each within their own areas of competency and in accordance with procedures laid down by the treaties, nevertheless it is for the PSC, in preparing the EU's response to a crisis, to propose to the Council the political objectives to be pursued by the Union and to recommend a coherent set of options aimed at contributing to the settlement of the crisis. In particular, it may draw up an opinion recommending to the Council that it adopt a joint action. Without prejudice to the role of the Commission, it supervises implementation of the measures adopted and assesses their effects. The Commission informs the PSC of the measures it has adopted or is envisaging. The member states inform the PSC of the measures they have adopted or are envisaging at national level. The PSC sends guidelines to the Military Committee and receives the latter's opinions and recommendations. In the event of a military response, the PSC exercises political control and strategic direction. On the basis of the opinions and recommendations of the Military Committee, the PSC evaluates strategic military options, the operation concept and the operation plan to be submitted to the Council. With a view to launching an operation, the PSC sends the Council a recommendation based on the opinions of the Military Committee.[477]

The Military Committee of the European Union (EUMC) is the highest military body within the Council of the EU. The EUMC is composed of the Chiefs of Defence (CHOD), represented by their military representatives (Milreps). It may meet at CHOD or Milrep level. The EUMC is the forum for military consultation and co-operation between EU member states in the field of conflict prevention and crisis management. It provides the PSC with advice and recommendations on military matters. Military advice is taken on the basis of consensus. In a crisis situation, the EUMC exercises military direction and gives military instructions to the Military Staff.[478]

The European Union Military Staff (EUMS) is the source of the EU's military expertise. The EUMS provides an early-warning capability. It plans, assesses and makes recommendations on the concept of crisis management and general military strategy. The EUMS is a Council Secretariat department under the military authority of the European Union Military Committee (EUMC). The EUMS implements the decisions and guidance of the EUMC and supports it in situation assessment and military aspects of strategic planning. This concerns the full range of Petersberg tasks, including the European security strategy and all EU-led operations. The EUMS is directly attached to the Secretary-General/High Representative (SG/HR) and provides support, on request from the Secretary-General/High Representative or the Political and Security Committee (PSC), for temporary missions in third countries or international organisations. Since 2004 the EUMS has been assisted by a civilian/military cell which, within the framework of the EUMS, performs such tasks as strategic planning in response to crises with a view to joint civilian/military operations. Working through the civilian/military cell, the EUMS is responsible for providing the capacity needed to plan and manage independent EU military operations. This enables the EUMS, acting on a recommendation from the EUMC, to set up an operations centre speedily in cases where a joint civilian/military response is required and no national HQ

---

477. See Council Decision 2001/78/CFSP of 22 January 2001 (OJL 27, 30 January 2001).
478. See Council Decision 2001/79/CFSP of 22 January 2001 (OJL 27, 30 January 2001).

has been designated by the Council. The civilian/military cell is the permanent hub of the EU's operations centre and helps to co-ordinate civil operations.[479]

Established in August 2007, the Civilian Planning and Conduct Capability (CPCC) has a mandate to plan and conduct civilian European Security and Defence Policy (ESDP) operations under the political control and strategic direction of the Political and Security Committee; to provide assistance and advice to the SG/HR, the Presidency and the relevant EU Council bodies and to direct, co-ordinate, advise, support, supervise and review civilian ESDP operations. CPCC works in close co-operation with the European Commission.

In addition, agencies have been set up to carry out very specific technical, scientific and management tasks within the framework of the European Union's Common Foreign and Security Policy: European Defence Agency (EDA), the European Union Satellite Centre (EUSC) and the European Union Institute for Security Studies (ISS).

The European Defence Agency was established under Joint Action 2004/551/CFSP of the Council of Ministers of 12 July 2004 and subsequently regulated in Article 45 of the EU Treaty of Lisbon. In conformity with this Article, the European Defence Agency shall have as its task to: (a) contribute to identifying the member states' military capability objectives and evaluating observance of the capability commitments given by the member states; (b) promote harmonisation of operational needs and adoption of effective, compatible procurement methods; (c) propose multilateral projects to fulfil the objectives in terms of military capabilities, ensure co-ordination of the programmes implemented by the member states and management of specific co-operation programmes; (d) support defence technology research, and co-ordinate and plan joint research activities and the study of technical solutions meeting future operational needs; (e) contribute to identifying and, if necessary, implementing any useful measure for strengthening the industrial and technological base of the defence sector and for improving the effectiveness of military expenditure.

The European Union Satellite Centre (EUSC) was set up in 2002, based on Council Joint Action 2001/555/CFSP of 20 July 2001 and became operational in January 2002. It is an agency of the Council of the European Union dedicated to the production and exploitation of information deriving from analysis of earth observation space imagery. It aims at supporting EU decision-making in the CFSP. The EUSC has its own legal personality in order to carry out its functions and is under the political supervision of the Political and Security Committee of the Council and the operational direction of the Secretary General.

---

479. See Council Decision 2001/80/CFSP of 22 January 2001 (OJL 27, 30 January 2001).

Finally, the European Union Institute for Security Studies (ISS) was set up in 2002 based on Council Joint Action 2001/554/CFSP of 20 July 2001. Its aim is to help create a common European security culture, to support the strategic debate by providing the best possible interface between European decision-makers and the diverse circles of non-official specialists. The Institute's activities are directed towards data analysis and recommendations necessary for EU policy-making. Consequently, the Institute contributes to the development of the CFSP by executing several main tasks: organising research and debate on key security and defence issues that are of importance to the European Union; bringing together academics, officials, experts and decision-makers from the EU member states, other European countries, the United States and Canada to provide a forward-looking analysis on defence issues for the EU's Council of Ministers and the High Representative for the CFSP; developing a transatlantic dialogue on all security issues among the countries of Europe, the United States and Canada to raise the profile of the transatlantic relationship and enrich both sides' approaches to security issues; and offering fellowships to expand its network of contacts and synergies with national think tanks. Visiting Fellowships are given to junior academics from all European countries, while Senior Visiting Fellowships are granted to well-known experts.

12.4. The legal instruments of the CFSP. The role of the Commission and European Parliament

Prior to the Lisbon Treaty, the objectives of this Second Pillar of the Union were set out in Article 11 of the EU Treaty and were to be attained through specific legal instruments (common strategies, joint action, common position and international agreements) which had to be adopted unanimously in the Council, though the Treaty of Amsterdam provided for qualified majority voting under certain conditions (Articles 23.2 and 24.3 of the EU Treaty, currently Article 31.2 of the EU Treaty of Lisbon). Likewise and according to current Article 31.1 of the EU Treaty, it provides the possibility of constructive abstention by allowing a member state to abstain on a vote in the Council on the common foreign and security policy (CFSP), without blocking a unanimous decision. If abstention is accompanied by a formal declaration, the member state in question is not obliged to apply the decision but must accept that it commits the Union. In a spirit of mutual solidarity, the member state must then refrain from any action likely to conflict with or impede Union action based on that decision and the other member states shall respect its position. If the members of the Council qualifying their abstention in this way represent at least one third of the member states comprising at least one third of the population of the Union, the decision shall not be adopted. On the other hand, if a member of the Council declares that, for vital and stated reasons of national policy, it intends to oppose the adoption of a decision to be taken by qualified majority, a vote shall not be taken. The High Representative will, in close consultation with the member state involved, search for a solution acceptable to it. If he does not succeed, the Council may, acting by a qualified majority, request that the matter be referred to the European Council for a decision by unanimity.

The European Council decided on common strategies to be implemented by the Union in areas where member states have important interests in common. Common strategies defined their objectives, duration and the means to be made available by the Union and the member states. The Council made the decisions necessary for defining and implementing the Common Foreign and Security Policy on the basis of the general guidelines defined by the European Council. Joint actions addressed specific situations where operational action by the Union was required. They laid down their objectives, scope, the means to be made available to the Union, if necessary their duration, and the conditions for their implementation. Common positions defined the approach of the Union to a particular matter, either geographical or thematic. Member states were required to ensure their national policies conform to the common position. When it was necessary to conclude an agreement with one or more states or international organisations to implement this policy, the Council could authorise the Presidency, assisted by the Commission as appropriate, to open negotiations to that effect. Such agreements were concluded by the Council on a recommendation from the Presidency. The Council acted unanimously when the agreement covers an issue for which unanimity was required for the adoption of internal decisions. When the agreement was aimed to implement a joint action or common position, the Council acted by qualified majority. No agreement is binding on a member state whose representative in the Council states that it has to comply with the requirements of its own constitutional procedure; the other members of the Council may agree that the agreement shall nevertheless apply provisionally. Agreements concluded under the conditions set out by this article are binding on the institutions of the Union.

With the Lisbon Treaty, these specific legal instruments are removed and are now replaced by decisions. Now, the European Council shall identify the Union's strategic interests, determine the objectives of and define general guidelines for the common foreign and security policy, including in matters with defence implications. It shall adopt the necessary decisions and *expressly the adoption of legislative acts shall be excluded* (Articles 25-26 and 31 EU Treaty). In conformity with Article 28 EU Treaty where the international situation requires operational action by the Union, the Council shall adopt the necessary decisions. They shall lay down their objectives, scope, the means to be made available to the Union, if necessary their duration, and the conditions for their implementation. If there is a change in circumstances having a substantial effect on a question subject to such a decision, the Council shall review the principles and objectives of that decision and take the necessary decisions. Decisions shall commit the member states in the positions they adopt and in the conduct of their activity. Whenever there is any plan to adopt a national position or take national action pursuant to a decision, information shall be provided by the member state concerned in time to allow, if necessary, for prior consultations within the Council. The obligation to provide prior information shall not apply to measures which are merely a national transposition of Council decisions. In cases of imperative need arising from changes in the situation and failing a review of the Council decision, member states may take the necessary measures as a matter of urgency having regard to the general objectives of that decision. The member state concerned shall inform the Council immediately of any such measures. Should there be any major difficulties in implementing a decision as referred to in this Article, a member state shall refer them to the Council which shall discuss them and seek appropriate solutions. Such solutions shall not run counter to the objectives of the decision or impair its effectiveness. For its part, Article 29 EU Treaty provides that the Council shall adopt decisions which shall define the approach of the Union to a particular matter of a geographical or thematic nature. Member states shall ensure that their national policies conform to the Union positions. Finally Article 37 of the EU Treaty provides that the Union may conclude agreements with one or more states or international organisations in areas covered by this policy. These agreements are subject to the rules laid down in Article 218 of the Treaty on the Functioning of the European Union (TFEU). According to this article, the Commission, or the High Representative of the Union for Foreign Affairs and Security Policy where the agreement envisaged relates exclusively or principally to the common foreign and security policy, shall submit recommendations to the Council, which shall adopt a decision authorising the opening of negotiations and, depending on the subject of the agreement envisaged, nominating the Union negotiator or the head of the Union's negotiating team. Likewise and in conformity with Article 218 TFEU, it provides that when the agreements relate exclusively to the common foreign and security policy, the Council shall adopt the decision concluding the agreement without requiring the consent of the European Parliament.

In a pre-Lisbon European Union without express recognition of its international personality, the European Council and the Council of the EU were the decisive organs in configuring the CFSP, assisted by the Secretary-General of the Council, the High Representative for Common Foreign and Security Policy, and the Political and Security Committee; these three exercised, under the responsibility of the Council, political control and strategic direction of crisis management operations.[480] Neither Parliament nor the Commission

---

480. Ongoing operations: EU Military Operation in Bosnia and Herzegovina (EUFOR-Althea); EU Police Mission in Bosnia-Herzegovina (EUPM); European Union rule-of-law mission in Kosovo (EULEX Kosovo); European Union Monitoring Mission (EUMM) in Georgia; EU Police

intervened in this control. Both institutions lacked capacity of decision in this area of the European Union.

The Commission was fully associated with the work carried out in the field of the CFSP. It could, in the same way as any member state, refer to the Council any question relating to the CFSP and could submit proposals to the Council – though it does not have the sole right to do so as in Community matters. The Commission could also, like any member state, request the Presidency to convene an extraordinary Council meeting and make suggestions to the Policy Unit for work to be undertaken. The Commission implemented the CFSP budget (under the EC budget) by means of appropriate financial proposals.

To the European Parliament a merely consultative statute was granted in this area. In agreement with the former Article 21 of the EU Treaty, the Presidency consulted the European Parliament on the main aspects and basic choices of the CFSP and ensured their views were duly taken into consideration. The European Parliament was to be kept regularly informed by the Presidency and the Commission of the development of the Union's foreign and security policy. The European Parliament could ask questions of the Council or make recommendations to it, and it held an annual debate on progress in implementing the CFSP.

With the Lisbon Treaty, the situation is essentially unchanged. Article 30.1 of the EU Treaty provides that any member state, the High Representative of the Union for Foreign Affairs and Security Policy, or the High Representative with the Commission's support, may refer any question relating to the common foreign and security policy to the Council and may submit to it initiatives or proposals as appropriate. On the other hand, the High Representative shall regularly consult the European Parliament on the main aspects and the basic choices of the common foreign and security policy and the common security and defence policy and inform it as to how those policies evolve. He shall ensure that the views of the European Parliament are duly taken into consideration. Special representatives may be involved in briefing the European Parliament. The European Parliament may ask questions of the Council or make recommendations to it and to the High Representative. Twice a year it shall hold a debate on progress in implementing the common foreign and security policy, including the common security and defence policy (Article 36 EU Treaty).

Mission in the Palestinian Territories (EUPOL COPPS); EU Border Assistance Mission at Rafah Crossing Point in the Palestinian Territories (EU BAM Rafah); EU Integrated Rule of Law Mission for Iraq (Eujust Lex); EU Police Mission in Afghanistan (EUPOL Afghanistan); EU mission in support of Security Sector Reform in Guinea-Bissau (EU SSR Guinea-Bissau); EUFOR Tchad/RCA; EUPOL RD Congo; EU security sector reform mission in the Democratic Republic of the Congo (EUSEC RD Congo); EU military operation to contribute to the deterrence, prevention and repression of acts of piracy and armed robbery off the Somali coast (EU NAVFOR Somalia, Operation Atalanta).

12.5. The scope of judicial review

There is no doubt of the intergovernmental and political character of this second pillar of the European Union. The Court of Justice of the European Communities (ECJ) has no jurisdiction with respect to review of the legality of provisions adopted under Title V of the EU Treaty, with the exception of its jurisdiction, under Article 46 EU Treaty, to prevent intergovernmental pillars invading the competencies of the Community pillar or vice versa. It follows then that individuals have no recourse to any effective legal remedy before the ECJ for the acts adopted by this pillar.[481]

In the *Segi* case, the European Court of Human Rights noted that common positions adopted in the framework of the CFSP are not directly applicable in the Member States and cannot form the direct basis for any criminal or administrative proceedings against individuals, especially as they do not mention any particular organisation or person. As such, therefore, the CFSP does not give rise to legally binding obligations for the applicant. In consequence, the Court considered that the situation complained of does not give the applicant the status of victim of a violation of the Convention under the meaning of Article 34 of the Convention. In any event, as added by the Court of Strasbourg, "the concrete measures of application of these positions (as community regulations or national laws) which have been adopted or might be in the future would be subject to the form of judicial review established in each legal order concerned, whether international or national".[482]

On the other hand, in Case T-228/02, *Organisation des Modjahedines du peuple d'Iran v. Council of European Union*, the Court of First Instance of the European Communities (Second Chamber) affirmed in its judgment of 12 December 2006 that

> In the Community legal system founded on the principle of conferred powers, as embodied in Article 5 EC, the absence of an effective legal remedy as claimed by the applicant cannot in itself confer independent Community jurisdiction in relation to an act adopted in a related yet distinct legal system, namely that deriving from Titles V and VI of the EU Treaty (*Segi and Others* v *Council* ...). Nor can the applicant rely on *Unión de Pequeños Agricultores* v *Council* .... In that judgment ..., the Court based its reasoning on the fact that the EC Treaty has established a complete system of legal remedies and procedures designed to ensure judicial review of the lawfulness of acts of the institutions. However, as indicated above, the EU Treaty has, in relation to acts adopted on the basis of Titles V and VI thereof, established a limited system of judicial review, certain areas being outside the scope of that review and certain legal remedies not being available.[483]

---

481. On this question, see F. Jiménez García, "Tutela judicial efectiva, Pilares intergubernamentales de la Unión Europea y Naciones Unidas o Viceversa", in *Nuevos Desafíos del Derecho Penal Internacional. Terrorismo, Crímenes Internacionales y Derechos Fundamentales*, ed. A. Cuerda Riezu and F. Jiménez García, Tecnos, Madrid, 2009, pp. 411-464.
482. European Court of Human Rights, Decision 23 May 2002, *Segi and Others v. 15 States of the EU.*
483. See paragraph 54.

The judgment also indicated that, at the outset, a common position is not an act of the Council adopted on the basis of the EC Treaty (and subject, as such, to the review of its lawfulness provided for by Article 230 EC), but rather an act of the Council, composed of representatives of the governments of the member states, adopted on the basis of Article 15 EU, under Title V of the EU Treaty relating to the CFSP. It is clear, the Court of First Instance continued, that neither Title V of the EU Treaty relating to the CFSP nor Title VI of the EU Treaty relating to justice and home affairs (JHA) makes any provision for actions for annulment of common positions before the Community Courts. Under the EU Treaty, the powers of the Court of Justice are listed exhaustively in Article 46 EU and that article does not confer any competency on the court in relation to the provisions of Title V of the EU Treaty.[484]

In such circumstances, the Court of Justice has jurisdiction to hear an action for annulment directed against a common position adopted on the basis of Articles 15 EU only strictly to the extent that, in support of such an action, the applicant alleges an infringement of the Community's competencies. The Community Courts have jurisdiction to examine the content of an act adopted pursuant to the EU Treaty in order to ascertain whether that act affects the Community's competencies and to annul it if it should emerge that it ought to have been based on a provision of the EC Treaty.[485] In this respect, however, we may note that, without its being necessary to consider the possibility of challenging the validity of a common position before the courts of the member states, the contested common position requires the adoption of implementing Community and/or national acts in order to be effective. It has not been contended, as indicated in the cited judgment, "that those implementing acts cannot themselves be the subject-matter of an action for annulment either before the Community Courts or before the national courts. Thus, it has not been established that the applicant does not have available to it an effective legal remedy, albeit indirect, against the acts adopted pursuant to the contested common position which affect it adversely and directly. In the present case, moreover, the applicant has availed itself of its right of action against the contested decision as indicated in the mentioned judgment".[486]

The Lisbon Treaty, as the failed Constitution for Europe, maintains essentially this situation of absence of judicial control.[487] However, the second

---

484. See paragraphs 46 to 48.
485. Paragraph 56. See, to that effect, Case C-170/96, *Commission v. Council* [1998] ECR I-2763, paragraphs 16 and 17; Case C-176/03, *Commission v. Council* [2005] ECR I-7879, paragraph 39; orders of 7 June 2004 in Cases T-338/02, *Segi and Others v. Council* and T-333/02, *Gestoras Pro Amnistía and Others v. Council*, paragraph 41; order of 18 Nov 2005 in Case T-299/04, *Selmani v. Council and Commission*, paragraph 56; also, by analogy, Case C-124/95 *Centro-Com* [1997] ECR I-81, paragraph 25.
486. See paragraph 55 Case T-228/02.
487. In accordance with Article 24 EUT and Article 275, paragraph 1 of the Treaty on the Functioning of the European Union, the Court of Justice of the European Union shall not have

paragraph of Article 275 of the Treaty on the Functioning of the European Union states that the ECJ shall have jurisdiction to review, in accordance with the conditions laid down in the fourth paragraph of Article 263 of this Treaty relating to action for annulment, the legality of decisions providing for restrictive measures against natural or legal persons adopted by the Council on the CFSP. Thus, the acts of other bodies or agencies working in this field are excluded from such control, reducing the scope of judicial review over acts adopted by the Council that have effects on third parties. On this issue, current Article 39 EU Treaty only provides that in accordance with Article 16 of the Treaty on the Functioning of the European Union and by way of derogation from paragraph 2 thereof, the Council shall adopt a decision laying down the rules relating to the protection of individuals with regard to the processing of personal data by the member states when carrying out activities which fall within the scope of common foreign and security police, and the rules relating to the free movement of such data. Compliance with these rules shall be subject to the control of independent authorities.

---

jurisdiction with respect to the provisions relating to the common foreign and security policy nor with respect to acts adopted on the basis of those provisions.

Chapter 13
The EU's third pillar – Police and judicial co-operation in criminal matters

F. Jiménez

13.1. The constitutional framework

Title IV of the EC Treaty and the third pillar (Title VI of the EU Treaty) thus together form the legal basis for the area of freedom, security and justice in which the free movement of persons is ensured in conjunction with appropriate measures with respect to external border controls, asylum, immigration and the prevention and combating of crime. Initially, Title VI of the EU Treaty, introduced by the Maastricht Treaty, contained provisions establishing co-operation on justice and home affairs. The Treaty of Amsterdam, however, reduced the number of matters covered by Title VI by transferring a number of them to the Treaty establishing the European Community (first pillar), specifically to Title IV: "Visas, asylum, immigration and other policies related to free movement of persons".

The Treaty of Lisbon, adopted 17 December 2007, integrates this pillar in the structure and community logic (Articles 67-89 TFEU), introducing parliamentary control and judicial review, the latter including acts and activities of agencies working in this area (for example, Europol and Eurojust). Nevertheless, the Treaty maintains the position that the Court of Justice of the European Union has no jurisdiction to review the validity or proportionality of operations carried out by the police or other law-enforcement services of a member state or the exercise of responsibilities incumbent on member states in the maintenance of law and order and safeguarding internal security (Article 276).[488] By the terms of the Lisbon Treaty, national parliaments ensure that Community proposals and legislative initiatives comply with the principle of subsidiarity, but the European Parliament and the Council may, by directives following ordinary legislative procedure, establish minimum rules in the definition of criminal offences and sanctions for particularly serious crimes that have a cross-border dimension, either because of their nature or impact or because of a special need to combat them on a common basis.[489]

---

488. See Title V and Articles 251-281 of the Treaty on the Functioning of the European Union (Official Journal C 115, the 9 May 2008 pp. 0001-0388).
489. See Articles 69 and 83 of the Treaty on the Functioning of the European Union.

In the area of freedom, security and justice, the aim of police and judicial co-operation in criminal matters is to ensure a high level of safety for EU citizens by promoting and strengthening speedy and efficient co-operation between police and judicial authorities. According to current Article 67 TFEU the Union shall constitute an area of freedom, security and justice with respect for fundamental rights and the different legal systems and traditions of the member states. It shall ensure the absence of internal border controls for persons and shall frame a common policy on asylum, immigration and external border control, based on solidarity between member states, which is fair towards third-country nationals. For the purpose of Title IV TFEU, stateless persons shall be treated as third-country nationals. The Union shall endeavour to ensure a high level of security through measures to prevent and combat crime, racism and xenophobia, and through measures for co-ordination and co-operation between police and judicial authorities and other competent authorities, as well as through the mutual recognition of judgments in criminal matters and, if necessary, through the approximation of criminal laws.

In the field of judicial co-operation in criminal matters (Articles 82-86 TFEU), the European Parliament and the Council, acting in accordance with the ordinary legislative procedure, shall adopt measures to: (a) lay down rules and procedures for ensuring recognition throughout the Union of all forms of judgments and judicial decisions; (b) prevent and settle conflicts of jurisdiction between member states; (c) support the training of the judiciary and judicial staff; (d) facilitate co-operation between judicial or equivalent authorities of the member states in relation to proceedings in criminal matters and the enforcement of decisions.

To the extent necessary to facilitate mutual recognition of judgments and judicial decisions and police and judicial co-operation in criminal matters having a cross-border dimension, the European Parliament and the Council may, by means of directives adopted in accordance with the ordinary legislative procedure, establish minimum rules. Such rules shall take into account the differences between the legal traditions and systems of the member states. They shall concern: (a) mutual admissibility of evidence between member states; (b) the rights of individuals in criminal procedure; (c) the rights of victims of crime; (d) any other specific aspects of criminal procedure which the Council has identified in advance by a decision. For the adoption of such a decision, the Council shall act unanimously after obtaining the consent of the European Parliament. Adoption of these minimum rules shall not prevent member states from maintaining or introducing a higher level of protection for individuals.

Also the European Parliament and the Council may, by means of directives adopted in accordance with the ordinary legislative procedure, establish minimum rules concerning the definition of criminal offences and sanctions in the areas of particularly serious crime with a cross-border dimension resulting from the nature or impact of such offences or from a special need to combat them on a common basis. These areas of crime are the following: terrorism, trafficking in human beings and sexual exploitation of women and children, illicit drug trafficking, illicit arms trafficking, money laundering, corruption, counterfeiting of means of payment, computer crime and organised crime. On the basis of developments in crime, the Council may adopt a decision identifying other areas of crime that meet the criteria specified above. It shall act unanimously after obtaining the consent of the European Parliament. If the approximation of criminal laws and regulations of the member states proves essential to ensure the effective implementation of a Union policy in an area which has been subject to harmonisation measures, directives may establish minimum rules with regard to the definition of criminal offences and sanctions in the area concerned. Such directives shall be adopted by the same ordinary or special legislative procedure as was followed for the adoption of the harmonisation measures in question.

Where a member of the Council considers that a draft directive as referred to above would affect fundamental aspects of its criminal justice system, it may request that the draft directive be referred to the European Council. In that case, the ordinary legislative procedure shall be suspended. After discussion, and in case of a consensus, the European Council shall, within four months of this suspension, refer the draft back to the Council, which shall terminate the suspension of the ordinary legislative procedure. Within the same timeframe, in case of disagreement, and if at least nine member states wish to establish enhanced co-operation on the basis of the draft directive concerned, they shall notify the European Parliament, the Council and the Commission accordingly. In such a case, the authorisation to proceed with enhanced co-operation referred to in Article 20(2) of the Treaty on European Union and Article 329(1) of this Treaty shall be deemed to be granted and the provisions on enhanced co-operation shall apply.

In the field of police co-operation, the Union shall establish police co-operation involving all the member states' competent authorities, including police, customs and other specialised law enforcement services in relation to the prevention, detection and investigation of criminal offences. For these purposes, the European Parliament and the Council, acting in accordance with the ordinary legislative procedure, may establish measures concerning: (a) the collection, storage, processing, analysis and exchange of relevant information; (b) support for the training of staff, and co-operation on the exchange of staff, on equipment and on research into crime-detection; (c) common investigative techniques in relation to the detection of serious forms of organised crime.

The Council, acting in accordance with a special legislative procedure, may establish measures concerning operational co-operation between the authorities referred to in this article. The Council shall act unanimously after consulting the European Parliament. The absence of unanimity in the Council will activate the enhanced co-operation procedure previously described (Article 86).

13.2. Organs of government of the third pillar

Besides the actions of Community institutions (analysed below), this policy is implemented mainly via agencies set up by the European Union under the third pillar: Eurojust, Europol, the European Police College and the European Judicial Network.

Europol is responsible for improving co-operation between the member states' police and customs authorities. The convention establishing Europol was signed in July 1995 and entered into force on 1 October 1998. That agency's field of competency is the combating of crime and terrorism, but it is not a European police force as such. It is an instrument at the service of the member states designed to help them deal with criminal phenomena. In practice, Europol's work consists of facilitating the flow of information between national authorities and providing them with crime analyses. Europol participates in joint investigation teams comprising representatives of the various member state authorities and provides the information they need on the spot. Article 88 TFEU provides that the European Parliament and the Council, by means of regulations adopted in accordance with the ordinary legislative procedure, shall determine Europol's structure, operation, field of action and tasks. These tasks may include: (a) the collection, storage, processing, analysis and exchange of information, in particular that forwarded by the authorities of the member states or third countries or bodies; (b) the co-ordination, organisation and implementation of investigative and operational action carried out jointly with the member states' competent authorities or in the context of joint investigative teams, where appropriate in liaison with Eurojust. These regulations shall also lay down the procedures for scrutiny of Europol's activities by the European Parliament, together with national parliaments.

The European Police College (CEPOL), established as an agency of the European Union in 2005 by Council Decision 2005/681/JHA, brings together senior police officers across Europe with the aim of encouraging cross-border co-operation in fighting crime and maintaining public security and law and order. It organises numerous courses, seminars and conferences.

Eurojust, a body for co-ordinating member states' national public prosecution services, comprises 27 national representatives: judges, prosecutors and police officers on secondment from each member state.[490] It can carry out its tasks through one or more national members or collectively. Each member

---

490. Eurojust was created by an EU Council Decision of 28 February 2002 No. 2002/187/JHA, amended by Council Decision of 18 June 2003 No. 2003/659/JHA.

state may appoint one or more national correspondents, who can act as contact points for the European Judicial Network (EJN). Eurojust's competency covers investigations and prosecutions of serious crime, particularly organised crime or cross-border crime. It aims to promote co-ordination between competent authorities in the member states, to facilitate international mutual legal assistance and to carry out extradition requests and European arrest warrants. That judicial agency also contributes to member states' criminal investigations on the basis of analyses carried out by Europol. There is some overlap in the two bodies' competencies with regard to computer crime, fraud and corruption, laundering of the proceeds of crime, environmental crime and participation in a criminal organisation. The Treaty of Lisbon adds that the European Parliament and the Council, by means of regulations adopted in accordance with the ordinary legislative procedure, shall determine Eurojust's structure, operation, field of action and tasks. These tasks may include: (a) the initiation of criminal investigations, as well as proposing the initiation of prosecutions conducted by competent national authorities, particularly those relating to offences against the financial interests of the Union; (b) the co-ordination of investigations and prosecutions referred to in point (a); (c) the strengthening of judicial co-operation, including by resolution of conflicts of jurisdiction and by close co-operation with the EJN. These regulations shall also determine arrangements for involving the European Parliament and national parliaments in the evaluation of Eurojust's activities.

The purpose of the EJN in criminal matters is to facilitate mutual judicial assistance in the fight against transnational crime. It originated in a joint action adopted by the Council on 29 June 1998. The judicial network is made up of contact points designed to enable local judicial authorities and judicial authorities in the other member states to establish direct contacts between themselves. These contact points also provide the legal or practical information necessary to help the authorities concerned to prepare an effective request for judicial co-operation. There is also an EJN in civil and commercial matters, established by Council Decision of 28 May 2001 and based on the network in criminal matters.

The TFEU introduces two new provisions. First, Article 86 provides that in order to combat crimes affecting the financial interests of the Union, the Council, by means of regulations adopted in accordance with a special legislative procedure, may establish a European Public Prosecutor's Office from Eurojust. The European Public Prosecutor's Office shall be responsible for investigating, prosecuting and bringing to judgment, where appropriate in liaison with Europol, the perpetrators of, and accomplices in, offences against the Union's financial interests. It shall exercise the functions of prosecutor in the competent courts of the member states in relation to such offences. The European Council may, at the same time or subsequently, adopt a decision amending to extend the powers of the European Public Prosecutor's Office to include serious crime having a cross-border dimension and amending as regards the perpetrators of, and accomplices in, serious crimes affecting more than one member state. The European Council shall act unanimously after obtaining the consent of the European Parliament and after consulting the Commission. Second, Article 71 provides that a standing committee shall be set up within the Council in order to ensure that operational co-operation on internal security is promoted and strengthened within the Union (COSI). Without prejudice to Article 240, it shall facilitate co-ordination of the action of Member States' competent authorities. Representatives of the Union bodies, offices and agencies concerned may be involved in the proceedings of this committee. The European Parliament and national parliaments shall be kept informed of the proceedings.

13.3. Legal instruments of the EU's third pillar

To pursue the objectives of the third pillar, the Council, acting unanimously on the initiative of a member state or the Commission, could adopt the following legal instruments:

–   common positions, defining the approach of the Union to a particular matter;

–   framework decisions, for the purpose of approximating the laws and regulations of member states. Framework decisions are binding on member states as to the result to be achieved but they leave to the national authorities the choice of form and methods. They do not entail direct effect;

–   decisions for any other purpose consistent with the aims of this title, excluding approximation of laws and regulations of member states. These decisions are binding and do not entail direct effect; the Council, acting by qualified majority, adopts measures necessary to implement these decisions at Union level;

–   conventions, which it recommends to member states for adoption in accordance with their constitutional requirements. Member states must begin the procedures applicable within a time limit set by the Council. Unless they provide otherwise, conventions, once adopted by at least half the member states, enter into force for those member states. Measures implementing conventions must be adopted in the Council by a majority of two-thirds of the contracting parties;

–   agreements with one or more states or international organisations to implement this title. When it is necessary to conclude such an agreement, the Council may authorise the Presidency, assisted by the Commission as appropriate, to open negotiations to that effect. Such agreements are concluded by the Council on a recommendation from the Presidency. The Council must act unanimously when the agreement covers an issue for which unanimity is required for the adoption of internal decisions. When the agreement aims to implement a joint action or common position, or when the agreement covers an issue for which a qualified majority suffices, the Council acts by qualified majority.

The Lisbon Treaty abolishes this "pillar structure" of EU legislation. Matters which were previously dealt with under the third pillar, such as judicial co-operation in criminal matters and police co-operation, will be treated under the same kind of rules as those of community law. However, according to Article 10 of Protocol 36 on transitional provisions concerning acts adopted on the basis of Titles V and VI of the Treaty on European Union prior to the entry into force of the Treaty of Lisbon, the legal effects of the acts of the institutions, bodies, offices and agencies of the Union adopted on the basis of the Treaty on European Union prior to the entry into force of the Treaty of Lisbon shall be preserved until those acts are repealed, annulled or amended in implementation of the Treaties. The same shall apply to agreements concluded between member states on the basis of the Treaty on European Union.

13.3.1. The role of the Commission and European Parliament

As with the CFSP, prior to the Lisbon Treaty police and judicial co-operation was conducted by intergovernmental arrangement; the powers of the European Commission, the European Parliament and the Court of Justice of the European Communities were limited in favour of the Council of the European Union and the member states. The Commission continued to be simply an associate with a limited power of initiative, whereas the European Parliament's role on these issues did not go beyond a merely informative and consultative nature. Notwithstanding the topics of this pillar are substantial questions that affect the constitutional power of the states and, even more, the rights and freedoms of individuals, both the Commission and the European Parliament were merely consultative organs.

In accordance with the former Article 39 EU Treaty, the Council had to consult the European Parliament before adopting any measure referred to framework decisions, decisions and conventions under Article 34.2. The European Parliament delivered its opinion within a time limit which the Council laid down, which could not be less than three months. In the absence of an opinion within that time limit, the Council could act. The Presidency and Commission had to also regularly inform the European Parliament of discussions in the areas covered by this title; and the Parliament could ask questions of the Council or make recommendations to it. Each year, it held a debate on the progress made in areas referred to in this pillar.

The Lisbon Treaty introduces the ordinary legislative procedure in the field of justice and home affairs (JHA). The main areas which move from unanimity to qualified majority voting in the Council and full co-legislative powers in the European Parliament (formerly co-decision procedure) are: judicial co-operation in criminal matters (Articles 82-86 TFEU), Eurojust (Article 85 TFEU), non-operational police co-operation (Article 87 TFEU) and Europol (Article 88 TFEU). Other areas remain subject to unanimity in the Council with the European Parliament only being consulted, for example, on operational police co-operation (Article 87 TFEU). As to the right of initiative, the EU's general rule is also valid in the field of JHA: it is up to the European Commission to propose new legislative acts. The Lisbon Treaty introduces, however, the possibility that an initiative can also come from a quarter of EU member states in three areas: judicial co-operation in criminal matters, police co-operation and administrative co-operation (Article 76 TFEU).

13.4. The third pillar's limited system of judicial review

The entry into force of the Treaty of Lisbon brings full judicial integration of this pillar, going beyond the limited judicial oversight provided by the Amsterdam Treaty. However, this general rule is limited by the exceptions specified above in section 13.1: judicial review of the validity or proportionality of operations carried out by the police or other law-enforcement services of a member state, on one hand, and the exercise of the responsibilities incumbent upon member states with regard to the maintenance of law and order and the safeguarding of internal security, on the other hand (Article 276 TFEU).

The former Article 35 of the EU Treaty stated that the Court of Justice shall have jurisdiction to give preliminary rulings on the validity and interpretation of framework decisions and decisions, on the interpretation of conventions established under this title and on the validity and interpretation of the measures implementing them. By a declaration made at the time of signature of the Treaty or at any time thereafter, a member state could accept the jurisdiction of the Court of Justice to give preliminary rulings as specified above. Under Article 35, a member state making this declaration should specify that either:

(i) Any court or tribunal of that state against whose decisions there is no judicial remedy under national law may request the Court of Justice to give a preliminary ruling on a question raised in a case pending before it and concerning the validity or interpretation of an act referred to in paragraph 1 if that court or tribunal considers that a decision on the question is necessary to enable it to give judgment; or

(ii) Any court or tribunal of that state may request the Court of Justice to give a preliminary ruling on a question raised in a case pending before it and concerning the validity or interpretation of an act referred to in paragraph 1 if that court or tribunal considers that a decision on the question is necessary to enable it to give judgment.

Nevertheless, the Court of Justice had no jurisdiction to review the validity or proportionality of operations carried out by the police or other law-enforcement services of a member state or the exercise of the responsibilities incumbent on member states in the maintenance of law and order and the safeguarding of internal security.

The Court of Justice had jurisdiction to review the legality of framework decisions and decisions in actions brought by a member state or the Commission on grounds of lack of competency, infringement of an essential procedural requirement, infringement of this treaty or of any rule of law relating to its application, or misuse of powers. The proceedings provided for in this article had to be instituted within two months of the publication of the measure. Likewise, it had jurisdiction to rule on any dispute between member states on the interpretation or application of acts adopted under Article 34.2 whenever such dispute could not be settled by the Council within six months of its being referred to the Council by one of its members. The Court also had jurisdiction to rule on any dispute between member states and the Commission on the interpretation or application of conventions established under Article 34.2d.

Judicial review of the activities of agencies, particularly Europol and Eurojust, was also limited. In the former EU, there is no general provision conferring jurisdiction on the Court of Justice to review the legality of acts of agencies,[491] though the national courts were competent to determine the liability of Europol and Eurojust for any damage caused to an individual which results from their unauthorised or incorrect processing of data.[492] The lack of democratic and judicial supervision of bodies such as Europol and Eurojust and the differences in the level of judicial review exercised in respect of the acts of agencies explain the debate originating with the Constitution for Europe.[493]

As mentioned, the Lisbon Treaty amended this situation. Article 263 TFEU extended actions for annulment to the legality of acts of bodies, offices or agencies of the Union intended to produce legal effects on third parties. Moreover, the act setting up bodies, offices and agencies of the Union may lay down specific conditions and arrangements for actions brought by natural or legal persons against acts of these bodies, offices or agencies intended to produce legal effects relating to them. The Lisbon Treaty also standardised judicial review not only to ensure the legality of EU agencies' and bodies' acts, but also to review their failure to act (Article 265), providing jurisdiction to the European Court to give preliminary rulings on the validity and interpretation of acts of institutions, bodies, offices or agencies of the Union (Article 267).

However, as already indicated, according to Article 10 of Protocol 36 on transitional provisions the full powers of the Court of Justice become applicable to

---

491. See Case C-160/03, *Kingdom of Spain v. Eurojust*, 15 March 2005, paragraphs 35 to 44.
492. See Article 38, Europol Convention, and Article 24, Council Decision on Eurojust.
493. See E. Nieto-Garrido, "Judicial protection: Union bodies and agencies" in E. Nieto-Garrido and I. Martín Delgado, *European administrative law in the constitutional treaty*, Oxford/Portland OR, 2007, pp. 161-164.

the existing "acquis" of the third pillar legislation five years after entry into force of the Treaty of Lisbon, that is, 1 December 2014.

13.4.1. Individuals lack *locus standi* before the Court of Justice in the field of third pillar

Thus, *ius standi* is not recognised to the individual to denounce the legality of acts adopted by the third pillar, even if the individual is directly and individually concerned by the decision adopted in this area. Only an indirect proceeding is possible, based on preliminary rulings or a hearing before the national courts or before the Court of Justice in Luxembourg for acts dictated in execution of Community law.

However, the characteristics of existing legal instruments and of the cited scope of jurisdiction of the Court of Justice in the EU Treaty underline the "Community vocation" of this pillar and point to important consequences in the area of judicial oversight. On the validity of Council Framework Decision 2002/584/JHA of 13 June 2002 on the European arrest warrant and the surrender procedures between member states, the Advocate General, Ruiz-Jarabo Colomer, declared that:

> The nature of the situation changes when assistance is requested and provided in the context of a supranational, harmonised legal system where, by partially renouncing their sovereignty, States devolve power to independent authorities with law-making powers. That approximation, which falls within the scope of the first pillar of the Union, also operates in the third, intergovernmental, pillar – albeit with a clear Community objective, as was demonstrated in *Pupino* – by transferring to framework decisions certain aspects of the first pillar and a number of the parameters specific to directives.[494]

On the other hand, such a community vocation appeared in Article 42 of the EU Treaty, which stated that "the Council, acting unanimously on the initiative of the Commission or a Member State, and after consulting the European Parliament, may decide that action in areas referred to in Article 29 shall fall under Title IV of the Treaty establishing the European Community, and at the same time determine the relevant voting conditions relating to it. It shall recommend the Member States to adopt that decision in accordance with their respective constitutional requirements".

This Community dimension has forced the European Court to adopt a jurisprudential teleological-systematic interpretation of the scope of the dispositions of the third pillar. In the *Pupino* case, the Court of Justice in Luxembourg transferred the direct effect specific to directives to a framework that, in conformity with Article 34 of the EU Treaty, does not entail direct effect.[495] In this respect, the Luxembourg Court affirmed that, irrespective of the

---

494. Opinion delivered on 12 September 2006, Case C-303/05, *Advocaten voor de Wereld VZW*, paragraph 43.
495. See CJEC (Grand Chamber), Case 105/03, judgment of 16 June 2005, paragraphs 36 and 42 to 44.

degree of integration envisaged by the treaty in the process of creating an ever closer union among the peoples of Europe within the meaning of the second paragraph of Article 1 EU Treaty, it is perfectly comprehensible that the authors of the Treaty on European Union should have considered it useful to make provision, in the context of Title VI of that Treaty, for recourse to legal instruments with effects similar to those provided for by the EC Treaty, in order to contribute effectively to the pursuit of the Union's objectives. It would be difficult for the Union to carry out its task if the principle of loyal co-operation, requiring in particular that member states take all appropriate measures, whether general or particular, to ensure fulfilment of their obligations under European Union law, were not also binding in the area of police and judicial co-operation in criminal matters, which is entirely based on co-operation between member states and the institutions. In the light of all the above considerations, the Court of Justice concluded that:

> The principle of conforming interpretation is binding in relation to framework decisions adopted in the context of Title VI of the Treaty on European Union. When applying national law, the national court that is called upon to interpret it must do so as far as possible in the light of the wording and purpose of the framework decision in order to attain the result which it pursues and thus comply with Article 34(2)(b) EU.

It should be noted, however, that the obligation on the national court to refer to the content of a framework decision when interpreting the relevant rules of its national law is limited by general principles of law, particularly those of legal certainty and non-retroactivity.[496]

On the other hand, in the cases *Gestoras Pro Amnistía and Others v. Council* and *Segi and Others v. Council*,[497] the Grand Chamber of the Court of Justice in appeal noted that a common position is not supposed to produce of itself legal effects in relation to third parties. That is why, in the system established by Title VI of the EU Treaty, only framework decisions and decisions may be the subject of an action for annulment before the Court of Justice. The Court's jurisdiction, as defined by Article 35.1 EU Treaty, to give preliminary rulings also does not extend to common positions, but is limited to rulings on the validity and interpretation of framework decisions and decisions, on the interpretation of conventions established under Title VI and on the validity and interpretation of the measures implementing them.

Nevertheless, given that the procedure enabling the Court of Justice to give preliminary rulings is designed to guarantee observance of the law in the interpretation and application of the Treaty, it would run counter to that objective to interpret Article 35.1 EU Treaty narrowly. The right to make a reference to the Court for a preliminary ruling must therefore exist in respect of all measures adopted by the Council, whatever their nature or form, which

---

496. See ibid., paragraph 44.
497. See CJEC, Cases C-354/04 P and C-355/04 P, judgments of 27 February 2007, paragraphs 52 to 57.

are intended to have legal effects in relation to third parties.[498] As a result, it has to be possible to make subject to review by the court a common position which, because of its content, has a scope going beyond that assigned by the EU Treaty to that kind of act. Therefore, a national court hearing a dispute which indirectly raises the issue of the validity or interpretation of a common position adopted on the basis of Article 34 EU Treaty, and which has serious doubts whether that common position is really intended to produce legal effects in relation to third parties, would be able, subject to the conditions fixed by Article 35 EU Treaty, to ask the European Court to give a preliminary ruling. It would then fall to that Court to find, where appropriate, that the common position is intended to produce legal effects in relation to third parties, to accord it its true classification and to give a preliminary ruling.

The Court of Justice would also have jurisdiction to review the lawfulness of such acts when an action has been brought by a member state or the Commission on the conditions fixed by Article 35.6 EU Treaty. Finally, we must remember that it is for the member states and, in particular, their courts and tribunals, to interpret and apply national procedural rules governing the exercise of rights of action in a way that enables natural and legal persons to challenge before the courts the lawfulness of any decision or other national measure relating to the drawing up of an act of the European Union or to its application to them and to seek compensation for any loss suffered.[499]

In the light of these conclusions, the reflections of the Advocate General, Paolo Mengozzi – formulated in his opinion in the *Gestoras* and *Segi* cases – are of great interest. First, the Union is based, *inter alia*, on the principle of the rule of law and respect for fundamental rights. The rule of law is based not so much on rules and the proclamation of rights as on mechanisms that make it possible to ensure respect for rules and rights (*ubi ius ibi remedium*). The "right to challenge a measure before the courts is inherent in the rule of law", is the "corollary" to it, and is both "a victory over and an instrument" of it. Hence, in Article 6.2 EU Treaty, Union law now expressly grants the individual a range of fundamental rights, which, as is clear from Article 46d EU Treaty, can be relied on before a court as criteria for the legality of acts of the Union.

The point of departure must therefore be that, under Articles 6.1 and 6.2 EU Treaty, the Union recognises judicial review of the legality of actions of its institutions and it guarantees the judicial protection of rights, especially those that can be classed as fundamental. Likewise, no provision of the EU Treaty

---

498. See, by analogy, Case 22/70 *Commission v. Council (ERTA)* [1971] ECR 263, paragraphs 38 to 42, and Case C-57/95 *France v. Commission* [1997] ECR I-1627, paragraph 7 et seq.
499. In consequence, the Court concludes that "It follows that the appellants are incorrect in maintaining that the contested common position leaves them without a remedy, contrary to the requirement of effective judicial protection, and that the order under appeal prejudices their right to such protection. That ground of appeal must, in consequence, be rejected".

to the contrary can be invoked to claim, in particular, that the authors of that treaty intended to exclude such review and protection from the field of police and judicial co-operation in criminal matters, where moreover the action of the Union may impair individuals' fundamental rights and freedoms more easily than in other fields within the jurisdiction of the Union and where the involvement of the European Parliament is still very limited.

Regarding the former third pillar, Mengozzi went on to state that it cannot be said that Title VI of the EU Treaty established a complete system of legal remedies and procedures designed to permit the Court of Justice to review the legality of the Council measures referred to in Article 34 EU Treaty. Indeed, it is clear that the jurisdiction conferred on the Court of Justice by Article 35 EU Treaty alone does not constitute a complete system of legal remedies and procedures such as to ensure review of the legality of such measures. As proof, one need only consider that a reference for a preliminary ruling on validity is not possible in member states that have not made a declaration in accordance with Article 35.2 EU Treaty , given the lack of provision for any direct recourse to the Court of Justice by individuals against such acts. This means that the judicial protection which individuals must be held to be able to exercise, under Union law, in national courts in relation to the action of the Union in the context of the third pillar is not limited to the mere possibility, expressly provided for in Article 35.1 EU Treaty, of indirectly challenging the validity of framework decisions and decisions (objection of invalidity in the context of a direct action against national implementing measures). It also includes, in particular, the right to challenge directly the validity of such acts and common positions mentioned in Article 34a EU Treaty, where, despite having no direct effects, they are nevertheless likely of themselves, irrespective of national implementing measures, to cause immediate harm to the legal position of individuals; the purpose of such a challenge is to obtain at least compensation for any damage such acts may have caused.[500]

References

Carrera, S. and Geyer, F., "Tratado de Lisboa y Espacio de Libertad, Seguridad y Justicia", *Revista de Derecho Comunitario Europeo*, Vol. 29 (2008), pp. 133-162.

Golsalbo Bono, R., "Some reflections on the CFSP legal order", *Common Market Law Review*, Vol. 43 (2006) No. 2, pp. 337-394.

González Sánchez, E., "El proceso de toma de decisiones en el ámbito de la política exterior y de seguridad común", *Revista de Derecho Comunitario Europeo*, Vol. 8 (2000) No. 2, pp. 383-415.

---

500. See Opinion of Advocate General Mengozzi delivered on 26 October 2006, Cases C-354/04 P *Gestoras Pro Amnistía and Others v. Council* and *Segi and Others v. Council*, C-355/04 P, paragraphs 101 to 135.

Jiménez García, F., "El control de legalidad en la ejecución de las sanciones internacionales antiterroristas por parte de la Unión Europea: ¿tutela judicial efectiva o vuelta a la doctrina de los actos políticos?, *Revista de Derecho de la Unión Europea* Vol. 15 (2008), pp. 81-136.

Jiménez García, F., "Tutela judicial efectiva, Pilares intergubernamentales de la Unión Europea y Naciones Unidas o Viceversa" in A. Cuerda Riezu and F. Jiménez García (eds), *Nuevos Desafíos del Derecho Penal Internacional. Terrorismo, Crímenes Internacionales y Derechos Fundamentales*, Tecnos, Madrid, 2009, pp. 411-464.

Jimeno-Blunes, M., "European judicial co-operation in criminal matters", *European Law Journal*, Vol. 9 (2003) No. 5, pp. 614-630.

Karolewski, I., "Constitutionalization of the common foreign and security police of the European Union: implications of constitutional treaty" in *The Unity of the European Constitution*, Ph. Dann and M. Rynkowski (eds), Springer, Berlin, 2006, pp. 263-282.

Kuijper, P. J. "The evolution of the third pillar from Maastricht to the European Constitution: institutional aspects", *Common Market Law Review*, Vol. 41 (2004) No. 2, pp. 609-626.

Liñán Nogueras, D. J., "El Espacio de Libertad, Seguridad y Justicia" in A. Mangas Martín and D. J. Liñán Nogueras, *Instituciones y Derecho de la Unión Europea*, Madrid, 2005, pp. 717-746.

Liñán Nogueras, D. J., "La Política Exterior y de Seguridad Común" in A. Mangas Martín and D. J. Liñán Nogueras, *Instituciones y Derecho de la Unión Europea*, Madrid, 2005, pp. 681-713.

Nieto-Garrido, E. and Martín Delgado, I., *European administrative law in the constitutional treaty*, Hart, Oxford and Portland, Oregon, 2007.

Peers, S., *EU justice and home affairs law*, 2nd edn, Oxford University Press, Oxford, 2006.

Sarmiento, D. "Un paso más en la constitucionalización del tercer pilar de la Unión Europea. La sentencia *María Pupino* y el efecto directo de la decisiones marco" in *Revista Electrónica de Estudios Internacionales,* No. 10, 2005 (www.reei.org).

Part IV
The European legal system: a complex legal order

Chapter 14
European legal tradition and the EU legal system: understandings and premises about the rule of law's requirements

S. Galera

14.1. European legal tradition

In the preceding chapters, we explained the legal conception for each type of legal order considered with regard to some essentials in the rule-of-law tradition: national laws, Council of Europe doctrine and the EU legal order, examining their legal tools and requirements which make possible the control of public – administrative – activity.

As Part I of this work shows, the current legal culture of Europe is the consequence of many years of development shaped by similar collective wishes – such as the separation of power and the law, the progressive pre-eminence of the latter,[501] and convergent principles of constitutional law all over Europe, especially in the fields of human rights and the rule of law.[502] Of particular importance is access to the courts, a right that has only recently come to be explicitly recognised in national constitutions. This recognition is an example of the emergence over time of the rule-of-law ideal.[503]

National laws have been greatly influenced by the legal corpus created by the Council of Europe through its executive bodies and the case law of the Judges in Strasbourg. The Organisation's continuous influence can be easily shown in all its members, even in older and well-established democracies. Due to the Strasbourg Court's interpretation of Convention provisions, the Council of Europe not only grants citizens "human rights" in a literal sense but also contributes to maintain democracy in Europe, being "a part of the cultural self-definition of European civilisation".[504] Its jurisprudence is based on a civil rights approach, meaning that the Strasbourg interpretation of rights provided by the Convention often goes beyond a word-for-word version. By

---

501. See B. Aguilera, "Law as a limit to power – origins of the rule of law", Chapter 1 of this work.
502. See R. Arnold, "Constitutionalism after the Second World War", Chapter 2 of this work.
503. E. Storskrubb and J. Ziller, "Access to justice in European comparative law" in F. Francioni (ed.), *Access to justice as a human right*, Oxford University Press, 2007, p. 180 and ff., distinguishing three broad categories of constitutional provision on this issue.
504. P. Alston and J. Weiler, "An 'ever closer union' in need of human rights policy: the European Union and human rights", Harvard Jean Monnet Working Paper 1/99, available at www.jeanmonnetprogram.org/papers/99/990105.html.

contrast, the Council of Europe has strictly interpreted the exceptions and limitations on the commitments and obligations imposed by the Convention, which represents the "constitutional instrument of European public order (*ordre public*) in the field of human rights".[505] In its own view,

> The Council of Europe is the oldest pan-European institution standing for democratic values and principles. Acceptance and realisation of the principles of democracy, the rule of law and human rights and fundamental freedoms area are a necessary condition for membership in the Organisation.[506]

The issues we are dealing with in these pages are good examples to illustrate this jurisprudential approach. From particular interpretations of specific rights,[507] the Court has outlined the essentials of the rule-of-law tradition in Europe, stating a huge list of guarantees for individuals affected by the activities of public administrations and their corresponding limits, a clear concept of "judicial independence" and detailed criteria for whether public activities can be legitimately excluded from judicial scrutiny.

In addition to the broad scope given by the Court's case law to the rights granted by the Convention, a further effect comes from the Court's judicial activities, especially the so-called "autonomous concepts" which outline the meaning and scope of basic terms in the Convention. Hence, the Judges in Strasbourg have gone a long way to creating a common European law by making good any gaps resulting from a word-for-word reading of the Convention, by implementing the uniformity needed to ensure its common application and by preventing national legal peculiarities from leading to different levels of guarantee.[508]

The convergence between the national laws of the European countries subscribing to the European Convention is particularly valuable in National Administrative Laws, a legal field which is especially influenced by national peculiarities.[509] Here it is necessary to mention the non-official code adopted by the Council of Europe summarising the principles which should be respected

---

505. *Loizidou v. Turkey (preliminary objections)*, judgment of 23 March 1995, paragraph 75; *Bosphorus Hava v. Ireland*, judgment of 30 June 2005, paragraph 156.

506. Parliamentary Assembly, Resolution 1547 (2007), State of human rights and democracy in Europe.

507. Article 6 grants "the right to fair and public hearing within a reasonable time by an independent and impartial tribunal established by law"; Article 8 grants the "right to respect private and family life, home and correspondence".

508. See F. Suder, "Le Recours aux 'notions autonomes'" in *L'interpretation de la convention européenne des droits de l'homme*, Brussels, Bruylant, 1998, p. 94 and ff., and Chapter 4 in this work.

509. In this regard, J. Schwarze identifies two main causes for the convergence of national procedural administrative law in Europe: the "growing importance of the European Court of Human Rights" and the enormous influence of German and French procedural rules in the rest of Europe. He also considers the influence of the case law of the ECJ, in "The role of the European Court of Justice in shaping legal standards for administrative action in the member states: a comparative perspective" in D. O'Keeffe (ed.), *Judicial Review in EU Law*, Kluwer Law International, The Hague, 2000, p. 459.

by public administrations and the basic principles of administrative justice.[510] These principles have arisen from the case law on the "right to a fair trial" granted by Article 6 of the Convention, even when, paradoxically, this article refers only to "civil and criminal proceedings", and, consequently, the relations involving the administration as public power are theoretically not under its scope.[511]

On the other hand, and in spite of their non-binding effects, all the acts together adopted by the Council of Ministers proposing common general rules on issues should be considered to cumulatively create the essentials of a common Administrative Law in Europe. From among them, it is worth mentioning those relating to the following issues:

– protection of the individual in relation to the acts of administrative authorities[512] where the right to be heard, the access to information, the statement of reasons and the indication of remedies were specifically stated;

– exercise of discretionary powers by administrative authorities,[513] establishing the basic aims of such powers, basic procedural guidelines for taking actions in the exercise of these powers and the supervision of their legality;

– measures facilitating access to justice,[514] detailing the kind of general information which should be provided to the public, measures of simplification and some requirements relating to court fees;

– judicial review of administrative acts, defining what "administrative act" and "judicial review" mean, and the conditions for bringing an action by individuals with reference to associations, among other matters;[515]

– good administration,[516] stating a Code of Good Administration which includes three groups of provision: principles of good administration, rules governing administrative decisions and basic rules on appeals, in

---

510. I refer to the well-known study *The Administration and you: Principles of Administrative Law concerning relations between administrative authorities and private persons, a handbook*, Strasbourg, Council of Europe, 1996. See also Resolution Res(2002)12 establishing the European Commission for the efficiency of justice (CEPEJ), specifically its Appendix 2 referring to the relevant Council of Europe recommendations on this issue.

511. See the interpretative ways through which the Strasbourg Court has enlarged the scope of this provision in S. Cassese, *La Globalizacion Juridica*, Inap-Marcial Pons, Madrid, 2006, p. 167.

512. Resolution (77) 31.

513. Recommendation (80)2.

514. Recommendation (81)7.

515. Recommendation (2004)20: the definition of "administrative act" enlarges its scope beyond that previously established in Recommendation (80)2 on exercise of discretionary powers.

516. Recommendation (2007)7. For its purposes, "public authorities" refer, on one hand, to any public law entity, including state, local and autonomous authorities providing a public service or acting in the public interest and, on the other hand, any private law entity exercising the prerogatives of a public authority responsible for providing a public service or acting in the public interest.

addition to the previously defined concept of the "public authorities" to whom the Code should apply.

Consequently, and due to the already noted difficulty in identifying a set of common legal principles of administrative law,[517] it would not be going too far to interpret the increasing mention in Community provisions of "principles of procedural law generally recognised in the member states" as fashioned to accord with this sort of code.[518]

It is in this context that later European regional organisations were set up facing the challenge of building a new European legal order which, because of history and geography, had to co-exist with the preceding one.

Initially, the only objectives of the European Communities were economic, and the original Treaties did not include any provisions relating to the individual's legal position, but the need for such provisions soon surfaced as increasingly Community activity directly involved the issue of citizens' legal status. In the late 1960s, the Luxembourg Court gave recognition to some procedural guarantees in particular and in general to fundamental rights, including them among the General Principles of Law which fall under Community law. Later, these "principles" evolved in Luxembourg's case law into "fundamental rights" and finally they achieved recognition in the EU's own catalogue of fundamental rights, the European Charter. It is useful to recall that, when Community law began to consider these non-economic issues, a sort of European public order on fundamental rights and rule of law had already been developed by the Judges in Strasbourg.

It is in this framework that we are going to consider the alleged equivalence of EU law in the preservation of such tradition and values, going beyond the formal recognition that the Maastricht Treaty has given to the "rule of law" values.

It is worthwhile to examine the regulatory details, looking at further developments in EU law and ECJ case law, following the traditional dialectics between constitutional values and principles and their further development by sub-constitutional regulation. As has been pointed out, the "agreement of ultimate values and objectives at the macro-level does not denote the absence at the micro-level of substantial variance".[519]

---

517. In this sense, M. Chiti, who considers the alleged "common administrative values" to be "historically artificial", in "Forms of European administrative action", *Law and Contemporary Problems*, Vol. 68, No. I, winter 2004, p. 42.

518. I agree with the identification made by E. Chiti, "Administrative proceedings involving European agencies", *Law and Contemporary Problems*, Vol. 68, p. 227, pointing out among these principles those added to the list of the ECJ.

519. C. Harlow, "Global administrative law: the quest for principles and values", *European Journal of International Law*, No. 17 (2006), p. 191.

The question underlying the next pages is whether it is possible to assert an equivalence between the EU legal system and a European legal tradition that preserves some of the most basic rule-of-law requirements, considering formal recognition at constitutional level but also the understanding built up by sub-constitutional sources of EU law. Is the EU legal system a further development of the nation-states in Europe, reflecting its legal tradition? Is the "European legal tradition" the foundation of the EU's legal system or, on the contrary, are they different phenomena born from very different premises which thus preserve very different values? Can the thousand-year-old palimpsest on which European legal culture is based survive the requirements of the primacy principle?

14.2. Fundamental rights: defence and due process

The process of recognising fundamental rights in the European Union has produced a huge volume of legal literature, of which it is advantageous to this discussion to refer to a recent European judgment which clearly describes and summarises this process:[520]

> the ECJ held as early as 1969 that fundamental rights were enshrined in the general principles of Community law protected by the ECJ. By the early 1970s the ECJ had confirmed that, in protecting such rights, it was inspired by the constitutional traditions of the member states and by the guidelines supplied by international human rights treaties on which the member states had collaborated or to which they were signatories. The Convention's provisions were first explicitly referred to in 1975 and by 1979 its special significance amongst international treaties on the protection of human rights had been recognised by the ECJ. Thereafter the ECJ began to refer extensively to Convention provisions (sometimes where the EC legislation under its consideration had referred to the Convention) and latterly to this Court's jurisprudence, the more recent ECJ judgments not prefacing such Convention references with an explanation of their relevance for EC law.

This process could be explained by the increasing number of issues covered by Community law and the sensitive nature of some of them.[521] Whereas ECJ case law first recognised the legal position of fundamental rights in the Community system, later it was the Community legislator who did so. Community law included specific guarantees for human rights, first in the Single European Act (1985) and later in the Maastricht (1992) and Amsterdam (1997) Treaties.

Recently, after the ECJ formally dismissed the possibility of the EU's accession to the European Convention because of a lack of legal basis in the Treaties,[522]

---

520. *Bosphorous Hava v. Ireland*, European Court of Human Rights 30 June 2006, pt. 73. This judgment is full of ECJ case law references: I have omitted them for easier reading.

521. See Vlad Constantinesco, "The ECJ as law-maker: *Praeter aut contra legem*?" in *Judicial Review in European Union Law*, ed. D. O'Keeffe, Kluwer, The Hague, 2000, pp. 73-79.

522. These criteria are described in the ECJ's well-known Opinion 2/94. However, I join those scholars who state that these reasons were "unpersuasive" (P. Alston and J. H. H. Weiler, op. cit., available at www.jeanmonnetprogram.org/papers/99/990110.html).

the EU began working on its own "Bill of Rights". First, the "Charter of Fundamental Rights of the European Union" was formally "proclaimed" in Nice in 2000. Later, it was included in the so-called "Constitutional Treaty" and, finally, it was definitively empowered by the Lisbon Treaty, which also provides the legal basis for the EU's further accession to the European Convention. This is not the right place for a detailed analysis of the effects of the Charter, which has been generally welcomed, despite some scepticism. We must hope it will increase the level of protection of fundamental rights in Europe, though a previous fear remains concerning legal sources granting fundamental rights in Europe.[523] Now, in addition to the protection provided by the national constitutions, we have two international texts – the Convention and the Charter – and three international interpreters, the Judges in Strasbourg, the ECJ and the Praesidium, governing this essential field.[524]

The pre-eminent role of the "right of justice" in developing the catalogue of fundamental rights has been pointed out. The ECJ has repeatedly stated its protection at Community level, distinguishing the following as included in this right: the right to a fair trial, "inspired in Article 6 of the ECHR" (ECJ 17 December 1998, C-185/95); the right to an independent court, particularly independent from the executive powers (ECJ 11 January 2000, C-174/98 and C-189/P); rights of defence relating to an administrative procedure and a judicial one (ECJ 11 July 1968, C-35/67); and the duty to state the reasons on which decisions are based, to allow the parties to defend their rights and the Court to exercise its supervisory jurisdiction (ECJ 14 December 1990, C-350/88).

It should be noted that, just as occurred with the right to a fair trial, the right of access to court has given rise to a cluster of other guarantees for individuals. As mentioned above, administrative law expands the right of access to a court as a set of due process principles, reflecting the classic rule-of-law preoccupations with equality before the law, the non-retrospectivity principle, an impartial and independent judge and a fair trial.[525] These principles, to

---

523. See F. Rubio Llorente, *La Carta Europea de los Derechos*, Claves de la razón práctica, No. 122, 2002; and L. Ortega Alvarez, *Fundamental Rights in the European Constitution*, European Public Law, Vol. 11, No. 3, 2005.
I underlined the unnoticed Praesidium as interpreter of the Charter in my work "Sobre el alma de Europa, derechos fundamentales y EuroSpeak", *Tiempo de Paz*, Madrid, No. 90, Fall 2008, pp. 33-39.
524. It should be pointed out that the Preamble of the Charter (fifth paragraph, last sentence, 2007/C 303 01)) once " the constitutional tradition and international texts" have been affirmed, states that *the Charter will be interpreted with due regard to the explanations prepared under the authority of the Praesidium of the Convention which drafted the Charter and updated under the responsibility of the Praesidium of the European Convention.* Such explanations were published in 2007/C303 02.
525. C. Harlow, "Global administrative law: the quest for principles and values", *European Journal of International Law*, No. 17 (2006), p. 190, stressing a direct link: rule of law–access to court–due process.

which the Strasbourg Court has been "a non-negligible source of influence and cross-fertilisation",[526] have found their way into modern human rights texts; specifically, the due process rights have became a "fourth generation" of human rights in the latest text, taking the shape of "principles of good administration".[527]

The "procedural rules" stated by the ECJ first arose during implementation of the Community's Competition Law, the most important substantive Community law contribution to a codification of procedural rights at the European level (especially in the first years after its passage). Implementation of the Competition Law was, and still is, the most important administrative activity directly managed by the European Commission's services. The law's provisions tend to be applied with great severity and frequently affect individuals' rights. Examples include inspections in a company building without staff permission, information requirements whose answers could cause self-incrimination, and access to the Commission's files during an investigation.

The ECJ has had to balance in such cases procedural rights and guarantees, on one hand, and public powers of investigation, on the other hand. It is not easy to identify general criteria applied in similar cases. Diverse strains exist in the serious academic literature, some that welcome the ECJ's criteria on procedural rights relating to competition law and others that have very critical opinions about it.

It has been pointed out that the protection of procedural rights was based on consideration of principle and on utilitarian or instrumental considerations, enhancing the effectiveness and efficiency of anti-trust enforcement.[528] From this perspective, an ECJ hybrid approach on this issue has recently been affirmed, wedding two opposing trends: an instrumental or pragmatic approach – describing boundaries by reference to their social functions – and an essentialist approach – which mainly applies to formal categorisation, taking into account the very substance of the right to a defence.[529]

---

526. Storskrubb and Ziller, "Access to justice in European comparative law" in F. Francioni (ed.), *Access to justice as a human right*, Oxford, 2007, p. 180. Following Cappelletti's asserts, they previously underlined the process of "constitutionalisation, socialisation and internationalisation of the protection of procedural guarantees" in Europe after the Second World War.

527. C. Harlow, "Global administrative law", op. cit.

528. See Wouter Wils, "Powers of investigation and procedural rights and guarantees in EU antitrust enforcement: the interplay between European and national legislation and case law" in *Competition Law and Economics. Advances in Competition Policy and Antirust Enforcement*, ed. Abel M. Mateus and Teresa Moreira, Kluwer Law International, 2007, p. 110.

529. See E. Barbier de La Serre, "Procedural justice in the European Community case law concerning the rights of the defence: essentialist and instrumental trends", *European Public Law*, 2006, Vol. 12, No. 2, pp. 225-250 *in toto*.

For a long time, the Court followed the "reluctant approach" to human rights issues,[530] meaning that, where human rights were involved in a case, the ECJ usually handed down a judgment that left questions about human rights unanswered. That is, ECJ decisions resolved the disputes in the end by avoiding any general criteria about the related procedural rights. This was because during its first decades the EC focused on implementation of the Common Market's basic rules. It was neither a fast nor an easy task to achieve the free movement of economic factors in the European market, and the Community legislators were much more concerned with efficient implementation of the competition rules than the elaboration of a sort of code of procedure. In fact, the general opinion is that in the early cases the ECJ was more focused on administrative action and only later turned to the subjective rights of individuals.[531]

Divergences are quite noticeable if we compare earlier ECJ case law with the standard of the Strasbourg Court concerning principles and values. Areas of divergence include: the lawfulness of administrative action; proportionality, objectivity and impartiality; legitimate trust and vested rights; access to documents; the right to be heard; notification, statement of reasons and indication of remedies.[532]

Significant examples concern the *non bis in idem* principle, which has been applied to cumulative effects of domestic and European competition penalties by the Strasbourg Court (Gradinger 1995), whereas the Luxembourg Court has declined to apply it in identical situations (Walt Wilhelm 1969). A similar restrictive approach is evident in relation to the protection for private homes (provided by Article 8 of the European Convention). The ECJ refused to recognise protection beyond individuals (Hoechst 1989), determining that Article 8 of the Convention concerns individuals' personal freedoms and therefore cannot be extended to business premises. The ECJ at that time observed that there was still no Strasbourg case law on the subject. Nevertheless, later (Niemietz case, 1992), the Judges in Strasbourg provided protection, based on Article 8, to a law firm, while affirming that protection for a professional or business site was inferior to that afforded to an individual's domicile.[533]

---

530. D. Spielmann, "Human rights case law in the Strasbourg and Luxembourg courts: conflicts, inconsistencies and complementarities" in P. Alston (ed.), *The European Union and human rights*, Oxford, 1999, p. 766, identifies Case 136-79 *Nacional Panasonic* as the most significant for this issue.

531. J. Schwarze, "The role of the European Court of Justice in shaping legal standards for administrative action in the member states: a comparative perspective" in D. O'Keeffe (ed.), *Judicial Review in EU Law*, Kluwer Law International, The Hague, 2000, at p. 450.

532. See a detailed comparative study of the two jurisdictions in D. Spielmann, "Human rights case law in the Strasbourg and Luxembourg courts" in P. Alston (ed.), *The European Union and human rights*, Oxford, 1999; and in the same book C. Harlow, "Access to justice as a human right, the European Convention and the European Union", at pp. 187 to 214.

533. European Court of Human Rights 21 February 2008, *Ravon and Others v. France*, mentions the later doctrine on Article 8 of the Convention relating to companies and legal persons. In

Recent case law embodies a more sensitive approach to procedural rights than was previously applied by EC courts. In addition to its general acknowledgement of human rights as a protected issue in Community law, the Court of Justice has emphatically limited some of the Commission's powers applied during inspection proceedings.

In *Limburge* and other cases (2002),[534] the ECJ overruled a CFI judgment on the basis of infringement of an applicant's right to defence resulting from the refusal to grant access to a document used as evidence against him. In this judgment we also see how the Luxembourg Court expressly refers not only to the European Convention, but also to the interpretation of it given by the Strasbourg Court which "must be taken into account by the Community judicature". Additional examples of this positive approach can be found. In 2000, in *Compagnie maritime belge* and other cases,[535] the ECJ over-ruled a CFI judgment considering the breach of the appellant's right to a fair hearing. This right, said the court, constitutes a fundamental principle of Community law which should be observed in all proceedings.[536] Earlier, in the *Orkem* judgment (1989),[537] the ECJ had protected the privilege against self-incrimination, denying that the Commission's power could be used to oblige companies to admit their infringement of Community law (though they are obliged to answer factual questions and to provide documents even if it implicitly means the existence of the infringement).

In general terms, it could be affirmed that in ECJ case law procedural rights have evolved from general principles (in the earliest case law) to fundamental rights (as clearly stated in 2002 in the *Limburge* case).[538] However, this general trend does not always bring about a predictable solution. Whatever the ECJ qualifies as procedural rights, nonetheless in Mannesmann (2007)[539] the

contrast, see Opinion of Mr Advocate General of 20 September 2001 (Case C-94/00, *Roquette Frères*) on the validity of Hoechst's criteria.

534. Judgment of the Court of 15 October 2002, joined Cases C-238/99 P, C-244/99 P, C-245/99 P, C-247/99 P, C-250/99 P to 252/99 P and C-254/99 P.

535. Judgment of the Court of 16 March 2000, joined Cases C-395/96 P and C-396/96 P.

536. Since the Commission had not clearly identified the persons on whom fines might be imposed in the procedural stage ("statement of objections"), but only identified an entity in which related companies took part, that principle was not fully respected. The ECJ considered that companies forming that entity were not sufficiently aware that fines would be imposed on them individually if the infringement occurred.

537. Case 374/87, judgment of 18 October 1989.

538. Passing through a halfway phase initiated in 1989 by Hoestch case; see Joseph H. H. Weiler and Nicolas J. S. Lockhart, "Taking rights seriously: the European Court and its fundamental rights jurisprudence", Part I, *Common Market Law Review*, Vol. 32 (1995), 51-92.

539. Mannesmann, C-411/04 P, judgment of 25 January 2007. In paragraphs 40 and 41, the ECJ declares that "the Court has recognised the general principle of Community law that everyone is entitled to a fair legal process … It has also held that that principle is inspired by the fundamental rights which form an integral part of the general principles of Community law which the Court of Justice enforces, drawing inspiration from the constitutional principles common to the Member States and from the guidelines supplied, in particular, by the European Court of Human Rights".

guarantee provided by the ECJ on procedural rights was once again less than those granted by the Strasbourg Court. The ECJ, taking into account "particularities" of competition procedures, refused to recognise a plea to invalidate proofs coming from an anonymous source, a principle of "right of justice" already stated by the Judges in Strasbourg.[540] Due to the sensitive nature of this issue, any oscillating trend in ECJ case law is not acceptable, especially since procedural rights have already achieved the highest legal recognition at the community level. The Charter is equivalent in legal status to treaties.

There are other considerations to suggest that careful scrutiny of Strasbourg case law is advisable. In the framework of increasingly complex administrative activity, it is a good idea to distinguish the double meaning of the right to a defence: the right to intervene in the course of an administrative proceeding; and the right that can be exercised at the end of the proceeding by challenging an administrative decision before a judge.[541]

In the first sense, the ECJ has produced a huge amount of doctrine on rights, which has been increased in recent years. However, and related to the second meaning, ECJ doctrine is far removed from that already established by the Strasbourg Court, whose doctrine is closer to the national ones.[542] It should be remembered that the Strasbourg Court's doctrine on the right to defence has been elaborated on the basis of the very sophisticated judicial systems of member states, a complex design involving a detailed distribution of jurisdictional competencies with regard to the nature of the issue, various instances of judicial review in each jurisdictional order and a varied catalogue of judicial bodies and their corresponding lawsuits – first instances, appellations, cassations and constitutional court remedies. The procedural design in the EU follows a unitary model with only two judicial bodies; the criteria and principles in this framework are necessarily less detailed and thus leave a wider margin of application when applied at the domestic level.

14.3. The judicial review: access and scope

We have explained the ways by which citizens can bring an action challenging the legality of Community law, directly before the ECJ and, indirectly, before the national courts examining a national measure which implements Community law. For direct actions – of annulment, for failure to fulfil obligations, for failure to act – citizens have very narrow access to the Community courts, if any. Addressing the national courts is the usual, albeit indirect, way

---

540. European Court of Human Rights case.

541. See Cassese, "European administrative proceedings", *Law and Contemporary Problems*, Vol. 68, No. 1, winter 2004, p. 33, with reference to Case C-78/01, Bunderverband Güterkraftverkehr.

542. Relating to the European Court of Human Rights' doctrine on procedural guarantees and the notion of fair trial, it has been affirmed that "even if these are not constitutionally entrenched and acknowledged, their contribution should be borne in mind" (E. Storskrubb and J. Ziller, "Access to justice in European comparative law" in Francioni, *Access to Justice*, Oxford, 2007, p. 180).

to get judicial protection in the framework of a collaborative system, putting the two jurisdictional levels in touch by a "preliminary reference". As the ECJ repeatedly states, "the Treaty has established a complete system of legal remedies and procedures designed to ensure judicial review of the legality of acts of the institutions and has entrusted such review to the Community Courts".[543]

However, the co-operative framework between both jurisdictional levels on which the "complete system of legal remedies" is settled does not work well enough in all the situations required for effective judicial protection or for full and effective judicial checks on the public power's compliance with the (Community) law. Neither the Constitutional nor the Lisbon Treaties put an end to these situations: the present Community judicial system is affected by the Lisbon Treaty much more from an organisational point of view than from a substantive one. More particularly, and taking into account the present challenges in an enlarged Union, the few amendments introduced by the Lisbon Treaty are still poor and insufficient, failing to increase in a significant way the judicial guarantees for individuals at the Community level or to provide a renewed, efficiently working judicial system.[544]

These gaps could be referred to at least two aspects of the procedural regulations: citizens' standing to sue, to directly bring an action before the ECJ; and the scope of judicial control exercised by the European jurisdiction. Here we briefly describe both.

14.3.1. Indirect access, such as (alleged) compensation

The narrow possibilities for citizens to go before the ECJ to directly challenge a measure implementing Community law are justified and explained on the basis of the complementary roles of national and community jurisdictions, specifically in the alleged balance provided by the wider access citizens have to national courts – access which has been reinforced at national level by the requirements deduced from the "right to a fair trial" by the ECJ. This explanation was used early on by the ECJ in the well-known case *Les Verts*,[545] where the judicial protection provided for individuals by the ECJ was presented as being based on the distinction between direct and indirect action, according to the level – Community or national – where the contested measure is applied.

However, a more detailed analysis of the content of the "effective judicial remedy" coming from such a co-operative model between the two judicial levels suggests some objections, which can be summarised in the three following considerations.

---

543. ECJ 25 July 2002, C-50/00 P, UPA, paragraph 40, and many earlier paragraphs.
544. See Ruiz-Jarabo Colomer, "El Tribunal de Justicia de la Unión Europea en el Tratado de Lisboa" in *Noticias de la Unión Europea*, No. 291, April 2009 p. 31 and ff. (Issue devoted to the Lisbon Treaty).
545. Case 294/83, Les Verts, paragraph 23.

One view is that the narrow access to the ECJ provided to citizens is offset by another method of pursuing an action before the national courts. If they do not comply with the demanding conditions of admissibility to bring an action before the ECJ, they can always initiate proceedings at national level. In this way, and through the preliminary reference of the national court, citizens always have indirect access to the ECJ. However, this assertion requires a previous condition: the equivalence in the judicial review provided by the two legal remedies, a conclusion which is far from being generally accepted. For this method of access, it is important to note once again the Opinion of a General Advocate stating the different levels of judicial control which can be achieved with one remedy or the other:

> Judicial review in an action for annulment, both before the Court of Justice and before the Court of First Instance, of individual administrative measures ... is more effective than that achieved by way of a reply to a reference for a preliminary ruling.[546]

> The approach taken by the Court of Justice (in preliminary reference) is purely legal. It is confined to the interpretation and assessment of the legality of legislative and individual acts of the Community institutions. Conversely, the procedural route of Article 230 (action of annulment) leads to the Community Court reviewing issues of substance such as the finding and assessment of facts.[547]

The faculties of the parties to participate in procedural debate differ substantially in the two types of action. First, a national court is not bound to stay a preliminary reference proceeding each time the parties ask for it. This decision belongs to the national courts, not to the parties. Secondly, the petitions, reasoning and observations made by the parties in an annulment procedure have a direct influence on the result; the observations presented in the preliminary reference procedure have a much more limited role.

Although the restricted access to the ECJ for citizens in annulment actions is probably the most criticised aspect of the Community judicial system, other serious limitations on access are identifiable. An action for failure to act is strictly reserved to privileged applicants: member states and the Commission. Citizens can require the Commission to bring action against a member state, but it has the discretion to decide whether to do so.[548] Its decision refusing to bring an action cannot be challenged by citizens either by an action of annulment or by an action for failure to act.[549]

Such a regulation sometimes leads to situations which are inconsistent with the general understanding of the right to a fair trial, as the Dangeville case illustrates:[550] A French company had been overtaxed on the basis of statutory

---

546. Opinion of Mr Advocate General Cosmas, 16 May 2000, Case C-344/98, paragraph 55. Similar statements and criteria in Jacobs UPA.
547. Ibid., paragraph 52.
548. See the Opinion of the Advocate General Ruiz-Jarabo in Case C-362/01.
549. See Order of the CFI 3 July 1997, Case T-201/96, among many others.
550. European Court of Human Rights, judgment of 16 April 2002, *Dangeville v. France*, confirmed in a similar case, *Cabinet Diot and Grus Savoye v. France*, European Court of Human

provisions that were incompatible with a Community Directive. However, both the claim based on the incorrect national implementation of the Community Directive and the action for damages caused by these illegal provisions were dismissed by the national courts. Yet there was no access for the taxpayer to the European courts in Luxembourg to challenge the incorrect national implementation, by way of an action for failure to satisfy a Community obligation. Thirteen years after the suit was initiated and only because the incorrect national implementation involved a fundamental right – the right of property – it was the Strasbourg Court that finally satisfied the applicant's claims, declaring that its right to peaceful enjoyment of its possession had been infringed. Would not the Luxembourg Court have been the natural jurisdiction to declare such infringements, avoiding 13 years of legal disputes before the national courts? Was this delay consistent with the ECHR's doctrine on reasonable delay and the right to a fair trial? Of the complementary role played by the Convention in such cases, it has been wisely observed that "we can perhaps agree that this is not the proper way forward for achieving access to justice for litigants who challenge law on fundamental rights-related grounds".[551]

Finally, just a short comment on the significant divergences in access to the Court for associations and NGOs, divergences found in the European legal tradition (Council of Europe and national laws) and the EU system. The Council of Europe recommends a careful examination of cases where access to judicial review is not provided for associations and other bodies empowered to protect collective or community interest,[552] a view that essentially coincides with that of the Aarhus Convention.[553] Likewise, national laws in general recognise standing to sue at least for certain categories of associations, mainly those involved in environmental and consumer interests. In contrast, the EU legal system holds a restrictive view on the requirements associations must comply with, in law and in the ECJ's approach. At best, the admissibility of group actions is "limited to particular sectors and extremely particular circumstances".[554]

Rights 22 October 2003.

551. Storksrubb and Ziller, in Francioni, *Access to justice*, op. cit., p. 198.

552. See Chapter 4 for comments on Rec(2004)20, which specifically encourages member states to grant associations the capacity to bring proceedings against decisions "which adversely affect not just one individual but also those which affect any community".

553. See Article 9.2 in relation to Article 2.5, linking the standing to sue for environmental NGOs with the "public concerned". See C. Redgwell, "Access to environmental justice" in Francioni, *Access to justice*, op. cit., particularly p. 166 and ff.

554. L. W. Gromley, "Public interest litigation" in D. O'Keeffe (ed.), *Judicial review in European Union law*, Kluwer Law International, The Hague, 2000, p. 192, adding that "in Greenpeace, both the CFI then the ECJ made it clear that the traditional hostile stance to public interest litigation would be maintained". He suggests to improve public interest litigation on a sector-by-sector basis, and to create a register for organisations which have standing to sue will have the additional effect of encouraging participation of interest groups in the global Community legislative process in a transparent way (p. 201).

14.3.2. Transnational administrative activity
and procedure

The second objection affects the premises on which the co-operative judicial model is based. According to the ECJ, different remedies are provided depending on who implements the Community regulation, a national or a Community administrative body. In other words, the model presupposes a clear distinction between direct and indirect implementation of Community law; however, it is currently exceeded in importance by the vastly different and more complex administrative activity.[555] As we have explained, beyond the two initial ways there are several administrative activities developed by many bodies linking them in horizontal and vertical relationships which do not fit with the original binary scheme. Consequently, since the "alleged distinction" could be objected to, the judicial architecture based on it and the efficiency of its functions deserve examination.

These new ways to implement Community law, known as Mixed Administration and transnational procedures, do not provide accurate regulation for private parties to deal with all the administrative authorities that affect them. These types of Community procedures are mainly focused on the efficiency of administrative action in the whole Community territory and on the participation of all authorities which could be involved by the national resolution. However, the position of private parties who have initiated a procedure before their national authority has not been definitively ruled on. Before adoption of the (national) resolution that private parties have petitioned for, a complex transnational procedure is set in motion, whereby many procedural acts can be adopted by foreign authorities and Community bodies. The Community procedures do not establish rules about the procedural rights of the parties with regard to these intermediate authorities, nor do they offer the possibility to challenge these procedural acts even when they have settled de facto the content of the final (national) acts. All these details are left to national administrative laws, which not only are not sufficiently harmonised[556] but which historically are law only within their own national territories.

There is a long list of controversial situations arising from transnational procedures: the difficulty of being heard before an administrative authority, whether it adopts a formal or informal resolution affecting the interest of the third party; difficulties and divergences in access to documents in different countries as a prerequisite to the full exercise of procedural rights because of the lack of harmonisation of national rules; different national regulations on

---

555. Relating these issues, I referred in Chapter 11 to the works of M. Chiti ("Forms of European Administrative action", referring to the "disappearing system of indirect administration", p. 51), G. J. Della Cananea ("The European Union's mixed proceedings"), S. Cassese ("European administrative proceedings") and my own work (Galera, *La aplicación administrativa del Derecho comunitario*).
556. M. Chiti, "Forms of European administrative action", op. cit., pp. 49 and ff.

procedural and final acts; difficulties for the private parties to access foreign courts, even when the administrative activity affecting their interest was carried out in that country; difficulties in identifying the right authority among the different participants to whom a damage is attributable in order to claim for responsibility.[557] On the other hand, a narrow interpretation of Community "decisions" that can be challenged by an action of annulment before the ECJ does not help to mitigate these situations.

This already complex situation becomes still more complicated if we consider the Community bodies and agencies participating in transnational procedures. In fact, their role is to assist the Commission in these administrative functions. As we mentioned above, no single rule states how, where and when the measures adopted by these administrative bodies can be challenged in order to verify their legality.

It is thus obvious that transnational administrative action which implements Community procedures requires specific rules for adequate control of this activity and on the correlative legal position of the parties involved. As has been suggested, a specific legal framework distinct from that of the entirety of European administration may not be necessary.[558] However, specific tools such as "arbitration" bodies could be convenient in order to deal with disputes stemming from international legal divergence – access to a document or judicial review of some interim resolutions, among others – and to provide access to the ECJ through actions brought against its decisions. In any event, official recognition is needed so that "though structurally distinct, the Commission and national administration constitute a procedural whole for the purposes of judicial review and safeguarding individual rights".[559]

14.3.3. Public activity excluded from judicial review

A final objection to the system of judicial review focuses on the areas of European activity outside the scope of common judicial controls. Beyond the exclusions coming from the rules governing administrative procedures and judicial processes – preparatory acts, normative acts, inactivity, acts confirming a previously adopted act, standing to sue and so on – historically there is a whole set of public activities which are not subject to judicial scrutiny, in some cases as a consequence of the principle of the division of powers. We have already presented the Convention doctrine on the acts of governments, also recognised in the national law with different scope.

---

557. Della Cananea ("The EU's mixed administrative proceedings", op. cit.), pointing out these types of difficulty in mixed proceedings concludes that "judicial review is not the only concern" (p. 215); M. Chiti ("Forms of European administrative action", op. cit.) underlines national divergences on administrative inaction, and the ground on which administrative acts can be declared void (pp. 49, 54).
558. Della Cananea, op. cit.
559. Cassese, "European administrative proceedings", p. 35.

In general terms, public activities involving sovereign attributes such as foreign affairs, national defence and general security are not under judicial scrutiny. However, this general rule is not without some limits, which are stated in the corresponding legal order, with a different scope.[560] In this regard, there are two kinds of limits established by the Convention. First, governmental powers should be exercised within the bounds laid down in the legal rules conferring such powers, which implies a check on whether these rules and bounds have been observed; secondly, respect for human rights constitutes a limit itself, and the possible exceptions to judicial review should be defined by the law in a specific and limited manner.[561]

Up to recently, there were in the EU system two fields where limited judicial control was provided: foreign and security policy (former second pillar) and police and judicial co-operation in criminal matters (former third pillar). The exclusion observes the legality principle which is required by the rule-of-law tradition, in that it is the EU Treaty itself which excluded the ECJ from jurisdiction in these fields. However, a sort of formal control was exercised by the ECJ, just to verify if the measures adopted in the framework of such pillars were capable of being adopted as Community measures, in which case the latter will prevail. This was just a check to preserve the Community competencies, but at least it exerted some control as a first limit, the importance of which was highlighted by the Convention for the acts of governments.[562]

The Lisbon Treaty introduces a few improvements in ways of reducing the exceptions:

–   with respect to the provision on common foreign and security policy, the Court remains without jurisdiction, with two exceptions: the current possibility to preserve Community competencies and the check on legality of restrictive measures adopted by the Council in this framework against natural or legal persons (Article 275);

–   in the provisions relating to police and judicial co-operation in criminal matters – now included in the area of freedom, security and justice – the general rule is full submission to the common judicial check provided by the Treaty. However, there is an important exception in the event of national implementation of such measures: According to the Article 276, is not is not for the Court to review the validity or proportionality of operations carried out by the police or other law-enforcement services

---

560. See above (Part II) for different national approaches to this issue. I want to underline the Spanish approach by which, notwithstanding the general rule that political acts are outside the scope of judicial review, such a check is always provided when fundamental rights are involved, to verify the formal legality of the decision or when compensation for damages is at stake.

561. See above, Part II, and the European Court of Human Rights 21 September 1994, *Fayed v. the United Kingdom*, where it was rejected that "a State could remove from the jurisdiction of the courts a whole range of civil claims, or confer immunities from civil liability on large groups or categories of persons without restraint or control by the Convention enforcement bodies".

562. See the case law referred to above in Part III, in Chapter 11.

of a member state or the exercise of the responsibilities incumbent on member states in maintaining law and order and safeguarding internal security.

We can expect future doctrine to be developed from these new provisions. For this task, the ECJ has the valuable reference of the Convention doctrine already stated on these issues.

14.4. Judicial independence

Judicial independence is granted in the European legal system as a rule-of-law requirement and a condition for the due exercise of the right to a fair trial. In addition to the constitutions granting this right, both European jurisdictions provide us with a complete doctrine about what judicial independence requires. The European Court of Human Rights has produced two types of case law covering the two separate historical understandings of "judicial independence": the conditions for an impartial decision on individual cases, and the framework in which the judges work, with respect to how they are appointed and removed, salaries and facilities, and so on.[563]

Once again there are a few nuances in the judicial independence standards as they are commonly understood which necessarily should be considered: specifically, some Community rules determining how some judicial functions should be handled at national level, their scope and limits, an issue that is strictly governed by national laws from a formal and from a substantive normative perspective.

In particular, there are grey areas in Community competition law, where controversial points arise; again, the "due implementation" of Community law is the explanation for such a regulation. We are going to refer to two of them: the regulation for the "search warrants" required by the Commission and provided by national courts; and the pre-eminence of the Commission's criteria over (national) judicial ones in the event of possible inconsistencies.

There is a new general provision in Community competition law – Regulation 1/2003 – replacing the older one, in force since 1962. This new regulation does not provide any new rules on the issue we are concerned with that are different from those previously established in ECJ case law, but it codifies this case law in a Community regulation with a primacy effect.

Community competition law foresees the possibility of a company opposing an inspection conducted by the Commission's official and, according

---

563. See J. Resnik, "Judicial independence" in Vikram David Amar and Mark V. Tushnet (eds), *Global perspectives on constitutional law*, Oxford University Press, 2009, who, beyond these two classical treats, underline that "during the 20th century, two new 'friends' of 'foes' of judicial independence have come to the fore – the media and 'repeat player' litigants" (p. 17).

to national law, a judicial search warrant is required.[564] It defines the task of national courts in providing this authorisation and delimits their power, clearly establishing that oversight by the national courts is just a "control of the proportionality of the coercive measure". It also adds that "national judicial authority may not call into question the necessity for the inspection *nor demand that it be provided with the information in the Commission's file*" [italics added].

These articles codify the criteria already established by the Luxembourg Court case law. The limits imposed on national courts to verify the Commission's request for a search warrant were recently challenged before the Luxembourg Court. In a 2002 judgment the ECJ decided a case about a preliminary reference sought by the French court, which clearly asked about national judicial powers in these situations.[565] A framework has been constituted by precedent in the *Hoechst* and *Niemietz* case law,[566] relating to whether home protection provided by Article 8 of the Convention extends to business companies or not.

Following its previous criteria and the specific rules to be applied, the ECJ finally determined that a national judge has limited powers to request information from the Commission. The national judge may only verify that the coercive measures are not arbitrary or disproportionate for the subject of the investigation ordered; but the judge is not able to review "the justification of those measures beyond what is required … The national court may not demand that it be provided with the evidence in the Commission's file on which suspicions are based".[567] The Court underlines that the necessity for an investigation – whether or not the arguments put forward by the Commission to justify it are convincing – is subject to a review by the Court of Justice each time it is disputed.[568]

Once again, "primacy of Community law and needs for its proper implementation" appear as the main reasons to support a solution which does not convince everybody. The General Advocate itself indicated the right solution, which was the search warrant provided by the ECJ or CFI[569] – having full control of the legality of the Commission's request – not by the national

---

564. Regulation 1/2003, Article 20, paragraph 7. Similar provisions are established in the event that private homes of directors, managers and other staff are involved in an investigation (Article 21).

565. Judgment of the Court of 22 October 2002, Case C-94/00, *Roquette Frères*. The French High court asked: "whether … the national court … cannot refuse to grant the authorisation requested where it considers that the information or evidence presented to it … is not sufficient to authorise such a measure."

566. See note 533 above.

567. See Judgment of the Court of 22 October 2002, Case C-94/00.

568. Strasbourg case law criteria are pertinent here, specifically *Funke v. France*, judgment of 25 February 1993, Application No. 10828/84. This relied on broad powers of administrative authorities "to assess the expediency, number, length and scale of inspections" and found that they were disproportionate to the private domicile right of the applicant.

569. Opinion of Mr Advocate General Mischo, Case C-94/00, point 46.

courts, which only have a limited and formal control over it. However, and failing this right and coherent solution, "consistency in the implementation of Community law"[570] should prevail, even when this implementation would affect such a sensitive question as jurisdictional functions.

This way to verify the legality of a search warrant hardly fits into the Strasbourg Court's criteria as stated in its *Ravon* judgment:[571] after recalling its previous case law recognising for legal persons and companies the right to a private domicile provided by Article 8 of the Convention, the Court stated that full and effective judicial control is required of measures ordering the inspection of private domiciles, both for relating facts and legal reasoning. According to the Court, it is not enough that the authorisation is provided by a court; rather, full judicial control of such a measure is required by the right to a fair trial granted by Article 6 of the Convention. As in a specific case full control was only provided once the inspection had taken place, the Court stated that such control did not comply with Article 6 requirements.

Another consequence of this regulation whose value is open to question is the dual legal regime on judicial functions applied by the national court. Full control of legality of search will be in the hands of the national court only if the national administrative authorities so request. When it is the Commission that asks for review, the national court is only allowed a limited control, even when the Community proceeding is coincidental with an ongoing national judicial proceeding. This duality has drawn severe criticism: "[T]here is a clear discrimination between investigation for breaches of Articles 81 and 82 only carried out by the French authorities, and the same kind of investigations carried out by the Commission with the assistance of the French authorities. This is certainly most unsatisfactory."[572]

These limits on national judges have recently been repeated by the CFI in a case where the appellant pleaded that relevant information had not been provided to a national judge before he approved a search warrant.[573]

If this provision limits the judicial functions of the national courts, the next provision we are going to mention goes further. The provision not only puts limits on national courts' functions, it also awards a sort of pre-eminence to the Commission's criteria in the event that they are inconsistent with the (national) judicial resolution. Under the label of "co-operation" between the national and Community levels, the competition rules state that "when national courts rule" on issues covered by European competition law "which

---

570. Ibid., point 52.
571. European Court of Human Rights, judgment of 21 February 2008, *Raven and Others v. France*, paragraphs 28, 30 and 34.
572. L. Idot, *Are NCAs investigation power?*, op. cit. p. 909.
573. CFI 8 Mar 2007, Case T-339/04, *France Telecom*. The *Roquette Frères* doctrine was applied, remanding limits on the national judge to request information and applying some formalist rules for dismissing this plea.

are already the subject of a Commission decision, they cannot make decisions running counter to the decision adopted by the Commission".[574]

The Regulation takes extra steps to avoid inconsistencies between the Community and national (judicial) authorities implementing competition law. It also foresees the possibility of proceedings initiated at both national (judicial) and Community level which are not already finalised by any decisions. In this event, the national judicial resolution cannot be inconsistent with decisions that the Commission is going to adopt in the future; the national courts "must also avoid giving decisions which would conflict with a decision completed by the Commission in proceedings it has initiated".[575]

In these situations, the expected and advisable national judge's "co-operative" behaviour is developed by the Commission itself.[576] The Commission states again that the judge "must avoid adopting a decision" inconsistent with the (future) Commission decision and indicates that the national judge "may ask the Commission and also consider staying its proceedings until the Commission has reached a decision".

These regulations suggest a pre-eminence of the Commission's decisions – the already adopted and the future ones – over the decisional power of a judicial (national) body handling its own proceedings, which hardly fits in with the common understanding of "judicial independence".

The Community system has its own explanation based on its particular legal premises, where the duty of "legal co-operation" enshrined in Article 4 TEU (former Article 5 EC Treaty) appears as pre-eminent. The ECJ case law gives its reasons about this peculiar collaborative way of implementing Community law, which can be found summarised in the Masterfood case,[577] where the Irish Supreme Court asked about the relationship between the national courts and the Community administrative and judicial institutions in such cases. Among others, we want to underline the following criteria:

–   The duties imposed on the national court, limiting its autonomy to decide the content of a judicial resolution, are part of the "loyal collaboration" imposed on member states whose duties "to take all appropriate measures … is binding on all authorities of Member States including, for matters within their jurisdiction, the courts";[578]

–   In these situations, the national courts appear as just a subordinate body to the Commission when the Commission deals with a coincidental case applying its competition law, which is explained on the basis of the "principles governing the division of powers between the Commission

574. Regulation 1/2003, Article 16.
575. Regulation 1/2003, Article 16, second paragraph.
576. In the already mentioned Commission Notice (2004/C 101/4), which replaces one from 1993.
577. ECJ judgment of 14 December 2000, Case C-344/98.
578. Paragraph 49, confirming the criteria already stated in Case C-2/97 *IP v. Borsana*.

and the national courts in the application of the Community competition rules".[579] According to the specific provisions which are legitimated on these principles:

-   "the Commission cannot be bound by a decision given by a national court"[580] as it is "entitled to adopt at any time a decision … even where an agreement or practice has already been subject of a decision by a national court and the decision contemplated by the Commission conflicts with the national courts' decision";[581]

-   on the other hand, the national court "cannot take a decision running counter to that of the Commission",[582] being compelled "to stay the proceedings in any case where there is a risk that the decision contemplated by it might conflict with an existing or future decision of a Community institution",[583] the preliminary reference appearing as a *deus ex machina* remedy "if the national court considered that it could not wait"[584] once it has stayed the national proceeding.

Additional comments are not necessary. Perhaps it would be a good idea just to point out the particular use given to the expression "division of powers". In the common general understanding, it refers to an essential of the rule-of-law tradition preserving the due and independent functioning of each of the three powers of the state – legislative, executive and judicial – paying special attention to the relationship between the executive and judicial branches. By contrast, in the above-mentioned comment, the "division of powers" appears to distribute the task between one executive body – the Commission, and a judicial one – the national court. Would this assertion be better expressed with the words "distribution of competencies" or "distribution of tasks"? It is worth recalling here the need to clearly distinguish the terms power, functions and competencies, which have a specific common meaning in public law.[585]

References

Alston P., and Weiler, J. H., "An 'ever closer union' in need of human rights policy: the European Union and human rights", Harvard Jean Monnet Working Paper 1/99, available at www.jeanmonnetprogram.org/papers/99/990105.html.

---

579. Paragraph 45.
580. Paragraph 48.
581. Ibid.
582. Paragraph 60
583. Paragraph 39, confirming the criteria already stated in case C-250/92 *Grotup-Klim v. Dansk Langbrugs*.
584. Paragraph 42 confirming the criteria already stated in Case 23/67 *Delimitis*.
585. A detailed and subtle distinction among these concepts is found in M. Baena del Alcázar, "Competencias, funciones y potestades en el ordenamiento jurídico español" in Sebastián Martín-Retortillo Baquer (ed.), *Estudios sobre la Constitución española: Homenaje al profesor Eduardo García de Enterría*, Vol. 3, Cívitas, Madrid 1991, pp. 2453-2466.

Baena del Alcázar, M., "Competencias, funciones y potestades en el ordenamiento jurídico español" in Sebastián Martín-Retortillo Baquer (ed.), *Estudios sobre la Constitución española: Homenaje al profesor Eduardo García de Enterría*, Vol. 3, 1991.

Barbier de La Serre, E., "Procedural justice in the European Community case law concerning the rights of the defence: essentialist and instrumental trends", *European Public Law*, 2006, Vol. 12, No. 2.

Cassese, S. *La Globalizacion Juridica*, Inap-Marcial Pons, Madrid, 2006.

Chiti, E. "Administrative proceedings involving European agencies", *Law and Contemporary Problems*, Vol. 68, p. 227, pointing out among these principles those added to the list of the ECJ.

Chiti, M., "Forms of European administrative action", *Law and Contemporary Problems*, Vol. 68, No. I, winter 2004.

Constantinesco, V., "The ECJ as law-maker: *Praeter aut contra legem?*" in *Judicial Review in European Union Law*, ed. D. O'Keeffe, Kluwer, The Hague, 2000.

Council of Europe, *The Administration and you: Principles of Administrative Law concerning relations between administrative authorities and private persons, a handbook*, Strasbourg, 1996.

Della Cananea, G. J. "The European Union mixed proceedings", *Law and Contemporary Problems*, Vol. 68 (2004), No. 1.

Galera Rodrigo, S., "Sobre el alma de Europa, derechos fundamentales y EuroSpeak", *Tiempo de Paz*, Madrid, No. 90, Fall 2008.

Galera Rodrigo, S., *La aplicación administrativa del Derecho comunitario*, Cívitas, Madrid 1998.

Gromley, L. W., "Public interest litigation" in D. O'Keeffe (ed.), *Judicial review in European Union law*, Kluwer Law International, The Hague, 2000.

Harlow, C., "Global administrative law: the quest for principles and values", *European Journal of International Law*, No. 17 (2006).

Harlow, C., "Access to justice as a human right, the European Convention and the European Union", in *The European Union and human rights*, Alston P. (ed.), Oxford, 1999.

Ortega Alvarez, L., "Fundamental Rights in the European Constitution", *European Public Law*, Vol. 11, No. 3, 2005.

Redgwell, C., "Access to environmental justice" in Francioni, *Access to justice as a human right*, Oxford University Press, 2007.

Resnik, J., "Judicial independence" in Vikram David Amar and Mark V. Tushnet (eds), *Global perspectives on constitutional law*, Oxford University Press, 2009.

Rubio Llorente, F., "La Carta Europea de los Derechos", *Claves de la razón práctica*, No. 122, 2002.

Ruiz-Jarabo Colomer, D., "El Tribunal de Justicia de la Unión Europea en el Tratado de Lisboa" in *Noticias de la Union Europea*, No. 291, April 2009 (Issue devoted to the Lisbon Treaty).

Schwarze, J., "The role of the European Court of Justice in shaping legal standards for administrative action in the member states: a comparative perspective" in D. O'Keeffe (ed.), *Judicial Review in EU Law*, Kluwer Law International, The Hague, 2000.

Spielmann, D., "Human rights case law in the Strasbourg and Luxembourg courts: conflicts, inconsistencies and complementarities" in P. Alston (ed.), *The European Union and human rights*, Oxford, 1999.

Storskrubb, E. and Ziller, J., "Access to justice in European comparative law" in F. Francioni (ed.), *Access to justice as a human right*, Oxford University Press, 2007.

Suder, F., "Le Recours aux 'notions autonomes'" in *L'interprétation de la convention européenne des droits de l'homme*, Brussels, Bruylant, 1998.

Weiler, J. H. H., and Lockhart, Nicolas J. S., "Taking rights seriously: the European Court and its fundamental rights jurisprudence", Part I, *Common Market Law Review*, Vol. 32 (1995).

Wils, W., "Powers of investigation and procedural rights and guarantees in EU antitrust enforcement: the interplay between European and national legislation and case law" in *Competition Law and Economics. Advances in Competition Policy and Antitrust Enforcement*, ed. Abel M. Mateus and Teresa Moreira, Kluwer Law International, 2007.

Chapter 15
The European contribution to an emerging global law

S. Galera

There are two elements shaping the current European legal outline, with common roots, though not fully coincidental. The constitutional text comes from the long legal tradition, preserved in its essentials by the Council of Europe, on the one hand, and a new institutional and political supranational experience constituted by the EU, on the other. We refer to this result as the European legal system, meaning an integrated whole formed by many interacting entities.

Undoubtedly, the EU experience constitutes the most complete institutional and legal experience attempted by the states to go beyond the classic international organisations scheme. The evolution of its institutional framework has to be taken into account because it works efficiently, merging the many players intervening in an organised procedural scheme; but it should also be considered because it has improved its democratic elements as the process has gone forward since the 1950s. The achievements and the imperfections of the EU's evolution are equally valuable references to the current attempts at economic and political integration all around the world.

The EU has an institutional architecture which is not equivalent to the states' systems in terms of democracy, control or rule-of-law requirements, although these differences do not exclude that possible EU contributions to the member states will improve the embodiment of these values. The link with the Council of Europe as a de facto prerequisite to become an EU member is evidence in this regard.[586] In addition, the impacts on national judicial systems coming from repeated ECJ case law have to be mentioned. Some significant changes in national law on essential issues came from these Community obligations, among them the national statutes ruling on the standing to sue, the delay to bring an action and the interim measures regime, among others.[587] Although this requirement has been mainly based on the "proper implementation of

---

586. Membership of the Council of Europe is evidence of compliance with the political criteria for EU membership stated in Article 48 of the EU Treaty – respect for the principles of liberty, democracy, human rights and fundamental freedoms, and the rule of law.

587. An updated version of such legal changes is in V. Cerulli Irelli, "Trasformazioni del sistema di tutela giurisdizionale nelle controversie di diritto pubblico per effetti della giurisprudenza europea", contribution to *XVII Congreso italo-español de Profesores de Derecho Administrativo*, Zaragoza 2008.

the Community law" and on the primacy principle, there is no doubt that procedural justice in the correspondent member states has been reinforced.

However, EU law occasionally reinforcing the rule-of-law tradition is not proof enough to identify EU law with the rule of law itself or with a later renewed version. We have referred to significant divergences between the two elements constituting the European system. The underlined persistent gaps in the EU judicial review system and the different understanding of what judicial independence or division of powers means cannot be simply interpreted as particular and different legal solutions on specific issues, but instead represent a serious divergence affecting values and principles that have been applied for a long time on the European institutional scene. The primacy principle or the "need for the due implementation of the community law" is only able to resolve a few particular judicial cases but cannot avoid the corresponding tensions within the whole legal system, as the constitutional court's warnings historically showed.[588] There is no need to endure such tensions since fortunately Europeans share a well-defined doctrine about the European understanding of rule-of-law requirements, initiated in 1949 by the Council of Europe.

On the other hand, there is a general understanding in Europe of what administrative law means and the main functions it has to comply with in the rule-of-law tradition. The different definitions of administrative law stress its control function, either when such definition is focused on this function or when it is administration-centred.[589] It is worth insisting on this coincidental element in the current legal atmosphere, when administrative action has to be developed in a territory where national borders have become increasingly diffuse. It appears the effectiveness of administrative action is a pre-eminent goal in the corresponding rules, whereas the consequent legal position of individuals dealing with the administration seems to remain at a second level. In effect, it has been pointed out that "the late-20th century free market experiment is an attempt to legitimate through democratic institutions severe limits on the scope and content of democratic control", making a "thin or procedural version of the rule of law doctrine likely to flourish in economic communities".[590]

---

588. An updated version of this controversial debate in W. Sadurski, "Solange: Chapter 3. Constitutional Courts in Central Europe", *European Law Journal*, January 2008, Vol. 14, No. 1, pp. 1-35.

589. See C. Harlow, "Global administrative law", *European Journal of International Law*, Vol. 17, No. 1 (2006), p. 191 and ff., referring to the classic definition by Shapiro, on one hand, and by Debbasch, Duguit and Cassese, on the other.

590. Both references (the first quoting John Gray) in Harlow, "Global administrative law", p. 195, considering that this "thin" economic version of the rule of law and the four community freedoms understood as an economic constitution "has influenced the way in which the ECJ set about its task of putting in place principles of administrative law".

However, there are possible "adapted versions" of the rule-of-law tradition that include the standard level of checks and guarantees suited to today's continually fast-changing society. This was foreseen by the European Court of Human Rights, which stated that the key concepts of the Convention, especially its "object and purpose, and in the light of present-day conditions in democratic societies", have to be interpreted by a dynamic approach.[591] However, a very different possibility, an adapted version of the rule-of-law tradition that reduces the scope of checks to which public power is submitted or the already consolidated guarantees to individuals facing public action, is hardly acceptable.

Furthermore, and from a wider perspective, the European legal system interacts with its legal environment as well. From this position, and considering both the European integration and the globalisation of legal issues, it has been underlined a current "order of order, implying a plurality of legal sources as well as of both legislatures and courts".[592]

It was not yesterday that states began to consider some issues on the basis of their "common interest" and consequently adopted common rules in intergovernmental treaties passed in the framework of international organisations. However, a profound change has emerged in recent years as the scope of common interest has been enlarged. Now common general rules are not enough: instead, common detailed regulations, going beyond the normal content of an international treaty, are required as well in specific fields. The effectiveness of these regulations on specific and an increasing number of issues imposes a certain consensus on how the public authorities are going to implement these regulations.

This phenomenon has been referred to as the "unnoticed rise of global administrative law", defined "as comprising the mechanisms, principles, practices and supporting social understandings that promote or otherwise affect the accountability of global administrative bodies, in particular by ensuring they meet adequate standards of transparency, participation, reasoned decision, and legality, and by providing effective review of the rules and decisions they make".[593]

---

591. European Court of Human Rights, judgment of 28 June 1978, *König v. Germany*, referred to above.

592. G. J. Della Cananea, "Beyond the state: the Europeanization and globalization of procedural administrative law", *European Public Law*, Vol. 9, No. 4, p. 577.

593. B. Kingsbury, N. Krisch and R. B. Stewart, "The emergence of global administrative law", *Law and Contemporary Problems*, 68/1, p. 17. Among fields with such common regulations, they identify (p. 16): "security, the conditions on development and financial assistance to developing countries, environmental protection, banking and financial assistance to developing countries, environmental protection, banking and financial regulation, law enforcement, telecommunications, trade in products and services, intellectual property, labour standards, and cross-border movements of populations, including refugees".

This *in fieri* global law has to resolve two important challenges. In the first place are the common detailed regulations, just mentioned, which will require great flexibility in the current legal orders, either as recipients of the new regulations or as contributors in their elaboration. In fact, the mutual influence which is shaping European administrative law – national principles influencing Community regulations which go back to the national orders,[594] can now be identified at classic international forums such as the World Trade Organization.[595]

On the other hand, this global law has to deal with a distinct understanding of the traditional state. In the international arena, states and international organisations still play the main roles, though the classical structure of the play can be hardly recognised in a more choral work. There is a new role played by the state, which increasingly takes part in a horizontal structure with other governmental representatives or with other kinds of participants, different from governmental representatives, also having a seat. In this framework, putting aside its authoritative nature and executive – national – prerogatives based on a hierarchy, the nation-state plays different functions. As such it interacts in a complex scenario "in which the state is just one of several public organizations existing alongside the legal order operating outside its border".[596]

Currently, the main challenge for the public law in the global era is to fashion the institutional architecture necessary for democracy to work,[597] balancing the needs arising from an increasingly complex and interdependent scenario with the universally accepted achievements of the rule-of-law tradition. The European contribution to this task is two-fold. First, from the EU experience, its institutional framework and its developments are an obligatory reference for any supranational integration experience. Specifically, and concerning emerging global administrative law, transnational administrative action has been developing for years on the European scene as national borders have become only formal boundaries for an increasing number of issues. Although current European administrative law requires adjustment and legal improvements, the "European administrative proceedings ruling the relationship among administrations according to different models based on co-operation"[598] form a valuable legal achievement. Thus, it is worthwhile that these proceedings are taken into account, both in relation to their parts that work correctly – such as the achievement of joint talks, negotiation and agreement among

---

594. See Cassese, "European administrative proceedings", *Law and Contemporary Problems*, 68/1, p. 35.
595. G. J. Della Cananea, "Beyond the state", op. cit., p. 575, underlining that principles of administrative law are applied by the instances to deal with disputes, pointing out particularly the trace of American law in the well-known *Shrimp and Turtles* case, decision adopted by the WTO Apellate body, October 1998.
596. G. J. Della Cananea, "Beyond the state", op. cit., p. 578 .
597. C. Harlow, "Global administrative law", op. cit., p. 208.
598. Cassese, "European administrative proceedings", p. 35.

many players – rather than in relation to those which have to be improved, as far as these last are likely to appear in similar transnational experiences.

On the other hand, we have referred to the European legal tradition, as integrated by European constitutional culture and the doctrine accepted by the Council of Europe, which is also an important source of possible contributions in a globalised world. In fact, this tradition can be identified far from Europe, as a result of well-known historical events. Also, the European rule-of-law tradition has the great advantage of being preserved, and adapted when necessary, by a specific entity set up for these purposes.

Thus, it is worthwhile to consider the whole complexity of the European legal system and to reach its two essential components merged finally in an efficient way without unwanted tensions. Of course, such an aim requires the emphatic dismissal of any simplistic attempt to summarise the rich European legal culture in a poor market-approach model.

References

Aguilera, B., "Law as a limit to power: the European origins of the rule of law", Chapter 1 of this work.

Alston, P. and Weiler, J., "An 'ever closer union' in need of human rights policy: the European Union and human rights", Harvard Jean Monnet Working Paper 1/99, available at www.jeanmonnetprogram.org/papers/99/990105. html.

Arnold, R., "European constitutionalism after the Second World War", Chapter 2 of this work.

Baena del Alcázar, M., "Competencias, funciones y potestades en el ordenamiento jurídico español" in Sebastián Martín-Retortillo Baquer (ed.), *Estudios sobre la Constitución española: Homenaje al profesor Eduardo García de Enterría*, Vol. 3, Madrid, Civitas, 1991.

Barbier de La Serre, E., "Procedural justice in the European Community case law concerning the rights of the defence: essentialist and instrumental trends", *European Public Law*, Vol. 12 (2006) No. 2, pp. 225-250.

Cassese, S., "European administrative proceedings", *Law and Contemporary Problems*, Vol. 68 (2004) No. 1.

Cassese, S., *La Globalizacion Juridica,* Inap-Marcial Pons, Madrid, 2006.

Cerulli Irelli, V. "Trasformazioni del sistema di tutela giurisdizionale nelle controversie di diritto pubblico per effetti della giurisprudenza europea", contribution to the *XVII Congreso italo-español de Profesores de Derecho Administrativo*, Zaragoza, 2008.

Chiti, E., "Administrative proceedings involving European agencies", *Law and Contemporary Problems*, Vol. 68, No. 1 (winter 2003-4).

Chiti, M., "Forms of European administrative action", *Law and Contemporary Problems,* Vol. 68, No. 1 (winter 2003-4).

Constantinesco, V., "The ECJ as law-maker: *praeter aut contra legem?*" in D. O'Keeffe and A. Bavasso (eds), *Judicial review in European Union law*, Kluwer Law International, Leiden, 2000.

Council of Europe, *The administration and you: principles of administrative law concerning the relations between administrative authorities and private persons. A handbook*, Council of Europe, Strasbourg, 1996.

Della Cananea, G. J., "The European Union: mixed proceedings", *Law and Contemporary Problems*, Vol. 68, No. 1 (winter 2003-4).

Della Cananea, G. J., "Beyond the state: the Europeanization and globalization of procedural administrative law", *European Public Law*, Vol. 9 (2003), No. 4.

Galera Rodrigo, S., *La aplicación administrativa del Derecho comunitario*, Civitas, Madrid, 1998.

Galera Rodrigo, S., "Sobre el alma de Europa, derechos fundamentales y EuroSpeak" in *Tiempo de Paz* [Madrid], No. 90 (autumn 2008).

Gromley, L. W., "Public interest litigation" in D. O'Keeffe and A. Bavasso (eds), *Judicial review in European Union law*, Kluwer Law International, Leiden, 2000.

Harlow, C., "Global administrative law: the quest for principles and values", *European Journal of International Law*, Vol. 17, No. 1 (2006), 187-214.

Kingsbury, B., Krisch, N. and Stewart, R. B., "The emergence of global administrative law", *Law and Contemporary Problems*, Vol. 68, No. 1 (winter 2003-4).

Nieto-Garrido, E. and Martin Delgado, I., *European administrative law in the constitutional treaty*, Hart, Oxford, 2007.

Ortega Alvarez, L., "Fundamental rights in the European constitution", *European Public Law*, Vol. 11 (2005), No. 3.

Redgwell, C., "Access to environmental justice" in F. Francioni (ed.), *Access to justice as a human right*, Oxford University Press, Oxford, 2007.

Resnik, J., "Judicial independence" in Vikram David Amar and Mark V. Tushnet (eds), *Global perspectives on constitutional law*, Oxford University Press, Oxford, 2009.

Rubio Llorente, F., "La Carta Europea de los Derechos", *Claves de la Razón Práctica*, No. 122, 2002.

Ruiz-Jarabo Colomer, D., "El Tribunal de Justicia de la Unión Europea en el Tratado de Lisboa", *Noticias de la Union Europea*, No. 291 (April 2009).

Sadurski, W., "Solange: Chapter 3. Constitutional Courts in Central Europe", *European Law Journal*, Vol. 14, No. 1 (January 2008), pp. 1-35.

Schwarze, J., "The role of the European Court of Justice in shaping legal standards for administrative action in the member states. A comparative perspective" in D. O'Keeffe (ed.), *Judicial review in EU law*, Kluwer Law International, The Hague, 2000.

Spielmann, D., "Human rights case law in the Strasbourg and Luxembourg courts: conflicts, inconsistencies and complementarities" in P. Alston (ed.), *The European Union and human rights*, Oxford University Press, Oxford, 1999.

Storskrubb, E., and Ziller, J., "Access to justice in European comparative law" in F. Francioni (ed.), *Access to justice as a human right*, Oxford University Press, Oxford, 2007.

Sudre, F., "Le Recours aux 'notions autonomes'" in *L'Interpretation de la convention européenne des droits de l'homme*, Bruylant, Brussels, 1998.

Weiler, J. H. H., and Lockhart, N. J. S., "Taking rights seriously: the European Court and its fundamental rights jurisprudence", Part I, *Common Market Law Review*, No. 32, 1995, pp. 51-86.

Wils, W., "Powers of investigation and procedural rights and guarantees in EU antitrust enforcement: the interplay between European and national legislation and case law" in Abel M. Mateus and Teresa Moreira (eds), *Competition law and economics: advances in competition policy and antitrust enforcement*, Kluwer Law International, Leiden, 2007.

Appendix

Council of Europe: Recommendation Rec(2004)20 of the Committee of Ministers to member states on judicial review of administrative acts

(Adopted by the Committee of Ministers on 15 December 2004 at the 909th meeting of the Ministers' Deputies)

The Committee of Ministers, under the terms of Article 15b of the Statute of the Council of Europe,

Considering that the aim of the Council of Europe is to achieve greater unity among its members;

Recalling Article 6 of the Convention for the Protection of Human Rights and Fundamental Freedoms which provides that "everyone is entitled to a fair and public hearing within a reasonable time by an independent and impartial tribunal established by law" and the relevant case law on administrative disputes of the European Court of Human Rights;

Considering that effective judicial review of administrative acts to protect the rights and interests of individuals is an essential element of the system of protection of human rights;

Having in mind that a balance should be struck between the legitimate interests of all parties with a view to providing for the procedure without delay and for efficient and effective public administration;

Taking into account the results of the monitoring of member states' observance of their commitments on the subject of "functioning of the judicial system" and of the decision taken by the Ministers' Deputies at their 693rd meeting on 12 January 2000 on the possibility and scope of judicial review of administrative decisions;

In the light of the conclusions of the First Conference of the Presidents of Supreme Administrative Courts in Europe, which had as its theme "The possibility and scope of the judicial control of administrative decisions in member states", which took place in Strasbourg on 7 and 8 October 2002;

Taking into account the legal instruments of the Council of Europe in the field of administrative law, and in particular Resolution (77) 31 on the protection of the individual in relation to the acts of administrative authorities;

Bearing in mind Recommendation R (94) 12 on the independence, efficiency and role of judges;

Recalling Recommendation Rec(2003)16 on execution of administrative and judicial decisions in the field of administrative law;

Seeking to strengthen the rule of law and human rights, which are fundamental values of the legal systems of Council of Europe member states;

Seeking to ensure effective access to judicial review of administrative acts;

Convinced that other methods of control of administrative acts, which may include internal appeal to the administrative authorities and control by the ombudsman institution as well as appeal to alternatives to litigation, set out in Recommendation Rec(2001)9 on alternatives to litigation between administrative authorities and private parties, are useful for improving the functioning of jurisdictions and for the effective protection of everyone's rights,

Recommends that the governments of member states apply, in their national legal system and in practice, the principles set out below:

A. Definitions

For the purposes of this recommendation,

1. By "administrative acts" are meant:

   a. legal acts – both individual and normative – and physical acts of the administration taken in the exercise of public authority which may affect the rights or interests of natural or legal persons;

   b. situations of refusal to act or an omission to do so in cases where the administrative authority is under an obligation to implement a procedure following a request.

2. By "judicial review" is meant the examination and determination by a tribunal of the lawfulness of an administrative act and the adoption of appropriate measures, with the exception of review by a constitutional court.

B. Principles

1. The scope of judicial review

   a. All administrative acts should be subject to judicial review. Such review may be direct or by way of exception.

   b. The tribunal should be able to review any violation of the law, including lack of competence, procedural impropriety and abuse of power.

2. Access to judicial review

   a. Judicial review should be available at least to natural and legal persons in respect of administrative acts that directly affect their rights or interests. Member states are encouraged to examine whether access to judicial review should not also be opened to associations or other persons and bodies empowered to protect collective or community interests.

b. Natural and legal persons may be required to exhaust remedies provided by national law before having recourse to judicial review. The length of the procedure for seeking such remedies should not be excessive.

c. Natural and legal persons should be allowed a reasonable period of time in which to commence judicial review proceedings.

d. The cost of access to judicial review should not be such as to discourage applications. Legal aid should be available to persons lacking the necessary financial resources where the interests of justice require it.

3. An independent and impartial tribunal

a. Judicial review should be conducted by a tribunal established by law whose independence and impartiality are guaranteed in accordance with the terms of Recommendation R (94) 12.

b. The tribunal may be an administrative tribunal or part of the ordinary court system.

4. The right to a fair hearing

a. The time within which the tribunal takes its decision should be reasonable in the light of the complexity of each case and of the procedural steps or postponements attributable to the parties, while respecting the adversary principle.

b. There should be equality of arms between the parties to the proceedings. Each party should be given an opportunity to present his or her case without being placed at a disadvantage.

c. Unless national law provides for exceptions in important cases, the administrative authority should make available to the tribunal the documents and information relevant to the case.

d. The proceedings should be adversarial in nature. All evidence admitted by the tribunal should in principle be made available to the parties with a view to adversarial argument.

e. The tribunal should be in a position to examine all of the legal and factual issues relevant to the case presented by the parties.

f. The proceedings should be public, other than in exceptional circumstances.

g. Judgment should be pronounced in public.

h. Reasons should be given for the judgment. Tribunals should indicate with sufficient clarity the grounds on which they base their decisions. Although it is not necessary for a tribunal to deal with every point raised in argument, a submission that would, if accepted, be decisive for the outcome of the case requires a specific and express response.

i. The decision of the tribunal that reviews an administrative act should, at least in important cases, be subject to appeal to a higher tribunal, unless the case is directly referred to a higher tribunal in accordance with the national legislation.

5. The effectiveness of judicial review

a. If a tribunal finds that an administrative act is unlawful, it should have the powers necessary to redress the situation so that it is in accordance with the law. In particular, it should be competent at least to quash the administrative decision and if necessary to refer the case back to the administrative authority to take a new decision that complies with the judgment. It should also be competent to require of the administrative authority, where appropriate, the performance of a duty.

b. The tribunal should also have jurisdiction to award costs of the proceedings and compensation in appropriate cases.

c. The necessary powers to ensure effective execution of the tribunal's judgment should be available in accordance with Recommendation Rec(2003)16.

d. The tribunal should be competent to grant provisional measures of protection pending the outcome of the proceedings.

Explanatory memorandum

I. Introduction

1. The rule of law is inconceivable without access for all citizens to an independent, impartial tribunal established by law and capable of meeting the requirements of a fair trial. This is particularly important where the possibility of challenging administrative acts is concerned because such measures or decisions are taken in the exercise of public authority and often directly affect the rights and freedoms secured under the European Convention on Human Rights (hereafter ECHR). Given the specific nature of administrative acts, the member States of the Council of Europe should ensure that their judicial organisation and control procedures are in line with the requirements of the ECHR in order to guarantee the effectiveness of the control of administrative acts.

2. Nevertheless, at a time when the expansion of the public sector in the member States and the effects of such expansion on people's lives are highlighting

the need for special new arrangements, the States remain free to define the framework and procedure for supervising administrative acts. However, given that the lack of a judicial remedy against administrative acts might be interpreted as a denial of justice, member States are required to guarantee the reality and efficacy of the control of such acts while not encroaching on the independence of the judge or of the competent court or tribunal.

3. For these reasons, and in the light of the results of the procedure for monitoring the honouring of commitments entered into by member States on the theme of "functioning of the judicial system", which showed that some member States had structural problems linked to the absence of judicial review of administrative acts, the Committee of Ministers, on a motion from the European Committee on Legal Co-operation (CDCJ), entrusted the Project Group on Administrative Law (CJ-DA) with the task of formulating an appropriate instrument on the judicial review of administrative acts.

4. On 7 and 8 October 2002, the Council of Europe organised a Conference of Presidents of Supreme Administrative Courts in Europe in order to secure a preliminary assessment of the problems arising out of the judicial control of the Administration. At the close of this Conference the participants adopted conclusions in which they proclaimed their support for the work assigned to the CJ-DA by the Committee of Ministers and came down in favour of continuing to study the issue of judicial review of administrative acts.

5. This Conference debated the optimum ways and means of ensuring effective control of administrative acts in the light of the case law of the European Court of Human Rights (hereafter European Court). It recalled that the ECHR had not originally been intended to apply to administrative proceedings, but that the European Court's case law had partly remedied this situation. The CJ-DA took account of the proceedings of the conference during its discussions on the content of the present Recommendation, and the explanatory memorandum is largely based on them.

II. General considerations

6. The Recommendation on the judicial review of administrative acts is aimed at establishing the principles governing judicial review of administrative acts in a State governed by the Rule of Law. It should be noted that in all States governed by the rule of law the Administration is subject to the law and supervision by the courts on the same basis as any individual and any citizen, in accordance with the principle of the pre-eminence of law. The Recommendation strives to present pointers for the desirable future development of administrative justice, while taking account of the disparities between administrative and judicial systems in the various member States. It attempts to avoid any traditional conception of judicial review of administrative acts, that is, acts adopted by the authorities having consequences for the rights

and interests of citizens. Its main aim is to ensure effective access to judicial review, thus helping to consolidate the rule of law and human rights in Europe.

7. The Recommendation draws on the principle that all administrative acts must be subject to judicial review. This requirement would in this way also be respected with regard to the acts and procedures which are not covered by the relevant provisions of the ECHR, in particular Article 6.1. As was emphasised by the Conference of Presidents of Supreme Administrative Courts in connection with the lawfulness of administrative acts, this obligation results from both their nature and their effects. By nature they are a prime means of action for the Administration on behalf of the public authorities, and members of the community are required to execute and implement them. On the other hand, the principles of democracy require the addressees of the acts to be able to enlist the services of a judge to verify their lawfulness, in formal and substantive terms. In terms of their effects, these acts may violate the rights and freedoms secured under national legislation and various international instruments. For instance, Article 13 of the ECHR states that "everyone whose rights and freedoms as set forth in this Convention are violated shall have an effective remedy before a national authority notwithstanding that the violation has been committed by persons acting in an official capacity".

8. The Recommendation sets out five groups of principles which are to be applied by the governments of member States. These principles concern the scope of judicial review, access thereto, the independence and impartiality of the courts, the right to a fair trial and the effectiveness of judicial review. It was decided to define the basic concepts used in the Recommendation, namely "administrative act" and "judicial review", in order to clarify the ambit of the principles and recommendations, which relate both to the national legal systems and to actual practice.

9. With a view to guaranteeing constant respect for Article 6 of the ECHR in administrative matters, this recommendation supplements the legal instruments adopted with reference to civil and criminal proceedings.

10. Taking account of the variety of legal traditions in member States in the field of administrative proceedings, the Recommendation sets out the general rules to be observed in organising the judicial review of administrative acts, without attempting to achieve complete harmonisation of the relevant legislation.

A. Comments on the definitions

11. The definitions adopted for the purposes of the Recommendation were drawn up on the basis of a functional criterion aimed at delimiting the scope of the text. This involves, firstly, protecting the rights and interests of citizens in respect of a wide range of acts adopted by the Administration vis-à-vis the constantly expanding area of administrative activity in parallel to the

increasing scope of State intervention, and secondly, guaranteeing the powers of the Administration. Consequently, the definitions adopted are not identical to those of similar concepts set out in other Council of Europe instruments.

1. Administrative acts

12. The administrative acts covered by the Recommendation are broadly defined in order to ensure judicial review of all administrative activities by the Administration. The definition of administrative acts does not include acts having a purely private law character and acts or proceedings of the Parliament in its legislative function. While the concept of administrative decision (*acte administratif*) has very specific connotations in some legal systems, the concept of administrative act (*acte de l'administration*) covers a wider area of activities conducted by administrations.

13. The Recommendation does not prevent States from defining very limited exceptions established by law, for example certain acts in the field of foreign affairs, international agreements, defence or national security.

14. The definition of administrative act adopted by the Recommendation embraces several possible actions by the public administration. It comprises individual administrative acts constituting decisions taken by the Administration in respect of specific individuals. It also covers prescriptive acts and statutory acts accompanied by general, non-personal regulations addressed to an unspecified number of persons. It further includes material actions which will have consequences in terms of the legal regulations governing natural or legal persons, on the understanding that changes to the legal situation entail creating both rights and obligations.

15. Lastly, the definition also covers situations of refusal or failure to act on the part of the public administration in cases where there is an obligation for the administrative authority to act. The Recommendation considers that the concept of administrative act also covers cases where the Administration fails to respond to a request or where it explicitly or implicitly refuses to adopt a given decision or act. The tribunal should be empowered to act in both these situations.

16. Under no circumstances may a citizen's interests be harmed by the administration's remaining silent. After a certain time prescribed by law, this silence should open access to a tribunal. In such cases the administrative authority will be required to explain to the tribunal, at the applicant's request or at the request of the tribunal, its reasons for refusing the applicant's request. If the authority fails to give grounds, the tribunal shall hold its act to be unlawful.

17. The Recommendation applies only to such administrative acts as have been implemented by the Administration in the exercise of public authority. Such authority allows the Administration to impose obligations, issue acts and confer rights. These acts have the effect of changing the legal and factual

situation of the persons concerned, depending on the scope of the act. The Recommendation specifically targets administrative acts which infringe the rights or interests of natural or legal persons. Private acts lie outside the ambit of the text.

2. Judicial review

18. The concept of judicial review covers different ideas in different countries. As mentioned at the Conference of Presidents of Supreme Administrative Courts, experience shows that the rule of law and the subjection of the public authority to law and the courts are not self-evident, and that there is a constant temptation to exempt administrative acts from legal rules and control by the courts. It is therefore vital to ensure that administrative acts can be controlled and set aside – or rebutted by exceptional remedy – if they prove unlawful.

19. The Recommendation is aimed at guaranteeing the right of everyone, in accordance with the ECHR, to a fair hearing by an independent and impartial tribunal also in administrative cases. This principle of a fundamental right to a tribunal is inherent in the rule of law, and it is imperative for the States having ratified the ECHR to respect it. Both the Statute of the Council of Europe and the Preamble to the ECHR stress the rule of law and genuine democracy. These two principles therefore involve judicial review of administrative acts, if only in order to mitigate the inequality of arms between the administration and the citizen.

20. The concept of judicial review adopted in this recommendation is broader than that consisting in merely examining the lawfulness of an act; it also encompasses the tribunal's power to annul an act following its review or to award compensation. The administrative court's role is to protect individuals by means of the law.

21. Therefore, the tribunal must be empowered to instigate proceedings to verify the lawfulness of administrative acts, including administrative silence or failure to act, and to draw the requisite conclusions from its findings.

22. The concept of lawfulness of an administrative act is broadly construed: it concerns infringements of interests which, by law, are worthy of protection. Infringing a protected interest accordingly amounts to breaking the law.

23. Judicial review is an objective activity which can be initiated at the request of an individual or of another body, particularly a public body. One of the functions of judicial review is the protection of the individual vis-à-vis the administration. However, such control is also geared to safeguarding and clarifying the administration's powers.

24. The subjects of judicial review comprise all the types of administrative act covered by the definition of such acts.

25. The Recommendation does not apply in cases where, in accordance with national legislation, the constitutional court exercises the review. In a number of countries review of certain normative administrative acts is entrusted to the constitutional court. In such cases, a specific procedure is followed, different to that before an administrative tribunal or ordinary court. This is why review of administrative acts by a constitutional court does not fall within the scope of the Recommendation. This does not affect the requirement of compliance with Article 6 of the ECHR.

B. Comments on principles

26. The field of administrative proceedings varies widely in the different member states' legal systems. This fact has highlighted the need to specify the general principles applicable to administrative proceedings in order to prevent Article 6 of the ECHR from being implemented in different ways in different countries.

27. It is true that the ECHR was not originally intended to apply to the administrative field. However, as early as 1971, the European Court stated the following in its *Ringeisen* judgment: "to be applicable to a case ["contestation"] it is not necessary that both parties to the proceedings should be private persons …. The character of the legislation which governs how the matter is to be determined (civil, commercial, administrative law, etc.) and that of the authority which is invested with competence in the matter (ordinary court, administrative body, etc.) are therefore of little consequence".

28. Taking account of the specific nature of judicial review of administrative acts, this part of the Recommendation lists the principles applicable to the exercise of such review, including those set out in the ECHR.

1. The scope of judicial review

Principle 1a

29. This principle mainly concerns the subject of judicial review, viz administrative acts as defined in this Recommendation. Review may take two forms. It is direct when it deals with the act contested before the court. It is by way of exception when, in proceedings concerned with an act, the tribunal reviews another act connected with it (for instance, when the tribunal reviews the lawfulness of the normative act on which the decision challenged is based). It should be noted that if an administrative act cannot be referred direct to a tribunal (as is the case with normative acts in several legal systems), the state should ensure that the act can be reviewed by way of exception.

30. With regard to administrative acts involving exercise of a discretionary power, although such a power is, in principle, exempt from judicial review, the tribunal may seek to determine whether the administration has overstepped

permitted limits in the use of its discretionary power or whether it has committed manifest errors.

31. Administrative sanctions are deemed equivalent to administrative acts and therefore subject to judicial review.

Principle 1b

32. This principle contains, firstly, a general assertion that the courts should be able to review any violation of the law and, secondly, examples of grounds for invalidating an act.

33. The arguments on which the applicants can base their complaints embrace violation of the law, including lack of competence, procedural flaws and abuse of authority. Violation of the law may take the form of a lack of legal basis, a direct violation of a legal standard or a legal error, in which latter case the administration has misjudged the scope of a rule. Lack of competence may stem from spatiotemporal considerations or the subject of the decision. Procedural flaws include such irregularities as a failure to conduct compulsory consultation. Lastly, abuse of power refers mainly to cases where an authority uses a power vested in it by law, but for another purpose than that provided for by law. The Recommendation draws a distinction at this point between formal violations and those arising out of lack of competence, on the one hand, and those involving misapplication, misinterpretation or ignorance of the law, on the other.

34. The function of the tribunal adjudicating in administrative proceedings is fundamentally different from that of civil and criminal courts because of the subject of the review. The issues to be addressed by administrative tribunals have already been the subject of a lawful or unlawful decision by an authority hypothetically so empowered by law. It is therefore unnecessary, in principle, for the judicial decision to deal directly with the questions that originated the dispute. The tribunal's primary function is to review the lawfulness of the decision taken by the administration in the exercise of its attributions. However, the legal systems of some member States do empower the administrative tribunal to examine the substance of cases involving individual acts, and to pronounce both on the merits and the appropriateness of the administrative act and to replace the administration's decision with a fresh ruling.

2. Access to judicial review

35. The Recommendation does not specify how judicial review should be organised. The States are free to organise judicial review in administrative cases in accordance with their specific legal tradition and culture: by specialised administrative tribunals, by the ordinary courts or by a combination of both.

Principle 2a

36. This principle defines capacity to bring court proceedings. Natural and legal persons can obtain judicial review of administrative acts that infringe any of their rights or interests worthy of protection.

37. In order to protect collective or community interests that have been jeopardised by an administrative act, the Recommendation encourages the member states to take into consideration the possibility of granting associations or other persons or bodies empowered to protect these interests the capacity to bring proceedings before a court. The reference is to administrative decisions which adversely affect not just one individual but also those which affect any community. Such decisions, which might relate, for instance, to the environment or consumers' rights, could be eligible for judicial review without the direct interests of any particular individual being at issue.

38. Each state is entitled to extend the capacity to bring court proceedings. This remedy may for example be available to third parties concerned by the act.

39. The Recommendation applies solely to cases where rights or interests are directly affected. This means that there must be a close link between the act and the rights or interests concerned. If the link between the challenged act and the right asserted is too tenuous and distant, the Recommendation does not apply (*Balmer-Schafroth* judgment, 1997). Such acts must therefore adversely affect the applicant and have the effect of altering his/her legal situation. This precludes certain categories of administrative acts from a judicial remedy, such as preliminary measures. It is for national law to give practical definition to the rights or interests protected under this Recommendation.

40. The Recommendation does not preclude states from adopting procedures for the early disposal of judicial review claims which are weak, brought by persons who do not have a sufficient interest in the administrative act in question, or otherwise undeserving of full consideration. Thus applicants for judicial review may be required to apply to the tribunal for permission to proceed with their claims, or may be required to show that they have an arguable case in a preliminary procedure.

Principle 2b

41. This principle stipulates the conditions of access to judicial review.

42. Natural and legal persons have access to a number of preliminary channels for settling the dispute before reaching the judicial review stage. The Recommendation states that the applicant may have to exhaust all internal remedies with the administration in order to gain access to judicial review.

43. The right of access to judicial review must be an effective right. The Recommendation seeks to ensure that the obligation for natural and legal

persons to exhaust other remedies first does not prevent them from seeking judicial review of the administrative act.

44. It specifies that the time needed to deal with the case must be reasonable even during the preliminary procedure, as from the taking of the initial act. It is true that the safeguards laid down by Article 6 of the ECHR have, in principle, only to be respected at the judicial proceedings stage. However, according to the case law of the European Court, the reasonableness of the length of proceedings conducted before one or more administrative bodies partly depends on the length of any preliminary proceedings before an administrative body, where such an administrative procedure exists as a remedy which must be exhausted before the case can be brought before the courts. The period to be taken into account can therefore begin as soon as an administrative appeal is lodged with an administrative appeal body (*König* judgment, 1978).

45. Exhaustion of other remedies before seeking judicial review makes it possible to prevent an excessive workload for the ordinary courts with a view to judicial efficiency. This is in the interests of both the judiciary and the administration and may also contribute to reducing the cost of the procedure for the individual.

Principle 2c

46. This provision aims to guarantee that parties are allowed a reasonable time for bringing the matter before the courts. If the time-limit is too short, the parties may be unable to lodge an appeal against an administrative act.

47. States are accordingly required to set a reasonable time-limit for challenging the lawfulness or legitimacy of an administrative act before a tribunal, in order to guarantee the applicant effective access to judicial review. National legislation generally specifies the reasonable time.[1] In certain justified circumstances this period may be extended.

48. The Recommendation makes no reference to the concept of taking cognisance of the act, but time naturally begins running from when the natural or legal person is deemed to have cognisance of the act's notification. The Recommendation does not specify any fixed period between the time of formal or implicit notification of the act and the application for judicial review, rather leaving this matter to the states' discretion.

Principle 2d

49. In order to make judicial review widely accessible to natural and legal persons, the cost of proceedings must not constitute a deterrent to judicial

---

1. For example, applicants usually have a period of 30 days in Albania, Azerbaijan, Finland, Hungary, Romania and Switzerland, of 6 weeks in Austria and the Netherlands, of 60 days in Belgium and Italy, and of 6 months in Malta and Norway.

action. The point at issue here is the cost of access to judicial review, rather than merely the cost of judicial review itself.

50. This effective access condition implies a right to legal assistance to guarantee access to court for applicants who cannot afford to pay the costs where the interests of justice require, whatever the judicial body competent to adjudicate in cases involving the Administration.

3. An independent and impartial tribunal

Principle 3a

51. This principle confirms that settlement of an administrative dispute is a matter for a tribunal established by law, in accordance with the requirements of the ECHR.

52. The principle of independent and impartial tribunals is confirmed by Article 6 of the ECHR. In order to reinforce respect for this principle, the Council of Europe drew up Recommendation R (94) 12 on the independence, efficiency and role of judges, which specifies the preconditions for judicial independence. Opinion No. 1 (2001) of the Consultative Council of European Judges (CCJE) concerning the independence of the judiciary and the irremovability of judges further develops the provisions of this Recommendation: in endorsing the requirements of the European Charter on the Statute for Judges in this respect, the CCJE considered that "the fundamental principles of judicial independence should be set out at the constitutional or highest possible legal level in each member state, and its more specific rules at the legislative level."

53. In view of the specific risks surrounding an administrative judge since he or she is required to settle disputes concerning the public authorities, this principle reasserts the requirement of both subjective impartiality (taking account of the judge's personal conviction or interest in a given case) and objective impartiality (which consists in ascertaining whether the judge offers sufficient guarantees to exclude all legitimate doubt in this respect), as upheld in the case law of the European Court (*Piersack*, 1982, *De Cubber*, 1984, *Demicoli*, 1991, *Sainte-Marie*, 1992, judgments). In this connection, the CCJE confirmed in its Opinion No. 3 (2002) that "judges should, in all circumstances, act impartially to ensure that there can be no legitimate reason for citizens to suspect any partiality."

54. Even though there are international legal instruments aimed at protecting such independence and impartiality, it appeared important to explicitly confirm this principle in the Recommendation on judicial review of administrative acts. The independence and impartiality of judges adjudicating in administrative cases are essential for guaranteeing the effective protection of citizens' rights.

Principle 3b

55. This principle supplements principle 3a; it specifies the characteristics of the body responsible for judicial review of administrative acts: it refers to both administrative tribunals and ordinary courts dealing with administrative proceedings, both categories of court having the same status. Each state will choose one or the other type of court to deal with administrative proceedings depending on its own system of organisation of the courts.

56. Both administrative tribunals and ordinary courts must satisfy the requirements of principle 3a.

4. Right to a fair trial

57. This section further develops the provisions of Article 6 of the ECHR with practical measures to be applied to the examination of administrative cases. The Recommendation takes account of the problems arising in some countries in connection with safeguarding the principles set out in Article 6 on proceedings relating to formal administrative acts.

Principle 4a

58. According to the case law of the European Court, the reasonableness of the time-limit stipulated in Article 6 of the ECHR must always be evaluated in the light of the specific circumstances of the case, such as its complexity, the applicant's conduct and the manner in which the case is dealt with by the administrative or judicial authorities (*O.*, 1987, *Tomasi*, 1992, *Poiss*, 1987, judgments). As stated in paragraph 42 above, the "reasonable" length of time stipulated in Article 6 of the ECHR does not refer solely to the duration of the proceedings conducted before the administrative tribunal. The time taken into consideration may begin on the day the party starts an appeal procedure within the administration, if this is a precondition for the judicial review in question.

Principle 4b

59. The concept of a fair trial necessitates respect for the principle of equality of arms between the parties to proceedings. In administrative cases there is a particular risk of infringement of this principle by the parties' relative positions, with one side representing the authorities and the other demanding that their rights be respected. Applicants should therefore have the full benefit of the protection provided by Article 6.1 of the ECHR in general in order to make good this inequality inherent in administrative proceedings.

60. The principle of equality of arms requires that each party have the same facilities for presenting its case under conditions which do not place it at a

clear disadvantage compared with the opposing party (*Dombo Beheer B.V.* judgment, 1993, *Stran Greek Refineries and Stratis Andreadis* judgment, 1994).

Principle 4c

61. This principle confirms that the administrative authority is obliged to make available all the documents in its case-file on which it bases its decision.

62. Access by parties to the administrative file is one of the preconditions for a fair trial. According to the case law of the European Court, this principle implies that a citizen must have access to the administrative file as forwarded to the tribunal by the administration (*Schuler-Zgraggen* judgment, 1993). This requires the administration to supply all the facts on which its act was based. The European Court has confirmed this requirement in connection with documents that might help the applicant in putting his/her case (*Bendenoun* judgment, 1994). It is essential for the fairness of the trial that the administrative file be forwarded in sufficient time.

63. Effect can be given to these requirements either by imposing a duty on the authority to disclose all the relevant documents to the tribunal, or by giving the tribunal the power to require disclosure of these documents.

64. In certain circumstances it should be possible to apply special protective measures to sensitive documents (for instance, where national security is at stake).

Principle 4d

65. The right to adversarial proceedings in administrative cases involves notifying the appeal to the opposing party and any other interested parties.

66. According to the case law of the European Court, the fundamental right to adversarial proceedings "means the opportunity for the parties to have knowledge of and comment on the observations filed or evidence adduced by the other party" (*Ruiz-Mateos* judgment, 1993). This includes documents and all information admitted by the tribunal. That does not prevent various means of protection being given by the tribunal to sensitive documents (for instance in order to protect national security, professional secrecy or intellectual property rights).

67. The adversarial nature of the proceedings must be safeguarded in cases where evidence concerning the case's admissibility is disputed.

Principle 4e

68. This principle confirms that a court must be in a position to examine all the arguments raised by the parties (*Ortenberg* judgment, 1994). The arguments relied on may concern points either of law or of fact.

69. Regarding questions of law, where the contested measure was taken under the administration's regulatory powers, the tribunal to which the case is referred must be empowered to examine whether the administrative authority remained within the limits of the law; in this connection, the tribunal must be able to review the challenged measure "in the light, *inter alia*, of principles of administrative law" (*Oerlemans* judgment, 1991).

70. Regarding the facts, the court must be competent to ascertain these (*Fischer* judgment, 1995) or at least to correct errors of fact (*Albert and Le Compte* judgment, 1983). One possibility is that the court should be able to ascertain the relevant facts itself by rehearing the case. However, Article 6.1 of the ECHR apparently does not preclude a system whereby the court must rely on the facts ascertained by the administrative authority. In that case it is nonetheless vital that the procedure before the administrative authority should offer guarantees concerning the decision-making process and also that the court should be able to ascertain, firstly, that the administration's findings of fact were based on sufficiently sound evidence and, secondly, that the administrative act did not result from a conclusion which no administrative authority, acting rightly, would have drawn from the facts (*Potocka* judgment, 2001).

71. A number of legal systems allow administrative tribunals to rule on the lawfulness of the contested act, even where the ground relied on in a finding of unlawfulness was not raised by a party, if it finds that the act is unlawful. This system strengthens judicial control of the administration by a tribunal and thus the judicial protection of applicants.

72. The administrative tribunal is entitled and obliged to offset any inequality between the parties. For instance, the tribunal may invite the parties to submit additional factual evidence (or to supplement the information available on the circumstances of the case). The tribunal should have the initiative in determining the progress of the administrative proceedings.

73. In annulment proceedings the tribunal should verify the existence of the facts. Where the administrative act involved the exercise of a discretionary power, it ascertains that the limits on the exercise of that power have not been overstepped. It also verifies application of the law to the facts.

Principle 4f

74. Proceedings must be public in order to protect the citizens against any secret, arbitrary judicial approach.

75. The right to public proceedings in principle includes the right to a public hearing, if none of the exceptions laid down in the second sentence of Article 6.1 of the ECHR apply (*Håkansson and Sturesson* judgment, 1990). Nevertheless, the question of whether a hearing is necessary is dealt with differently in different national laws, particularly for administrative proceedings

as they are often written proceedings and mainly concern questions of law. The right to a public hearing is particularly important where the tribunal examines contested questions of fact.

76. Both written and oral procedure should be public. All members of the public should be able to acquaint themselves with the proceedings, in particular their course and conduct.

77. Where a case is examined at different levels by different bodies and is of a highly technical nature, it may be justifiable not to hold a public hearing in the final stages of the proceedings (*Eisenstecken* judgment, 2000). In proceedings before a court of first and only instance "exceptional circumstances" must be shown in order to justify dispensing with a hearing (*Göç* judgment, 2001). Such circumstances are difficult to prove where the court deals with questions not only of law but also of fact (*Fischer* judgment, 1995).

78. Where it is in the public interest, the procedure should be oral. The choice between a written or an oral procedure in specific cases should be determined by national law.

79. The parties should be able to waive the right to a public hearing of their own free will, either expressly or tacitly. However, this waiver should be ineffective where it runs counter to an important public interest (*Schuler-Zgraggen* judgment, 1993).

Principle 4g

80. The principle that judgments should be pronounced in public, which is confirmed by Article 6 of the ECHR, requires all interested parties to have access to a judgment in which they have a legitimate interest, whereby judgments of general scope should also be accessible to a broad public, taking account of language considerations and such facilities as publication in a journal or in the electronic media (*Pretto* judgment, 1983).

Principle 4h

81. Reasons must be given for the judgment pronounced by the tribunal. The reasoning of the judgment should be presented in writing and relate to the tribunal's response to all of the applicant's arguments, justifying the decision reached. The scope of this obligation may vary in accordance with the nature of the judgment. The reasons given must be specific and suited to the facts of the case, not confined to mere references to certain pieces of legislation. However, no detailed reply is required to each argument, as the European Court confirmed in its *Ruiz Torija* judgment (1994). Any lack of or inadequacy in the reasons given is liable to invalidate the judgment in formal terms.

82. The terminology used in the reasons is extremely important for the parties' understanding of them. Special attention must be paid to the use of terms from other fields which might prove inappropriate in the judicial context.

Principle 4i

83. Proper judicial protection involves the right to two-tier proceedings. Nevertheless, while appeal facilities are not compulsory under the ECHR, they are still possible with a view to reducing the risk of arbitrary decisions, *inter alia* within the judicial system. This principle should be applied to the most important cases, particularly those involving heavy administrative sanctions, subject to any exceptions provided for in domestic legislation. The applicant's right to appeal against the judgment pronounced should be recognised in each State within a reasonable time-limit defined by the individual national system. States will decide the extent to which appeals can be lodged with higher courts.

84. The Recommendation accordingly goes further than the ECHR and requires a right of appeal in the most important cases. National law should specify the conditions of appeal and the jurisdiction of the appeal body, which must satisfy the requirements of Article 6 of the ECHR. Involvement of a higher instance in administrative proceedings is essential to guarantee the consistency of administrative case law.

85. This principle does not apply where a case is referred directly to the higher tribunal pursuant to national law.

5. The effectiveness of judicial review

86. The Recommendation recognises that judicial review of administrative acts must be effective so that citizens' rights and interests are afforded genuine protection and to ensure the credibility vis-à-vis society and the efficiency of the administration itself.

Principle 5a

87. The Recommendation seeks to guarantee that a tribunal may take the necessary measures to restore a lawful situation. It covers provisional measures, procedural and substantive decisions, that is, the power to prevent potentially prejudicial material actions; the power to order the adoption of a material action which should have been but was not adopted, particularly in connection with enforcing administrative decisions already taken; the power to order the adoption of administrative acts and decisions, in the case of limited discretion; and the possibility of preventing the adoption of decisions in cases of limited discretion, where the Administration has acted *ultra vires*.

88. The Recommendation does not exclude the possibility of the tribunal replacing the administrative act where such a measure would be compatible

with national legislation. The case law of the European Court does not require the administrative tribunal to substitute an act held to be unlawful. Nevertheless, the tribunal must be in a position to impose its judgment on the administrative authority when the latter issues a fresh decision, on referral after the original judgment has been set aside. This rule does not apply to cases where after annulment of an act the administration is not required to take a new decision (for instance, in appointment matters, if an appointment decision is annulled, the administration has discretionary power to decide whether to resume the appointment procedure).

Principle 5b

89. This principle recognises that the tribunal has jurisdiction not only to deal with the substance of a complaint, but also, where the complainant is successful, to award some form of redress. Where appropriate, compensation for both pecuniary and non-pecuniary damage resulting from a violation must in principle be possible. In general, compensation is made by setting the decision aside.

90. The tribunal should also be empowered to exempt parties from liability for costs where justified.

Principle 5c

91. The execution of judgments is an important aspect of the effectiveness of control, and it is imperative to ensure that the administrative authorities in question execute the tribunal's judgments. This Recommendation endorses Recommendation R (2003) 16 on the execution of administrative and judicial decisions in the field of administrative law.

92. The possibility of enforcing the administrative authority's compliance with the judicial decision should be guaranteed. Means of enforcement should be consistent with national legal tradition.

Principle 5d

93. This principle is aimed at ensuring that implementation of the contested measure can be suspended in cases where its enforcement would place the person concerned in an irreversible situation (*Jabari* judgment, 2000, and *Čonka* judgment, 2002).

94. The Recommendation recognises that the tribunal should have authority to grant provisional measures of protection pending the outcome of judicial proceedings. Such measures can include the full or partial suspension of the execution of the disputed administrative act, thus enabling the tribunal to re-establish the de facto and de jure situation which would prevail in the

absence of the administrative act or to impose appropriate obligations on the administrative authorities.

95. In this respect this principle is consistent with Recommendation R (89) 8 of the Committee of Ministers to member states on provisional court protection in administrative matters, which provides that an applicant may request the court or another competent body to take measures of provisional protection against the administrative act.

Sales agents for publications of the Council of Europe
Agents de vente des publications du Conseil de l'Europe

BELGIUM/BELGIQUE
La Librairie Européenne -
The European Bookshop
Rue de l'Orme, 1
BE-1040 BRUXELLES
Tel.: +32 (0)2 231 04 35
Fax: +32 (0)2 735 08 60
E-mail: order@libeurop.be
http://www.libeurop.be

Jean De Lannoy/DL Services
Avenue du Roi 202 Koningslaan
BE-1190 BRUXELLES
Tel.: +32 (0)2 538 43 08
Fax: +32 (0)2 538 08 41
E-mail: jean.de.lannoy@dl-servi.com
http://www.jean-de-lannoy.be

**BOSNIA AND HERZEGOVINA/
BOSNIE-HERZÉGOVINE**
Robert's Plus d.o.o.
Marka Maruliça 2/V
BA-71000, SARAJEVO
Tel.: + 387 33 640 818
Fax: + 387 33 640 818
E-mail: robertsplus@bih.net.ba

CANADA
Renouf Publishing Co. Ltd.
1-5369 Canotek Road
CA-OTTAWA, Ontario K1J 9J3
Tel.: +1 613 745 2665
Fax: +1 613 745 7660
Toll-Free Tel.: (866) 767-6766
E-mail: order.dept@renoufbooks.com
http://www.renoufbooks.com

CROATIA/CROATIE
Robert's Plus d.o.o.
Marasoviçeva 67
HR-21000, SPLIT
Tel.: + 385 21 315 800, 801, 802, 803
Fax: + 385 21 315 804
E-mail: robertsplus@robertsplus.hr

**CZECH REPUBLIC/
RÉPUBLIQUE TCHÈQUE**
Suweco CZ, s.r.o.
Klecakova 347
CZ-180 21 PRAHA 9
Tel.: +420 2 424 59 204
Fax: +420 2 848 21 646
E-mail: import@suweco.cz
http://www.suweco.cz

DENMARK/DANEMARK
GAD
Vimmelskaftet 32
DK-1161 KØBENHAVN K
Tel.: +45 77 66 60 00
Fax: +45 77 66 60 01
E-mail: gad@gad.dk
http://www.gad.dk

FINLAND/FINLANDE
Akateeminen Kirjakauppa
PO Box 128
Keskuskatu 1
FI-00100 HELSINKI
Tel.: +358 (0)9 121 4430
Fax: +358 (0)9 121 4242
E-mail: akatilaus@akateeminen.com
http://www.akateeminen.com

FRANCE
La Documentation française
(diffusion/distribution France entière)
124, rue Henri Barbusse
FR-93308 AUBERVILLIERS CEDEX
Tél.: +33 (0)1 40 15 70 00
Fax: +33 (0)1 40 15 68 00
E-mail: commande@ladocumentationfrancaise.fr
http://www.ladocumentationfrancaise.fr

Librairie Kléber
1 rue des Francs Bourgeois
FR-67000 STRASBOURG
Tel.: +33 (0)3 88 15 78 88
Fax: +33 (0)3 88 15 78 80
E-mail: librairie-kleber@coe.int
http://www.librairie-kleber.com

**GERMANY/ALLEMAGNE
AUSTRIA/AUTRICHE**
UNO Verlag GmbH
August-Bebel-Allee 6
DE-53175 BONN
Tel.: +49 (0)228 94 90 20
Fax: +49 (0)228 94 90 222
E-mail: bestellung@uno-verlag.de
http://www.uno-verlag.de

GREECE/GRÈCE
Librairie Kauffmann s.a.
Stadiou 28
GR-105 64 ATHINAI
Tel.: +30 210 32 55 321
Fax.: +30 210 32 30 320
E-mail: ord@otenet.gr
http://www.kauffmann.gr

HUNGARY/HONGRIE
Euro Info Service
Pannónia u. 58.
PF. 1039
HU-1136 BUDAPEST
Tel.: +36 1 329 2170
Fax: +36 1 349 2053
E-mail: euroinfo@euroinfo.hu
http://www.euroinfo.hu

ITALY/ITALIE
Licosa SpA
Via Duca di Calabria, 1/1
IT-50125 FIRENZE
Tel.: +39 0556 483215
Fax: +39 0556 41257
E-mail: licosa@licosa.com
http://www.licosa.com

MEXICO/MEXIQUE
Mundi-Prensa México, S.A. De C.V.
Río Pánuco, 141 Delegacíon Cuauhtémoc
MX-06500 MÉXICO, D.F.
Tel.: +52 (01)55 55 33 56 58
Fax: +52 (01)55 55 14 67 99
E-mail: mundiprensa@mundiprensa.com.mx
http://www.mundiprensa.com.mx

NETHERLANDS/PAYS-BAS
Roodveldt Import BV
Nieuwe Hemweg 50
NE-1013 CX AMSTERDAM
Tel.: + 31 20 622 8035
Fax.: + 31 20 625 5493
Website: www.publidis.org
Email: orders@publidis.org

NORWAY/NORVÈGE
Akademika
Postboks 84 Blindern
NO-0314 OSLO
Tel.: +47 2 218 8100
Fax: +47 2 218 8103
E-mail: support@akademika.no
http://www.akademika.no

POLAND/POLOGNE
Ars Polona JSC
25 Obroncow Street
PL-03-933 WARSZAWA
Tel.: +48 (0)22 509 86 00
Fax: +48 (0)22 509 86 10
E-mail: arspolona@arspolona.com.pl
http://www.arspolona.com.pl

PORTUGAL
Livraria Portugal
(Dias & Andrade, Lda.)
Rua do Carmo, 70
PT-1200-094 LISBOA
Tel.: +351 21 347 42 82 / 85
Fax: +351 21 347 02 64
E-mail: info@livrariaportugal.pt
http://www.livrariaportugal.pt

**RUSSIAN FEDERATION/
FÉDÉRATION DE RUSSIE**
Ves Mir
17b, Butlerova ul.
RU-101000 MOSCOW
Tel.: +7 495 739 0971
Fax: +7 495 739 0971
E-mail: orders@vesmirbooks.ru
http://www.vesmirbooks.ru

SPAIN/ESPAGNE
Mundi-Prensa Libros, s.a.
Castelló, 37
ES-28001 MADRID
Tel.: +34 914 36 37 00
Fax: +34 915 75 39 98
E-mail: libreria@mundiprensa.es
http://www.mundiprensa.com

SWITZERLAND/SUISSE
Planetis Sàrl
16 chemin des Pins
CH-1273 ARZIER
Tel.: +41 22 366 51 77
Fax: +41 22 366 51 78
E-mail: info@planetis.ch

UNITED KINGDOM/ROYAUME-UNI
The Stationery Office Ltd
PO Box 29
GB-NORWICH NR3 1GN
Tel.: +44 (0)870 600 5522
Fax: +44 (0)870 600 5533
E-mail: book.enquiries@tso.co.uk
http://www.tsoshop.co.uk

**UNITED STATES and CANADA/
ÉTATS-UNIS et CANADA**
Manhattan Publishing Co
2036 Albany Post Road
USA-10520 CROTON ON HUDSON, NY
Tel.: +1 914 271 5194
Fax: +1 914 271 5886
E-mail: coe@manhattanpublishing.coe
http://www.manhattanpublishing.com

Council of Europe Publishing/Editions du Conseil de l'Europe
FR-67075 STRASBOURG Cedex
Tel.: +33 (0)3 88 41 25 81 – Fax: +33 (0)3 88 41 39 10 – E-mail: publishing@coe.int – Website: http://book.coe.int